LEISURE IN A CHANGING AMERICA

Multicultural Perspectives

Richard Kraus

Department of Sport Management
and Leisure Studies
Temple University

Macmillan College Publishing Company
New York

Maxwell Macmillan Canada
Toronto

Maxwell Macmillan International
New York   Oxford   Singapore   Sydney

Cover photos: (clockwise from upper left) Myrleen Ferguson/PhotoEdit; Wolfgang
    Spunbarg/PhotoEdit; Jose Carrillo/PhotoEdit; Tony Freeman/PhotoEdit
Editor: Ann Castel Davis
Production Editor: Mary Harlan
Photo Editor: Anne Vega
Text Designer: Marilyn Wilson Phelps
Cover Designer: Robert Vega
Production Buyer: Patricia A. Tonneman
Electronic Text Management: Marilyn Wilson Phelps, Matthew Williams, Jane Lopez,
    Vincent A. Smith

This book was set in Galliard by Macmillan College Publishing Company and was printed and
bound by R. R. Donnelley & Sons Company. The cover was printed by Phoenix Color Corp.

Macmillan College Publishing Company
160 Gould Street,
Needham Heights, MA 02194-2310.

Macmillan College Publishing Company is part of the
Maxwell Communication Group of Companies.

Maxwell Macmillan Canada, Inc.
1200 Eglinton Avenue East, Suite 200
Don Mills, Ontario M3C 3N1

Library of Congress Cataloging-in-Publication Data
Kraus, Richard G.
        Leisure in a changing America : multicultural perspectives / Richard Kraus.
                        p.   cm.
        Includes bibliographical references (p.   ) and index.
        ISBN 0-02-366302-2
        1. Leisure—United States—History. 2. Leisure—History. 3. Leisure—Social aspects—
United States. 4. Leisure—Social aspects. 5. Minorities—United States—Recreation.
I. Title.
GV53.K73   1994
790'.01'35—dc20   93-31963
                                                                                    CIP

Printing: 2 3 4 5 6 7 8 9   Year: 4 5 6 7

Photo credits appear on page 394.

To Galina

About the Author

Dr. Kraus is primarily known as an educator, having taught at the University of Utah and Cortland College, New York, and headed recreation and leisure-service curricula at Teachers College, Columbia University, Lehman College of the City University of New York, and Temple University. He has written more than 35 textbooks and monographs, including several widely used texts in recreation fundamentals, program planning and leadership, and therapeutic recreation. Dr. Kraus has received the Distinguished Fellow Award of the Society of Park and Recreation Educators, was selected the Jay B. Nash Scholar of the American Association for Leisure and Recreation, and was given the National Literary Award of the National Recreation and Park Association.

Preface

Most textbooks on leisure and recreation in American life take one of three perspectives: (1) leisure as an individual, personal experience, seen from a psychological or philosophical vantage point; (2) leisure as a social system, using sociological methods of analysis; or (3) leisure as a function of government or other agencies, in terms of providing recreational facilities and programs.

In contrast, this text seeks to provide a diversified, contemporary picture of the role of leisure and recreation in American culture. It confronts the dramatic changes in the nation's population in terms of ethnic or racial makeup, shifting gender roles, and such factors as social class and life-style groupings, generational trends, and the impact of disability and residence on leisure behaviors. Throughout, it shows the linkage of leisure with religion and family life, business and employment, environmental concerns, and political and governmental issues.

Leisure in a Changing America: Multicultural Perspectives is designed to serve as a text in upper-level undergraduate and graduate courses in major departments of recreation and leisure studies. It may also be used in non-major courses that are part of general undergraduate degree or core curriculum requirements in American studies, or those concerned with women's or African-American studies.

The reader should be warned—unlike texts that paint a rather limited and glossy picture of leisure's role in American life or of the nation itself, this book presents a more critical and realistic view. While leisure and recreation are seen as highly enriching and creative aspects of modern life, it is also shown that leisure may encompass seriously self-destructive or societally damaging forms of play, such as addictive gambling, substance abuse, and commercialized and exploitative sex. Similarly, although the United States is credited for the generosity with which it has accepted immigrants from every part of the world and for its rich and complex culture, the text also depicts the racial or gender-linked prejudices and inequities of the past—some of which still linger today.

The text is divided into four sections. Part One includes Chapters 1 through 4, which deal with basic concepts of time, work, leisure, and recreation, tracing them through earlier periods of history to the end of the twentieth century in America. Part Two includes Chapters 5 through 8, which describe the major demographic categories in which change is occurring in American society: race and ethnicity, gender, social class, and stages of the life cycle. Part Three includes Chapters 9 through 12, which present detailed analyses of outdoor recreation and tourism, sports and games, the arts and entertainment, and what the author describes as "morally marginal" or potentially harmful forms of play. Part Four includes Chapters 13 and 14, which examine the leisure-service system and recreation, park, and leisure-service profession in terms of both challenges facing the field and future projections.

Several important themes recur throughout the book. First is the ongoing struggle of people throughout history to obtain more discretionary time, including the "shorter-hours" movement during the industrial era in the United States and the recently reported "time famine" that affects particularly upper-level professional and managerial personnel. Next, the commodification of leisure—its emergence as an industry that brings vast revenues and employment rewards to the nation's economy—is discussed; this is linked to technological innovation, which helps to create new forms of play and make possible additional nonwork time.

A third important theme has to do with religion, in terms of its historical role in condemning and seeking to control various forms of play and, more recently, serving as a sponsor of leisure pursuits. A fourth critical trend has been government's acceptance of leisure and recreation as significant responsibilities on federal, state, and local levels, particularly in terms of providing parks and other opportunities for outdoor recreation.

A fifth and overriding concern of the book stems from its multicultural perspective. It shows how America, starting from its essential white, Protestant, Anglo-Saxon identity, in which those of other backgrounds were regarded as subordinate inferiors, moved through a "melting pot" phase that stressed the need for all citizens to become blended in a single homogeneous society—and ultimately became today's "mosaic" that accepts the reality that we are a nation of many respected racial and ethnic backgrounds and customs. Similarly, the impact of the feminist movement on the status and life opportunities of girls and women is examined—particularly as it relates to leisure and recreation. The concept of androgyny and fuller acceptance of homosexuality within the culture are described, recognizing that they continue to represent controversial and emotion-laden issues. The nature of past and present social class structures and leisure life-styles in the United States and the changing roles of different age groups and family constellations are also examined.

A final major concern of *Leisure in a Changing America: Multicultural Perspectives* focuses on the marked contrast between the nation's inner cities, plagued as they are by poverty, broken families, drug dealing, and other pathologies, and the surrounding suburbs and small towns, which are generally much more prosperous and stable. The effect of this "have" and "have-not" dichotomy in American life—particularly vivid in terms of leisure and recreation opportunities and life-style patterns—represents a critical challenge to professionals and agencies in this field of community service.

In dealing with all of these issues, this text seeks to be as accurate, honest, and carefully documented as possible, recognizing that many of them are controversial and that some of the subjects covered may be viewed from sharply varying perspectives. As a single example, college and university sport, which represents an extremely popular area of spectator interest in the United States, is shown to be a highly exploitative and morally dubious enterprise—although sport itself is viewed as a fascinating and potentially valuable leisure experience.

As an aid to the reader, photographs are presented in 25 photo essays that illustrate many of the key points of the book. Within the text, a number of passages begin with a *To the Point* heading; these sections provide examples or stress important concepts. These, along with the questions at the end of the chapter, should be used as the basis for class discussions or the subject of written papers.

To ensure the book's authenticity, the author has carried out extensive research in a wide range of sources. Scholarly journals like the *Journal of Leisure Research, Leisure Sciences,* and *Leisure Studies* have been reviewed, along with journals in the social and behavioral sciences, and more professionally oriented publications like *Parks and Recreation,* the *Journal of Physical Education, Recreation and Dance,* and the *Journal of Park and Recreation Administration.* General-interest publications like *Time, Newsweek, U.S. News and World Report, Harper's, Atlantic Monthly,* and *The Christian Century,* and several leading newspapers have also been studied to ensure coverage of leisure-related subjects well into the early 1990s.

The author has also benefited from the published writings of dozens of leading recreation, park, and leisure studies educators, including M. Deborah Bialeschki, John Crompton, Daniel Dustin, Geoffrey Godbey, Thomas Goodale, Karla Henderson, Benjamin Hunnicutt, John Kelly, Leo McAvoy, James Murphy, and H. Douglas Sessoms. Finally, material has been gathered from dozens of other sources, such as directors of public recreation and park departments, nonprofit youth-serving agencies, therapeutic recreation programs, outdoor recreation sponsors, theme parks and commercial recreation businesses, armed forces bases, and educational institutions, who provided brochures, program reports, and photographs.

The author gratefully acknowledges the assistance of several individuals who reviewed the manuscript or proposal and provided criticism and helpful suggestions, including Gene Bammel and Lei Lane Bammel, West Virginia University; Kathleen Cordes, Miramar College; Geoffrey Godbey, Pennsylvania State University; Michael Jackson, Temple University; and Charles Yaple, State University of New York, Cortland. At Macmillan, Ann Castel Davis and Mary Harlan provided consistent and generous guidance and support. To them, and to his fellow faculty members and students through the years at Teachers College, Columbia University, Lehman College of the City University of New York, and Temple University in Philadelphia, he expresses his deep appreciation.

Contents

CHAPTER 10
Sports in American Life   235

CHAPTER 11
Arts and Entertainment in Popular Culture   267

PART FOUR
The Leisure-Service System:
Goals, Professionalism, and Future Challenges

CHAPTER 13
The Leisure-Service System:
Agencies, Philosophy, and Professionalism   331

⫸ PART ONE

Setting the Stage: Basic Concepts and Historical Background

1 Leisure in American Life

Now we stand on the threshold of an age that will bring leisure to all of us, more leisure than all the aristocracies of history, all the patrons of art, all the captains of industry and kings of enterprise ever had at their disposal. . . . What shall we do with this great opportunity? In the answers that we give to this question the fate of our American civilization will enfold.[1]

Just what is leisure, and why is it an appropriate subject for scholarly investigation and social concern?

Seen simply as free time, leisure represents an important force in contemporary American life, from a personal, societal, and economic point of view. However, leisure is more than simply freedom from work. This chapter presents several concepts of leisure that show its true dimensions. They make clear that leisure provides a mirror that reflects America's traditional beliefs and customs, as well as a channel that helps to redirect and transform the society's evolving values and behaviors.

Given the complex and changing nature of American culture, it is essential not to rely on a single discipline such as sociology or psychology to understand leisure, but rather to take a multidisciplinary approach that captures the varied aspects of leisure in modern life. History, sociology, anthropology, economics, and other disciplines are part of this approach. They are used to identify the impact of America's increasingly pluralistic makeup—in terms of ethnic and racial identity, changing gender roles, generational trends, and social-class shifts—on leisure values and behaviors.

■ MID-CENTURY EXPECTATIONS OF LEISURE

In the mid-twentieth century, expectations for the growth of leisure in the United States were high. It was widely predicted that leisure—usually defined as nonwork or discretionary time—would expand dramatically for all. The workweek would be shorter, vacations and holidays would be increasingly available, and retirement would come at a much earlier age.

Beyond such predictions, it was also assumed that leisure would represent an increasingly important source of personal values and life satisfaction for most Americans. Sociologists agreed that the work ethic had declined sharply, with labor in the industrial era having become overly specialized, boring, and unfulfilling. Proponents of a new humanistic approach to leisure argued that it was rapidly becoming the focal point of our lives, playing a critical role with respect to work, family relations, education, and religion.

Although such views may have seemed visionary to many Americans, they had their roots in past centuries. In ancient Athens, Socrates concluded that leisure was the best of all possessions, and Aristotle wrote that in a well-ordered state, the citizen should have leisure. In nineteenth-century America, Thoreau praised enrichment of the spirit through leisure, and Walt Whitman's great poem, "Leaves of Grass," had the line, "I loaf and invite my soul." In 1876, journalist Horace Greeley pointed out the need for "professors of play," and asked, "Who will teach us incessant workers how to achieve leisure and enjoy it?" Four years later, President James Garfield declared, "We may divide the whole struggle of the human race into two chapters: first the fight to get leisure, and then the second fight of civilization—what shall we do with our leisure when we get it?" Numerous other influential public figures continued to hail the growth of leisure and its potential contribution to national well-being in the decades that followed.

In the final years of the twentieth century, have these glowing expectations of leisure been realized? At best, the trend has been mixed. Despite predictions that the workweek would continue to become shorter, it remained relatively stable in the post–World War II decades. Then, in the mid and late 1980s, a series of reports indicated that many Americans were actually working longer hours, and that the nation was suffering from a "time famine"—a trend that will be discussed more fully later in this text. Nonetheless, leisure continues to be a critical element in contemporary American life. Our free-time pursuits provide a major source of life satisfaction, healthful personal development, and rewarding social involvement. In the broadest sense, leisure helps to assure the quality of everyday life. It provides the opportunity for pleasure, relaxation, release from stress, and creative self-fulfillment.

When constructively used, leisure promotes a sense of community and civic pride and helps to build constructive relationships among people of different ethnic, racial, and religious backgrounds. Overall, it provides the space in which we come together as friends, family members, or neighbors to explore our talents and skills, compete and cooperate, celebrate our lives, and express our finest human qualities.

⫸ TO THE POINT

Beyond these personal and social values, leisure has become an immense economic force in the modern world. Spending on varied forms of leisure activity involves hundreds of billions of dollars each year and is responsible for millions of jobs. Such activities have a profound impact on Americans, not only at home but throughout the world. American entertainment, for example, has "gone global," and is changing both those who consume it and those who create it:

> America is saturating the world with its myths, its fantasies, its tunes and dreams. . . . American entertainment products—movies, records, books, theme parks, sports, cartoons, television shows—are projecting an imperial self-confidence across the globe.
>
> Entertainment is America's second biggest export (behind aerospace), bringing in a trade surplus of more than $5 billion a year. American entertainment rang up some $300 billion in sales last year, of which an estimated 20 percent came from abroad. By the year 2000, half of the revenues from American movies and records will be earned in foreign countries.[2]

Today, government at all levels assists in the provision of varied forms of recreation by establishing national and state parks and other sites for outdoor recreation, local playgrounds, sports and arts complexes, senior centers, and other facilities and programs. Similarly, numerous nonprofit agencies have been developed to meet community needs for wholesome leisure activity. Major corporations, the armed forces, religious denominations, and real estate developers all sponsor recreation services to meet the needs of their constituencies. Within the fields of health care and rehabilitation, therapeutic recreation service has evolved as a recognized professional discipline.

Leisure represents a giant industry today, estimated to involve several hundred billion dollars in spending each year. Above, the Annual Convention and Trade Show of the International Association of Amusement Parks and Attractions features nearly two thousand booths and six hundred amusement industry companies from around the world. Many companies are involved in providing water-based recreation. Left, White Water, Inc., markets huge, futuristic waterplay parks around the world. Below, the Sylvan Corporation designs and builds thousands of residential swimming pools.

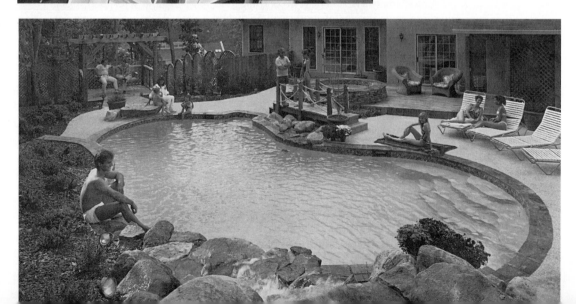

However, it would be wrong to assume that leisure represents a totally positive force in American life. Many forms of play—such as those involving compulsive gambling or drug abuse—degrade or injure those who engage in them. Beyond this, as a nation, Americans spend a great bulk of their free time in passive and unimaginative ways, often relying on stereotyped entertainment with an overwhelming emphasis on violence or other tawdry themes. Summing up, the case may be made that leisure in modern American life represents a blessing or a curse—with the potential for either enriching individual and societal well-being or for undermining and damaging it.[3]

Until recently, few efforts were made to examine leisure systematically. The sociology of leisure tended to be regarded as a minor adjunct of work in industrial society, and the study of leisure's past was conducted chiefly by amateur historians as a colorful, even amusing branch of history to which few serious scholars would devote their energies.

Over the past four decades, however, there has been a marked turnaround in the recognition of leisure as a significant area of academic study. Scholars in a dozen academic specializations have explored the meaning of leisure and recreation and their impact on society. Through their efforts, it has become increasingly clear that leisure represents an important aspect of national and community life. Its role may be described in two ways: (1) leisure serves as a *mirror* that *reflects* our national character and cultural values; and (2) leisure constitutes a powerful force in *shaping* and *changing* our way of life.

■ LEISURE AS A MIRROR OF NATIONAL VALUES

Leisure in American culture offers a diverse panorama of pastimes, hobbies, rituals, competitive events, excursions, social groups, and other voluntarily chosen free-time pursuits. For those who think of it chiefly as casual relaxation and respite from work, it is instructive to recognize that millions of people engage regularly in strenuous sports or demanding outdoor recreation activities—not as work but as a form of play. Millions of others participate in community arts activities or volunteer in a host of community-service roles in their leisure hours.

All of our nation's traditions and values are clearly illustrated in such free-time involvements. In our hobbies, the games we play, the television shows or movies we watch, the tourist attractions we visit, and the toys and games we give our children, our character as a society is exposed. Our love of the land, sense of civic responsibility, aesthetic standards, attitudes toward winning and losing, and other traits all come into play in our leisure.

A vivid example of this lies in the way we have transformed leisure into a commodity. In the early days of the republic, foreign visitors commented on the materialistic values of the American people and their fervent worship of business. Today, almost every form of organized leisure activity has been transformed into a vigorously marketed commercial enterprise. Huge conglomerates and mom-and-pop businesses alike develop games and toys, campgrounds, fitness centers, and varied forms of play and entertainment that saturate the free hours of the nation. Increasingly, universities sponsor competitive sports networks that have little to do with the legitimate goals of higher education, but instead feed into the high-powered world of professional sports. In numerous other ways, the leisure activities we pursue reflect our nation's values, both positive and negative.

■ LEISURE AS SHAPER OF THE CULTURE

At the same time that leisure mirrors national traditions and values, it also transmits and shapes them. In ancient Athens, Plato argued that the laws of adulthood were taught through the games of childhood. In modern America, we have established numerous organizations, both sectarian and secular, that use recreation as a means of teaching responsible citizenship and moral values to children and youth. Similarly, we have established museums, libraries, theaters, art galleries, and opera and concert halls that carry on the cultural heritage of the past and contribute to new forms of creative expression.

Too often, however, we permit the private and commercial domination of leisure programming, particularly in urban ghettos where socially constructive forms of leisure opportunity are lacking. Three decades ago, economist John Kenneth Galbraith suggested that in well-organized communities with strong school systems, recreation programs, and other needed services, the diversionary forces operating on youth might do little harm. But, he wrote, in communities where public services failed to keep abreast of private consumption, things were quite different:

> Here, in an atmosphere of private opulence and public squalor, the private goods have full sway. Schools do not compete with television and the movies. . . . The hot rod and the wild ride take the place of more sedentary sports for which there are inadequate facilities. . . . alcohol, narcotics and switchblade knives [or today, semiautomatic weapons] are . . . part of the increased flow of goods, and there is nothing to dispute their enjoyment.[4]

To illustrate the power of popular entertainment to influence youth today, we find an incessant display of obscenity and often sexist violence displayed on the television screen or in the rock music that appeals to vast numbers of young people. It is widely believed that the growing incidence of violence against women and the mindless slaughter of the young by gunfire in inner-city slums are at least partly attributable to such causes. Certainly, when society fails to provide attractive and positive leisure outlets for disadvantaged youth today, it permits them to fall easy victims to the lures of drug culture, gang allegiances, and other forms of contemporary social pathology.

■ MEANING OF LEISURE

At its simplest level, leisure is usually thought of as time free of work commitment. A related meaning is that it is an attitude or state of being that is relaxed and free of care or obligation. The German philosopher, Josef Pieper, described leisure as:

a mental and spiritual attitude. . . . not simply the result of external factors [such as] spare time, a holiday, a week-end or a vacation. . . . It is . . . an attitude of mind, a condition of the soul, and as such utterly contrary to the ideal of [work].[5]

It was usually assumed that leisure activities were relaxed and undemanding; Rom Harré suggests that they

should be unhurried, idle, unstructured, perhaps even a mode of resting. They are thus defined in contrast to frantic, busy, structured, demanding activities in which time appears as some kind of discipline.[6]

A number of authors have suggested highly complex perspectives through which to understand and analyze leisure, including "humanistic," "epistomological," "existential," and "political" models. In the present text, the author presents six of the most useful perspectives, leading to a composite definition of the term.

Classical View of Leisure: Athenian Scholē

Historically, the earliest recorded references to leisure were in ancient Athens, where wealthy citizens did not work, but instead were free to engage in study, the arts, philosophical and literary discussion, and athletics. For them, leisure—or *scholē,* as it was called—was a way of life spent in the pursuit of virtue and civic contribution. It excluded the possibility of work, which was regarded as ignoble and unworthy of the Athenian citizen. Kelly comments that Greek towns were carefully designed to serve leisure needs:

Not only did a central area for markets and government provide a "forum" for discussion and argumentation, but the town plan generally provided parks, baths, theaters, sports arenas, gymnasium and exercise grounds. Added to these were the academies for the learning and practicing of the arts and philosophy and music. Stress was placed on [enabling the free person to] develop both mind and body.[7]

Veblen's Theory of the Leisure Class

Extending the concept of leisure as an aristocratic possession, the late-nineteenth-century scholar, Thorstein Veblen, concluded that throughout history only the rich and powerful social classes had possessed leisure. This practice originated, he wrote, among earlier predatory societies that ultimately evolved into "pecuniary" cultures based on economic power. In the modern era, the wealthy engaged in what Veblen called "conspicuous consumption"; their elaborate homes and summer retreats and their ostentatious entertainment and pastimes all demonstrated their superior status.

Some critics have argued that the existence of a leisure class was essential to the development of culture through the ages. Clive Bell wrote:

Civilization requires the existence of a leisured class and thus of slaves—of people, I mean, who give some part of their surplus time and energy to the support of others. . . . As a means . . . to civility, a leisured class is essential.[8]

Veblen was less charitable in his view, considering leisure itself as a decadent example of economic exploitation. He deplored the extravagance of the rich in an era when vast numbers lived in hovels and toiled long hours in factories, in mines, or on farms.

Leisure as Discretionary Time

The most common understanding of leisure today is that it consists of time free from work or work-related responsibilities, such as study, travel, or union activity. Typically, when the workweek is shortened or when holidays or vacations are added, economists conclude that employees have gained increased leisure.

Other tasks required for self-maintenance, such as eating, sleeping, shopping, housekeeping, cleaning, or obtaining medical care, are also regarded as obligatory uses of time, and so are not considered to be forms of leisure. Thus, the French sociologist Joffre Dumazedier described leisure as time apart from the obligations of work, family, and society.

Leisure as Free-Time Activity

A related view is that leisure is more than discretionary time; instead, it is often considered to be the activities we engage in voluntarily during such periods of time. The *International Dictionary of Sociology* has defined leisure as the pursuits that people carry on in their free time, and many sociological studies of leisure have sought to identify and analyze the recreational involvements of different population groups.

Leisure activities range from games and hobbies to sports, creative pastimes, and varied forms of entertainment, outdoor play, and travel. They may also include volunteer activity and community service, education that is not career-directed, and religious involvement. In the view of some social critics, most such activities are trivial and unworthy of the term *leisure*. For example, Sebastian de Grazia concluded that the tendency of modern Americans to fill their free hours with hobbies, community tasks, personal chores, and other forms of light amusement meant that they had no real leisure, in the classical sense.[9]

Leisure as Personal Experience
and State of Being

The same activity may or may not constitute a form of leisure involvement, depending on the reasons for engaging in it and the circumstances under which it is enjoyed. An activity pursued primarily for gain—monetary or otherwise—is not usually considered leisure. Beyond this, leisure motivations may be listed by the dozen, including the need to achieve varied forms of emotional satisfaction—to gain a sense of accomplishment, pleasure, release or escape, self-discovery, excitement, mastery, or challenge.

In recent years, social psychologists have identified two basic characteristics of the leisure experience: (1) it must involve perceived freedom in selecting activities without compulsion or the hope for extrinsic rewards; and (2) it has the potential to involve all aspects of the individual's personality and, in its highest form, to reach a state of what has been called "self-actualization"—achieving one's fullest potential as a human being.

The Leisure Industry

The most recent and influential shift in our thinking about leisure has been to characterize it as an industry—a huge, diversified area of business opportunity, employment, and economic return. Butsch points out that two centuries ago, Americans purchased comparatively few leisure goods or services. They played their own games, created their own music, and made their own toys. Commercial amusements, while they existed, did not dominate daily life. Today, most of our leisure activities depend on some organized form of sponsorship or provision of service, much of it involving the purchase of commodities:

> a television set, a baseball, tickets to the theater. We spend much of our free time watching and listening to programmed entertainment distributed by large corporations; we use sports and recreational equipment distributed by oligopolistic industries. Toys, now a multibillion-dollar industry, are produced by major corporations and retailed through national chains. As we have become more and more dependent on purchased goods and services for our fun, so too has leisure become a source of profit for corporate enterprise, and an integral part of the economy.[10]

To illustrate, Table 1.1 sums up national expenditures on leisure goods and services in the United States extending over a recent twenty-year period. While impressive, these statistics do not report the full range of leisure spending, since they do not include a number of important areas of leisure activity, such as travel and tourism, casino gambling, alcohol consumption, adult education, or spending by government and nonprofit agencies on recreation and park facilities and programs. The actual amount, if it were possible to measure all leisure spending accurately, would be closer to $700 billion, rather than the *Statistical Abstract*'s consumer expenditure sum of $256.6 billion.[11]

Unlike other industries, leisure does not represent a single clearly identifiable service, manufacturing, or distributing process. Instead, it involves the provision of a remarkably diverse set of services and programs by several different kinds of sponsors: governmental, commercial, nonprofit, educational, and therapeutic.

■ LEISURE: A COMPOSITE DEFINITION

Recognizing that leisure may be conceptualized in many different ways, the following statement suggests its key elements, as it is portrayed throughout this text:

> Leisure is defined as that portion of a person's life that is marked by: (1) freedom from the necessity for carrying on paid work or other obligated tasks; and (2) the opportunity to engage in pursuits that bring a sense of pleasure and self-enrichment, or that meet other important personal or social needs.

However, leisure involves much more than purely personal experience. It also represents an important social institution and is both a recognized function of government and a complex industry that provides substantial employment opportunities in the United States and around the world.

TABLE 1.1
Personal consumption expenditures for recreation, 1970–1990

Type of Product or Service	1970	1980	1985	1990
Total recreation expenditures	91.3	149.1	195.5	256.6
Percent of total personal consumption	5.0	6.1	6.8	7.9
Books and maps	10.5	10.2	11.4	15.4
Magazines, newspapers, and sheet music	13.2	18.4	17.9	20.8
Nondurable toys and sports supplies	9.5	17.4	22.3	28.3
Wheel goods, sports and photographic equipment	10.3	20.2	24.4	27.7
Video and audio products, computer equipment, and musical instruments	8.8	17.5	29.7	52.5
Radio and television repair	2.7	3.5	3.3	3.4
Flowers, seeds, and potted plants	4.0	5.9	7.0	9.6
Admissions to specified spectator amusements	8.2	9.9	10.2	11.2
Motion picture theaters	4.2	3.8	3.6	3.4
Legitimate theaters, opera, and entertainments of nonprofit institutions	1.3	2.7	2.8	4.1
Spectator sports	2.8	3.4	3.7	3.7
Clubs and fraternal organizations except insurance	3.8	4.0	6.3	7.8
Pari-mutuel net receipts	2.8	3.6	3.2	3.1
Commercial participant amusements	6.3	12.5	16.1	19.2
Other	11.3	25.8	43.5	57.5

SOURCE: *Statistical Abstract of the United States*. 1992. Washington, DC: U.S. Government Printing Office, p. 234.
NOTE: Expenditures are given in billions of constant (inflation-adjusted) dollars, with 1987 as base. Figures represent market value of purchases of goods and services by individuals and nonprofit institutions.

Beyond this point, a number of other questions must be considered. First, is *all* free time leisure? Does the person who has lost a job and is unable to find a new one really have leisure? Do prisoners in penitentiary cells or people with serious disabilities in long-term care facilities have leisure? Throughout the industrial era, leisure was generally regarded as a complement to work; one worked in order to gain leisure, and used it to restore oneself for further work. Do individuals who do not, or cannot, work have leisure?

Another issue deals with the idea of freedom and the understanding that leisure activities must be chosen without compulsion or pressure. But is this always possible? Many children engage in sports or other forms of recreation because their parents want them to or because of peer pressure. If one's environment lacks needed recreation resources, such as golf courses or swimming pools, is one truly free in making leisure choices?

Is it always possible to distinguish between work and leisure or between maintenance tasks and recreation? Is the mere fact of monetary payment enough to distinguish work from leisure? Often a person who is essentially a hobbyist may begin to earn money at it, as in the case of an amateur potter who occasionally sells his or her work at craft shows. Would such involvement be legitimate leisure as long as the individual is creating works that do *not* sell—and does it suddenly turn into work when the first salable pieces are created?

Any definition of leisure must be treated rather flexibly and must take into account the possibility of "semi-leisure"—that is, experiences that are chosen under certain constraints or pressures, or that may have practical or extrinsic purposes apart from pleasure or personal satisfaction. Religion might be an illustration of semi-leisure, in that it usually consists of a voluntarily chosen activity carried on in one's discretionary time. At the same time, many devout individuals might consider religious practice an important form of self-maintenance, essential to healthy living.

■ RELATED TERMS: *RECREATION* AND *PLAY*

Two other terms that are closely related to leisure and are often used synonymously are *recreation* and *play*. *Recreation* customarily refers to the activities that one carries on in leisure for pleasure or to achieve other important personal outcomes. It may also be described as a process or personal experience and in that sense is very similar to definitions of *leisure*. The distinction between the two concepts is that leisure provides the *opportunity* for several different kinds of involvements, *including* recreation—but also including such pursuits as continuing education, community service, or religious worship, which are not normally thought of as recreation. Another distinction is that the term *recreation* is often used to describe the provision of leisure services, or the network of agencies that offer sports, social activities, the arts, or other forms of enjoyable participation.

The term *play* has often been used synonymously with *recreation,* although over time what was called the "play movement" came to be known as the "recreation movement." *Play* was thought to refer to the casual amusement of children; today it is recognized that adults may play, and that play may be serious, organized, and purposeful, rather than light and spontaneous activity. Generally, play is believed to be based on several specific elements, such as competition, playacting, and exploratory or creative behavior. Usually, it implies a degree of active involvement; thus, while games and sports would be forms of play, attending a lecture or reading a book—which might be forms of recreation—would not be considered play. For children, psychologists confirm that play is often an important developmental experience. For adults, it may represent an essential break from tedious or monotonous work; it may also be a way of approaching work creatively.

■ LEISURE AS A SOCIAL CONCERN

The realization that leisure may have both positive *and* negative potential, in terms of societal and human outcomes, led to government's accepting responsibility for providing recreation and park facilities and programs beginning in the late nineteenth and early twentieth centuries. It was widely believed that such programs would help build desirable character traits among young people, assist in preventing juvenile delinquency, and improve community life in general.

By the mid-twentieth century, there was widespread recognition that one of the important social challenges facing the United States had to do with the "new leisure." Planning agencies confidently predicted that the expanded use of automation in industry would result in an immense block of added free time for all groups in society. Based on these expectations, a new academic discipline emerged. In the years after World War II, several hundred colleges and universities throughout the United States and Canada established new degree-granting curricula in recreation and leisure studies. These programs had two major thrusts: (1) to prepare individuals to direct recreation, park, and leisure-service programs in governmental, voluntary, commercial, therapeutic, and other types of agencies; and (2) to conduct scholarly investigations of leisure as a human experience and social institution.

■ SCHOLARLY STUDY OF LEISURE

The study of leisure—or, more broadly, recreation, parks, and leisure studies—is linked to three broad areas of higher education, the humanities, the natural sciences, and the social sciences. However, its primary emphasis has been within the realm of the social sciences. Historians, for example, have documented the past development of recreation and leisure in Europe and North America. Some have focused on a particular era, such as the colonial period, while others have examined the history of the recreation and park movement, the role of women in leisure, the functions of government in park development, or the evolution of a particular form of leisure activity, such as sports.

Sociologists have taken the lead in analyzing the overall role of leisure in contemporary society. They have explored the relation of leisure to work, to different occupational groups and social classes, to gender, race, life-cycle and life-style patterns, and to numerous other social variables.

Economists have examined the market behavior of leisure consumers, monetary measures of benefits and costs of recreational participation, equity in resource allocation by public recreation and park agencies, and problems of financing and operating recreation facilities and programs.

Anthropologists have long maintained an interest in pursuits such as games, music, rituals, oral and written literature, and other folklore elements, in preliterate and tribal societies and in more developed cultures as well.

Philosophers have formulated concepts of leisure, recreation, and play and have studied the linkage between religion and leisure, the ethics of sports, the appropriate role of government in leisure, and other theoretical issues underlying this field.

Psychologists have been particularly active in defining the nature of the play experience, the goals and outcomes of leisure involvement, and other aspects of individual and group recreation. In a host of other scholarly disciplines, including political science, urban planning, and environmental studies, significant leisure research is being conducted today.[12]

Interdisciplinary Approaches

In addition to research within such specialized disciplines, a number of social scientists have begun to ask broader questions about the place of leisure in the modern community. Butsch, for example, asks: Why has leisure developed in particular ways? Did interpersonal social or economic forces, such as the dynamics of capitalist economy, constitute the engine of change?

> As consumers of leisure products, have we lost control of our own free time? Does leisure represent the interests and values of participants—that is, is it an area of self-expression? Or have capitalists or reformers designed leisure to control the behavior of lower classes?[13]

▮▶ TO THE POINT

Far from being a "fun-and-games," trivial kind of concern, leisure is now recognized as an important part of the play of ideas and public policy, with government, religious groups, businesses, and other organizations all having a stake in its development. Polish sociologist Bohdan Jung points out that leisure has become closely linked to major problems of cultural and economic development and to international relations. Writing in the late 1980s, he described the "globalization" of leisure, embodying the following elements:

> its internationalization, transcending local cultures and value systems, together with applications not just to industrialized urban societies (First World), but also to the Second (socialist) and the Third World; increasingly broader conceptualization of "leisure" as a social time, a period for enjoyment of culture and recreation, self-actualization and human development, as opposed to . . . passive idleness [and] growing awareness that in terms of human development and creation of non-material values, leisure can have as much impact on the generation of well-being as purely economic measures . . .[14]

Jung argues that the marketing of leisure goods and services worldwide, the creation of transnational entertainment conglomerates, and the promotion and delivery of leisure services in both developed and developing countries are having profound impact on the world economy. In a number of nations, he points out, tourism has become the largest employer after agriculture and the most important means of earning foreign exchange.

Beyond this, we now recognize the complex influences that affect leisure in the modern community. Chris Rojek, for example, points out that in the past, leisure and recreation were seen largely as a reaction to or spillover from work. Today, he writes, leisure is clearly related to:

> social constructs of health and illness, virtue and idleness, propriety and profanity. . . .
> To understand these influences, we need to examine the processes of class and sexual

struggle, rationalization, civilization and citizenship. . . . [and to] get away from mono-chromatic pictures of leisure and recreation which present these very complicated activi-ties as determined [by single systems] such as class, gender, race and bureaucracy. Leisure and recreation experience is not the product of a single system. Rather, it arises from the interaction between systems.[15]

Accepting this view, it is clear that a full understanding of leisure's role in modern life cannot be obtained through any single mode of inquiry. While it might be con-venient to rely exclusively on sociology or psychology, the reality is that the subject is too complex for any one discipline to be successful in dealing with all its issues. Burton points out that a central problem in current leisure planning and research efforts is the investigators' unquestioning reliance on the scientific method:

coupled with an overwhelming felt need to identify, demonstrate and quantify causality, and a dominating desire to separate "facts" from "values"—with the erroneous pre-sumption that, not only *can* the two be separated, but also that "scientific facts" . . . should form the sole basis for forecasting, policy-making and planning for leisure.[16]

Benjamin Hunnicutt agrees, pointing out that reliance on empirical research methods compels scholars to rely on "measurable attitudes," "observable behavior," and narrowly conceived hypotheses, rather than explore broader and more signifi-cant aspects of leisure. He writes:

play and leisure are surely the most complex and even irrational aspects of human expe-rience. They are also the most individualistic. Can behavioral science . . . ever avoid reducing play and leisure to categories and behavioral patterns so that they are no longer recognizable? Does not the essence of play and leisure lie in their very irrational-ity, their individual quality, their complexity and their changing nature? Can one ever measure and predict fun or pleasure?[17]

Instead, Hunnicutt suggests that a more humanistic approach that makes use of varied disciplines involving literature, the arts, and history should be used in explor-ing leisure. Accepting this principle means that a truly comprehensive review of the field cannot be limited to any single discipline, and should incorporate two kinds of research—the subjective, anecdotal, and humanistic method of inquiry, as well as the quantitatively oriented, empirical method.

■ FOCUS ON LEISURE IN HUMAN CULTURE

Linked to this approach is the conviction that leisure in America can best be under-stood by examining it as a part of contemporary culture. But what does the term *cul-ture* mean? It is sometimes narrowly understood to be concerned with intellectual knowledge and aesthetic awareness and sensitivity. However, a better understanding for our purpose is that of Robin Williams, Jr., who suggests that culture comes down from the past and is not created by any single person or generation—although it may be modified over time. He writes:

culture is social heredity—the total legacy of past human behavior effective in the pre-sent, representing the accumulation, through generations, of the artifacts, knowledges, beliefs and values by which men deal with the world. It is the precipitate of *learned* human adjustments to the physical environment and to society . . . that complex whole which includes knowledge, belief, art, morals, law, custom and any other capabilities and habits acquired by man as a member of society.[18]

Not only does culture change through the years; there are many different cultures or subcultures within any given society. A strong case can be made for "cultural relativism," meaning that there is no single, universal truth or set of values, customs, or moral codes among nations, or even within a single nation. Clearly, culture and leisure are closely linked. John Kelly writes:

> When culture is defined as what is learned in a society—the values, language, thought forms, role definitions, world views, art, organization and all that is taught in its institutions—then leisure and culture are obviously inseparable. . . . Culture is . . . the stuff out of which leisure experiences are made.[19]

The Multicultural Perspective

Within American society, while we may share certain common values and traits, we also vary greatly in terms of such factors as socioeconomic class, racial or ethnic identity, gender, age, degree of health or disability, region, and educational background.

If one is to understand the full meaning of leisure in America today, it is essential to take these factors into account. This book is therefore written from a multicultural perspective. The term *multiculturalism* has become almost a catchword over the last several years and has been the basis for heated debate with respect to educational goals and policies. There has been violent controversy over the effort to supplant what have been called Eurocentric approaches to the teaching of history, literature, and the other humanities with a new, more diverse emphasis on the contributions of Americans of many racial and ethnic origins. This effort has been linked with the demands of women and those with alternative life-styles for new curricula and teaching content representing their history and societal roles more fully.

Leisure represents an ideal medium for framing this debate. America's history is marked by a tradition of racial and sexual discrimination that kept minorities and women from participating fully in community life. Yet today, as part of a new drive toward equality within various spheres of personal opportunity, African Americans have made spectacular gains—as women have—in terms of sports participation, the arts and media of popular entertainment, and other sectors of leisure involvement.

But multiculturalism—or pluralism—involves far more than these two groups alone. Other racial or ethnic minorities, those with alternative sexual life-styles, members of different socioeconomic classes, people at each stage of the life cycle, those with disabilities, and those living in different regions of the country, all comprise an immensely varied society. Sharply contrasting leisure interests, values, and patterns of involvement help to make American society a rich mosaic of nonwork experience and personal enrichment. As Jesse Jackson puts it:

> America is not like a blanket—one piece of unbroken cloth, the same color, the same texture, the same size. America is more like a quilt—many pieces, many colors, many sizes, all woven and held together by a common thread.[20]

Throughout this book, American culture will be examined and illustrated from this pluralistic leisure perspective. We will see how the struggle for civil rights broke down the pattern of rigid racial segregation that had prevailed through most of the country until the 1960s and 1970s—and how much covert discrimination continues even today. We will review the progress made by girls and women in areas such as sports and outdoor recreation, and how much of this is still threatened by charges of lesbianism and male resistance to giving women equal opportunity in varied fields of daily life. As other demographic variables are brought into play, our growing reliance on technology in play, and the commodification of leisure in American culture will also be studied.

Beyond these emphases, we will review the history of leisure in the United States from the colonial era to the present day. The struggle on the part of labor leaders and political and social reformers to shorten the workweek and obtain more free time will be examined, along with the current, widely publicized "time famine." An analysis of the emerging profession of recreation, parks, and leisure services will be presented, ending with a projected scenario of future trends.

■ CHANGING VIEWS OF LEISURE

At the same time, we will see how the concept of leisure itself has changed sharply in recent years. First, the narrow view of leisure as nonwork time has shifted to a strong emphasis on leisure as participation in a host of athletic, cultural, social, and other pursuits.

The assumption that leisure is quiet and relaxing has been supplanted by the realization that free-time involvement may be demanding, exciting, and physically challenging. The linked concept of leisure being unstructured and free of commitment also has been replaced by the reality that many leisure pursuits necessarily involve scheduling, organization, and personal commitment over time.

The concept of leisure choices being totally free of compulsion and carried on solely for intrinsic purposes no longer applies; many leisure activities are constrained either by outside pressures or limitations, or are carried on to achieve practical personal goals.

Veblen's concept of leisure as an aristocratic possession, illustrated in the familiar term, *the leisure class,* has been reversed in modern society, in that the upper classes in society tend to have the least amount of free time, while the lower socioeconomic groups have the most.

In general, we have thought of leisure as an unmitigated "good," permitting relaxation from toil and the opportunity for self-enrichment and pleasure. Yet, as this text will show in detail, leisure may also provide the vehicle for a number of serious personal problems or social pathologies.

Traditionally, leisure was justified in industrial society as a reward for working well and was intended to refresh the worker for new toil. Today, leisure is no longer regarded as a secondary value, but assumes a primary role in many people's lives.

Finally, the view of leisure as a primarily personal kind of experience has given way to the understanding that it has become a social institution. Frey and Dickens point out that leisure has become transformed by the growth of organizations that sponsor it and by the opportunity it offers the public for a sense of community and bonding. They write:

> research . . . demonstrates that leisure in advanced societies is shaped by a highly visible network of commercial and public organizations encompassing a wide range of activities. These organizations have clearly defined arrangements of statuses and roles (e.g., organizers, schedulers, players, coaches, spectators, managers, promoters and referees) comparable to statuses and roles in the more traditional institutions. [They] also include, in varying degrees, virtually all members of society.[21]

■ SUMMARY

Leisure represents a major use of time today, has important social and personal values in contemporary society, and is part of a pervasive marketing system that shapes our lives in many ways. It has strong links to politics, family life, education, religion, and economics and has become an accepted responsibility of government and other social agencies.

In the chapters that lie ahead, we will explore three key concepts—time, work, and leisure—as they evolved throughout history and as they are understood in contemporary America. Throughout, we will see how the major forms of popular recreation illustrate the way in which leisure reflects dominant values of American culture—on the one hand materialistic, hedonistic, aggressive, and competitive, and on the other hand generous to others, spiritual, sensitive, and cooperative.

■ QUESTIONS FOR DISCUSSION

1. Justify the formal study of leisure in college or university curricula. Why is it a significant topic for analysis and understanding in higher education? What broad areas of academic study is it related to?
2. Leisure is said to be both a mirror of national values and a shaper of the culture. Give several examples of how specific forms of leisure illustrate the society's ideals and behavioral norms, and how these leisure pursuits influence or change the nation's values over time.
3. Draw a contrast between earlier, classical views of leisure, as exemplified in the Athenian *scholē,* and the contemporary approaches to it—particularly those that see leisure as a major industry and economic force.
4. Leisure has traditionally been thought of as slow-paced, freely chosen, and unstructured, carried out for its own sake. How has our modern-day view of leisure diverged sharply from this view?
5. This chapter argues that subjective, interdisciplinary approaches to the study of leisure may be more useful than empirical, statistically based, single-discipline approaches rooted in the physical or social sciences. What are the advantages of each of these two differing methods?
6. Define *culture* and explain how this chapter introduces the idea of multiculturalism as a focus for the study of leisure in a changing America.

■ NOTES

1. GRISWOLD, W. A. (President, Yale University). 1959. *Life Magazine* (December): 59.
2. BERNSTEIN, C. 1990. The leisure empire. *Time* (December 24).
3. This contrast was first made explicit in J. CHARLESWORTH. 1964. *Leisure in America: Blessing or curse?* Lancaster, PA: American Academy of Political and Social Science.
4. GALBRAITH, J. K. 1958. *The affluent society.* Boston: Houghton Mifflin, pp. 256–257.
5. PIEPER, J. 1952. *Leisure: The basis of culture.* New York: Pantheon, p. 52.
6. HARRÉ, R. 1990. Leisure and its varieties. *Leisure Studies* 9: 187.
7. KELLY, J. R. 1982. *Leisure.* Englewood Cliffs, NJ: Prentice-Hall, pp. 43–44.
8. BELL, C. 1958. How to make a civilization. In *Mass leisure,* ed. E. Larrabee and R. Meyersohn. Glencoe, IL: Free Press, p. 32.
9. DE GRAZIA, S. 1952. *Of time, work and leisure.* New York: Twentieth Century Fund.
10. BUTSCH, R., ed. 1990. *For fun and profit: The transformation of leisure into consumption.* Philadelphia: Temple University Press, p. 3.
11. See R. KRAUS. 1990. *Recreation and leisure in modern society.* Glenview, IL: Scott, Foresman, pp. 272–273.
12. For example, see A. GRAEFE and S. PARKER, eds. 1987. *Recreation and leisure: An introductory handbook.* State College, PA: Venture.
13. BUTSCH, *op. cit.,* p. 4.
14. JUNG, B. 1990. Globalization of leisure: A new set of issues. *Society and Leisure* (Spring): 77.
15. ROJEK, C. 1989. In *Understanding leisure and recreation: Mapping the past, charting the future,* ed. E. L. Jackson and T. L. Burton. State College, PA: Venture, p. 82.
16. BURTON, T. L., in Jackson and Burton, *op. cit.,* p. 48.
17. HUNNICUTT, B. K. 1988. Problems raised by the empirical study of play and some humanistic alternatives. Arlington, VA: *Abstracts of the 1988 NRPA Leisure Research Symposium* 8.
18. WILLIAMS, R. M., JR. 1970. *American society: A sociological interpretation.* New York: Knopf, pp. 25–26.
19. KELLY, J. R. 1987. *Freedom to be: A new sociology of leisure.* New York: Macmillan, p. 165.
20. JACKSON, J. 1992. The fabric of a nation. *Modern Maturity* (June-July): 23.
21. FREY, J., and D. DICKENS. 1990. Leisure as a primary institution. *Sociological Inquiry* 60 (August): 265.

2 Time, Work, and Leisure: Concepts and Early History

[Michael Fortino] says he has determined that over a lifetime the average American spends seven years in the bathroom, six years eating, five years waiting in lines, four years cleaning house, three years in meetings, one year searching for things, eight months opening junk mail, six months sitting at red lights. He also says that the average married couple spends four minutes a day conversing and the average working parent converses 30 seconds a day with children.[1]

Columnist George Will suggests that whether or not Fortino's numbers (see preceding page) describe the life of the typical reader, they underscore in a depressing way the fact that life is cumulative, and that we measure out our daily existences in coffee spoons of trivial activities. Any effort to comprehend the meaning of leisure in contemporary culture should begin with an examination of *time* itself—what it is, how it rules our lives, and how it is apportioned to varied human activities, including both work and play. This chapter traces the changing roles of time, work, and leisure through earlier periods of human history, showing their relationship to social class, religion, and economic life. It concludes with an analysis of the blurring of the line between work and leisure, and with the emergence of leisure as an important business element in American culture.

■ MEANING OF TIME

Time that is free of work or other obligated tasks is at the heart of leisure. Yet, what is time itself? It is essentially an abstract concept; it can't be touched, photographed, or weighed, yet we permit it to govern our lives. Wilbert Moore argues that the only close rival of money in terms of desirability and scarcity for humans is time.[2] However, there is no commonly acceptable term for the study of time and its uses. The closest is *chronology,* which describes the ordering and dating of past events, but does not analyze the rhythms and cycles that mark the use of time in human life.

Early Awareness of Time

The concept of time itself was probably understood at first by preliterate humans through such elements as the rhythm of breathing, the beat of the pulse, and other physiological phenomena. They became aware of the alternation of day and night and of the seasons of the year. Gradually, human beings must have learned to accept the need for ordering and synchronizing events within a time framework. The idea of a seven-day week is attributed to the ancient Babylonians, with the names of its successive days linked to seven gods and, through them, seven heavenly bodies that were believed to have power over humans. Similarly, the idea of hours having sixty minutes and minutes sixty seconds is attributed to the Babylonian mathematical system.

In earlier periods of history, work schedules were largely determined by the seasons of the year and the availability of daylight, rather than by formal time measurements. However, the invention of the clock made it possible to develop regularity in organizing and scheduling work. Historian Michael O'Malley describes the growing reliance on the ordering of time in America. At first, he writes, clocks were not respected and were widely regarded as a poor representation of the real time found in nature:

> But as the nation expanded westward and became more interconnected through the telegraph and the railroad, using nature's rhythm as the course of time became a problem. In the nineteenth century, clocks became the authority for time and a system of regional time zones developed. . . . Well into the nineteenth century there were dozens of local time zones across the country.[3]

Ultimately, throughout the world, agreement on major time zones was established and it became possible to schedule business activities and coordinate other societal functions more efficiently than during the earlier agricultural era. Today, time is at the heart of how we organize our lives, with appointments and deadlines for all tasks and events, including work and study hours, rates of speed on the highway, meal times, religious worship, and thousands of other functions.

■ DISCRETIONARY TIME: SOURCE OF LEISURE

Time that is unencumbered by work or other obligated tasks is referred to as discretionary time, in that we are able to decide for ourselves how to use it. Typically, we allow a major portion of our discretionary time *for* leisure, whether it be watching television, scheduling a tennis match or orchestra rehearsal, taking a trip, or simply loafing.

Leisure planners and managers must be acutely aware of time as they organize and schedule activities. A race track program or swimming meet must be precisely timed, both in terms of the individual events and the overall program. In analyzing the market appeal of a theme park or other tourist attraction, planners must factor in the time required to travel to a given site as part of the cost that consumers will be willing to pay to visit the attraction. In selling television advertising time for a major sports event, a single minute may cost many hundreds of thousands of dollars.

The most obvious application of time to the study of leisure, however, has to do with the free time that people have to engage in leisure pursuits. This tends to be available in differing amounts through one's lifetime. Typically, younger children and the elderly have the most free time, while working parents, particularly single parents, have the least. Leisure also fits within certain patterns of availability through the year and from day to day during the week. Summer tends to be a time when most families have substantial blocks of free time. This pattern is influenced by school vacation periods, which were originally instituted during an agricultural era to permit schoolchildren to work on farms during the summer months. In terms of daily and weekly schedules, for most individuals leisure is usually found during the late afternoon and evening hours and on weekends.

Special Leisure Times: Weekend and Saturday Night

The Canadian architect, Witold Rybczynski, points out that the modern two-day weekend evolved in the Industrial Revolution, when many British workers took what was wryly called "Saint Monday" off to sober up from a very unsober Sunday.[4] The weekend as Americans now enjoy it was the product of social reformers and labor leaders, who lobbied for a half-day off on Saturday, and entrepreneurs like Henry Ford, who realized that giving workers a two-day weekend would promote the sale of his inexpensive motorcars.

The catchphrase "TGIF" (Thank God It's Friday) reflects employees' boredom with work or their desire to escape from its stresses, and their anticipation of fun and relaxation to come on the weekend. For many, leisure is at its height on Saturday night. Susan Orlean points out that Saturday is the one night that neither follows nor precedes work, when people expect to have a good time doing what they want to do, not what they have to do:

> Saturday night is different from any other. On Saturday night, people get together, go dancing, bowling, drinking, out to dinner, get drunk, get killed, kill other people, go out on dates, visit friends, go to parties, listen to music, sleep, gamble, watch television, go cruising, and sometimes fall in love—just as they do every other night of the week. But on Saturday night they do all these things more often and with more passion and intent.[5]

Summing up, while some leisure may be spent casually or without preplanning, most deliberate uses of it involve the commitment and organization of time. We must reserve a campsite six months in advance, race along the highway to reach a motel for the night, schedule a bowling alley or racquetball court, and often cram our recreational and social obligations into too brief a span of time. The individual who attends a sports, music, or other special-interest camp, presumably for "fun," is likely to find that he or she is subjected to a demanding schedule of lectures, practice, and performance or competition extending over eight or ten hours each day. Thus, the fact that our leisure pursuits are so closely tied to time makes them seem much more like work than in the past. Indeed, it is impossible to understand the role of leisure in American culture today without also reviewing the place of work in our lives.

■ WORK IN SOCIETY

By definition, leisure is nonwork time, activity, or experience. But what *is* work? Our daily conversations reflect a broad preoccupation with it, using terms such as *homework, busywork, workouts, workshops, workhorses, schoolwork, work force, works of art, workrooms, worksheets, workups, work schedules,* and dozens of similar words and phrases.

Work may simply be defined as carrying out purposeful, organized tasks designed to provide material goods and services and usually compensated by payment. In a broader sense, it may suggest any systematic or focused activity; one may work at improving one's own fitness or learning a new language for pleasure and personal enrichment, rather than for pay.

Within the Protestant work ethic, work has historically been regarded as a religiously imposed task, essential to social progress and personal salvation. Theologians John Raines and Donna Day-Lower point out that humans evolved over thousands of years as toolmakers and users, developing skills that enabled them to master the natural world and achieve safer, healthier, and more comfortable life-styles. They cite the biblical mandate, "Be fruitful and multiply, and fill the earth and subdue it," as a way of saying that the human species' way of taking up residence on earth is through work. Labor, they write, is not simply a means of gaining wealth, but is instead an expression of a unique human excellence:

> In work and through work we humans express our human essence. And over time we transform and evolve that essence—biologically, technologically, and also religiously. . . . We are uniquely a species that lives by way of skill. It is by human skills that we establish our presence upon the earth and transform and perfect that presence.[6]

In the modern world, work has a number of important values beyond the obvious ones of providing needed goods and services or earning a livelihood. The American philosopher, George Santayana, suggested that there were three basic motivations for work: want (economic need), ambition (the drive for power, or to get ahead), and the love of occupation (intrinsic satisfaction in one's craftsmanship).

Clearly, work in the industrialized Western world has provided men and women not only financial reward but also a sense of self-respect. Beyond these values, having a job or other daily work commitment provides needed structure in one's life; often, when people retire, their lives seem to be empty and without purpose. Work also provides a social milieu; often the company office, factory, or other workplace gives employees a sense of "belonging," camaraderie, and being part of a larger whole.

■ EARLY PERSPECTIVES ON WORK AND LEISURE

To fully understand the relationship between time, work, and leisure, a brief review of earlier periods of human history will be helpful. In preindustrial, tribal societies, past and present, the line between work and leisure is not sharply drawn. The orientation of daily life is toward periods of intense effort—a mass hunt, a battle, planting and harvesting a crop—interspersed with periods of relative rest. Throughout, the rhythm of life is influenced by the seasons of the year and is marked by rituals, songs, dances, games, and ceremonies that are closely linked with practical tasks.

Historically, the first societies of which we have direct, detailed knowledge were in the Middle East—ancient Assyria, Babylonia, and Egypt. In these cultures, thousands of years before the Christian era began, social stratification led to the definition of several classes within a hierarchy of wealth and power. Jay Shivers points out, for example, that the upper classes in ancient Egypt constituted a relatively small elite composed chiefly of a hereditary caste of priests, soldiers, bureaucrats, and occasional gifted commoners who rose to power.[7] These individuals did not toil as such, but instead enjoyed entertainment, hunting, fishing, banquets, and other pastimes.

For the lower classes, work was required, and here we find the first detailed accounts of the days and hours of labor within specific occupations. Papyrus records tell of contracts between employers, apprentices, and journeymen, including details of pay, holidays, work hours, and obligations. In a historical description of Roman Egypt, Lindsay writes:

> A papyrus dated A.D. 48 allows an apprentice boy three free days a month, thirty-six a year. The method of computation shows the Egyptian division of the month into three . . . ten-day weeks.
>
> In [another contract] a lad is apprenticed for five years. Wages begin after six years and seven months, and the weaver provides clothes on a rising scale. "The boy shall have twenty holidays a year on account of festivals without any deduction from his wages . . . but if he exceeds this number of days through idleness, bad health, disobedience, or for any other reason he must work for an equivalent number of days."[8]

It was also at this time that the earliest recorded holidays prohibited work. Rybczynski describes an Egyptian calendar that has survived from about 1200 B.C., that lists a series of forbidden activities for specified days throughout the year:

"These include injunctions against travel, sexual intercourse, washing, and eating certain kinds of food. Among the most frequent injunctions is 'do no work.'"[9]

Rybczynski points out that "unlucky" days when work was proscribed were also identified in the Greek and Roman calendars; vestiges of this ancient practice have survived to the present day, as in the current prejudice against Friday the thirteenth.

In ancient Greece, there was a sharp distinction between those who were free citizens of Athens, Sparta, and the other city-states and those who were not. Although the Athenian *scholē* was an aesthetically rich experience, praised by such philosophers as Aristotle, Plato, and Socrates, the Greek citizen's leisure was purchased at the expense of others. In Athens, for example, there was estimated to be a ratio of four slaves to every free male; women were considered lesser beings whose functions were largely related to the home and childrearing, and leisure was described chiefly in male terms. The Greek attitude toward work itself was revealed in the words used to describe it:

> One is *ponos,* which has the connotations of toil in our sense . . . of fatiguing, sweating, almost painful manual effort. The other is *ascholia,* which has less of the painful physical element. In origin the word really denotes the absence of leisure . . . or the state of being busy or occupied.[10]

The early Romans were a vigorous and courageous people—talented agriculturalists, engineers, planners, and soldiers, who instituted a regular cycle of festivals in the arts and religiously based athletic competitions. However, at the height of its power, as Rome became increasingly wealthy through conquest, its economy came to depend on the importation of food and other goods, slave labor, and the military assistance of mercenaries. The continued influx of cheap grain and slave labor created a powerless class of free citizens—an urban proletariat with lives of squalor and bare existence, placated by the state's provision of "bread and circuses." Wilensky writes:

> In the old Roman calendar, out of 355 days, nearly one third were marked as unlawful for judicial and political business. In the last two centuries of the republic, festival days were stretched to accommodate more spectacles and public games. The Roman passion for holidays reached its climax in the middle of the fourth century when days off numbered 175. . . . Whatever the work schedules of slaves and women, leisure for the ruling classes . . . was never again so abundant.[11]

Without the philosophical idealism of the Greeks, Romans were entertained by violent spectacles of chariot racing, mock sea battles, and the cruel slaughter of men, women, and animals in huge arenas. Based on this historical example, later scholars concluded that one of the significant causes of the dissolution of the powerful Roman empire, which had conquered most of Europe, the Middle East, and North Africa, was its misused and decadent leisure.

Work and Leisure in the Christian Era

The Dark and Middle Ages that followed the collapse of Rome were marked initially by the disintegration of the legal and military controls that the Romans had established and by the abandonment of many of their advanced practices in agriculture, architecture, industry, and law. Throughout Europe, civilization was at a low ebb, with many minor nobles and military leaders claiming power and forming temporary allegiances to control shifting territories. The Catholic church gradually spread its influence over Europe by converting the formerly pagan populations and linking its power with that of local rulers; as larger, more unified states emerged, their rulers were regarded as divinely appointed.

In the monasteries that served as centers of religious life, a doctrine of toil and worship was promoted as essential to the spiritual life. The church, in its opposition to all that imperial Rome had represented, condemned various forms of entertainment, including the theater, secular music and art, dance, gambling, and sports. As in earlier societies, although a doctrine of work was preached, it was largely carried out by serfs or poorly paid craftsmen; typically, lower-class women were assigned "drudge" tasks. In Western Europe during the early Middle Ages, there was no word for labor as such, but by the twelfth century it was custom to identify workers *(laboratores)* as one segment of society, along with prayer-sayers *(oratores)*, and warriors *(bellatores)*. Byrne writes:

> Throughout the Middle Ages the clergy (the prayer-sayers) monopolized intellectual functions and demeaned other endeavors as "servile" (appropriate for serfs, if not slaves), from which they were—all too conveniently, perhaps—banned by law.[12]

■ DECLINE OF LEISURE DURING INDUSTRIALIZATION

For the common folk, such as peasants working on manorial farms, life was harsh, with an incessant cycle of plowing, planting, and harvesting crops. However, as the Catholic church grew more powerful, it instituted a continuous cycle of holidays and religious festivities throughout the year, which reached a peak in the Renaissance period. Gary Cross writes:

> In preindustrial society, leisure time was not so much scarce as it was irregular. Religious holidays and seasonal festivals . . . consumed up to 164 days per year in seventeenth-century France. And while the workday often encompassed twelve or more hours, it generally was limited by the number of daylight hours; the day was broken up by two or more hours for meals, which were often the center of family leisure time.[13]

With the beginnings of industrialization and the need to develop regularity in the hours and days worked in factories and mines throughout Europe, a conflict began to develop between the Catholic church and the growing employer class. Reinforced by the Protestant work ethic, businessmen and government gradually reduced the number of holidays throughout the year to a handful. The process began in the sixteenth-century Reformation and was extended by the Puritans in seventeenth-century Britain. The French Revolution in the 1790s not only gave legal control of work time to employers, but even temporarily suppressed the Sunday holiday. As Europe and Great Britain became increasingly industrialized, many workers sought to gain more free time; when work was done in the artisan's own cottage, employers' efforts to reduce the hours of leisure often failed. Some employers tried to force craftsmen to commit longer periods of time to work by reducing payment for piece-

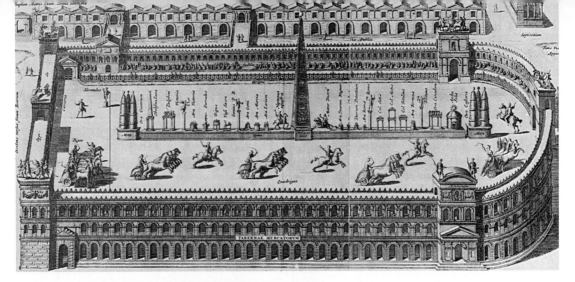

Throughout history, humans have enjoyed varied forms of entertainment and spectacular events, often keyed to the tastes of different social classes. Above, chariot racing in the huge Circus Maximus appealed to all classes in ancient Rome. Center, Flemish painter Pieter Brueghel depicted the common folk attending street theater in the Middle Ages. Below, the royal court in Renaissance France took part in festive ballet and opera performances in palace courtyards, as the nobility watched.

work. And, as the factory system spread, they were able to impose stronger time discipline directly through the central management of labor in the factory or mill.

In the widespread shift from rural life and home industry to urban centers and
factory-based jobs, the old tradition of the natural workday that extended from sun-
rise to sunset was abandoned. Bailey writes that in the shift from a predominantly
agricultural society leisure became a separate sector in an increasingly compartmen-
talized way of life. Work and play were no longer intertwined as they had been in
the closed world of the small, homogenous traditional rural village:

> In the populous and extensive industrial city, leisure was time clearly marked off from
> work, to be pursued elsewhere than in the workplace and its environs, and undertaken
> in company no longer . . . comprised [chiefly] of workmates. Moreover, the activities of
> this leisure time were no longer regulated as a whole by the tight mores and collective
> obligations of traditional social life.[14]

In the earlier period, the lower classes had enjoyed traditional games and sports,
fairs, entertainments, and social pastimes that were passed down from generation to
generation through the years, often linked to past religious customs and celebrations.
Many of these practices were abandoned in the new industrial era. Bailey points out
that when a man walked out of the factory gates in the urban manufacturing centers,
he was freer than in any previous age. However, part of what now was available to
him consisted of such activities as drinking, gambling, vice and such pastimes as
horse racing, prize-fighting, and so-called blood sports, such as bull- or bear-baiting
and dog- and cockfights.

Attempts to Control Leisure

This new freedom led to conflict about how leisure should be used. In the Protestant
nations of northern Europe, and particularly in Great Britain, there was a growing
effort on the part of the church, the business establishment, and other influential
groups to control the leisure of the lower classes. In England, for example, religious
and civil authorities attempted repeatedly to prohibit amusements on the Sabbath, to
eliminate gambling and worldly sports, to punish the poor severely for poaching
(hunting or trapping illegally on the estates of the wealthy), and to bar the use of
public lands that had formerly been available for traditional forms of recreation.
Bailey writes:

> Viewed from above, leisure constituted a problem whose solution required the building
> of a new social conformity—a play discipline to complement the work discipline
> that was the principal means of social control in an industrialist capitalist society. In
> contrast to the harsh offensive of the earlier period of industrialization, however, this
> policy was now to be pursued through the reform of popular recreations rather than
> their repression. . . .[15]

⟫ TO THE POINT

In England during the nineteenth century and ultimately in the United States, this new effort took the form of so-called rational recreation for the working classes—the provision of youth organizations, supervised sports programs, workers' clubs, and similar groups that linked religion, education, social welfare, and morally desirable forms of play. This effort was only partially successful; many workers resisted such forms of circumspect leisure and continued to engage in gambling, drinking, and other "sporting" forms of play.

Increasingly, during the early and middle years of the Industrial Revolution, theologians preached that work was the source of moral and social values, and was in effect "divine." The principle that "hard work would lead one to heaven" represented both a social counterrevolutionary influence (work rather than revolution) and a form of personal motivation (work portrayed as the mainspring of character). Work was also seen as vital to national economic advancement and expansion. Throughout the Western world, life came to be seen as an ever more sober business. The Scottish philosopher and historian, Thomas Carlyle, expressed the spirit of his times by writing, "All work, even cotton-spinning, is noble; work is alone noble . . . a life of ease is not for any man." John Ruskin, the English social critic, agreed, stating, "Life without industry is guilt" and "When men are rightly occupied, their amusement grows out of their work."

Increasingly it was believed that the wealth of a nation lay in a large and properly employed working class—but not necessarily a prosperous one. While some liberals, like Adam Smith, believed that "no society can surely be flourishing or happy, of which the far greater part of the members are poor and miserable," they were outweighed by others who held to the doctrine of poverty as the most effective spur to labor and social control. Thus, the age of "laissez-faire" capitalism was fully under way; the price of labor would be determined in the marketplace and workers themselves came to be viewed as little more than a commodity, subject to employer exploitation.

Throughout the nineteenth century, the working classes fiercely desired more free time. With the widespread adoption of the factory system, wage-and-hour issues became a point of conflict between employees and employers and a focus of political controversy. As early as 1815, there were proposals for reducing work time as part of negotiations for an international work-hours standard in Europe; these were renewed by working men's associations in the decades that followed. At the same time, with the continuing efforts of the business establishment and its allies in the church and government to indict idleness as a sin and vagrancy as a crime, fears of increased leisure gave many workers a sense of guilt in their free time.

■ SHIFTING RELATIONSHIPS BETWEEN WORK AND LEISURE

As this chapter has shown, despite the values of work described earlier, throughout history work has often been seen as unpleasant and onerous. It has generally been relegated to the lower social classes, and leisure reserved for the upper classes. Customarily, the two kinds of experiences—work and leisure—were sharply divided in public thinking and moral pronouncements. Robert Lee comments that those who regarded leisure as the opposite of work and dependent on it failed to see the correct relationship between the two. The older views, he writes:

> imply that leisure is a reward for sweat—something that must be earned through productive effort—much as a beast of burden deserves food and a night's rest as a reward for the day's toil. Leisure need not be viewed as subordinate to work or as a restorative for work, but may be seen as an end in itself, something valued for its own sake.[16]

Today the linkage between work and leisure may be illustrated in several ways. These include: (1) the fact that many recreational activities are based on work behaviors; (2) the infusion of many forms of play into work settings; (3) the existence of "semi-leisure," forms of free-time activity that include both practical and playlike elements; (4) adjustments that have been made in work schedules to provide much flexible time for leisure uses; and (5) the fact that leisure itself has been transformed into a major form of business enterprise.

Play Forms Descended from Work Activities

Throughout history, many forms of play have evolved from human activities that were serious in purpose, such as work, religion, or warfare. For example, music, drama, and dance were all originally part of religious worship in pre-Christian cultures, and costumed parades and other lively forms of play have been part of holiday celebrations, particularly in Latin countries, throughout the Christian era. In terms of links with warfare, ancient Greek warriors performed Pyrrhic dances, a stylized form of training for hand-to-hand combat. In medieval Europe, the jousting tournament was a form of practice for battle and ultimately became, in a watered-down version, a sort of garden-party game. Many other elements of warfare, such as archery, fencing, throwing the javelin, and horsemanship, have simply become sports in the modern era.

In North America, other work activities have been transformed into forms of play and entertainment. Agricultural pursuits like sheepshearing, oxen-, horse-, or truck-pulling, and similar skills have become play competitions carried on at country fairs. The real work of lumberjacks in northern forests has been converted to contests pitting men against each other in timber-cutting, log-splitting, or log-rolling events. On the western plains, cowboys in their spare time competed at such workaday tasks as bronco-busting, calf-roping, and similar skills, which in time became a popular form of entertainment—the rodeo.

So, throughout history, work and other practical tasks have been interfused with play, as real-life functions became the substance of play and the occasion for celebration and sport.

Leisure in the Work World

Turning the coin over, many forms of leisure activity have entered the work setting in recent years. One obvious example involves employee recreation; thousands of companies today sponsor leisure programs for their employees. Their purposes are to improve employee health and fitness, build positive morale and loyalty to the organization, reduce absenteeism and problems of drug or alcohol abuse, and assist in employee recruitment and retention. To accomplish these goals, companies often establish recreation and fitness centers, sponsor bowling and softball leagues, company choruses and hobby clubs, chartered vacation flights, and similar activities.

In addition to such efforts, there is a significant blurring of the gap between work and leisure in many companies. Lee describes:

> conventional and institutionalized morning and afternoon coffee breaks, the lunch "hour" among business and professional people . . . the card games among night shift employees, the piping of soft background music into factories and offices . . . the "customer" golf game for sales executives. . . .[17]

Today, numerous corporations, business associations, and professional societies regularly hold conferences or special meetings that mingle work and pleasure—often at resorts with elaborate recreation facilities and entertainment. A growing number of industrial psychologists claim that serious, unrelenting work, epitomized by a workaholic life-style, is often self-defeating. Instead, a relaxed, creative, and playlike life-style tends to be more productive than its grim alternative.[18]

Semi-Leisure

Another example of the blurring of the gap between work and leisure is found in life activities that have elements of both work and play. Numerous hobbies may be carried on for purely recreational purposes at the outset, but evolve into financially rewarding pursuits. For example, an amateur collector of stamps, coins, or baseball cards may gradually become an entrepreneur who sells or trades profitably at flea markets or trade fairs. Even clearly recreational pursuits like sport fishing may be approached in a serious, competitive way, with winners of national fishing contests earning substantial sums through personal appearances, testimonials for fishing equipment, and television shows.

Work itself may be regarded as a form of challenging play. Michael Maccoby, an authority on business management life-styles, points out that many company executives are compulsively driven to succeed and are "jungle fighters" who enjoy challenges of business competition:

> Unlike other business types, the leader is energized to compete not because he wants to build an empire, not for riches, but rather for fame, glory, the exhilaration of running his team and gaining victories. His main goal is to be known as a winner, and his deepest fear is to be labeled a loser.[19]

Adjustment of Work Schedules

A fourth example of how the barrier between work and leisure has been breached in recent years lies in the alterations that have been made in work schedules to allow employees more leisure time. In addition to increasing holidays and vacations and improving retirement benefits, some companies have developed schedules to permit employees to work four or even three days a week. Others have developed flex-time plans that enable workers to set their own work hours flexibly.

Economic Importance of Leisure

Finally, instead of regarding leisure as a nonproductive or morally dubious "frill," economists and business leaders now respect it as an important force in national life and a major source of profits and jobs.

Today, state governments vigorously promote their resort and vacation areas and advertise widely to attract tourists. When companies seek to recruit high-level employees, they often stress the cultural and recreational advantages of their surrounding regions. Recreation has evolved as a key selling point in real estate developments, with target-marketing of condominiums, town houses, and other housing units linked to swimming pools, golf and tennis facilities, fitness, boating, and other leisure resources.

■ SUMMARY

We have explored the meaning of time, work, and leisure, and have seen how work has historically been regarded as tedious and unpleasant and been assigned to the lower social classes. During the Protestant Reformation and the Industrial Revolution that followed, a work ethic evolved that promoted toil as the basis of personal salvation and national well-being. While leisure was seen initially as a social danger or, at best, a means of recovering for renewed labor, in the late twentieth century it was recognized that work and leisure were closely related forms of human endeavor, and that leisure itself represented a major form of economic enterprise.

■ QUESTIONS FOR DISCUSSION

1. If leisure is viewed primarily as a form of discretionary or nonobligated time, what special periods of time in modern America are primary sources of leisure?
2. What was the impact of industrialization on free time during the eighteenth and nineteenth centuries in Europe? Why did the business-oriented middle classes seek to control working-class uses of free time, and how was their effort linked to the religious establishment?
3. Traditionally, work has been seen as a major focus in human lives, and leisure has been seen as distinctly subordinate to it. Show how this view has changed in recent years, including a discussion of the ways in which work and play have become intermingled in modern life.

4. The distinction between work and leisure was philosophically based on the idea that purposeful activity carried out for pay was work, and that leisure was carried out for its own sake, without any sort of extrinsic purpose or other compensation or gain. The term *semi-leisure* implies that there is a middle ground between these two extremes. Discuss this point, giving examples of semi-leisure.

5. There is a widely shared belief that work is dull, boring, and exhausting. However, psychologists today point out that work may be challenging, creative, stimulating, and even playlike. From your own experience, which of these views is closer to the truth? Provide examples of both kinds of work situations.

■ NOTES

1. WILL, G. 1988. In keeping time, life's many duties leave few moments for pleasure. *Philadelphia Inquirer* (Sept. 1): 22–A.
2. MOORE, W. 1963. *Man, time and society.* New York: Wiley, p. 6.
3. O'MALLEY, M. 1990. Conversation: The time of our lives. *U.S. News and World Report* (Oct. 22): 66.
4. RYBCZYNSKI, W. 1991. *Waiting for the weekend.* New York: Viking.
5. ORLEAN, S. 1990. Saturday night. *New York Times Magazine* (Feb. 11): 37.
6. RAINES, J., and D. DAY-LOWER. 1986. *Modern work and human meaning.* Philadelphia: Westminster, pp. 15–16.
7. SHIVERS, J. S. 1981. *Leisure and recreation concepts: A critical analysis.* Boston: Allyn & Bacon, p. 31.
8. LINDSAY, J. 1965. *Leisure and pleasure in Roman Egypt.* New York: Barnes & Noble, p. 1.
9. RYBCZYNSKI, *op. cit.,* pp. 60–61.
10. DEGRAZIA, S. 1962. *Of time, work and leisure.* New York: Twentieth Century Fund, p. 14.
11. WILENSKY, J. L. 1963. The uneven distribution of leisure. In *Work and leisure,* ed. E. O. Smigel. New Haven: College & University Press, p. 109.
12. BYRNE, E. 1990. *Work, Inc.: A philosophical inquiry.* Philadelphia: Temple University Press, p. 50.
13. CROSS, G., ed. 1988. *Worktime and industrialization: An international history.* Philadelphia: Temple University Press, p. 25.
14. BAILEY, P. 1978. *Leisure and class in Victorian England.* London: Methuen, p. 4.
15. *Ibid.,* p. 5.
16. LEE, R. 1964. *Religion and leisure in America.* New York and Nashville: Abingdon, p. 29.
17. *Ibid.,* p. 30.
18. HARRIS, T. G., and R. TROTTER. 1989. Work smarter, not harder. *Psychology Today* (March): 33–38.
19. MACCOBY, M. 1977. *The gamesmen: The new corporate leaders.* New York: Simon & Schuster, p. 100.

3 Leisure in America: Colonial Era to Twentieth Century

By the turn of the [twentieth] century the managers of mass culture sensed new markets both within the urban middle class and spilling beyond its borders to "high society" and the largely untapped working class, all eager to respond to amusement in a less earnest cultural mood: more vigorous, exuberant, daring, sensual, uninhibited, and irreverent. As a result, American mass culture embraced activities which had previously existed only on the margins of American life.[1]

This chapter describes the transformation of America from the time when tiny bands of colonists struggled to survive on the edge of a vast and unknown wilderness to the emergence of the United States as a rich and powerful industrial nation. Throughout, leisure played a key role in providing release from toil and the opportunity for civic celebration, cultural enrichment, and family involvement in games, sports, and hobbies. Five major forces influenced the evolution of leisure and recreation during this three-hundred-year period: religious efforts to control leisure and play; social-class distinctions that were vividly expressed in free-time pursuits; the continuing struggle of working-class men and women for more free time; the deprivation of women and racial minorities in the realm of leisure; and, finally, government's acceptance of responsibility for providing constructive forms of community play.

■ LEISURE AND PLAY IN THE COLONIAL ERA

During the early years of settlement on the North American continent, the Puritans in particular condemned play as sinful and prohibited pastimes linked to holidays associated with the old Catholic church calendar, which had been traditional times for common folk to participate in sports, dancing, and other customs that reflected the "pagan" past. In part, the condemnation of play and idleness stemmed from the urgent need to build homes, plant crops, and survive in a harsh new land. Their disapproval of play also reflected the Puritans' past resentment of the pleasures of the rich—the landed aristocracy and dissolute court circle in England.

Thus, throughout the New England colonies, dice, cards, bowling, and other "unlawful" games were banned, as were "unprofitable fowlers" and "tobacko takers," along with singing and dancing, theatrical entertainment, and similar pursuits. Similar ordinances were passed in other colonies. In 1619, for example, the Virginia Assembly decreed that any person found idle should be bound over to compulsory work; it prohibited gambling, regulated drinking, and even provided penalties for those wearing excessively elaborate clothing.

Gradually, many of these rules and prohibitions were relaxed. By the mid and late 1700s, a colonial aristocracy had developed in the mid-Atlantic colonies that engaged in banquets, concerts and theatergoing, pleasure boating and riding in sleighs, horse racing and card parties, and balls and assemblies. In the southern colonies, where the land was rich and fertile and substantial land grants had been given to upper-class British settlers who had indentured servants and slaves to work on tobacco, cotton, and sugar plantations, a luxurious way of life developed. Sports in particular gained acceptance and were practiced throughout the colonies, often influenced by the traditional games that the new settlers had played in their homelands. In Boston, New Amsterdam, Richmond, and Philadelphia, new theaters were built, and teachers of music, dancing, and fencing established schools. Gradually opposition to leisure and play diminished throughout the colonies, and by the time of the American Revolution, varied pastimes were widely accepted. In rural villages and along the major turnpikes that led from town to town, country inns offered entertainment, games, and drinking, and popular sports were enjoyed at times of community celebration.

Colonial Morality: Sex, Drinking, and Gambling

Particularly in Puritan New England, there were severe attempts to prevent various types of moral lapses among the settlers. Sexual misbehavior was harshly punished; sinners were placed in the stocks, whipped, fined, and imprisoned. However, research in the birth and marriage records of colonial towns shows that in the 1700s, pregnancy was frequently a prelude to marriage. Larkin concludes that the condemnation of illicit sex was at least partly based on economic grounds. If a young unmarried woman who had become pregnant married before the birth of the baby, so that it would not become a financial "burden" for the community, she could be easily forgiven.[2]

Americans in the colonial era were heavy drinkers on all occasions, although preachers constantly inveighed against drunkenness. Larkin writes:

> Americans drank not only nearly universally but in large quantities. . . . After 1790 American men began to drink even more. By the late 1820s their imbibing had risen to an all-time high.[3]

Gambling was also extremely popular, particularly in larger cities and in the southern colonies, where horse racing was widespread. The life-style for many resembled that of the English aristocracy. George Washington typified the leisure pursuits of his class. He liked to dance, attend prizefights and the theater, and was said to have a "keen eye for the ladies." His favorite pastime was gambling; he played cards, sometimes twice a day, and kept a detailed personal record of his wins and losses.

■ EARLY DAYS OF THE NEW REPUBLIC

Following the American Revolution, life continued much as before. Traditional diversions remained popular, with drinking, gambling, and sports flourishing, along with the theater and other forms of amusement. Nonetheless, the original precepts of industry and hard work continued, with the moralistic writings of Benjamin Franklin typifying the American belief in hard work and thrift.

Meanwhile, life in the newly formed nation was generally harsh, dirty, and crude for most citizens. Particularly in rural areas and along the frontier in the early nineteenth century

> America was a bawdy, hard-edged and violent land. We drank more than we ever had before or would again. We smoked and chewed tobacco like addicts and fought and quarreled on the flimsiest pretext. The tavern was the most important gateway to the primarily male world of drink and disorder . . . excited gambling and vicious fights, and always hard drinking, heavy smoking and . . . alcohol-stimulated talk.[4]

Entertainment was often violent and cruel. In the early decades of the nineteenth century, public hangings were a popular and festive spectacle that brought huge crowds of onlookers—including women and children—to the seats of justice. Gallows were often erected on a hill or set up at the bottom of a natural amphitheater, to allow thousands of spectators an unobstructed view. Criminals were punished with public flogging, although this practice was gradually abandoned.

Efforts at Reform

Drives to curb cruder or more morally dubious forms of play began to take effect. In the 1820s and 1830s, religious forces gained strength, with frequent revival meetings and the establishment of many new churches. In smaller cities and towns, prayer meetings and evening worship came to take the place of other amusements.

The American Temperance Society was established in 1826, and promptly initiated campaigns against "demon rum," using literature, sermons, lectures, and local ordinances to curb drinking. Alcohol, formerly thought of as "fortifying," was now depicted as a physical and moral poison, and liquor consumption declined. There were also campaigns against gambling, racing, and blood sports like cockfighting, although these tended to persist in and around cities, where there were larger numbers of unattached men, and religious influences were weaker.

■ THE DRIVE FOR FREE TIME

During the early decades of the nineteenth century, as factories and mills were widely established, many employers imposed longer hours and stricter scheduling of work. At first, employees sought to resist these demands through absenteeism, irregular work habits, and clinging to traditional holidays. Gradually, they banded together to combat the drudgery or danger of their jobs and to gain more free time from work in the factory, mine, or mill.

Teresa Murphy points out that the struggles for a shorter workday were at the heart of much labor unrest throughout the nineteenth century. The effort to reduce hours was particularly sustained and difficult in New England, where employers had extended the workday both openly and surreptitiously—"lighting up" mills in the winter months, and purposely setting back clocks in shipyards and factories to keep workers at their tasks beyond normal quitting hours. Murphy writes:

> Housewrights in Boston struck for a shorter workday in 1825. Machinists, carpenters, and shipwrights led the way in a regionwide movement during the early 1830s, creating an organization that united industrial workers with artisans in traditional trades. . . . In the mid-1840s, the movement gained new impetus as factory operatives . . . formed the New England Workingmen's Association. . . . Yet, despite a broadening basis of support, their efforts met with failure during this period. New England mechanics would finally achieve a ten-hour day in the 1850s, but factory operatives would have to wait until the 1870s for meaningful legislation to be passed.[5]

⮕ TO THE POINT

The struggle between labor and management was often couched in moral, patriotic, and religious terms. Workers transformed the issue of long workdays from one of economic exploitation to one of perfection and salvation.

When the women of Lowell, Massachusetts, formed a Female Labor Reform Association, they spoke of the mind given all human beings, "capable of eternal progression and improvement," and argued for a shorter workday to improve their intellectual attainments: "It now only remains for us to throw off the shackles which are binding us in ignorance and servitude and which prevent us from rising to that scale for which God designed us." [6]

Others stressed that free time was necessary for family prayer, reading of the Scriptures, and church attendance. From a practical point of view, labor economists have concluded that a major purpose of the drive for shorter hours was to create more jobs, counter technological unemployment, and force up wages. However, it is also clear that worker desire for more leisure was heavily based on the need for more cultural, religious, and educational involvement.

In response, employers used moralistic arguments against giving workers shorter hours. The new industrial morality emphasized self-discipline, sobriety, self-denial, and respect for authority—all essential traits for the growing business economy. It was believed that human beings were easily tempted to sin, and that they needed to be held in check by a stable hierarchical society led by ministers, merchants, and masters, and by long work hours.

Gradually the struggle for more free time broadened to include claims that the new machines and rapid work pace caused accidents, chronic fatigue, and sickness, and that long factory hours disrupted family life and caused social instability and spiritual decay. By the mid-1800s, as modest reductions in work hours began to be made, labor unions stressed the job-improvement and economic values of shorter hours, rather than leisure as such. Seen in perspective, however, the struggle for shorter hours had been instrumental in establishing a social climate in which workers banded together and were able to bargain with their employers in a unified way.

■ THE EMERGING AMERICAN CHARACTER

All of these changes took place during a period in which the character and fundamental values of Americans were becoming more clearly defined. A French aristocrat, Alexis de Tocqueville, who visited the United States in 1832 and wrote a classic work, *Democracy in America,* admired what he described as the independence, peacefulness, and enterprise of Americans. However, he also considered them prosaic and boring and excessively occupied with making money. Foster Dulles quoted one observer:

> In no country are the faces of the people furrowed with harder lines of care. In no country that I know is there so much hard, toilsome, unremitting labor; in none so little of the recreation and enjoyment of life. Work and worry eat out the heart of the people, and they die before their time.[7]

This situation was a natural outgrowth of the Puritan condemnation of idleness and worship of work and material accomplishment, reinforced by the wave of religious conservatism throughout the country. It also stemmed from the fact that as a democracy the United States had never had a royal sovereign or nobility that patronized the arts and encouraged popular leisure. At an early point, John Adams commented that his generation had to "study Politicks and War," so that *his* sons might be free to study mathematics, geography, natural history, navigation, commerce, and agriculture, and *their* sons to study painting, poetry, music, architecture, and other arts. A foreign visitor, Michael Chevalier, wrote in 1833:

> Democracy is too new a comer upon the earth, to have been able as yet to organize its pleasures and amusements. In Europe, our pleasures are essentially exclusive, they are aristocratic like Europe itself. In this matter then, as in politics, the American democracy has yet to create everything fresh.[8]

So, in the early and middle nineteenth century, Adams's dream was not yet realized, and America was not ready to cultivate the arts of gracious living. Its values lay in a different direction—opening the West, laying inland waterways and roads, and becoming an economic power in the world.

During the mid-1800s the Industrial Revolution gave rise to a growing middle class and a higher standard of living. Transportation by rail, water, and highways speeded travel. Standards of personal hygiene were raised, as cities installed running water systems in middle- and upper-class neighborhoods. John Gordon writes:

> The newly affluent, able to afford leisure, greatly increased the market for books and magazines, while gaslight and oil lamps greatly improved the ease of reading and the time available for it. Publishers began to pour out new and inexpensive works of fiction and travel.[9]

The upper classes became obsessed with manners, etiquette, fashion, and household management, and increased their interest in the arts, theater, and music. While the Protestant church generally condemned commercial amusements as the "door to all the sinks of iniquity," specifically attacking the stage, the concert hall, and the circus, nonetheless these pastimes continued to be widely enjoyed. As the working day was reduced to twelve hours and then to ten, new time was available to engage in recreation and cultural pursuits.

Restrictions on Leisure for Women

However, while men enjoyed increased leisure opportunities, women became more restricted in the mid-nineteenth century. As Chapter 6 will show in detail, popular ideas on the delicacy of females and a heightened degree of sexual prudery meant a far more limited life for women than in the 1700s. In colonial days, they had entered more fully into both work and leisure pursuits, due to the nature of life in rural agricultural areas, which integrated women in farm tasks, as well as in holiday celebrations, harvest-related social events, and similar experiences. But in the new industrial age that sharply separated work, play, and family life, middle- and upper-class women were increasingly restricted in their lives. "Once married," an observer of the time reported, "the young lady entirely changes her habits. Farewell gaiety and frivolity." Whatever their position in society, women were expected to devote themselves to domestic tasks. If they had any hobbies at all, most women took up such pastimes as embroidery or painting, but most leisure was sacrificed to narrow standards of proper female decorum.[10]

For working-class women who toiled in factories or the service trades, life in slums and crowded tenements offered few comforts and little leisure. And for those who sought out new lives on the frontier, as waves of immigration settled new territories to the west, existence was harsh and barren, often marked by poverty, danger, and disease. But for no group in American society was life as limited or leisure as lacking as for African-American slaves in the southern states.

Slavery in America

Slavery was a key phenomenon in American life, with profound social implications that led to the tragic war between the states and to changes that affect the nation even today.

In America, colonial New England pioneered in the African slave trade. By 1700, Rhode Island merchants were sending out eighteen slave ships annually, equipped with the necessary chains, handcuffs, and rum, to trap or trade for black slaves to be sold in the American South and the West Indies. Although New England's soil and climate were not suited to the plantation system, by the 1760s this region had about fifteen thousand black slaves employed as seamen, lumberjacks, farmhands, craftsmen, and domestic servants.

Economic conditions and the efforts of Quakers and other liberals brought about the abolition of slavery in the northern states in the first half of the nineteenth century. However, the southern states refused to give up slavery, both for economic reasons and because of concern about social control. By 1860 about one-third of the population in the South consisted of African Americans, who outnumbered whites in some states.

Some apologists for slavery have claimed through the years that it was not as cruel as popularly depicted, and popular folklore presented an image of happy slaves dancing to the banjo music of Stephen Foster tunes. The reality was much more brutal. The greater number of field hands dreaded the cruelty of their white owners and plantation foremen—as evidenced by the number of slaves running away and taking part in uprisings. Families were broken up at the slave owner's whim, and black girls and women were often used as concubines by their white owners.

⠿➡ TO THE POINT

In terms of work and living conditions, existence was harsh for most field hands. Often they lodged in log or frame huts, without furniture, sleeping on the bare floor—ten or twelve to a room, adults and children, male and female. Based on accounts of the period, published by former slaves who had escaped to the North, plantation life had severe work demands. One writer, Solomon Northrup, described the task of raising and harvesting cotton as an unending process of back-furrowing, planting, hoeing, and picking—with the added ingredient of constant physical punishment:

> . . . the overseer or driver follows the slaves on horseback with a whip. . . . The faster hoer takes the lead row. He is usually about a rod in advance of his com-

panions. If one of them passes him, he is whipped. If one falls behind or is a moment idle, he is whipped. In fact, the lash is flying from morning until night, the whole day long. The hoeing season thus continues from April until July.[11]

The cotton-picking season was equally harsh. All hands were required to be in the fields as soon as it was daylight and, with the exception of a few minutes at noon to swallow a simple lunch, they continued to labor steadily until it was too dark to see. If there was a full moon, they might work until late into the night. Only then, Northrup recounted, when the work had been completed and the cotton weighed, were slaves assigned to their other chores—feeding livestock, cutting wood, preparing a late meal, and, at last, sleep. As a rule, the only respite slaves had throughout the year was during the Christmas holidays, when owners would allow a few days—usually less than a week—for suppers to be given to slaves of adjoining landowners, with feasting, dressing up, dancing, music, and games. Thus, for millions of African Americans who were slaves within the plantation system, leisure had little meaning during this period.

■ GROWTH OF POPULAR CULTURE

During the middle decades of the nineteenth century, the American character continued to become more sharply defined. Within a climate of steadily rising prosperity, several national traits became evident: patriotism, aggressiveness, religion, and humanitarianism.

In the 1860s, the Civil War put an end to slavery and had a profound impact on the lives of many Americans, who were exposed to new environments, customs, and pastimes. For soldiers in the field, apart from marching, drilling, and periods of combat, there were often long stretches of relative idleness. At these times, soldiers played games and sports, gambled, and enjoyed music and other forms of popular entertainment.

During the decades after the war, there was a steady growth of interest in varied forms of cultural activity. Although Americans readily conceded their inferiority to European nations in the arts, organizations like the American Art Union encouraged contemporary painting, sold reproductions, published art magazines, and drew thousands of spectators to their galleries. Better taste began to prevail in public and domestic architecture, household furniture, and interior design.

The American theater became more centralized in New York, with professional Broadway producers putting on both classical and new plays featuring actors and actresses who began to develop national reputations. At the same time, stock companies toured the country. MacArthur writes:

> Throughout the nineteenth century, little acting companies tramped across the country. Towns often lacked theaters, so performances took place in meeting halls, dining rooms, and even barns. Conditions demanded versatility. Actors served as their own directors, musicians, stagehands, and publicity agents.[12]

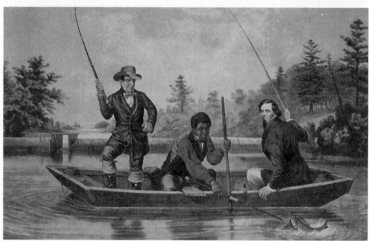

Americans enjoyed varied forms of outdoor recreation in the mid and late nineteenth century. Here, New Yorkers of all ages skated on a frozen pond in the city's newly opened Central Park. Hunting and fishing gained growing numbers of enthusiasts, and horse racing and trotting races attracted crowds of spectators.

Other forms of stage entertainment, including melodramas, vaudeville, and minstrel shows were widely popular, and circuses featuring clowns, animals, daredevil acts, and "freak" shows followed the lead of P. T. Barnum in finding huge new audiences. Amusement parks and beer gardens also sprang up around cities and in new resort areas.

Sports as Leisure Activity

During the mid and late nineteenth century, sports also became increasingly popular, although religious and civic authorities often condemned them. Thoroughbred horse racing gradually lost favor and tended to be replaced by trotting racetracks, which were more acceptable to the moralistic middle class. Boxing was often banned by local authorities and bouts were held secretly in nearby wooded areas or resort communities. Tenpin bowling and billiards became popular with all classes during the 1830s and 1840s; however, both pastimes were associated with saloons and taverns and were regarded as morally dubious pursuits. Other sports included rowing and foot races, as well as traditional team games that had been brought by settlers from their European homelands.

Gradually sports gained respectability both in the United States and in England, where religious and educational leaders accepted their value in building character by teaching team play, obedience to rules, and self-discipline. Encouraged by the new "muscular Christianity" movement, which supported games and outdoor recreation as a means of achieving the "sound mind in the sound body," sports were now seen as helpful in resisting the temptation to take part in less desirable leisure pursuits.

A key factor was the immigration from different European countries, which served to introduce new kinds of games and sports to the American scene. Scottish settlers sponsored Highland or Caledonian Games in a number of cities, with annual festive gatherings that featured music, dance, and athletic contests. German immigrants founded the Turnverein, a network of gymnastic clubs. Czech settlers brought the Sokol clubs with them, and other groups of immigrants brought their traditional games and sports.

Each sport underwent a process of evolution during this period. Baseball, for example, began primarily as a game played by amateurs in small towns, villages, and in the outskirts of large cities. Clubs were formed in the 1840s and rules and strategy were improved and made uniform over the next two decades. Many of the early clubs were made up of players drawn from a particular trade; there were teams of merchants, white-collar and blue-collar workers, shipwrights and mechanics. Baseball soon became known as the national pastime. It had the advantage over its British cousin, cricket, that it was simpler and could be played in a much shorter period of time. Later analysts concluded that baseball reflected American business practices and social values that would emerge in the oncoming scientific-management approach to business and manufacturing.[13]

Other sports found new sponsors—basketball in YMCAs and football in schools and colleges. An extremely violent pastime, football resulted in numerous injuries and deaths, and was at first resisted by college administrators. However, before long many presidents and deans came to see it as a way of building school spirit, capturing alumni support and contributions, and establishing the reputation of their institutions. For the public at large, individual and dual sports like tennis and golf gained popularity, particularly among the upper classes, while bicycling and skating were also widely enjoyed pastimes.

■ EMERGENCE OF THE PLAY MOVEMENT

In the latter half of the nineteenth century, the play movement—later to be known as the park and recreation movement—gained visibility. It owed much of its support to the efforts of upper-class reformers who sought to promote culture throughout the nation and to improve the lives of the less fortunate. A leading example was the so-called Brahmin class of elite society in Boston. Members of this native aristocracy took the lead in founding hospitals, schools, charitable societies, libraries, museums, orchestras, and youth organizations designed to promote culture, build character, and assist in the Americanization of the waves of immigrants arriving on the nation's shores each year. Under their leadership, and stimulated by other civic leaders and social reformers, the emerging play movement took several forms.

One of these was the Lyceum movement, a form of adult education that sponsored lectures on artistic, literary, and scientific subjects throughout the Midwest during much of the nineteenth century. Linked to it was Chautauqua, a cultural and educational network of touring lecturers, musical and drama groups, and other programs that enriched the lives of numerous communities well into the twentieth century.

Establishment of Parks

A second major thrust had to do with the development of parks on national, state, and local levels. During the second half of the nineteenth century, the federal government acquired a number of major wilderness areas, scenic wonders, and historical sites, including Yosemite and Yellowstone, and continued to build a network of parks and forests that would later become the prized possessions of the National Park Service.

As a parallel development, many large cities established new, attractive parks. Before 1850, Boston and Philadelphia had been the only major cities with significant amounts of open space for public recreation. However, in the late 1850s, New York City established an outstanding new park, Central Park, designed by landscape architect Frederick Law Olmstead. Initially, it was intended to bring nature and even wilderness to the city; it offered carriage rides, band concerts, and boating, but not active use of the park itself. But before long, tenement dwellers were enjoying the park's footpaths, picnicking, holding footraces, sledding and ice skating in the winter, and playing ball games on the open greens. In time, Central Park was seen as having health, aesthetic, and social-control values; it was lauded as a "necessary sanitary provision" and a "great preventative of crime and vice." In the years following, many other cities, including New Haven, Baltimore, St. Louis, New Orleans, and San Francisco, created large new public parks, and the parks movement was well under way.

Urban Playgrounds: The Leisure Needs of Children

Following the establishment of municipal park systems, there was increasing awareness of the need for spaces to play in the crowded cities of the nation. Knapp and
Hartsoe describe the need in New York City:

> With vacant lots gone, the wagon and trolley-filled streets became dangerous play-
> grounds. Central Park was miles away and inaccessible. . . . Police often disrupted
> harmless street play, and children drifted into gangs of delinquents.[14]

⮕ TO THE POINT

In the 1890s, groups of public-spirited citizens, urged on by social reformers,
editorial writers, ministers, and educators, spearheaded a movement to establish
playgrounds in several eastern cities. At first they were privately funded and
staffed, but before long metropolitan school systems and newly established
municipal park or recreation departments began to build public playgrounds.
Over time, playground programs expanded from a limited range of summertime
and after-school play designed primarily for children and youth, to a fuller variety of year-round activities to serve all age groups in both indoor and outdoor
activities. Their efforts supplemented the work of numerous youth-serving organizations, including Boy Scouts, Girl Scouts, Y.M.C.A. and Y.W.C.A., Campfire Girls, and others that were established in the late 1800s and early 1900s.

During the first decades of the twentieth century, a number of pioneers of
the play movement, including Luther Halsey Gulick, Jane Addams, and Joseph
Lee, argued convincingly that play represented a vital element in the lives of
children, and that organized recreation was a critical need for healthy communities. They were joined by educational authorities, newspaper editors, police
officials, and judges who agreed that playgrounds were instrumental in protecting the lives of children who were, as social surveys had shown, increasingly
being drawn into gambling, drinking, petty crime, and prostitution.

With growing public awareness and support, cities throughout the country established networks of playgrounds, making use of standards and leadership-training
programs developed by the newly formed Playground Association of America. A
number of women, including May Eliza MacDowell, Marie Ruef Hofer, Beulah
Kennard, and Ellen Mussey, were prime movers in the developing playground
movement. At the same time, many writers began to link play and leisure with religious values and outcomes. In a review of books and articles written during the early
decades of the twentieth century, Charles Sylvester found many references to leisure
as a means of achieving spiritual values. Discussions of work, play, love, and worship
referred frequently to God and other religious themes, and "play (defined as self-
expression for its own sake) was seen as a means of preparation for the religious life
. . . an end subordinate to God and a means of celebrating God . . . to realize the
divine. . . ."[15]

The 1918 Bulletin of the Commission on the Reorganization of Secondary School Education of the National Education Association, titled *Cardinal Principles of Secondary Education,* made clear that the unworthy use of leisure was a threat to health, home life, vocational efficiency, and civic-mindedness. It argued that education for the "worthy" use of leisure was of increasing importance as an educational objective.[16] Throughout the early 1900s, the recreation and park movement continued to grow. More and more cities developed major park and recreation systems, often under separate departments. Congress created the U.S. Forest Service in 1905 and the National Park Service in 1916. States established park and conservation agencies, and family camping and other forms of outdoor recreation became increasingly popular. World War I represented a major impetus in promoting community recreation, when the War Camp Community Service accepted responsibility for creating recreation opportunities for military personnel and war plant workers.

■ MASS LEISURE IN THE JAZZ AGE

The years that followed World War I were a time of rapid economic growth and dramatic shifts in social values and behavior. Known as the "Jazz Age" and the "Roaring Twenties," it was an optimistic, prosperous period, with the stock market booming and businesses flourishing everywhere. People had money to spend, and they did so—on automobile trips, motion pictures, radio and phonograph records, jazz music and dancing, and a host of games, sports, and hobbies. Although Prohibition, enacted by the Eighteenth Amendment in 1919, had made alcoholic beverages illegal, the nation thumbed its nose at the new law and bootlegging (both through the illicit manufacture of bathtub gin and corn whiskey and the smuggling of liquor from outside) was widespread.

There was a new aura of sexual freedom and defiance of old rules. Women, who had gone to work in great numbers during and after World War I, bobbed their hair, shed their corsets and wore short skirts, drank and smoked cigarettes in public, and in other ways declared their independence. Fads came and went—roller skating, miniature golf, crossword puzzles, and a dozen other crazes of long or short duration. Both college and professional sports continued to expand, as giant stadiums were built across the land, and professional baseball and college football teams gained new fans.

Inevitably, there were concerns about the new mass leisure. Kasson points out that the efforts of primarily Protestant, white, middle-class community leaders to guide public play in genteel and moral directions had largely failed. Instead, working-class men and women were embracing activities that had formerly existed only on the margins of respectable American life:

> Examples of this transformation abound. Beginning with the ragtime and the cakewalk in the 1890s, Afro-American music and dance emerged out of black communities and the demimonde to be commercialized and transformed for white urban audiences. Vigorous, violent sports such as prizefighting, earlier confined to gentlemen's clubs or working-class saloons, gained increased popular acceptance . . . literature broke with the genteel code of delicacy, domesticity and decorum . . . and the movies in the space of a

few years moved from penny arcades, billiard parlors and crude storefront "nick-elodeons" in working-class and immigrant neighborhoods to captivate an immense audience by the time of the First World War.[17]

Prominent educators like George Counts pointed out that before the rise of industrial civilization, recreation had been almost completely a function of the family, the neighborhood, or the community. But in the modern city, commercialized amusements had taken over in the form of dance halls, houses of prostitution, pool and billiard parlors, and other for-profit leisure enterprises. Linked to this concern was the view that leisure in the 1920s had become increasingly spectator-oriented. Influential writers like Jay B. Nash, a leading physical educator and camping expert, argued that "spectatoritis" might result in America's growing weak and decadent, like ancient Rome.

Characteristically, two sociologists, Martin and Esther Neumeyer, warned that modern life was being rapidly revolutionized by the expansion of leisure, but that too much free time without adequate preparation for its use might present a great menace to American society. They wrote:

> The civilizations of the world have been made and unmade by the way in which people have used their free time. . . . If people engage in creative and constructive activities during their leisure, civilization is advanced; if they indulge in useless and destructive activities, the social order deteriorates and progress is retarded.[18]

■ IMPACT OF THE GREAT DEPRESSION

Following the prosperous, upbeat period of the 1920s, the United States was convulsed by a stock market crash and an economic collapse that lasted for almost a decade—the Great Depression of the 1930s.

Fifteen million people, almost a third of the labor force, were suddenly unemployed. Many thousands of businesses failed, and banks closed their doors, with depositors losing their savings. Unable to make mortgage payments, millions lost their homes. Breadlines formed everywhere, and shantytowns of the unemployed sprang up around cities and towns.

President Franklin Roosevelt's New Deal attacked the emergency on several levels—enacting a temporary bank "holiday," instituting Social Security and new housing programs, and creating widespread public job programs for youth and adults. Leisure became a major focus of the New Deal, in an effort to raise the spirits of people who were demoralized by unwanted free time, and to provide employment for many hundreds of thousands. The Federal Emergency Relief Administration financed construction of recreation facilities like parks and swimming pools, and workers for the Public Works Administration built or improved 3,500 playgrounds and athletic fields. Civilian Conservation Corps youth developed camps, trails, and other facilities in state and federal parks. Overall, Works Progress Administration projects included 12,700 playgrounds, 8,500 gymnasiums and recreation centers, 750 swimming pools, 1,000 ice skating rinks, and 64 ski jumps—greatly enriching the nation's public recreation resources.

In terms of leisure programs, a peak of almost 50,000 recreation leaders were employed by the Recreation Division of the Works Progress Administration and, as late as 1940, 60,000 youth between the ages of eighteen and twenty-four worked in National Youth Administration Recreation centers.

■ SCHOLARLY STUDIES OF LEISURE

At the same time, beginning in the 1920s and extending through the decades that followed, leisure became a subject of serious scholarly study by American sociologists. For example, in their study of a midwestern city that they called Middletown, Robert and Helen Lynd compared the changes that had occurred over a ten-year period, from the mid-1920s to the mid-1930s.[19] Although some organized programs had been abandoned, they found that in many respects the leisure life of Middletown had expanded. There was a new Civic Theater group as well as several women's clubs concerned with the arts, self-improvement, and public affairs.

High school sports had also expanded during the decade, with a new basketball arena seating 9,000, and with numerous other team and individual sports added to the extracurriculum. But the most pronounced change from the mid-1920s involved public recreation facilities and programs. In 1925, there had been only two school playgrounds and a park that offered supervised play for 200 children. By the summer of 1936, there were nine play centers for older boys and girls and fifteen for smaller children, with over 9,800 children taking part in a full range of games, sports, and events.

In another landmark study, August Hollingshead analyzed the influence of class structure, religion, and other factors on youth behavior in a community that he called Elmtown.[20] He described the approved "character-building" organizations serving adolescents in Elmtown—the churches, American Legion and Farm Bureau, the Boy Scouts, the Girl Scouts, and the Camp Fire Girls. Within all youth organizations, a widely recognized system of social class affiliation prevailed. Patterns of snobbery and exclusion were widespread, including anti-Catholic prejudice that served to restrict or discourage membership.

Hollingshead found that young people engaged in many forms of "forbidden pleasures," including smoking, drinking, gambling, and sex play, despite the efforts of churches and other civic groups to encourage more socially approved forms of recreation. There was a hypocritical effort, he wrote, to hide their behavior under the bland exterior of a conventional, conforming life-style:

> The clandestine pursuit of pleasure is fostered, in opposition to official protestations, by a set of conspiratorial rules which encourage the breaking of these taboos by adolescents as well as by adults. What we called the *conspiracy of silence* . . . may be summarized in the following way: One must not admit publicly the existence of tabooed behavior traits except in condemnatory terms, for to recognize their existence is bad, to condone them is abhorrent to respectable people, and to admit any knowledge of their violation is wicked.[21]

As an example of the willingness to accept disapproved behavior provided that it was kept out of sight, male high school athletes were heavy drinkers; yet little effort was made to prevent their alcoholic adventures. There were distinct differences also in terms of male and female leisure participation. While it was understood that boys would drink, smoke, and gamble, and might stay out late at night, girls were far more limited in their behavior.

■ GENDER DISCRIMINATION IN LEISURE

The leisure restrictions for girls in Elmtown were part of a larger pattern in many communities. Earlier in the century, Kathy Peiss writes, boys of working-class families in tenement neighborhoods were free to enjoy a wide range of daring and semi-delinquent play activities. However, girls were generally expected to stay closer to home and to carry out domestic duties. In time, many young women in immigrant families who were working and earning their own livelihood began to develop a degree of independence in their leisure:

> The alluring world of urban amusements drew young women away from the ugliness of tenement life and the treadmill of work. Not content with quiet recreation in the home, they sought adventure in dance halls, cheap theaters, amusement parks, excursion boats, and picnic grounds. Putting on finery, promenading the streets, and staying late at amusement resorts became an important cultural style for many working women.[22]

With the growth of freer behavior for females during the 1920s and 1930s, reformers expressed increasing concern about their leisure activities. New recreation organizations for girls were established, usually based on the structure of boys' groups, and older ones were expanded. Most such organizations were gender-segregated. Even in public recreation programs, it was customary to develop separate classes or clubs in handicraft or homemaking activities for girls, and to have separate divisions of girls' and women's athletics.

The Middletown studies showed how middle- and upper-class women were generally active in two areas of leisure involvement: (1) civic organizations that promoted the arts, such as literary or current-events discussion clubs, or the boards of performing arts groups; and (2) participation in social-service, volunteer programs that assisted the poor, elderly, or disabled populations, or met other community needs. In rural environments, women living on farms or ranches tended to have relatively little leisure and to be heavily caught up in work—including caring for children and cleaning and cooking for family and farmhands, as well as chores involving the care of farm animals, vegetable gardening, and helping bring in crops at harvest time.

■ RACIAL SEGREGATION IN LEISURE

The patterns of leisure restriction based on social class or gender that were found in the Middletown and Elmtown studies were relatively minor compared to the degree of racial, ethnic, and religious discrimination that prevailed in the United States during the first half of the twentieth century. Much of this was directed against Jews and Catholics or against Americans of other than northern European ancestry. However, for no ethnic or religious group was discrimination as severe as it was for Americans of color. Prejudice against African Americans was widespread in the United States, and was enforced by law in the southern states and by community custom in northern or border states.

⟫ TO THE POINT

Recreational opportunity represented a major area of such racial discrimination. Throughout the South, for example, blacks were automatically excluded from playgrounds, public parks, beaches, swimming pools, and organized sports serving whites. C. Vann Woodward, in *The Strange Career of Jim Crow,* points out that during the first two decades of the twentieth century, a huge bulk of legislation piled up at state and municipal levels that effectively prohibited social contact between the races. Examples included:

> The Separate Park Law of Georgia, adopted in 1905 [was] the first venture of a state legislature into this field, although city ordinances and local custom were quite active in pushing the Negro out of the public parks. Circuses and tent shows . . . fell under a law adopted in Louisiana in 1914, which required separate entrances, exits, ticket windows and ticket sellers that would be at least twenty-five feet apart. . . .
>
> North Carolina and Virginia interdicted all fraternal orders or societies that permitted members of both races to address each other as brothers.[23]

A Birmingham ordinance in 1930 made it "unlawful for a Negro and a white person to play together or in company with each other" at dominoes or checkers. An Atlanta ordinance in 1932 prohibited "Caucasians" and "Africans" from boxing and wrestling together, and films depicting interracial boxing events might not be shown. In 1935, Oklahoma required that the races be separated while fishing or boating.

By 1944, Gunnar Myrdal was able to write in his exhaustive examination of race relations in the United States that "Segregation is now becoming so complete that the white Southerner practically never sees a Negro except as his servant and in other standardized and formalized caste situations."[24]

Meanwhile, what of the northern states? Here too there was an unmistakable record of segregation and inadequate provision of recreation facilities and programs for African Americans that was deeply rooted in community customs. In the city of Chicago, for example, Drake and Cayton documented the exclusion of black residents from public parks, playgrounds, pools, and beaches in white neighborhoods through the resistance of white residents who were supported by police and recreation officials.[25] While the Playground Association of America was aware of this problem and had formed a Bureau of Colored Work in 1920, this effort continued for only six years, and had limited success in improving public recreation programs for blacks—chiefly on a segregated basis. Even in voluntary-agency programs sponsored by nonprofit community agencies like the YMCA, YWCA, or the Boy Scouts or Girl Scouts, programs were generally segregated and often there was *no* provision at all for African-American children and youth.

■ LEISURE AT MID-CENTURY

A final important development in the mid-twentieth century was the end of the "shorter-hours" movement that had succeeded in achieving an eight-hour workday and providing American workers with a huge bulk of free time. This had been accomplished through a combination of labor union pressure and negotiation, legislation, and voluntary compliance on an industry-wide basis. For example, in 1868, Congress had set the eight-hour day by law for mechanics and laborers employed by or for the federal government, and in the summer of 1872, union leaders in New York City staged a general walkout to reduce the workweek. In 1890, the American Federation of Labor carried out a major drive to achieve the eight-hour day. Peter Henle describes its successes:

> In particular, the carpenters union, selected as the chief target union, reported that they were able to establish shorter hours for their members in 137 cities, altogether affecting almost 50,000 members of their trade as well as many others in other building trades crafts.[26]

During the years from 1850 to 1950, the labor movement succeeded in reducing the average number of weekly work hours in industrial employment from 65.7 hours in 1850 to 38.8 hours in 1950, and in agriculture, from 72.0 to 47.2 hours per week. Obviously, the shorter workweek was not the only source of increased leisure in the twentieth century. Paid holidays and vacations and a trend toward earlier retirement had also begun to add substantial amounts of free time to the nation's work force.[27]

Although this trend was justified as a natural result of technological improvement and heightened productivity, the same factors began to create a new problem for American business—overproduction and what began to be called "economic maturity." This forced labor leaders, social reformers, and politicians to consider exactly how the society should regard its wealth of newly available free time.

Benjamin Hunnicutt points out that in many ways, the union thrust for shorter hours had been prompted by concern for improving job safety and working conditions—and particularly for protecting women and children from overwork and exploitation.[28] The reformers who supported labor's efforts had usually justified them in economic rather than idealistic or cultural terms. In fact, despite the growth of the recreation movement, the term *leisure* was not widely used (except by educators, intellectuals, and utopian novelists) and was sometimes given a negative connotation, as in references to the "idle rich" living in ease and supported by the toil of the working classes.

In the 1920s, however, leisure began to be regarded as a national concern—not just as free time, but as a positive social trend. Linked with terms like *play, recreation,* and *entertainment,* books, newspapers, and magazines used the term at a rate ten times that of the preceding years. During the prosperity of the 1920s, increased free time was seen as the way to a rich, full life and valuable in its own right, and not simply as a means of improving work conditions. Union leaders now saw leisure as a unique opportunity for the nation; William Green, president of the American Federation of Labor, predicted:

> "a dawn of a new era, leisure for all," and a "revolution in living" for workers who could at last have enough time for the "finer things in life" in a democratic culture. Time wealth promised "music, arts, literature, travel," physical excellence and health to every American. . . . [It] would shame previous cultural advances that had been based on privilege and on the slavery of the masses.[29]

Beyond this type of justification, labor leaders argued that leisure could either be given to all workers in the healthy form of shorter hours, or it would enter the economy in the form of chronic unemployment or national depressions. Shorter hours were seen as a precondition for better wages and for creating more jobs that would then support the national economy. When the Great Depression began, there was intensified pressure for reduced work hours in order to spread the available work among more employees. Known as the "share the work" plan, this effort took the form of legislation before Congress that would make the thirty-hour week a national law. It was argued that the economy had matured, with industrial growth reaching a plateau; the so-called Gospel of Consumption that had driven the nation's prosperity during the 1920s was now regarded as a failure.

However, many business leaders and economists rejected these arguments as defeatist, claiming that the shorter-hour movement was simply a cosmetic device intended to disguise the tragedy of unemployment by distributing its misery. They concluded that the Depression could only be cured by full recovery and robust economic growth. Congress rejected the legislation and instead approved work relief through new jobs on public projects.

Although the shorter-hours movement essentially came to a halt at this point, the dialogue about the role of leisure in national life was in full ferment. Popular writers criticized the nation's new patterns of mass leisure; in a widely read article on "Free Time and Extra Money," an influential social critic, Walter Lippmann, decried the sterility that he found in the nation's free-time play.[30] He concluded that the problem of leisure had arisen because modern industrialization had weakened traditional social structures like the family and the community and undermined moral and cultural codes. He renewed the argument for fuller education for leisure, enriched hobbies, and meaningful free-time pursuits, availability of better public recreation facilities, and trained people to direct community leisure—all couched within a framework of individual choice and positive self-direction. These themes were to be more fully explored by the nation in the years following World War II, as recreation became an even more significant element in public life.

■ SUMMARY

This chapter depicts the nation's changing attitudes toward leisure and recreation during the nineteenth and twentieth centuries. Along with a continuing struggle for more free time through a shorter workweek and more holidays and vacations, Americans were caught up in a new wave of enthusiasm for sports, outdoor recreation, arts and entertainment, hobbies, and other social pastimes. At the same time, the emerging play movement, as evidenced in the establishment of parks and playgrounds, voluntary youth-serving agencies, and professional recreation societies, sought to guide the direction of American play toward socially constructive, "approved" pursuits. Sociologists and other scholars examined the role of recreation in American communities and documented the constriction of leisure opportunities for girls and women and for African Americans, well into the twentieth century. At the same time, the federal government made purposeful use of organized recreation during two world wars and in the Great Depression of the 1930s. Although the "shorter-hours" movement came to a close at this time, the stage was set for a tremendous expansion of recreation participation and organized sponsorship in the second half of the twentieth century.

■ QUESTIONS FOR DISCUSSION

1. Although Puritans and other Protestant sects sought to limit leisure severely in the early American colonies, in many ways they could not control popular behavior. How were the early settlers freer or more unrestrained in their play than is generally known?

2. Even during the early years of industrialization in the United States, there was a strong drive for more free time by American workers. How did they press for it, and what were the arguments cited on either side of the dispute?

3. Despite the idealized view of America as a land of democratic equality, both women and racial minorities—particularly blacks—were widely discriminated against throughout much of our history. What forms did this discrimination take with respect to leisure, in both the nineteenth and early twentieth centuries?

4. The recreation and parks movements had their roots in the late nineteenth century and began to flourish during the early decades of the twentieth. What were several of the key elements in this trend, and what were the social purposes ascribed to government-sponsored recreation and parks?

5. Although recreation participation (in terms of sports, hobbies, entertainment, travel, and other forms of popular culture) expanded rapidly during the Jazz Age, social critics expressed great concern about the impact of leisure on American society. Describe their fears.

■ NOTES

1. KASSON, J. 1978. *Amusing the millions: Coney Island at the turn of the century.* New York: Hill & Wang, p. 6.

2. LARKIN, J. 1988. The secret life of a developing country (ours). *American Heritage* (Sept.-Oct.): 60.

3. *Ibid.,* p. 54.

4. *Ibid.,* p. 58.

5. MURPHY, T. 1988. Work, leisure and moral reform: The ten-hour movement in New England, 1830–1850. In *Worktime and industrialization: An international history,* ed. G. Cross. Philadelphia: Temple University Press, p. 59.

6. *Ibid.,* p. 70.

7. DULLES, F. R. 1965. *A history of recreation: America learns to play.* New York: Appleton-Century-Crofts, p. 86.

8. CHEVALIER, MICHAEL, in Dulles, *op. cit.,* p. 85.

9. GORDON, J. S. 1989. When our ancestors became us. *American Heritage* (Dec.): 116.

10. DULLES, *op. cit.,* p. 96.

11. NORTHRUP, S. 1964. Slavery and the southern plantation system. In *Slavery in the South,* ed. H. Wish. New York: Noonday, p. 39.

12. MACARTHUR, B. 1984. *Actors and American culture.* Philadelphia: Temple University Press, p. 3.

13. BAKER, W. J. 1988. *Sports in the western world.* Urbana & Chicago: University of Illinois Press, pp. 115–117.

14. KNAPP, R. F., and C. E. HARTSOE. 1979. *Play for America: The National Recreation Association 1906–1965.* Arlington, VA: National Recreation & Park Association, p. 9.

15. SYLVESTER, C. 1987. The ethics of play, leisure and recreation in the twentieth century, 1900–1983. *Leisure Sciences:* pp. 173–188.

16. *Cardinal Principles of Secondary Education (1918).* Washington, DC: Department of the Interior, Bureau of Education Bulletin No. 35.

17. KASSON, *op. cit.,* p. 6.

18. NEUMEYER, MARTIN, and ESTHER NEUMEYER. 1936, 1949. *Leisure and recreation: A study of leisure and recreation in their sociological aspects.* New York: A. S. Barnes, p. 13.

19. LYND, ROBERT, and HELEN LYND. 1937. *Middletown in transition.* New York: Harcourt Brace.

20. HOLLINGSHEAD, A. B. 1949. *Elmtown's youth: The impact of social class on adolescence.* New York: Wiley.

21. *Ibid.,* p. 288.

22. PEISS, K. 1986. *Cheap amusements: Working women and leisure in turn-of-the-century New York.* Philadelphia: Temple University Press, p. 57.

23. WOODWARD, C. V. 1955. *The strange career of Jim Crow.* New York: Oxford University Press, p. 84.

24. MYRDAL, G., in Woodward, *op. cit.,* p. 104.

25. DRAKE, ST. C., and J. CAYTON. 1945, 1962. *Black metropolis.* New York: Harper and Row, pp. 102–106.

26. HENLE, P. 1965. The quiet revolution in leisure time. *Occupational Outlook Quarterly. U.S. Department of Labor* (May): 9.

27. DEWHURST, J. F., in de Grazia, *Of time, work and leisure.* New York: Twentieth Century Fund, p. 441.

28. HUNNICUTT, B. K. 1988. *Work without end: Abandoning shorter hours for the right to work.* Philadelphia: Temple University Press, pp. 19–22.

29. WILLIAM GREEN, cited in B. K. Hunnicutt. 1980. Historical attitudes toward the increase of free time in the twentieth century: Time for work, for leisure, or as unemployment. *Leisure and Society* 3: 201.

30. HUNNICUTT, *Work without end,* pp. 262–265.

4 The New Leisure: Counterculture to Century's End

In 1959, a year of lofty tail-fins and boundless optimism, the editors of Life magazine proclaimed that American civilization was on the brink of becoming "freer and bolder than the Greek, more just and powerful than the Roman, wiser than the Confucian . . . saner than the French, more responsible than the Victorian and happier than all of them together."

What was the mighty engine that was presumed to be ushering in this platinum age? It was not military conquest or political progress or, except indirectly, scientific advances. It was leisure; more specifically, The New Leisure.[1]

In the second half of the twentieth century, it was apparent that the nation had gained a vast reservoir of free time, through workweek reductions, the addition of holidays, vacations, and paid retirement, and new labor-saving devices that made daily life less onerous. There was a huge wave of enthusiasm for varied forms of play, as Americans spent lavishly to satisfy their personal interests and to expand parks, playgrounds, and other leisure facilities and programs.

During the decades after World War II, leisure and recreation were important elements in the civil rights movement, the War on Poverty, the urban riots of the 1960s, and the social changes that occurred during the counterculture movement. Members of racial and ethnic minorities, women, those with alternative life-styles, the aging, and the disabled all fought for fuller opportunities in community life, including leisure and recreation. The work ethic lost support for a time, but was revived in the 1980s in a new form—marked by "yuppy" careerism, greedy profit-taking, and deal-making. In the closing decades of the century, many members of the nation's work force found that, instead of gaining huge new amounts of leisure for all, as economists had predicted in the 1950s, work had increased and free time had declined. At the same time, recreation continued to increase steadily in terms of participation and spending on a broad range of pursuits.

■ LEISURE IN THE POST–WORLD WAR II ERA

World War II, coming in the fifth decade of the twentieth century, had been a watershed in the history of the United States. It was a time of immense testing of the country and its people, with all of the nation's labor-power diverted to amassing a huge war arsenal and sending millions of military personnel abroad to fight against Nazi, Fascist, and Japanese aggression. When the war ended successfully in 1945 and servicemen and servicewomen returned to their homes, a number of major societal shifts followed inevitably. First, the industrial power of the nation swung into action to meet civilian needs that had been long deferred—to make cars and homes and other consumer goods.

Next, huge numbers of newly formed families moved out of the major cities of the country, bought small suburban homes built on what had shortly before been farmland, and began to raise children in earnest—the "Baby Boom" generation. As part of the new good life, they put up backyard swings and slides, joined square dance clubs and the Parent-Teacher Association, formed scout troops and Little League baseball clubs, and accepted a doctrine of "family togetherness." In thousands of newly developed suburban communities, local recreation or park departments were established that built parks, playgrounds, swimming pools, and indoor centers, and offered clubs, day camps, special events, and varied leisure programs that served all ages throughout the year.

■ GROWTH OF DISCRETIONARY TIME

Writing in the May 1965 *Occupational Outlook Quarterly,* Peter Henle, a U.S. Labor Department official, summed up some of the key developments. In 1940, for example, only about one-fourth of all union members and a smaller proportion of all employees had received annual vacations with pay; for most, the maximum period was one week. The average number of paid holidays was about two per year, although many workers received additional holidays without pay. By the mid-1960s, paid vacations had expanded greatly, with three-, four-, and five-week vacations becoming the standard for longer-service employees. The number of paid holidays had increased well beyond the six days that were recognized nationally; a number of holidays were rescheduled to permit three-day weekends. As a result, Henle reported that the average American now had more leisure hours than working hours in a year—2,175 hours compared to 1,960 hours of paid work.[2]

In addition, earlier retirement, based on Social Security and company pension plans, had greatly increased leisure time for older workers. Another source of free time consisted of new labor-saving devices for the home, like power lawn mowers, automatic heating and air-conditioning systems, dish- and clothes-washers, and frozen foods that made daily chores less time-consuming.

■ AWARENESS OF THE "NEW LEISURE"

As free time continued to expand, there was a new awareness of leisure as a force in American life. Planning bodies like the Rand Corporation, the Hudson Institute, and the National Commission on Technology envisioned futuristic scenarios with such alternative possibilities as the lowering of the retirement age to thirty-eight, reduction of the workweek to twenty-two hours, or extension of typical paid vacations to as many as twenty-five weeks a year.[3]

Some concluded that, thanks to the growing use of automation—highly sophisticated, self-governing, and electronically guided forms of production—it would soon be possible for only 2 percent of the population to meet all the material needs of society, thus providing an immense amount of new leisure. More conservatively, the U.S. Chamber of Commerce predicted that employers should expect a four-day, thirty-two-hour workweek for most employees, along with new increases in vacations and holiday free time.[4]

Emerging Leisure Ethic

Linked to the expansion of nonwork time was the confident expectation that leisure would give rise to a new set of values for society that would replace the old work ethic. Historian Daniel Rodgers pointed out that, while work had held moral predominance in society, within the new industrial world it was easily possible to produce goods in great supply, and work itself had become increasingly monotonous.

As a consequence, he wrote, "a sizable number of Northern Protestant moralists had begun to argue that it was not in self-discipline that a man's spiritual essence was revealed, but in the free, spontaneous activity of play."[5]

Gradually this idea gained popular acceptance. In the mid-1970s, a spokesperson for the National Manpower Commission reported research showing that only one of five persons surveyed found work a greater source of satisfaction than leisure. In a landmark study of the American social structure, C. Wright Mills described the alienation that many workers felt. He wrote:

> Each day men sell little pieces of themselves in order to try to buy them back each night and weekend with the coin of "fun." With amusement, with love, with movies, with vicarious intimacy, they pull themselves into some sort of whole again, and now they are different men. Thus, the cycle of work and leisure gives rise to two quite different images of self: the everyday image, based on work, and the holiday image, based on leisure.[6]

Typically, Mills pointed out, the public's "idols" had shifted from business, professional, and political figures to individuals who were successful in areas of leisure consumption—entertainment, the movies, and baseball. Martha Wolfenstein confirmed this view, suggesting that Americans now accepted a "fun morality." Play was something not just to be tolerated, but instead a social necessity that contributed to personal health. According to Wolfenstein:

> fun, from having been suspect if not taboo, has tended to become obligatory. Instead of feeling guilty for having too much fun, one is inclined to feel ashamed if one does not have enough. Boundaries between play and work break down. Amusements infiltrate into the sphere of work, while in play, self-estimates of achievement become prominent.[7]

With this shift from a work ethic to a value system centered on leisure and play, play itself began to be used increasingly for practical purposes. Typically, in the life of the organization man or woman, leisure began to be used to build business contacts, cultivate the "right" people, make sales, or build a positive image of oneself. In *The Decline of Pleasure,* Walter Kerr wrote:

> We are all of us compelled to read for profit, party for contacts, lunch for contracts, bowl for unity, drive for mileage, gamble for charity, go out for the evening for the greater glory of the municipality, and stay home for the weekend to rebuild the house.[8]

■ GROWTH OF LEISURE-SERVICE AGENCIES

To meet the steadily growing demand for diversified leisure opportunities, several different types of organized recreation sponsors evolved during the post–World War II years. In addition to governmental, voluntary, and commercial organizations, these included such specialized kinds of agencies as therapeutic recreation providers, corporations sponsoring recreation for their employees, private membership organizations, and campus recreation—all described more fully in Chapter 13 of this text.

To coordinate and promote the work of these leisure-service sponsors, a number of national associations had been formed in the earlier decades of the century. In the mid-1960s, several of these groups merged to form the National Recreation and Park Association, representing chiefly the many thousands of recreation and park managers, leaders, and planners employed throughout the country in public local, state, and federal agencies. In addition to NRPA's specialized branches, which met such needs as programming for disabled persons and providing professional education in leisure service, numerous other national organizations concerned with recreation continued to expand during this period.

Influence of Growing Affluence

A key factor in promoting the growth of organized leisure services was the national affluence of the post–World War II years. The Gross National Product rose from $211 billion at the war's end to over a trillion dollars annually by 1971. In the late 1950s, it was reported that Americans were spending $30 billion a year for leisure—a sum that seemed astounding but was just one-tenth of what it was to become in the 1980s.

Involvement in varied forms of recreation exploded during this period. Visits to national forests increased by 474 percent between 1947 and 1963, and to national parks by 302 percent during the same period. Overseas pleasure travel increased by 440 percent and attendance at sports and cultural events also grew rapidly. Sales of golf equipment increased by 188 percent, of tennis equipment by 148 percent, and use of bowling lanes by 258 percent. Hunting and fishing, horse-racing attendance, and copies of paperback books sold all gained dramatically and—most strikingly, the number of families with television sets grew by 3,500 percent over this sixteen-year period.

■ POVERTY IN THE NATION'S CITIES

However, prosperity had not reached all Americans. For, just as millions of families, primarily young, white, and middle-class, moved from the central cities to attractive new suburban communities in the post-war period, so the neighborhoods they left began to be populated by increasing numbers of economically disadvantaged people—many of them black or Hispanic workers and their families from the rural South, Central America, and the Caribbean. Within a complex economy where manual and other low-level jobs were disappearing, unemployment rates were high, resulting in growing welfare dependency, crime and delinquency, deteriorated housing, and other severe forms of social pathology.

The suburbs and small towns of the nation generally moved ahead to develop rich park and recreation resources and programs, with swimming pools, golf courses and tennis courts, recreation centers, and other facilities. However, the urban sector of the nation was far less fortunate. Living chiefly in cities, the poor suffered from inferior municipal services, including recreation and parks. With increased costs of welfare, law enforcement, and health services, budgets to support other human services were cut. Parks and recreation centers were often poorly maintained, and leadership staffs were slashed.

Places for play. Above, the San Diego Zoo attracts millions of visitors each year. Children's playgrounds may feature traditional slides, swings, and merry-go-rounds or these fanciful giant lizards, designed by the Larson Company in Arizona. The Recreation, Parks and Conservation Department of Westchester County, New York, offers indoor skating rinks, golf courses, swimming pools, sports fields, and other leisure facilities.

Beyond this, it became apparent that in many American cities, park and recreation acreage and facilities were more unevenly distributed than personal income. Based on an analysis of a sample of cities across the nation, Clawson and Knetsch found that in comparison to low-income areas, which often had impacted housing neighborhoods and few parks and playfields,

> the higher income sections had relatively generous parks and recreation areas. This situation is made still worse by the racial pattern of urban living. . . . The low-income central city areas so deficient in recreation space are likely to be Negro; the suburban and outer city ring areas, generously supplied with recreation, are likely to be white. One of the great myths of the outdoor recreation field is that free public parks are a boon to "poor" people; actually it is the poor who frequently lack them.[9]

This disparity between the recreation and park opportunities accessible to Americans of different racial backgrounds had come about initially as part of the process of urban growth. As cities expanded, they tended to add parks on their periphery, where land was inexpensive and available and where new housing was being built. In the central areas of cities where old industrial plants and run-down tenements existed side-by-side, there were few parks.

Despite such inequities, a number of advocates for the "new leisure" in the post–World War II years enthusiastically described its potential contribution to the nation's welfare. They argued that recreation offered new ways of combatting problems like poverty, poor health, family breakup, and crime. They urged that recreation and park professionals adopt a humanistic ethic and become forceful agents in attacking such pathologies.

■ ENVIRONMENTAL PROGRESS

There was a particularly strong linkage between the recreation and park movement and environmental activists. In the 1950s, Americans came to realize that the nation's wildlands had been despoiled by uncontrolled lumbering, grazing, strip-mining, and oil-drilling; that breeding grounds and wetlands for wildlife had been destroyed or ravaged by pesticides or herbicides; and that there had been a steady loss of ocean frontage to private development and commercial exploitation.

Although we had set aside huge tracts of federally owned parkland for outdoor recreation, the bulk of these were in the western states and Alaska, far from the urban populations who needed them. In 1958, the Outdoor Recreation Resources Review Commission was appointed by Congress to review the situation and develop recommendations. Its extensive report, presented to President John F. Kennedy in 1962, documented the seriousness of the situation and offered major recommendations for legislation and new agencies to reclaim and protect the environment—with outdoor recreation a key priority.

With stimulation and fiscal support from the federal government through the new Land and Water Conservation Fund, states and communities throughout the nation acquired, developed, and rehabilitated major new tracts of land for outdoor recreation. Lakes, streams, and formerly wild rivers and trails were all revived; new national parks, seashores, and recreation areas were established, many close to crowded cities; and environmental beauty became a major concern in American life and public policy.

■ RECREATION IN THE WAR AGAINST POVERTY

A second major thrust for the recreation and park movement came during the 1960s, when the Lyndon Johnson administration initiated a War on Poverty that embraced a range of programs designed to provide job opportunity, improve living conditions, and bring the poor—particularly those in the inner cities—more fully into the mainstream of national life. The Office of Economic Opportunity was created in 1964 to coordinate all antipoverty programs on the federal government level.

The rationale for supporting recreation as part of the antipoverty program had several components. It was believed that recreation was particularly important to poor people, who were unable to pay for private or commercial forms of play. It was also recognized that past patterns of discrimination in providing adequate inner-city public facilities had deprived disadvantaged persons—particularly members of racial minorities—of adequate leisure opportunity. Beyond this, recreation offered a useful alternative to socially destructive forms of play, and both cultural enrichment and job training for many young people. It also had emerged as an important issue in the civil rights movement of the 1950s and 1960s.

■ CIVIL RIGHTS AND RECREATION

As was pointed out in Chapter 3, racial segregation had actually increased in intensity in the United States during the early decades of the twentieth century. It took a concentrated drive by many groups and individuals from the 1940s through the 1960s to bring about both federal legislation and Supreme Court decisions to end segregation in education, housing, public accommodations, and other areas of public life.

The first breakdown in recreational segregation came about during World War II, when army hospitals and armed forces centers moved toward desegregation. Based on presidential executive orders in the late 1940s, living quarters and schools for dependents, bars, clubs, athletic fields, and swimming pools were all gradually desegregated. The cracking of the color line in professional baseball shortly after World War II had a major effect on both professional and amateur sports. Not only did large numbers of black athletes join major league teams in baseball, football, and basketball, but increasing numbers also became active in college athletics.

Throughout the southern and border states, places of public accommodation, including libraries, museums, parks, and beaches, began to be opened to integrated participation. In some cities, black artists, entertainers, and speakers appeared before unsegregated audiences. Private lawsuits, sit-ins, demonstrations, and boycotts were all used to open up public and private facilities to integrated use. In some situations, African-American college students who entered segregated facilities in the face of angry opposition were beaten, attacked by police dogs, and arrested. However, they persisted and, ultimately, in three 1963 decisions the Supreme Court affirmed that no municipally owned and operated facilities might be segregated, and that this practice must be promptly reversed.

Throughout the late 1950s and early 1960s, southern and border states responded to such pressures in varied ways. In some cases, all municipal areas were thrown open to use by African Americans. In other cases, cities closed down swimming pools or golf courses rather than integrate them. In still others, publicly owned facilities were changed to pseudo-private ownership and operated in this way. However, gradually the majority of publicly owned bathing beaches and tennis and golf facilities that were formerly legally segregated were quietly opened to general use, and the principle of desegregation became generally accepted.

The 1964 Civil Rights Act stipulated that places of public accommodation (such as theaters, sports arenas, or other places of public exhibition or amusement) or publicly supported facilities like parks or libraries might no longer be racially segregated. Some ambiguity remained with respect to privately operated amusement parks, dance studios, bowling alleys, billiard parlors, or skating rinks.

Urban Riots as Racial Protest

In the mid-1960s, the country was torn by a series of major urban riots. Protesting against discriminatory forms of education, justice and law-enforcement practices, health and welfare services, and limited job opportunity, rioters burned buildings, looted stores, and had violent confrontations with police and National Guard units in dozens of inner-city areas—in Los Angeles, Newark, Chicago, Cleveland, Detroit, and many other communities. In a number of such cases, the flash point came when African Americans were denied access to adequate recreation opportunities during the long, hot summer months. For example, an account of one of the first riots, in Jersey City, New Jersey, in 1964, reported:

> Three recreation centers are being reopened today in the riot-scarred Negro areas of Jersey City as the start of a civic effort to ease racial tensions there. . . . The playgrounds opening today are at housing projects which were at the center of several riot incidents. They were among several the city had decided not to open this summer for economy reasons. Lack of recreational facilities was one of the grievances cited by Negro leaders as contributing to the bitterness behind the rioting.[10]

Within a Chicago slum area where over three hundred thousand African Americans were crowded into eight hundred square blocks, the lack of adequate recreation facilities was one of the key factors that led to bloody rioting in July 1966. The rioting began when police turned off a fire hydrant being used by black children during a particularly oppressive and sustained heat spell.

> The park district has 20 pools on the West Side, four of them within walking distance of the hydrant over which the first disorder began. Officially, none of the pools has a racial restriction. But practically, authorities concede, only one of the four has been readily available to Negroes because of hostility in white neighborhoods near the others.[11]

In numerous other cities, the demand for improved recreation was one of the key factors in the summer rioting. It was also apparent that the riots themselves represented an ugly form of play, a discharging of tensions that had built up for years, and in large measure, the result of boredom and frustration. Life in ghetto slums provides a setting in which such flare-ups can easily occur. In an analysis of poverty in America, Michael Harrington wrote:

> Harlem is distinctive because it lives so much of its life in the streets. The statistics on Negro unemployment may be abstract and distant. An afternoon block of milling waiting men is not. The rooms of Harlem are, more often than not, small, dingy, and mean. . . . So the bars are doing a good business in the afternoon, and there are men on the streets, simply standing talking. . . . Many of the fights of Harlem, or of any slum, are the consequences of mass enforced idleness.[12]

Riots themselves often have a curious air of holiday about them. In 1967, a policeman commented bitterly about Puerto Rican rioters in New York City's East Harlem district (although begun by African Americans, riots in the 1960s and in later years were often joined by Hispanic Americans and, in some cases, white looters): "They're like kids. They get a big kick out of the riots. It's like a carnival to them." In Newark, New Jersey, the state's governor commented that he found the "holiday atmosphere" of the riots most repelling. A passing nun commented, "They were doing it out of sport, you know, not maliciously. They were laughing like: 'Isn't this great fun, getting something for free.'"[13]

Congress voted hundreds of millions of dollars each year that the riots continued for community action programs to keep the summers "cool." The bulk of these emergency funds were granted to special antipoverty neighborhood programs to provide new jobs, light playgrounds, provide portable swimming pools, and support recreational programs for blacks and Hispanics in impacted inner-city areas. Recreation was widely recognized as a useful means of encouraging residents to take responsibility for upgrading their own communities and for reducing delinquency, tension, and gang violence. However, as the riots declined during the late 1960s and early 1970s, the sense of urgency about the problems of African-American and Hispanic city residents declined, and efforts to provide enriched leisure and social-service programs for the poor were sharply reduced.

■ YOUTH REBELLION AND THE EMERGING COUNTERCULTURE

During the same period in which the urban riots occurred, but extending beyond them well into the 1970s, there was also a widespread protest movement among the nation's young. Fueled by resistance to the Vietnam War, this rebellion took the form of a broad attack on establishment values and the powerful institutions of society.

The young people who spearheaded it challenged what they saw as the artificial constraints and values that governed their lives—the rigid curricula and lack of opportunity for self-governance in schools and colleges, the materialistic values that made money and economic success the keystone of success in life, and the traditional but often hypocritical sexual values that adults professed. Many young people became involved with drugs; rock music became increasingly popular, and the Beatles and the Rolling Stones helped to create an atmosphere symbolized by such popular slogans as "Do your own thing," "Let it all hang out," and "Don't trust anyone over thirty." Even younger teenagers were caught up in the rebellion, and many naive "flower children," wearing beads and long hair, flocked to neighborhoods like the East Village in New York City or Haight-Ashbury in San Francisco, where they often were preyed on by pimps, drug pushers, and other hardened slum residents.

Older students led antiwar and curriculum-change demonstrations in schools and colleges throughout the country, in some cases occupying administrative offices and sometimes shutting down entire universities. As a result, curriculum requirements were abandoned in many institutions and more flexible and "relevant" courses and requirements substituted; social-life restrictions, including those on sexual behavior, were also widely relaxed, and students were given a fuller role in campus governance.

Within the larger society, the youth rebellion stimulated other groups in the population to initiate drives for fuller recognition and societal status. Feminists became increasingly active in the fight for equality in all spheres of American life. Women formed support groups and established national organizations and lobbying mechanisms to attempt to overcome male dominance in government and politics, the job world, and family life. For the first time in America, homosexuals began to demand fuller civil and political rights and to lobby successfully for the decriminalization of alternative forms of sexual behavior. As Chapter 6 points out, gay groups emerged openly on college campuses and homosexuality gained a degree of acceptance as a legitimate life-style choice, rather than a form of mental illness—although it continued to be opposed by major religious denominations and many "mainstream" Americans.

Similarly, in the 1960s and 1970s there was growing social concern about mentally and physically disabled persons in the United States. The first important step came when President John F. Kennedy supported new legislation to serve developmentally disabled persons, and when organizations like Special Olympics and the Kennedy Foundation began to provide needed community programs for this population. There was a massive drive toward deinstitutionalization—getting hundreds of thousands of mentally retarded and mentally ill persons out of long-term custodial institutions into community-based residential facilities where they might become more fully functioning members of community life. Public Law 94-142, the Education for All Handicapped American Children Act, resulted in sharply improved services for disabled persons, including support for physical and occupational therapy, along with recreation as a "related service." Section 504 of the Rehabilitation Act of 1973, often called the "Nondiscrimination Clause," made it clear that schools and colleges were required to provide interscholastic athletics and extracurricular programs for disabled students, in "least restrictive" settings, and mandated that athletic, cultural, and entertainment events be made more fully accessible to all persons.

The elderly, who had long been demeaned and economically vulnerable in American society, also began to mobilize to improve their status in community life. Led by such individuals as Maggie Kuhn of the Gray Panthers, older Americans joined organizations like the American Association of Retired Persons, lobbied vigorously for fuller community services, and gained, through the Older Americans Act, new federal and local programs to assist the aged in terms of health care, retirement and housing assistance, and other social services.

For each of these special populations, one of the battlegrounds in which greater opportunity was a target was the broad area of leisure. Women, for example, sought support for fuller involvement in sports, outdoor recreation, and career employment in recreation. Advocates for physically and mentally disabled persons pressed for the integration of special populations in recreation on all levels in community life. Homosexuals began to present themselves openly in gay social clubs on university campuses and in community settings and exerted pressure to gain a more positive image in the mass media of communication and entertainment.

For all members of society, this period also came to be known as the time of "consciousness-raising" and of the "human potential" movement. Influenced by the writings of psychotherapists like Erich Fromm and Abraham Maslow, growing numbers of Americans sought to explore their own identities more fully. There was a lemming-like surge toward involvement in a host of workshops, retreats, cult-like organizations like est, Insight, Lifespring, and other groups that preached a doctrine of "self-actualization." Millions of Americans entered such therapies or interpersonal experiences as transactional analysis, primal scream, bioenergetics, gestalt therapy, psychosynthesis, nude marathons, or yoga—many of them linking modern Western psychotherapeutic methods with ancient disciplines linked to Eastern religions.

■ IMPLICATIONS FOR LEISURE AND RECREATION

What did these radical changes in social values and behavior have to do with leisure and recreation? Obviously, they sharply challenged many of the traditional beliefs and shibboleths that had governed past recreational practices. For example, most youth sports programs had typically been conducted within a highly competitive, gender-segregated structure that strongly emphasized winning as a goal and ignored the needs of less-skilled youngsters. Under the impetus of the humanistic thinking that gained popularity at this time, greater efforts were made to promote play for all, within a noncompetitive, corecreational framework.

Organizations like the Boy Scouts, which had always stressed conservative middle-class values, and which had a semi-militaristic aura in terms of uniforms, troops, and similar accoutrements, found their enrollments dropping sharply during the Vietnam War era. In response, they sought to reach a broader audience of urban, disadvantaged, and minority-group youth, and modified their program content to meet more contemporary needs of young people.

▥➤ TO THE POINT

For adolescents and young adults, as sex became more acceptable, pornography gained legal status, and drug use became endemic, a new vista of hedonistic leisure possibilities beckoned that made the traditional games, hobbies, and social activities of earlier generations seem pallid and boring. Increasingly, college courses were added that dealt with new life-style values and interests. Students at the University of Connecticut at Storrs established an Experimental College that sought to be responsive to the "real" needs of youth. Instead of courses, it offered "learning collectives," and instead of teachers it had "resource persons." Its curriculum included sessions in how to grow marijuana, build an atomic bomb, and play the banjo, as well as other collectives in massage, welding, yoga, automobile electrical systems, belly dancing, Chinese cooking, guitar playing, bread baking, vegetarian cooking, sewing, and stargazing.[14]

Many women who faced lives as single parents because of divorce took courses or joined support groups that helped them deal with their need for economic independence, roles as working women and mothers, and other challenges in the rapidly changing society. Both men and women by the millions joined support groups dealing with assertiveness training, stress management, weight loss, and dozens of other themes linked to consciousness-raising. One critic commented that whatever the motive—"pleasure, profit, or paradise now"—America in the mid-1970s had embarked on the biggest "introspective binge" any society in history had undergone.

Decline in Work Values

The traditional acceptance of work's being at the moral and religious core of life came under increasing attack at this time. The instinct of "workmanship" no longer motivated employees in boring and uncreative jobs. A nationwide study of work attitudes in the United States showed that college students voiced growing resistance to authority and to being "bossed around" on the job. In 1968, 60 percent of respondents accepted the view that "hard work will always pay off," but in 1971 only 9 percent supported it.[15] In offices and factories, absenteeism increased dramatically and growing numbers of employees refused overtime work. In *Work and Its Discontents,* Daniel Bell had concluded that if "conspicuous consumption" had been the badge of a rising middle class, "conspicuous loafing" was now the hostile gesture of a tired working class.[16] In a later book, *Rivethead: Tales from the Assembly Line,* an ex-automobile-assembly-line worker tells how he and other "shoprats" devised schemes to overcome job boredom and beat the time clock. Ben Hamper and his fellow "weekend warriors" invented death-defying games such as "rivet hockey" and developed clever plans to catch sleep while on the job or slip off to the nearest bar.[17]
   By 1981, a Harris Poll revealed that:

- 78 percent of all working Americans felt that "people take less pride in their work than they did 10 years ago."
- 73 percent believed that the "motivation to work hard is not as strong today as it was a decade ago."
- 69 percent felt that workmanship had declined significantly, and 63 percent felt that people did not work as hard as they had in the past.[18]

The ultimate expression of the Protestant ethic, what psychiatrists had begun to call *workaholism,* was now widely scorned as neurotic behavior. Instead of commitment to work, Bell wrote, many employees had embarked on a desperate "drive for leisure":

> The themes of play, of recreation, of amusement are the dominant ones in our culture today. They are the subject of the "hard sell." Sports clothes, travel, the outdoor barbecue, the portable TV set, all become the hallmarks of the time.[19]

A number of investigators sought to explore the changing relationship between work and leisure. In one study, Spreitzer and Snyder explored what they called a "compensatory" hypothesis—that when work failed to provide self-actualization and the opportunity for rewarding self-expression, leisure would tend to take on enriched meaning. They found that, while leisure activities may be useful in compensating for job dissatisfaction, they were not as psychologically encompassing as work experiences that were fully self-actualizing.[20] Other studies examining the relationship between leisure and work were carried out by John Kelly at the University of Illinois. Kelly suggested two contrasting concepts: (1) the *dualist* view, which sees leisure as a sphere of human activity that is distinctly separate from work; and (2) the *holistic* view, which sees a close relationship between leisure and work. He developed an analysis of leisure that took into account both societal constraints and pressures that affect it and also its degree of work-relatedness. Based on these variables, there were four ways of defining leisure:

1. Unconditional leisure: carried on for its own sake, and for intrinsic satisfaction, with a minimum of expectations related to family or community values.
2. Coordinated leisure: freely chosen, but similar to the participant's involvement in work, in its form or content.
3. Complementary leisure: strongly influenced by work; may be either role-related (similar to work) or compensatory (contrasting with work).
4. Required activities carried on in nonwork time: not really regarded as leisure, but done to prepare for work, maintain household, etc.[21]

Throughout this period, accompanying the decline of interest in work, Americans showed a steadily growing fascination with play—both in the search for pleasure and other personal values, and as a means of asserting their own individuality.

■ LEISURE—THE SEARCH FOR HAPPINESS

In a special seventeen-page feature in May 1977, *Newsweek* described the economic impact of the "dazzling world of play" that Americans had embarked on:

> Almost unnoticed, leisure-time activities have become the nation's No. 1 industry, as measured by people's spending. Latest figures . . . show that Americans will spend more than 160 billion dollars on leisure and recreation in 1977. By 1985, the total is expected to climb to 300 billions. The expenditure is a clear indication, sociologists say, of how avidly Americans pursue "the good life" beyond the bounds of work and home.[22]

As examples of the growth in leisure involvement, *Newsweek* reported that sports activities—including boating, tennis, football, archery, jogging, hunting, bowling, and others—drew more than 700 million participants a year. Attendance at sporting events had risen during the past decade to 314 million, and participation in cultural activities also had climbed by leaps and bounds; 78 million Americans visited museums each year, and 62 million attended at least one performance of live theater. Active hobbies were also growing, with 36 million households involved in gardening; there were 16 million participants in stamp collecting and 10 million in bridge and chess. An estimated 40 million Americans were spending leisure time in volunteer and religious activities.

Some social critics were skeptical of the meaning of the nation's growing involvement in leisure pursuits. Daniel Bell, for example, felt that much of the new American life-style represented the influence of relentless advertising and pressure to consume lavishly. He wrote:

> The American citizen, as *Fortune* once noted, lives in a state of siege from dawn until bedtime. "Nearly everything he sees, hears, touches, tastes, and smells is an attempt to sell him something. . . . Advertising is the handwriting on the wall, the sign in the sky. . . ."[23]

Similarly, psychiatrist Erich Fromm argued that many individuals were passive, alienated, and controlled by others in their free time, just as they were in their work:

> [The individual] "consumes" ball games, moving pictures, newspapers and magazines, books, lectures, natural scenery, social gatherings, in the same alienated and abstractified way in which he consumes the commodities he has bought. . . . Actually, he is not free to enjoy "his" leisure; his leisure-time consumption is determined by industry, as are the commodities he buys; his taste is manipulated. . . . entertainment is an industry like any other, the customer is made to buy fun as he is made to buy dresses and shoes. The value of the fun is determined by its success on the market, not by anything which could be measured in human terms.[24]

Certainly many forms of play were marked by mass conformity and passivity at this time, just as they were in earlier periods. However, given the impact of the consciousness-raising period of the 1960s and 1970s, growing numbers of Americans were determined to assert their own individuality through leisure. So, instead of relying on mass-produced toys or free-time gadgets or the world of electronic entertainment that had become increasingly popular, a sizable segment of the population sought out unique hobbies in their leisure:

> Retired individuals who live in travel trailers and go South in the winter and North in the summer, backpacking enthusiasts, scuba divers, antique collectors, swamp buggy racers, body builders, craftsmen and craftswomen, snowmobile racers, skydivers, folk music performers and fans, tailgating fans at professional football games, collectors, artifact searchers who use metal detectors, mummy dusters who volunteer in archaeological museums, hang gliders, performers in little theaters, people who practice "creative anachronism" (enacting lives of past or mythical cultures)—all illustrate such absorbing hobbies.[25]

In addition to providing facilities, public recreation and park departments offer a huge range of classes, events, tournaments, and other organized recreation activities. Left, the Portsmouth, Virginia, Recreation Department sponsors a community bicycle event. Below, residents enjoy a Polish folk dance demonstration and a women's volleyball tournament in Westchester County, New York.

Harvard sociologist David Riesman concluded that the herd instinct had largely disappeared when it came to life-style behaviors, and the director of the values-and-life-style program at SRI International, a California think-tank agency, summed it up: "The trend is that there is no trend. We're in the midst of a celebration of diversity."[26]

Search for Self: The "Me" Generation

Sociologist Robert Bellah suggested that individualism had been allowed to "run rampant" in the society by the mid-1980s. He attributed much of this to the role of psychologists in emphasizing almost exclusively the needs, interests, and feelings of the individual, rather than those of the broader society.[27] John Hewitt agreed, writing that the "self" is omnipresent in contemporary life. Everyday conversations are filled with references to identity, self-concept, self-esteem, self-image, self-fulfillment, self-actualization. He continued:

> Therapists and best-selling books promise to teach assertiveness, raise consciousness, enhance self-esteem, or improve relationships. Celebrities parade their psychic wounds before television audiences, and the language of self-reference has become a widely acceptable part of popular vocabularies of motive. Men and women . . . speak of "finding themselves" and of their "real" selves, as if the self could lose itself or be mistaken for another self.[28]

Inevitably, the 1980s became known as the "Me Decade." While work was no longer viewed as a moral imperative, to be successful and make money became increasingly important. So-called Yuppies (Young Urban Professionals) became the model for many young people. These success- and career-oriented individuals were out to make a killing by whatever means, including junk-bond speculation, leveraging companies, making high-flying deals, and enjoying a flashy, hedonistic life-style. As the nation itself went deeper and deeper into debt, Donald Trump, a glamorous real estate, gambling, and airlines tycoon, became a widely admired folk hero. Only when the economy cooled at the end of the 1980s did the decade of money fever come to an end, with a number of lawless inside traders, arbitrageurs, and savings-and-loan officers going to jail and Trump's financial empire nose-diving perilously toward bankruptcy.

■ CONTEMPORARY TRENDS AFFECTING LEISURE AND RECREATION

By the early 1990s, a number of societal trends that strongly affected leisure and recreation had become evident. For several years, a number of social critics had been protesting against what they saw as an era of selfishness and greed. Daniel Yankelovich, a leading pollster, suggested that the search for self-fulfillment had led to self-indulgence for many and that the nation now had a sense of social drift. He argued that a new "ethic of commitment" had begun to develop and that the permissiveness and decline of family and work values would be replaced by a return to civic responsibility.

With the economy declining and with growing problems of budget deficits on all levels of government, along with problems of drug abuse and urban crime, it was recognized that a retreat from the era of the "Me Decade" was in order. As part of this trend in thinking, work began to regain its positive image—and research reports indicated that Americans *were* working longer hours than they had a decade or two earlier. For some time, economists and political scientists had pointed out that America's shorter-hours movement was selective in its impact. Sebastian de Grazia had reported that, while average weekly hours of work had declined in the post–World War II years, this was due to the increase in holidays and paid vacations—and that professionals and business executives were now working disproportionately long hours.[29] Similarly, Staffan Linder had written in the 1970s of the "harried leisure class," and of "leisure for the masses and toil for the classes."[30]

The Shifting Work-Leisure Balance

In 1987, pollster Louis Harris reported that the number of hours the average American was working had risen from 40.6 hours weekly in 1973 to 48.4 in 1985, and that the leisure hours available to most Americans had declined from 26.2 hours to 17.7. The number of weekly work hours was particularly high for professional people, those with incomes of $50,000 a year and over, and for women, who often have both jobs and home-based responsibilities. Harris concluded:

> Clearly, a phenomenon has emerged among the country's most affluent sectors: they work the longest hours and have the least time for leisure. This trend toward longer work hours and shorter leisure time runs counter to all the predictions that were made 10 to 20 years ago, when it was widely assumed that automation and technology would shorten the workweek and would give most people more and more leisure time. Precisely the opposite has happened.[31]

A number of other reports supported the Harris Poll findings. A Wall Street Journal/NBC News survey in 1986 showed that, however Americans defined leisure, twice as many claimed to have less of it than those who claimed to have more, than in the past. The survey found that professionals and managers had less vacation time—two weeks a year on the average—than in any other industrial nation but Japan. A management training concern in Canada surveyed over 1,200 American and foreign business executives and found that 57 percent of them worked six to twenty hours beyond the forty-hour week, 20 percent longer on average than ten years before.

III⯈ TO THE POINT

In the early 1990s, Juliet Schor, a Harvard economics professor, wrote a book that summed up the trend—*The Overworked American: The Unexpected Decline of Leisure.*[32] In an article in *Newsweek,* Schor concluded that from the end of the 1960s to 1992, Americans had increased the amount of time they spend at work by about 160 hours, or nearly one month per year. This was equally true, she wrote, for workers in service jobs and those in "glamour" positions, and for both women and men. In part, Schor felt, the change had occurred because of employment practices within the competitive capitalist system:

> Businesses would rather employ fewer workers and pay overtime than hire more and pay fringe benefits. And as productivity increases, business would rather give employees more money than more time off.[33]

Lawrence Shames agreed; in the late 1950s, he wrote, leisure, rather than the job, seemed to be the wave of the future. By the late 1980s, however, work had become the opiate of the ruling class. Shames continued:

> In the 1980s . . . the work ethic staged an impressive comeback. No longer was a job just a job; it was a Career, the closest thing to a Quest. "The Pride Is Back," a carmaker proclaimed. "Your Money Should Work as Hard as You Do," spieled a financial services firm. Hard work was sexy again.[34]

■ DECLINE OF LEISURE: REALITY OR MYTH?

But *was* the reported expansion of work and decline of leisure a reality? A number of reputable authorities challenged the Harris Poll findings on several grounds. For example, economist Robert Samuelson concluded that the Harris statistics were unreliable, citing the data drawn from elderly respondents as evidence:

> Although few of them hold jobs, they recorded the largest drop in leisure in the latest survey. And they say they have only about an hour more of daily leisure than working-age Americans. How can this be? It can't. People don't offhandedly know how much free time they have and Americans are reluctant to admit they spend too much time relaxing.[35]

Samuelson went on to point out that the Harris data on work and free time were drawn from two questions taking about a minute to administer, in a seventy-two-question telephone interview on another subject entirely. Asked to give information of this type, respondents can easily provide subjective, inaccurate responses. Similarly, in a critique of Schor's book on the overworked American, Robert Sobel concludes that she had oversimplified the problem, in drawing inferences about the decline of leisure: "Schor ignores this matter [complexity of the country's population], preferring instead generalization, stereotype and recourse to aggregate statistics followed by [carefully selected] anecdotes."[36]

The most effective approach to gathering valid statistics in this field is to collect precise information from employees using daily diaries of time use. The most systematic and comprehensive studies of this type have been carried out by sociologist John Robinson of the University of Maryland. Based on surveys conducted in the 1960s, 1970s, and 1980s in cooperation with the University of Michigan and funded by the National Science Foundation, Robinson found that free time—defined as everything that excluded work, self-maintenance, or family care—had actually risen about 10 percent over this period.[37]

Robinson also suggested several reasons why many Americans feel that they have less leisure—including the growing number of working women, single parents, latchkey children, and parents working separate shifts—all of which create time pressures.[38]

The likelihood is that the so-called time famine is in part a reality, stemming from the increase in workload for individuals in companies that were downsizing during difficult economic times and from the pressure on many wealthy and successful professionals and business executives to compete in a heightened work climate. Indeed, surveys by Northwestern National Life, a major insurance company, found that twice as many workers found their jobs highly stressful in 1992 as those who did in 1985. Four out of ten private-sector employees reported that they suffered from extreme stress on the job and had considered quitting.[39]

Certainly time pressures have increased for many Americans, particularly those in the childrearing, career-building, debt-assuming years. Fax machines, overnight mail, computers, car phones, microwave ovens, and other technological innovations may have made life easier, but they also tend to wipe out time that is spent waiting for things to happen. Writing in *Time Magazine,* Nancy Gibbs suggests that the pace of life has become faster, faster, faster. The idea of instant gratification dominates our lives, and family schedules become overpowering. But much of the frenzy, the pressure, she writes, may be self-imposed, as part of the American ethos to be busy.[40]

Particularly in the transition from an industrial to a global service economy, many professionals such as lawyers, bankers, and accountants must work harder than ever to meet their clients' needs. Simply to remain competitive, Gibbs suggests, many professionals find that their lives have become one long, continuous workday that "squeezes out" any leisure time: "Workers are weary, parents are frantic, and even children haven't a moment to spare; leisure could be to the '90s what money was to the '80s."[41]

Leisure Impact on Time "Scarcity"

A paradox of the current work-leisure scene is that leisure, which was supposed to contribute to a sense of relaxation and escape from work pressures, today provides pressures of its own. Despite the findings that leisure time declined during the 1970s and 1980s, numerous sources have documented the continuous *rise* in spending on sporting goods, travel, recreational reading, music cassettes, electronic entertainment, and other leisure pursuits.

TO THE POINT

But the very nature of much modern play has transformed fun into work, writes Witold Rybczynski in *Waiting for the Weekend.*[42] Once free time was intended to be just that: freedom from the need to be busy, from commitments and pressure. With a new emphasis on fitness and health, many adults commit themselves to regular workouts in jogging, aerobics, or racquetball. There has been an evolution from casualness to intensity, from the simple to the intricate, in almost every form of contemporary play, whether it's bicycling, roller-skating, cross-country skiing, or boating. Technical gadgetry and advanced play equipment, often becoming obsolete within a year or two, emphasize not only the marketing of leisure as an industry, but also the serious meaning we assign to play. Rybczynski suggests that the reason we place so much energy and effort into play is because we do not believe that our work is really significant. But what it means in the long run is that leisure itself contributes to the sense of pressure in daily life and to the contemporary belief in the time famine.

Summing up, while reports of declining leisure may have been seriously exaggerated, they reflect the fact that for many individuals there is a clear sense of pressure and a real overload in work. The predictions of the post–World War II years about the future growth of leisure have not been realized for the society as a whole. They were dependent on the assumption that all groups would share the new leisure equally; instead, one segment of the population continues to work long hours, while another, larger group has a growing concern about the availability of work.

■ SHIFT IN LEISURE VALUES AND GOALS

Meanwhile, what has happened to the optimistic and visionary dreams that were expressed earlier in the century about the social and spiritual impact of leisure? In the 1960s and 1970s, for example, it was widely defined as a unique, holistic state of existence, marked by freedom and the opportunity for reaching one's fullest human potential.

However, such expectations have clearly not been realized in the final years of the twentieth century. Instead, many Americans shape their free time so it becomes as much like work as possible—segmented, purposeful, and routinized. For others, leisure has become a highly passive experience; a 1982 survey reported by United Media Enterprises suggested that Americans spent more than half their free time in front of the home television set. Increasingly, television had become like a fireplace, "the new American hearth—a center for family activities, conversation and companionship."

As far as leisure's providing an opportunity for spiritual and moral growth is concerned, the harsh reality is that many of the most common uses of leisure today are socially destructive or degrading. To illustrate, three of our most widely found uses of leisure involve gambling, substance abuse, and commercialized sex. As Chapter 12 will show in detail, each of these pursuits has gained a measure of popular acceptance and involves a tremendous financial outlay by the public.

It is clear that leisure, far from providing an idealized life-style for Americans, tends rather to reflect national attitudes and values that tolerate varied forms of play and entertainment that are morally dubious but driven by the dollar. A prime example was the quiz-show scandals of the late 1950s, when the five leading television network programs were exciting and suspenseful quiz shows. Huge prizes built up from week to week on programs like "The $64,000 Question" and instant-celebrity contestants were the focus of national attention. However, the bubble was pricked when a contestant revealed the truth—that in the effort to build big audiences and keep leading players in action, sponsors had pressured the game-show producers to "fix" the quizzes. The scandal ended with Congressional investigations and criminal trials for over a hundred contestants and producers who were prosecuted for perjury.

Similarly, sports have become so commercialized that the buying and selling of professional athletes and the skipping of sports franchises to more lucrative markets, along with the conscienceless exploitation of college athletes, are taken for granted. Such examples point up the fact that, far from representing a spiritually enriching experience in contemporary America, leisure is today regarded primarily as a business—a huge, interlocking system of personal products and services that is vigorously marketed by public, commercial, and voluntary agencies alike.

LEISURE AS AN INDUSTRY

It was first clearly recognized in the 1960s that recreation had become one of America's leading businesses. The financial columnist, Sylvia Porter, pointed out that such factors as climbing income, growing free time, physical fitness concerns, and a longer life span had resulted in the dramatic growth of spending and employment in the leisure field.

By the early 1980s, *U.S. News and World Report* estimated that annual consumer spending on leisure was over $300 billion (by way of comparison, spending on public education and the nation's defense budget were each approximately the same amount).[43] Recreation expenditures continued to climb in the years that followed. When all of the difficult-to-record forms of leisure spending are included, such as spending on gambling and other sub-rosa or semilegal pursuits, or travel and tourism, or the operating expenses of government and voluntary recreation agencies, it is clear that leisure represents a major economic force in the nation.

Fiscal Austerity and Leisure's Marketing Identity

Despite the impressive sums that are spent privately on leisure, many public recreation agencies have been forced by economic austerity trends—stemming from higher costs of welfare, personnel costs, crime- and drug-fighting measures, as well as lower tax revenues—to cut back sharply on human-service programs.

TO THE POINT

Today, both public and nonprofit voluntary leisure-service agencies are making increased use of varied revenue sources, such as admission charges or registration fees, along with concessions and leases of publicly owned areas, sales or rental of equipment, and other special-service charges. In so doing, leisure-service managers are following a national trend. Respected professionals like doctors and lawyers frankly advertise their services and in some cases operate as part of regional or national chains. Churches and cultural institutions all market their products and services today. Hospitals often house subsidiary industries, such as food or laundry services, while television evangelists not only provide entertainment directly to huge audiences but in some cases establish resorts or theme parks based on religious themes.

Perhaps the most striking example of how America had adopted a marketing orientation came in 1990, when Congress approved an Immigration Act that had been proposed by the Heritage Foundation, a Washington-based conservative think tank. In an ironic rejection of the nation's promise—symbolized by the Statue of Liberty—to "bring me your tired, your poor, your huddled masses yearning to breathe free," this act made it possible to *buy* American citizenship. Foreigners who were willing and able to invest at least one million dollars in American business were granted immediate permanent residency, leading to full citizenship—while desperate Haitian boat people seeking asylum in the United States were routinely being turned away by the thousands.[44]

The American Association for Leisure and Recreation, a national body representing thousands of leisure professionals who work in an educational framework, accepted its new identity in the mid-1980s, in its use of the term *recreation industry* to describe the leisure-service field.[45] Similarly, *Trends*, a publication of the National Recreation and Park Association and the federal government's National Park Service, has concluded that public recreation and park administrators are inseparable from their commercial counterparts:

> Managed recreation is a profession that provides services to consumers of all demographic stripes and shades. Under this designation, a public park superintendent is in the same business as a resort owner, as are a theme park operator and the fitness director of a YMCA. . . . There are many changes overtaking the industry. . . . [and it is becoming] more competitive, more complex and more in need of a high degree of professionalism to manage these changes.[46]

Recreation directors in public agencies, military morale and welfare units, hospitals, nursing homes, and employee-service programs are now urged to adopt an "entrepreneurship" approach, along with their openly commercial counterparts in profit-seeking businesses. They are regarded as part of the total spectrum of business-sponsored entertainment and play, including major motion-picture and music recording companies, professional sports teams and stadiums, theme parks and cruise-ship owners, television networks, magazine publishers, and toy and sports-equipment manufacturers.

If all members of the public were equally able to pay for the use of this variegated leisure system, the accommodation that has been made would be entirely appropriate. However, the reality is that great numbers of Americans—over thirty-five million in the early 1990s—are living below the poverty line. Millions of others, including the elderly, the physically and mentally disabled, at-risk children and youth in urban ghettos, and other special populations, are clearly unable to pay more than the most minimal costs of leisure involvement. Within a dominant marketing and revenue-seeking orientation, it is likely that the poor and those with other disabilities will have limited access to positive recreational opportunities, and will seek less socially desirable forms of play.

■ SUMMARY

As we approach century's end, it is clear that the leisure and recreation field has gone through a unique series of changes—from being regarded initially as a social evil or at best a subordinate adjunct to work, to being considered an important form of human experience and a valuable social service, and, most recently, to its identity as an economic commodity, or industry. Leisure has proven to be a battleground for groups that seek fuller opportunity in American life, including racial, ethnic, gender-related, and other minorities, and has become increasingly less available to the social classes that traditionally had it as their special possession. To understand the role of leisure and recreation in American life more fully, we will examine them in the chapters that follow in two major contexts: the key demographic variables that influence leisure participation, and the major forms of organized play enjoyed by the public today.

■ QUESTIONS FOR DISCUSSION

1. How were leisure and recreation linked to the War on Poverty, the civil rights movement, and efforts to control urban race riots in the 1960s? Respond to the statement that America had become a "have" and "have-not" society, with specific reference to recreational opportunities in cities and suburbs.
2. How did the counterculture movement, particularly as it involved challenges to establishment values in the family, educational settings, and the work world, affect the leisure behavior of youth in the 1970s?
3. During the second half of the twentieth century, American attitudes regarding work and other forms of social obligation went through a series of dramatic changes. What were these, and how did they affect leisure involvement?
4. Numerous reports in the 1980s and early 1990s indicated that work demands had increased for Americans and that leisure hours had declined. Critically review these reports, and indicate the degree to which they are based on reality in your view, as well as the degree to which they reflect popular perception of work trends.
5. With recreation now being viewed as an industry, dominated by a marketing orientation, what effect has the new trend in viewing leisure had on the government sponsorship of recreation programs to meet community needs?

■ NOTES

1. SHAMES, L. 1988. A greed for work. *New York Times Business World* (Dec.4): 30.

2. HENLE, P. 1965. The quiet revolution in leisure time. *Occupational Outlook Quarterly.* U.S. Department of Labor (May): 1–9.

3. NANUS, B., and H. ADELMAN. 1975. Forecast for leisure. In *Leisure Today: Selected Readings.* Washington, DC: American Association for Leisure and Recreation, p. 30.

4. WOLMAN, J. 1978. The future of working: Less of it for more of us. *Philadelphia Inquirer* (Sept 3).

5. RODGERS, D., cited in B. K. Hunnicutt. 1988. *Work without end: Abandoning shorter hours for the right to work.* Philadelphia: Temple University Press, p. 29.

6. MILLS, C. W. 1956. *White collar, the American middle classes.* New York: Oxford University Press, p. 237.

7. WOLFENSTEIN, M. 1958. The emergence of fun morality. In *Mass leisure,* ed. E. Larrabee and R. Meyersohn. Glencoe, IL: Free Press, p. 86.

8. KERR, W. 1965. *The decline of pleasure.* New York: Simon and Schuster, p. 39.

9. CLAWSON, M., and J. KNETSCH. 1960. *Economics of outdoor recreation.* Baltimore: Johns Hopkins Press and Resources for the Future, Inc., p. 151.

10. *New York Post* (Aug. 6, 1964), p. 50.

11. *New York Times* (July 18, 1966), p. 17.

12. HARRINGTON, M. 1962. *The other America.* Baltimore: Penguin, p. 177.

13. For several eyewitness accounts of summer riots in major cities, see: *New York Times,* July 15, 1967, pp. 10–11; July 26, 1967, pp. 18, 19; and April 7, 1968, p. 62.

14. Pot, bombs, banjos studied at U. Conn. *Associated Press* (Nov. 7, 1977).

15. YANKELOVICH, D. 1978. The new psychological contracts at work. *Psychology Today* (Nov.): 46–50.

16. BELL, D. 1959, 1988. Work and its discontents. In *The end of ideology.* Cambridge: Harvard University Press, p. 239.

17. HAMPER, B. 1991. *Rivethead: Tales from the assembly line.* New York: Warner.

18. YANKELOVICH, D. 1982. The public mind: The work ethic is unemployed. *Psychology Today* (May): 6.

19. BELL, D., *op. cit.,* pp. 257–258.

20. SPREITZER, E. A., and E. E. SNYDER. 1974. Work orientation: Meaning of leisure and mental health. *Journal of Leisure Research* (Summer): 207–219.

21. KELLY, J. R. 1975. Leisure decisions: Exploring extrinsic and role-related orientations. *Society and Leisure* 4: 45–61.

22. The boom in leisure: Where Americans spend 160 billions. *Newsweek* (May 23, 1977): 62.

23. BELL, *op. cit.*

24. FROMM, E. 1955. *The sane society.* New York: Fawcett, p. 124.

25. Summarized from JURY, M. 1977. *Playtime: Americans at leisure.* New York: Harcourt, Brace, Jovanovich.

26. Lifestyle of the '80's: Anything goes. *U.S. News and World Report* (Aug. 1, 1983): 45.

27. SANOFF, A. 1985. A conversation with Robert Bellah. *U.S. News and World Report* (May 27): 45.

28. HEWITT, J. 1989. *Dilemma of the American self.* Philadelphia: Temple University Press, p. 3.

29. DEGRAZIA, S. 1952. *Of time, work and leisure.* New York: Twentieth Century Fund, pp. 131–135.

30. LINDER, S. 1970. *The harried leisure class.* New York: Columbia University Press.

31. HARRIS, L. 1987. *Inside America.* New York: Vintage, Random House, p. 20.

32. SCHOR, J. 1991. *The overworked American: The unexpected decline of leisure.* New York: Basic Books.

33. SCHOR, J. 1992. Are we really that lazy? *Newsweek* (Feb. 17): 42–43.

34. SHAMES, *op. cit.,* p. 30.

35. SAMUELSON, R. 1989. Rediscovering the rat race. *Newsweek* (May 15): 57.

36. SOBEL, R. 1992. Working in America. Book review, *Philadelphia Inquirer* (Feb. 23): K-1.

37. KOLSON, A. 1989. A question of time. *Philadelphia Inquirer* (Oct. 26): 1–C. See also J. Robinson. 1991. How Americans use time. *The Futurist* (Sept.-Oct.): 23–37.

38. ROBINSON, J. 1989. Time's up. *American Demographics* (July): 33–35.

39. PARKER, J. 1992. Workplace is a 'pressure-cooker' of stress, study finds. *Knight-Ridder News Service* (June 3).

40. GIBBS, N. 1989. How America has run out of time. *Time* (Apr. 24): 58–61.

41. *Ibid.,* p. 59.

42. RYBCZYNSKI, W. 1991. *Waiting for the weekend.* New York: Viking.

43. Business gets healthy from athletics too. *U.S. News and World Report* (Aug. 13, 1984): 27.

44. DOWIE, M. 1991. Bring us your huddled millionaires. *Harpers Magazine* (Nov.): 58–59.

45. Recreation industry strong. *American Association for Leisure and Recreation Reporter* 11, 4 (Aug. 1986): 1.

46. ZENGER, J. 1987. Leadership: Management's better half. *Trends* 4: 3.

⫸ PART TWO

Multiculturalism and Four Demographic Variables

5 Racial and Ethnic Influences on Leisure

As a result of the political and social changes of recent decades, cultural pluralism is now generally recognized as an organizing principle of this society. In contrast to the idea of the melting pot, which promised to erase ethnic and group differences, children now learn that variety is the spice of life. . . . They learn that . . . the unique feature of the United States is that its common culture has been formed by the interaction of its subsidiary cultures. It is a culture that has been influenced over time by immigrants, American Indians, Africans (slave and free) and by their descendants. American music, art, literature, language, food, clothing, sports, holidays, and customs all show the effects of the commingling of diverse cultures in one nation.[1]

We turn now to an examination of several demographic elements in American life that have had a powerful influence on leisure values and behavior. The first of these has to do with race and ethnicity, factors that have played a key role in determining the social status and life-styles of many Americans. This chapter explores earlier American attitudes with respect to race, ethnicity, and national origin, such as the harsh biases against people of color and those from southern and eastern Europe. It reviews the influence of the melting pot approach, which has largely been replaced by a multicultural view of American life and education. Four minority populations— African Americans, Hispanic Americans, Native Americans, and Asian Americans— are examined, in terms of the role leisure has played in their lives and the impact they have had on other Americans' use of free time.

■ DEFINITIONS OF RACE AND ETHNICITY

The term *race* is frequently misused; we tend to think of people who share common languages or religious beliefs or who have similar national origins as belonging to the same racial group. However, such factors have little to do with race. Instead, a race is a statistical aggregate of people who share a composite of genetically transmissible *physical* traits, such as:

> skin pigmentation, head form, facial features, stature, and the color, distribution and texture of body hair. Since gross similarities are to be noted among human populations, many attempts have been made to classify the people of the world racially. Estimates of racial types range from three—Caucasoid, Mongoloid, and Negroid—to thirty or more.[2]

In contrast, *ethnicity* involves having a unique social and cultural heritage that is passed on from one generation to another. Ethnic groups are often identified by distinctive patterns of language, family life, religion, recreation, and other customs that differentiate them from other groups. To illustrate the point, Americans of different European origins would normally be regarded as of the same racial stock— Caucasoid. However, they would have different ethnic backgrounds because of their distinctive customs, values, or cultural traits.

Hess, Markson, and Stein identify three factors that serve to keep people apart, based on racial or ethnic differences: *prejudice, discrimination,* and *institutional racism.* The first two are primarily individual reactions, while the third involves a widespread structural arrangement or behavioral system:

> *Prejudice* literally means "prejudging" without knowledge. Thus, ethnic, racial, religious, or other social categories are *stereotyped.* A stereotype is an image in which a single set of characteristics, favorable or unfavorable, is attributed to an entire group. Stereotypes are overgeneralized; that is, behavior that may be true of some members is taken as typical of the whole group.[3]

One major purpose of prejudice is to improve one's own position in competition for such benefits as jobs, wealth, or housing, at the expense of another group. This is done through practices of discrimination.

Whereas prejudice is a set of attitudes, discrimination is the practice of treating people unequally. The two are closely related. That is, prejudice often leads to discrimination. Discrimination, in turn, reinforces prejudice in a vicious circle that limits opportunity and produces a self-fulfilling prophecy.[4]

Finally, *institutional racism* involves actual practices of discrimination that are based on a larger structure of societal norms and behavior and that are reinforced by both formal and informal agents of social control in areas such as housing, education, job opportunity, and leisure.

It should be stressed that throughout America's history prejudice and discrimination have affected not only people of color, but also those of European origin or of certain religious affiliations. Terms like *dago, kike, hunky,* or *wop* illustrate such attitudes; during their early periods of migration, the Irish were often greeted by signs like "No Irish need apply." Reactionary politicians frequently leveled charges of "Papist" against their opponents, meaning that they were tools of the Roman Catholic church. Although Jews were generally well accepted in the American colonies, by the latter part of the nineteenth century, anti-Semitism was widespread in social circles and the business world.

■ ETHNICITY AND SOCIAL STATUS IN THE AMERICAN PAST

Although the democratic principles outlined in the Declaration of Independence and the Constitution expressed belief in the equality of humankind, the reality is that from the very beginning the North American colonists had a distinct hierarchy of status. To be white, male, and of European stock tended to place one in the higher ranks, although many English convicts and prostitutes were transported to the colonies for forced or indentured labor. Others who came from the British Isles, such as the Irish or Scotch Irish, came from conditions of extreme poverty and famine, and other European settlers often faced prejudice and discrimination.

As the young nation developed, despite the antagonism toward Great Britain that stemmed from the American Revolution and the War of 1812, admiration of the British was widespread, particularly among the upper classes, who held the conviction that it was important to be white, Protestant, and of Anglo-Saxon heritage. Sociologist Digby Baltzell points out that during the nineteenth century a closed WASP elite came to dominate the United States in terms of banking, major corporations, education and religion, literature, politics, and other elements of culture.

Linked to American admiration for Great Britain was a tacit acceptance of that nation's role as a colonial power, which embodied an ideology of racial superiority— later to be described by Rudyard Kipling as "the white man's burden." This ideology held that whites were racially superior, and that it was their mission to rule the colored peoples of the world. In time, Furnas writes, this tradition led to

an explicit American imperialism to imitate Britain's. The position was that only by creating a large navy, acquiring colonies and ruling dark-skinned peoples could the American branch of Anglo-Saxonism live up to its family heritage.[5]

Within this mind-set of total Anglo-Saxon superiority, ethnocentrism flourished, and immigrants from central and southern Europe were regarded as second-class citizens. Racial and ethnic prejudices found a home in the Know-Nothing political parties that opposed the immigration arriving on America's shores throughout the nineteenth century and virulently expressed their hatred for Catholics and Jews. It continued for a major part of the twentieth century, as Congress extended a ban on Asian immigrants that had been enacted in the 1880s and established new formulas that sharply favored the admission of northern Europeans from such countries as Sweden, Germany, and the British Isles.

The Melting Pot Ideal

In contrast to this ethnocentric view, a different thrust in American life, literature, and politics was the concept of the "melting pot"—the idea that America's greatness stemmed from the contribution of newcomers of many nationalities who would all become blended into a new and unique citizen, the American. The melting pot idea stemmed from the very first days of the republic, when a naturalized New Yorker of French origin, Jean de Crèvecoeur, wrote in 1782 of individuals of many nations being "melted" into a new race of men. Much later, in 1908, a play titled *The Melting Pot* was a smash success on Broadway. Its hero, a Russian-Jewish immigrant who had fled from persecution, exulted in his new country, praising America as "God's crucible," where all the nations of Europe were melting and reforming, despite past "blood hatreds and rivalries." Historians agreed that the nation's history was largely the result of its vast folk migration; it was a society created by the intermingling of migrants and what the country did to them. Michael Kraus quotes the novelist Herman Melville:

> Settled by the people of all nations, all nations may claim her for their own. You cannot spill a drop of American blood without spilling the blood of the whole world. . . . We are not a nation, so much as a world. . . . We are the heirs of all time and with all nations we divide our inheritance.[6]

The melting pot vision opposed the idea of having "hyphenated" Americans who maintained even a vestige of their old loyalties and customs. Only English was to be taught in schools, and settlement houses and other agencies sought to help new immigrants become assimilated as quickly as possible. Under its pressures, the children of immigrants learned to be ashamed of their parents and grandparents, who spoke with accents and were perceived as "foreign."

By the mid-twentieth century, however, it was apparent that many Americans continued to retain ancestral ties and loyalties, often through national folklore societies or religious affiliations. Beyond this, the melting pot idea had never really applied to Americans of other than European origin. Indeed, miscegenation—the intermarriage or interbreeding of whites with those of color, including African Americans, Native Americans, and Orientals—was illegal by statute in a number of states. The great Supreme Court justice, Thurgood Marshall, commented, "The dream of America as the great melting pot has not been realized for the Negro; because of his skin color he never even made it into the pot."

Cultural Pluralism

A new concept came into being: *cultural pluralism*. This concept held that the United States was really a checkerboard or mosaic of different minority groups, and that it was strengthened, rather than weakened, by its continuing diversity. It helped to promote favorable attitudes toward those of different European origins and to create a hospitable climate toward improving race relations generally throughout the United States. For the first time, serious questions were raised about the place of African Americans and other nonwhites within the American mosaic.

Until the 1940s only a few scholars or political leaders like W. E. B. DuBois and Marcus Garvey had fought to promote black pride and a sense of unity among Americans of African ancestry. However, as the civil rights movement gained momentum in the 1950s and 1960s, a new doctrine of "black is beautiful" began to be preached. There was increased interest in African art, history, religion, and folklore, and when the television series "Roots" captured a huge, multiracial audience in its portrayal of a single African-American family's history from slavery days to the present, interest was redoubled. Blacks began to demand fuller and more accurate treatment of the role of color in American life.

There was growing pressure to revise and improve textbooks and courses dealing with the history and contributions of African Americans, in terms of their achievements in science, industry, and the armed forces. Before long, the demands grew to include new courses in black history, literature, art, and music—and then to have wholesale revision of other courses and the addition of new curricula in schools on all levels.

■ THE DRIVE TOWARD MULTICULTURALISM

It was clear that the nation's educational system had presented a rigidly one-sided view of American life. Many educators attested to their own past experience, not only as African Americans, but as members of other ethnic, racial, and sexual minorities as well. At a campus forum on multiculturalism, Renato Rosaldo, Professor of Anthropology at Stanford University, wrote about his experience as a Hispanic-American child in the Southwest:

> If the pain of changes under way is great, the pain of no change is even greater. I remember what it was like as a Chicano in junior high school during the 1950s in Tucson, Arizona. The punishment was bending over, holding your ankles, and getting swats with a board. The crime was speaking Spanish on the playground.[7]

Another writer, Ji-Yeon Mary Yuhill, expressed an Asian-American child's view:

> I grew up hearing, seeing and almost believing that America was white. . . . The white people were everywhere in my 1970s Chicago childhood: founding fathers, presidents, explorers and industrialists galore. The only black people were slaves. The only Indians were scalpers. . . .
>
> I never heard one word about how Asian immigrants were among the first to turn California's desert into fields of plenty. Or about Chinese immigrant Ah Bing, who

bred the cherry now on sale in groceries across the nation. Or . . . that Asian immigrants were the only immigrants denied U.S. citizenship, even though they served hon-
orably in World War I. All the immigrants in my textbook were white. . . .

So when other children called me a slant-eyed Chink and told me to go back where I
came from, I was ready to believe that I wasn't really an American because I wasn't
white.[8]

Writing in 1990 in *The American Scholar,* Diane Ravitch, Chancellor of the
University of Texas, summed up the background of the controversy: that for years,
schools and colleges had attempted to neutralize issues related to race, religion, or
sexuality largely by ignoring them:

. . . textbooks minimized problems among groups and taught a sanitized version of history. Race, religion, and ethnicity were presented as minor elements in the American
saga; slavery was treated as an episode, immigration as a sidebar, and women were
largely absent. The textbooks concentrated on presidents, wars, national politics, and
issues of state. An occasional "great black" or "great woman" received mention, but the
main narrative paid little attention to minority groups and women.[9]

The struggle became more bitter, as proponents of the new multiculturalism
began to condemn as Eurocentric the entire system of education with its emphasis
on the writings of great white, male classicists like Plato, Aristotle, Milton, and
Shakespeare, and to urge that major portions of it be replaced by materials drawn
from other cultures, races, and religious traditions.

Resistance to Multicultural Pressures

A number of writers and educational authorities came out in defense of classical education and against the new trend toward "political correctness"—the compulsive
avoidance of any statement or even phrase that might offend the new multicultural
orthodoxy. Apart from their resistance to what they viewed as the unconscionable
rewriting of history, such traditionalists sought to defend what they considered to be
the great treasures of world literature and art. They feared that the emphasis on the
contributions of each separate racial or ethnic group in American society would
mean that the nation would be fragmented and would lose its core of common
values.

On the other hand, those who argued for overthrowing the traditional content of
American education saw the need to resist the "patriarchy" of the white, male
Eurocentric elite that had dominated women and minorities in the past. By the early
1990s, it appeared that a consensus was developing; while the great literature and art
that had characterized Western cultural education would *not* be abandoned, there
would be a greater effort to present fully and fairly the contributions of all the cultural groups that made up the American mosaic. Beyond this, it would be imperative
to give a more honest picture of the nation's history, including the aggressions
and cruelties that had been part of American "manifest destiny" and economic
expansionism.

America's growing racial and ethnic diversity is illustrated in the smiling faces of these Oroville, California, schoolchildren, and a group of participants in the U.S. Space Camp's Aviation Challenge program in Huntsville, Alabama. Left, children of U.S. military personnel enjoy a summer camp program in Japan. Below, the Long Beach, California, Department of Parks, Recreation and Marine sponsors a human relations workshop.

Population trends made this approach inevitable. In April 1990, a *Time* cover story, "Beyond the Melting Pot," made it clear that in the rapidly approaching twenty-first century, racial and ethnic groups in the United States would outnumber whites for the first time. It predicted that the "browning of America" would alter everything in society, from politics and education to industry, values, and culture. Demographers reported that within twenty years, Hispanics would be the nation's largest minority group, and that the substantial influx of Asians meant that there were more Muslims in the United States than Episcopalians.[10] Indeed, religion linked to ethnicity was altering the face of popular culture throughout America, with Hindu temples, Muslim mosques, Buddhist shrines, and other Eastern religious centers springing up around the nation.

■ LEISURE AND ETHNICITY

Why is the drive toward multiculturalism particularly relevant to the study of leisure in American life? One answer is that leisure can represent a positive force toward achieving full intergroup understanding and more constructive relationships among Americans of different racial and ethnic origins.

In the past, this view of the role of community recreation was presented uncritically by authors in the field of recreation and leisure. For example, educators like Harold Meyer and Charles Brightbill argued that recreation provided a powerful influence in the "assimilation" of immigrant groups and achieving "social well-being" among those of different races. Programs of Americanization and the constant process of "infiltration and blending" (a clear reference to the melting pot idea) were said to find in recreation a strong ally.[11]

Similarly, a respected researcher in the recreation and park field, George Butler, claimed in a widely used textbook that community recreation was an important tool in promoting democracy and overcoming the gulf between different races and social classes:

> The young man who excels in swimming or basketball is recognized, regardless of his creed or color, by followers of these sports, and the woman who can act or paint scenery is welcomed by the drama group, without reference to her social position. The banker and the man on relief are found singing in the community chorus. . . .[12]

But were Americans ever as color-blind or unconcerned about race or socioeconomic status as Butler's statement suggests? The reality is that race has historically been a powerful force in dictating one's life-style patterns and social roles. In earlier chapters, we reviewed the way in which African Americans were deprived of leisure and forced to work under harsh and cruel circumstances as slaves, and later were barred from many forms of recreational opportunity—by law, community custom, and the inadequate provision of facilities and programs in black neighborhoods.

We must now ask—does institutional racism still exist in recreation and leisure and, if so, in what form? Do members of ethnic and racial minorities differ from the larger white population in their leisure interests and behaviors? How have members of different minority groups contributed to the national culture in such leisure-related fields as sports, the arts, and popular entertainment? To what degree does leisure serve as a catalyst for improving intergroup understanding or for providing channels for social mobility or career development for African Americans and other minority groups?

■ LEISURE INVOLVEMENTS OF AFRICAN AMERICANS

Some critics may object to singling out any racial or ethnic subgroups for special study or concern. Opponents of affirmative action, for example, frequently argue that, while America was guilty of widespread racial discrimination in the past, this is no longer the case. Today, they say, the "playing field" is level for all. Certainly, considerable progress has been made in recent years. In the last decade or two we have seen the first black presidential candidate, first black astronaut, first black mayors of many major cities, and numerous other evidences of positive change in the nation's racial philosophy and practice.

However, in many respects, African Americans continue to be second-class citizens. Racial discrimination in housing is endemic, despite efforts to eliminate redlining and other real estate practices that bar blacks from traditionally white neighborhoods. A 1991 Federal Reserve Board report shows that racial and ethnic minorities, particularly blacks, are rejected for mortgages at a far higher rate than whites, even when they are in the same income categories. While it is true that many African Americans have moved up the economic ladder, roughly a third of blacks are still mired in poverty. Even among those who have reached management positions in American businesses, few have achieved the highest ranks of responsibility. According to the *Harvard Business Review,* a study of the nation's leading corporations showed that of 1,362 senior business executives in the mid-1980s, there were only four blacks, six Asians, three Hispanics, and twenty-nine women.[13]

In terms of health, while the longevity of African-American men and women has improved in recent years, on average they die about six years younger than whites. Far fewer blacks, Mexican Americans and Puerto Ricans than whites have private health insurance, and elderly African Americans have greater difficulty in being admitted to nursing homes—despite the fact that they have the same Medicaid reimbursement eligibility as whites.[14]

Another major area of institutionalized racism is found in the American criminal justice system. The National Commission on Crime and Justice reported in June 1991 that persons of color and the poor are subject to disadvantages at every stage of the justice system. A study of the National Prison Project of the American Civil Liberties Union reported that minority-group individuals typically lacked adequate legal assistance and were penalized by much harsher sentences than whites, for similar infractions.[15] Linked to such disparities were widespread practices of police brutality toward persons of color—involving picking up many blacks on mere suspicion, the regular use of racial slurs, violent beatings, and similar abuses.

Thus, decades after the report of the National Advisory Commission on Civil Disorder in February 1968, which concluded that "Our nation is moving toward two societies, one black, one white—separate and unequal," there is continuing evidence that the problem continues unabated.[16]

■ CONTINUING BARRIERS TO LEISURE OPPORTUNITY

Clearly, much of the racist segregation of the past in community recreation has been eliminated through legislation and court decisions. Through the 1970s and 1980s, however, resistance to the integration of varied types of recreation facilities continued.

In 1972, for example, the Supreme Court upheld the right of private clubs, such as the Loyal Order of Moose, to exclude blacks from membership, despite lawsuits that sought to deny such clubs from having state-issued liquor licenses. On the other hand, in 1973 the Supreme Court ruled that privately owned community pools that customarily served those living close by might not exclude black neighborhood families. In another decision, the court ruled that an Arkansas amusement park had illegally excluded blacks from entering, because it was a "public accommodation" involved in interstate commerce and therefore forbidden by the Civil Rights Act of 1964 to discriminate on racial grounds.

⯈ TO THE POINT

Most voluntary, nonprofit organizations, which tended to be racially segregated before World War II, have now accepted the principle of desegregation and some have dedicated themselves vigorously to the elimination of racism in all their programs and facilities. In contrast, there continue to be numerous examples of discriminatory policies in commercially operated recreation businesses. For example, in the 1970s and 1980s, it was revealed that in suburban Washington, D.C., home of the nation's capital, the exclusive Chevy Chase Country Club permitted black-skinned members of the foreign diplomatic corps to join, but refused to allow black Americans—even the city's mayor—to be admitted. Numerous other prestigious clubs have continued to practice racial exclusion—a policy highlighted in the press in 1990, when the Shoal Creek Country Club in Birmingham, Alabama, scheduled to host the Professional Golf Association championship, was revealed as having a whites-only membership. As a result, six major sponsors withdrew their advertisements from the scheduled telecasts of the tournament, and Shoal Creek was forced to admit honorary black members.

There have been other examples of private businesses such as dance studios or swim clubs continuing to exclude blacks until compelled to do so by court decisions. A leading example came in the late 1980s, when a U.S. District Court found that U.S. Health, Inc., in Towson, Maryland, operator of a successful chain of fitness spas, had engaged in widespread practices of discriminating against black applicants who sought to join its clubs. Following court action, U.S. Health accepted a consent order documenting that it had committed the following types of violations of civil rights law: (1) employees at the Holiday clubs had been instructed to discourage black persons from joining and to make it difficult for them to schedule appointments; (2) black persons were often told about the most expensive membership options and were not informed of favorable financing methods; (3) salespersons were reprimanded for selling memberships to black persons and often were denied commissions for such sales; and (4) black members who did join were treated rudely to discourage them from attending the clubs, or recommending them to other black persons.[17]

As a second example of how long-standing traditions of racial exclusion continued to be challenged within the sphere of leisure activity, the discriminatory practices of the famous New Orleans Mardi Gras celebration came under concerted attack in the late 1980s. Historically, Mardi Gras had been carried on by "krewes" (clubs formed by the city's white male aristocracy) that paraded in the streets every year before Lent, wearing the elaborate costumes of kings, lords, and jesters. Membership in the krewes was controlled by unwritten laws—there might be no blacks, no Jews, no women, no Italians. As a reaction to these policies of exclusion, middle- and upper-class African Americans in New Orleans formed the Zulu krewe in 1909:

> Unable to join the white krewes, or even march in the same path during Mardi Gras, the blacks in Zulu donned grass skirts and wooly wigs, and paraded with rubber spears and coconuts in hand, to mock white prejudices. Even as they paraded with their most famous member, famous trumpeter Louis Armstrong, the Zulus were not allowed to parade the same route as whites until the late 1960s. [In time they came to hold] a prime slot on Mardi Gras Day as one of the most famous krewes.[18]

Through the years, the white krewes had constituted an inner circle of prestige and power, where many of New Orleans' most influential business leaders met and exchanged contacts, constituting a *de facto* chamber of commerce. However, by the late 1980s the city had become 61 percent black, with an African-American-dominated City Council and a black mayor. Unwilling to accept the existence of a publicly assisted institution like Mardi Gras in which all but white Christian males were barred from the elite clubs, the City Council passed an ordinance that banned krewes from discrimination on the basis of race, sex, religion, disability, or sexual orientation.

■ COMPARATIVE STUDIES OF LEISURE INVOLVEMENT

A second area of scholarly concern focuses on the degree to which members of racial minorities differ from whites in terms of leisure values and behaviors. For example, a study of consumer expenditures conducted by the Wharton School of Finance in the 1950s showed significant differences in black and white spending on such items as admissions, radio and television purchases, and other leisure pursuits. The 1962 Outdoor Recreation Resources Review Commission found that African Americans engaged in outdoor recreation activities like camping or hunting far less often than whites.[19]

A study by Short and Strodtbeck in 1965 examined the leisure behavior of several hundred black and white youthful gang members in Chicago. This report showed distinctly different patterns of involvement based on race. Black gang members tended to be more frequently involved in antisocial activities related to physical violence and heterosexual activity. On the other hand, white gang members were more frequently involved in homosexual activity, the use of hard narcotics and alcohol, gambling, auto theft, and other kinds of delinquent acts.[20] A 1967 study by Kraus examined participation in public recreation and park programs in the tri-state metropolitan area of New York, New Jersey, and Connecticut.[21] It found marked differences between black and white urban and suburban residents in such activities as sports, cultural programs, and activities for specific age groups.

One of the first studies to examine the issue of social class with respect to race was reported by E. Franklin Frazier, whose book, *Black Bourgeoisie,* examined the lives of middle-class African Americans.[22] Frazier concluded that many middle-class blacks were "excessively" preoccupied with sports, gambling, drinking, and the numbers game. He speculated that the exclusion of middle-class African Americans from meaningful participation in many areas of community life meant that they used such pursuits as a means of escape from frustrations that stemmed from second-class citizenship.

A number of other comparative studies were carried out in the decades that followed. In 1985, Stamps and Stamps reviewed seventeen different studies that examined African Americans' leisure in terms of urban-suburban, regional, or social-class factors or compared them to white populations.[23] In summarizing their findings, they reported: (1) southern blacks usually participating in inexpensive, close-to-home forms of leisure; (2) the leisure patterns of blacks persisting over time, even after migration from rural to urban areas; (3) a heavy involvement in church activities for all African Americans, regardless of class; and (4) middle-class blacks typically participating in such activities as bridge, travel, and both participation and spectator involvement in sports, comparable to whites. In other studies, Stamps and Stamps found a higher participation rate by blacks than whites in group-oriented pursuits, and a higher rate for whites in outdoor activities such as winter sports, camping, waterskiing, and golf.

Michael Woodard focused on the influence of regionality on the leisure behavior of American blacks, summarizing earlier reports showing that social life in the South relied heavily on the home, church, and fraternal halls, while in the North, there was more emphasis on leisure activities in the streets, in schools, and commercial settings like pool or dance halls.[24] Woodard also reported that the most popular leisure activities among urban black Americans were domestic pursuits, such as socializing with friends or family, radio and television, having barbecues, and other low-cost and communal activities.

In 1992, Dwyer and Gobster reported on a number of other studies by Washburn, Klobus-Edwards, Dwyer and Hutchison, and others, which continued to show generally lower participation among African Americans in dispersed outdoor recreational activities such as camping and hiking, and higher participation in active, social, and urban-oriented activities like ball playing and picnicking.[25] Similarly, in 1992, Henderson and Bedini summarized research studies by Warnick on participation trends among African-American adults, and Brown and Tedrick dealing with the outdoor recreation involvement of elderly black Americans.[26] The question arises—are differences among ethnic and racial groups due to innate or inherited cultural traits, or to other environmental factors? Hutchison suggests two possible theoretical explanations for them: *ethnicity* and *marginality*. He writes:

> The ethnicity perspective argues that an identifiable set of black activities results from a distinctive black subculture—a set of cultural patterns which are somehow different from that of the majority of white Americans. This is a cultural explanation for intergroup differences, and involves a complex interplay of social values, social organization, and normative elements passed from one generation to the next through the socialization processes of the family, local schools, and community.[27]

Langston Hughes, the black poet and folklore authority, essentially argued against the ethnicity perspective in concluding that African Americans have been so modified by their exposure to American life and culture that they have been radically transformed and have lost their original "negritude." Other sociologists agree that so-called black cultural traits are chiefly characteristic of lower-socioeconomic-class urban or rural blacks, and tend to disappear among middle- or upper-class African Americans.

In contrast, the marginality perspective suggests that the different values and leisure behavior of American blacks stem from their generally disadvantaged position in American society—more limited income, inadequate provision of recreational opportunity, and other social factors. Illustrating the marginality perspective, West found that black residents tended to use Detroit city parks more than whites, and that whites from Detroit used parks in the wider tricounty regional area more than blacks.[28] Poorer access to transportation as well as feelings of being unwelcome or unsafe in the regional parks because of interracial prejudice were apparent reasons for African-American residents failing to make use of the broader park system.

In some cases, traditional cultural behaviors or practices may be deliberately revived or even created to promote a distinctive culture. For example, in the 1960s and 1970s, many communities established courses, workshops, exhibitions, and events dealing with African art, music, history, religion, and other aspects of black culture. An example of such efforts is the festival of *Kwanzaa,* a seven-day-long non-religious celebration of black culture which has been accepted as a form of holiday celebration by more than five million African Americans. Originated in Los Angeles in 1966, *Kwanzaa* (a Swahili term meaning "first fruits of the harvest") stresses the importance of the black community and family, and is based on the *Nguzo Saba,* a framework of seven principles designed for black people to live by through the year. Examples of these principles are: *umoja* (collective work and responsibility), *kujichagulia* (self-determination), and *imani* (faith). Patterned after various African agricultural festivals, Kwanzaa is intended to help black people rescue and reconstruct their own history and culture.

■ RACE AND SPORTS

We turn now to an examination of American blacks in several specific areas of leisure participation, beginning with sports. Their history in different forms of athletic competition was a unique and tragic one. As Arthur Ashe, Jr., the tennis champion, recounted, many African Americans were highly successful in sports in the early and middle decades of the nineteenth century, but were gradually frozen out of participation by increasing racial discrimination at the end of the century. Ashe wrote:

> The saddest case is that of the black jockeys. When the first Kentucky Derby was run in 1875, 15 thoroughbreds were entered and 14 of their riders were black. Black domination of horse racing then was analogous to the domination of the National Basketball Association today. Subsequently the Jockey Club was formed in the early 1890s to regulate and license all jockeys. Then one by one the blacks were denied their license renewals. By 1911 they had all but disappeared.[29]

For over a hundred years, whites went to extraordinary lengths to discredit and discourage black participation in sports. When the National Association of Base Ball Players was formed in 1858, there were many black ball players in organized baseball. In 1867, the same year the Ku Klux Klan was established, the members of the National Association—all northerners at this point—met in Philadelphia and decreed that blacks should be totally banned from the sport. Although a few African Americans managed to stay in the professional game by representing themselves as Cubans, Rader writes:

> According to the *Sporting News* in 1889, "race prejudice exists in professional baseball ranks to a marked degree, and the unfortunate son of Africa who makes his living as a member of a team of white professionals has a rocky road to travel." Indeed, he did. Black players had to withstand withering ridicule from fellow players, their managers, and the white spectators.[30]

In the 1880s, blacks organized several professional baseball teams, a number of which regularly barnstormed the country year after year, often playing against white teams in exhibition games. In addition, separate Negro leagues were established. Despite the fact that many black players were recognized by sports fans as outstanding performers, segregation enforced by both association edicts and state Jim Crow laws prevented black athletes from playing on white professional baseball teams. In football, an occasional black athlete was permitted to play on college teams during the early 1900s. One of the great stars of this period was Paul Robeson, a black youth who had grown up in Somerville, New Jersey, where he was the top-ranked student in his high school, a soloist in the glee club, a member of the debate and drama clubs, and an outstanding athlete on several teams. After attaining the highest score on a statewide scholarship examination, Robeson entered Rutgers where, David Wiggins writes, on the first day of football practice

> Robeson's teammates made it clear they did not want a black man on the club by punishing him so severely his nose was broken, shoulder dislocated, and body lacerated with cuts and bruises. He spent the next ten days in bed before returning to practice.[31]

At other points in his football career at Rutgers, Robeson suffered from racial prejudice—by being barred, for example, from games against southern colleges. However, he went on to win twelve varsity letters in four different sports, was chosen twice as a football All-American, had a distinguished academic career capped by being elected to Phi Beta Kappa, and ultimately became a world-famous singer, actor, and social activist.

▰▰▶ TO THE POINT

A notable highlight of the progress of African Americans toward equal opportunity in sports came with the striking victories of the great track star, Jesse
Owens, at the 1936 Olympics in Berlin—an event that infuriated Adolf Hitler
and confounded his theories of Aryan racial superiority. The reign of Joe Louis
as a superb heavyweight champion led to fuller acceptance of blacks in boxing.
After Branch Rickey brought Jackie Robinson, who had starred in basketball,
baseball, football, and track at the University of California at Los Angeles, to
the Brooklyn Dodgers, racial barriers began to break down in both college and
professional sports.

A milestone was reached at the NCAA national basketball championship's
final game in March 1966, when little known TWC (Texas Western College)
played the mighty University of Kentucky team, coached by the famous
Adolph Rupp. Until that year, not a single African-American athlete had
played varsity basketball in the Southeast Conference, and Rupp had stead-
fastly resisted pressures to recruit them. Texas Western started five black players and used two substitutes, both black—and beat Kentucky handily.
Afterward, Adolph Rupp reportedly said, "TWC? TWC? What's that stand
for—Two White Coaches?" But before long, all conferences were recruiting
black players and they began to dominate both college and professional basketball.[32] In the period from the 1960s through the 1990s, the greatest American
sports idols included such names as Muhammed Ali, Henry Aaron, Jim Brown,
Wilt Chamberlain, Michael Jordan, Willie Mays, Bill Russell, and hundreds of
other outstanding black stars.

In such sports as tennis and golf, which tended to be nurtured in private clubs
and were regarded as middle- or upper-class pastimes, there began to be outstanding
professionals like Althea Gibson and Arthur Ashe in tennis, and Charlie Sifford and
Lee Elder in golf, but even here, black tournament players frequently met humilia-
tion or discrimination in terms of housing arrangements, as well as the lack of sponsors or lucrative advertising contracts.

Negative Aspects of Sports Success

Despite their dramatic success in college and professional athletics, a convincing
argument can be made that many young African Americans are severely exploited
through sports, and that covert discriminatory practices continue to operate
throughout the sports establishment.

David Wiggins points out that the first black athletes on white college campuses
were an elite group of individuals who came for the most part from middle- or
upper-class families that placed a heavy emphasis on education as preparation for
professional success. In the 1960s and 1970s, however, many poorly prepared young
black athletes were admitted to colleges throughout the country. Often they came
from inferior ghetto schools and had limited academic skills or motivation. Entering

colleges that had formerly admitted few African Americans, they were often academically neglected, socially isolated, and permitted to play out their eligibility and leave school without having made real progress toward a degree.

In addition to such practices, a number of studies have also shown that positions of leadership and authority in sports have been held chiefly by white males, as evidenced by the decades-long unwillingness to hire black quarterbacks in professional football. For example, a 1987 study of major league baseball by the Center for the Study of Sport in Society at Northeastern University identified the following percentages of black American-born, non-Hispanic players at each position in major league baseball: pitcher, 5; catcher, 0; first base, 29; second base, 25; shortstop, 20; third base, 11; outfield, 48.[33]

Much attention has been drawn recently to the reluctance of college and professional sports teams owners or administrators to hire African Americans in head coaching roles. In the late 1980s, the percentage of black head coaches at predominantly white institutions was as follows: baseball, 0; football, 1.5; women's basketball, 3.4; men's basketball, 10.9. Between 1989 and 1992, nineteen head coaching jobs opened up in the National Football League. All but one went to white men, despite the fact that over 60 percent of the players in the league were African Americans. In the National Basketball Association, in 1992, 80 percent of the players were black—but there were only two African-American coaches.[34] Finally, few black individuals have been hired in front-office and administrative positions in team sports. This issue was dramatized in 1987, with the widely broadcasted views of Al Campanis, a former baseball player and Los Angeles Dodgers executive, about black players lacking management "necessities."

In the spring of 1993, as professional athletes representing the baseball, football, and basketball players' unions formed a coalition with the heads of the NAACP, the national Urban League, and the Southern Christian Leadership Conference, national attention focused more sharply on the need to eliminate racist practices in professional sports. The owner of the Cincinnati Reds, Marge Schott, was suspended for one year because of her reported racist comments. In response to growing pressure, six African-American and Hispanic managers were now employed in major-league baseball, and increased numbers of minority-group managers, front-office personnel, and television commentators were being hired in the other sports leagues.

■ OTHER AREAS OF LEISURE INVOLVEMENT

While sports are the most obvious area in which African Americans have made a strong impact on American life, they have also been preeminent in the fields of music, dance, and stage entertainment.

African-American Musical Influences

Historically, when black slaves were brought to America, they brought with them distinctive African cultural practices that they retained and blended with American customs to create unique kinds of folk expression. In music, both spirituals and secular songs were part of an oral tradition that expressed the religious beliefs of slaves during the pre–Civil War period. They evolved a type of music called the blues, based on both traditions, that dealt with the personal and social concerns of African Americans. Later, a new, lighter and more improvisatory form of black music emerged, influenced by nineteenth-century dance, military band, and ragtime music. Called jazz, it flourished in New Orleans, later moving to the northern cities, where it was played by white musicians and was called Dixieland music.

Among black audiences, gospel music, an emotional form of religious song, and so-called rhythm-and-blues music continued to appeal. In time, white musicians and singers like Elvis Presley and Bill Haley were strongly influenced by rhythm-and-blues, and created a musical style known as rock-and-roll that gained national popularity among both blacks and whites. Other black artists like James Brown and Aretha Franklin stayed closer to their gospel roots, with "soul" music that was derived from African-American musical traditions. In addition to such artists, a number of black musicians were able to overcome white prejudice and become recognized in the realm of classical music. Marian Anderson, a great soprano who faced harsh early discrimination, had a brilliant career as a concert soloist and was the first African American to sing in a major role at the Metropolitan Opera in New York. Leontyne Price and Paul Robeson were among other great black singers, and pianist André Watts was a leading African-American concert performer. Conductor Dean Dixon was the youngest artist to direct a major symphony orchestra, but spent most of his professional life in Europe, because of prejudice against blacks in America.

African Americans in Dance

From the earliest colonial days, African-born slaves danced to entertain their masters, and often would play the fiddle or banjo as well. A number of dances created by black slaves were later transformed into popular social dances of the late nineteenth and early twentieth centuries, such as the Cakewalk, Turkey Trot, Black Bottom, and Ballin' the Jack. African-American dance forms also became the basis for many minstrel show routines, although, ironically, blacks were usually barred from performing in such shows. Instead, white performers in these popular stage presentations usually were made up in exaggerated blackface, and performed in comic routines that ridiculed blacks as lazy, superstitious, and cowardly.

Black dancers were able to perform in segregated theaters or on African-American vaudeville circuits during the early twentieth century and in time a number of black dancers, singers, and musicians were accepted more widely in all-black musical reviews and Broadway shows.

In addition to their role in creating and performing dances as part of the entertainment world, other African Americans devoted themselves to exploring their cultural roots. Katherine Dunham was one of the first to do this; an anthropologist, folklorist, author, and leading choreographer, she produced a number of popular touring reviews that featured colorful African, Caribbean, and Latin American dance forms. Another leading performer was dancer-choreographer Pearl Primus, who combined authentic dances drawn from African sources with dances that depicted the harsh reality of black life in America, and used thematic material taken from poems and other writings by black authors.

In the post–World War II period, many black choreographers and dancers emerged in the modern dance movement, a twentieth-century form of concert dance. Despite these successes, few blacks have entered the more exclusive field of traditional ballet, an aristocratic art form that has been identified with upper-class audiences and board members in the United States. A key exception was Arthur Mitchell, who became a leading black dancer with the New York City Ballet and went on to found the Dance Theater of Harlem, with the assistance of the Ford Foundation and other major grants. This company became a leading American artistic institution; it has toured widely and been acclaimed one of the nation's most impressive international arts ambassadors.[35]

Blacks in Literature and Fine Arts

In the modern era, a number of African Americans have achieved literary distinction, including Richard Wright, author of *Black Boy;* James Baldwin, author of *Giovanni's Room* and *The Fire Next Time;* and Ralph Ellison, author of *The Invisible Man.* Alex Haley's *Roots,* which led to a tremendously popular television miniseries, along with works by black militants Eldridge Cleaver and Malcolm X, helped to focus the eyes of white America on issues surrounding race in modern society. More recently, a number of African-American women have become popular authors, including Alice Walker, Toni Morrison, and Paula Marshall. Playwrights like Lorraine Hansberry, Imamu Amiri Baraka (LeRoi Jones), Charles Fuller, and August Wilson have also authored works about the black experience in America. Maya Angelou, a distinguished poet and playwright, inspired the nation with her poetry at the 1993 presidential inaugural ceremonies.

Through the nineteenth and early twentieth centuries, there were relatively few African-American artists; some of the more successful ones traveled to Europe to study and pursue careers. Beginning in the 1930s, a number of black painters, including Jacob Lawrence and Romare Bearden, began to capture critical acclaim. During the Depression, numerous other black artists were employed in the Federal Art Project; they painted murals and taught art in community centers around the country. One such artist, Frank Stephens, typified the race consciousness that was emerging. Stephens later designed a drawing that became a symbol of the civil rights movement in America—a black fist encircled by an American flag linked to a chain, based on a James Baldwin quotation: "To be black and conscious in America is to be in a constant state of rage."

Blacks and the Popular Media: Radio, Films, Television

A critical aspect of leisure as it affects African Americans involves the popular electronic media of entertainment—radio, films, and television, both in terms of how they have depicted blacks and contributed to widespread stereotypes of minorities, and with respect to the careers that they have offered over time to talented blacks as actors, directors, and producers.

In early radio and film programming, African Americans were presented in extremely limited and demeaning roles that reflected their subordinate role in American society at large. While there were a number of comedy shows that involved blacks, the most popular one was "Amos and Andy," a daily program written and acted by two white men, which ridiculed blacks as impractical, lazy, and pompous. The first silent films tended to portray blacks in negative ways, a prime example being "Birth of a Nation," which showed them as ignorant and brutal creatures after the Civil War and fanned antiblack hostility across the nation. Too often, African Americans were depicted as shuffling, stupid, and cowardly menials. In the 1940s and 1950s, films began to deal more realistically with blacks and the issue of race relations in American life. Hansberry's "A Raisin in the Sun" depicted African-American family life, and Sidney Poitier, Lena Horne, and Harry Belafonte appeared in films dealing with black-white relationships in a serious and positive way.

The period of the 1960s and 1970s took a different turn. Under the impact of the civil rights movement and the urban race riots, black males began to be perceived as threatening and dangerous, and a series of films portrayed them as gangsters and "macho" men—in so-called blaxploitation films. Others showed them in more sympathetic roles in films about prizefighters, adventure, and war exploits. These themes continued in the treatment of blacks in films of the 1980s and 1990s with a new factor entering in—the emergence of a new group of young African-American directors. Until this time, there had been few black producers and directors, notably the independent filmmaker Oscar Michaux, who made forty feature-length films for all-black audiences and with all-black casts between 1918 and 1948. However, Michaux never could break into the white film world, and died relatively unknown and in poverty.

In the 1980s the situation changed when a young black filmmaker, Spike Lee, produced a number of entertaining films that reached a broader audience and began to open the door for other African-American directors like John Singleton and Mario Van Peebles, who in turn created films that showed the harsher and more realistic side of urban ghetto life, like "New Jack City," "Boyz N the Hood," and "Colors." Lee's major 1992 work on Malcolm X forced many Americans to confront troubling issues of racism in the nation's past and present.

Television followed much the same course as motion pictures, with the early roles given to blacks perpetuating racial myths and stereotypes, or presenting an unrealistic picture of their lives. Gradually, a conscious effort was made to cast African Americans in more positive and diversified roles. Popular shows in the 1960s and 1970s showed blacks and whites together as buddies in adventure series, interracial friendships, or adoptive families—all at a time marked by tremendous racial tension in the society at large.

The long-running, highly rated Bill Cosby sit-com depicting the Huxtable family was clearly intended to counter the prevalent negative images of African Americans by showing stable, loving, and affluent black parents and their endearing brood. However, some critics commented that the show totally disregarded the social problems that affected the rest of black America. A research study by two University of Massachusetts professors found that the Huxtables had apparently led many white

Americans to believe that African Americans had made it—and that racial injustice no longer needed to be addressed in the United States.[36]

Relatively few television programs, apart from occasional documentaries and such series as "All in the Family" and "I'll Fly Away" dealt honestly with problems of racial discrimination and hostility. Although talk-show hosts like Oprah Winfrey have proved popular with white and black audiences alike, the overall treatment of African Americans on television has tended to be superficial and misleading. John O'Connor comments that many black young people are presented as dim-witted and ridiculous, and that the realities of life for the struggling black poor are simply ignored on television:

> For too many viewers, blacks are still simply the people who get busted the most on all those police "reality" shows. The diversity of the black community, the social and political ferment within that community, is reflected only occasionally. Both white and black viewers end up short-changed.[37]

A final point about the relationship between American blacks and television is that they have a substantially higher rate of TV-watching than other Americans. In addition, a 1992 report by a leading advertising agency showed that the top ten television shows among black viewers differed sharply from the general population's favorites. With few exceptions, African Americans preferred shows with mostly black casts, while general audiences did not.

Blacks as Leisure Consumers

The disparity between black and white Americans in terms of television tastes suggests another question about minority populations in American society—how different are they as leisure consumers? Certainly, blacks are less interested than whites in the more "highbrow" forms of culture like opera, serious theater, and ballet. However, this may be a reflection of generally lower socioeconomic class factors; few blue-collar families are likely to be patrons of the arts in American society.

Frances Callaway Parks cites detailed statistics drawn from the Bureau of Labor Statistics Consumer Expenditure Survey that show that black Americans spend proportionately less than white Americans on entertainment and recreation—although more on in-home entertainment, such as the purchase of television, radio, and sound equipment. She continues:

> Recreational activities which occur in parks reflect the greatest racial differences. For example, black Americans spend only 13 percent as much as white Americans on camping equipment, 17.5 percent as much on hunting and fishing equipment, and 6.2 percent as much on water sports equipment.[38]

⫸ TO THE POINT

A factor influencing African-American leisure behaviors negatively is the intensive target marketing of consumer products like alcohol and tobacco at minority-group youth. As one drives along any major avenue into inner-city neigh-borhoods today, one sees an unrelenting lineup of billboards advertising beer, cigarettes, and varied forms of hard liquor. Featuring popular entertainers, sports stars, or models in alluring poses, many of the ads are deliberately manipulative. For example, malt liquor makers have used rap artists like the popular Ice Cube with pitches aimed at under-21 audiences, with sexually slanted messages. A given malt liquor "will put you in the mood and make you wanna go oooh!" or "get your girl in the mood quicker."

In the late 1980s, the Center for Science in the Public Interest issued a report sharply critical of the liquor industry for targeting blacks, whose death rates for illnesses relating to smoking and alcoholism are significantly higher than those of whites. In cities like Chicago and Philadelphia, neighborhood task forces and clergymen have joined forces to protest targeting of black and Hispanic-American youth in low-income neighborhoods. Such practices repre-sent an extension of a long-standing tradition—that poor neighborhoods, par-ticularly those where minority-group populations live, were often places where city fathers permitted vice to exist. In such settings, houses of prostitution, speakeasies, and illegal gambling activities could all flourish, protected by bribes to the police. It was assumed that, if such enterprises could be confined geographically, other parts of the city would be protected. What it usually meant was that the Harlems of the nation were places where whites could go for illicit forms of pleasure. Today, this is still a common practice with respect to the drug trade. In some cities, white suburbanites drive regularly into black and Hispanic neighborhoods to satisfy their need for crack cocaine or heroin.

Other Changes in Popular Consumer Products

In a number of other less-destructive ways, racial awareness has made an impact on the design of many artifacts of popular culture. For example, in the past, children's dolls used to reflect racial stereotyping; dolls of black characters were invariably based on slave-day stereotypes, such as Aunt Jemima or Black Sambo types. In the late 1960s the Mattel toy company brought out its first African-American doll, Christie. However, she looked just like a dark-skinned Barbie, with Caucasian facial features. Today, dolls are being produced to more accurately reflect authentic black or Asian images. In the early 1990s, Mattel brought out *Shani* (meaning "mar-velous" in Swahili), a new fashion doll with black features, including a broader nose and fuller lips.

Similarly, instead of simply putting out colors like black, brown, or white, which make coloring drawings of people rather limited, the Columbia, Maryland, company that produces Crayola crayons, used in schools and recreation programs throughout the country, now has brought out a set of "multicultural" crayons, with eight that reflect the skin tones of the world—mahogany and peach, tan and sepia, burnt sienna and apricot, black and white.

As a final example of the changes in American popular culture, there are now a number of comic strips in the daily papers that are drawn by African-American artists and feature black characters. In the past, blacks were usually seen only as minor characters in such settings, if at all. Now, they have become part of the everyday reading habits of newspaper readers—presented in a light that is relaxed, humorous, and noncontroversial. Thus, varied forms of consumer products, along with changes in sports, arts, and entertainment all illustrate the degree to which African Americans have more fully entered the mainstream of American popular culture.

■ LEISURE AND HISPANIC AMERICANS

Although African Americans represent the most visible and numerous racial minority in the United States, there are obviously other important minority populations that have unique leisure values and interests. One of these groups is the Hispanic-American population—often referred to as Latinos. There are about twenty-three million Americans with Spanish surnames or Spanish-speaking backgrounds in the United States today, and it is estimated that the number will grow to over fifty million by the year 2020.

Although they come from many different ethnic and racial strains, and usually prefer to be identified in terms of their specific national origins (as Cubans, Mexicans, Colombians, Puerto Ricans, or Dominicans), most Latinos tend to be proud of their Spanish ancestry. For example, the October 12 holiday, Columbus Day, is known throughout the Spanish-speaking world as *Día de la Hispanidad* (Hispanic Day) or *Día de la Raza* (Day of the Race). Although the majority of Hispanics in America speak English as their main language and consider themselves loyal citizens of the United States, Nielsen surveys indicate that three out of four American Hispanics between ages eighteen and forty-nine watch Spanish-language television. Economically, Hispanics have made considerable strides in the United States, although many, particularly Puerto Ricans, are still below the poverty line, labor as migrant workers, and are poorly educated. Often images of them are stereotyped in the popular media of television and movies. Rene Abelardo Gonzalez writes:

> Speedy Gonzalez and the Frito Bandito did not die, they just underwent a transformation. . . . Witness the latest commercial for a tortilla chip, with the principal actor unshaven, dirty, cartridge belts crossing his chest, big hat, "peasants" in the background, etc. . . . The media have yet to explore the richness of the Mexican and Mexican-American contributions to this country.[39]

Similarly, such stereotypes as Cuban-American drug lords are often perpetuated in popular culture. To understand the leisure roles of Hispanic Americans, it is helpful to examine separate ethnic blocs, which vary greatly from each other. James Abreu, for example, describes the lives of Mexican Americans in southwestern rural villages and small towns as heavily influenced by traditional customs and by affiliation with the Catholic church.[40] Their culture tends to be a unique blending of Indian, Spanish, Mexican, and Anglo elements. Religious holidays and church fiestas, including Nativity Plays (simple folk dramas that were used by early Spanish missionaries to instruct newly converted Indians), are frequently held. Rodeos and horse-racing events are popular forms of entertainment. Family activities, including traditional foods and music, are common. Many youths enjoy sports like boxing and basketball, while middle- and upper-class Latinos are gradually adapting to the dominant Anglo pursuits, such as tennis and golf.

In contrast, leisure activities of the young in the inner-city areas of such cities as Los Angeles, San Antonio, and El Paso tend to be less constructive. In crowded *barrios* (the term *mi barrio* refers equally to "my gang" and "my neighborhood"), poverty and unemployment are common. Mexican-American youth are slow to assimilate and tend to join fighting and drug-using gangs at an early age, affiliating with *klikas* or age-cohort groups. Joan Moore points out that efforts made to transform these groups into social and sports groups emphasizing baseball, boxing, or other club activities have proved largely unsuccessful.[41] Often sports groups evolve into criminal gangs, promoting gambling on handball games, running bootleg whiskey, smuggling marijuana, and pimping. Some gangs engage regularly in cruising enemy territories, fighting with knives, tire irons, chains, and baseball bats.

A number of other studies have examined the lives of Mexican Americans in other regions and cities of the United States. Some yielded research findings showing that Mexican Americans typically valued vacations and free time more than whites or African Americans, and that their leisure usually involved extended-family and large group pursuits. Beyond this, Hispanic activities made heavy use of neighborhood leisure facilities and programs, and followed cultural traditions by having sharply segregated gender- and age-groupings. Among all Hispanic-American populations, the most popular sports activities tend to be baseball and boxing, with less interest in football and basketball, which place a premium on the player's size. These interests reflect a carryover from Caribbean and Latin American origins, where baseball is a major interest and boxing has proven to be a career choice of many Hispanic youths. While Mexican-American groups differ from region to region, they generally acknowledge common background ties with respect to cultural history, music, folk heroes, sports, and food. These are illustrated in the *Cinco de Mayo* patriotic holiday that is celebrated in many Spanish-speaking communities.

In terms of outdoor recreation, a number of studies have examined the differences between participation patterns and interests of different groups of Hispanic Americans, such as those who were born in the United States, in Mexico, or in other Central American countries.[42] Other studies have compared the interests, group makeup, and campsite preferences of Hispanic Americans, Anglos, and Asian park visitors to the Angeles National Forest in Southern California.[43] In a later study of three different groups of Los Angeles residents' outdoor recreation interests, designed to develop effective visitor management strategies for urban user groups, Debbie Chavez reported the following:

- Anglos were more likely to have tried picnicking, hiking, and swimming, while African Americans were least likely to have tried these activities.
- Anglo and Hispanic Americans reported a stronger desire to try natural history hikes.
- Hispanic and African Americans reported a greater desire to try shooting ranges; African Americans reported a greater desire to try off-road riding.[44]

In a number of cities, such as Santa Monica, California, public recreation departments have developed extensive programs to serve Latino populations, including senior citizens and parent-education bilingual programs, sports, excursions, and other cultural pursuits. Esther Wolf writes that goals of the Santa Monica Latino outreach program include:

> promoting the Latino culture, eliminating negative stereotypes, utilizing the Spanish language, providing accessible recreation programs for three age groups (youth, adult, and seniors), promoting Latino participation in city activities and establishing a referral and support system within the Latino community.[45]

On a broader scale, Hispanic Americans have made a strong impact on American culture through their popular music and dance. Latin-American dance music—particularly drawn from Cuba and Puerto Rico—such as the rumba, merengue, mambo, pachada, and Lambada, has for long been featured at resorts and on cruise ships, in nightclubs and movies, and on television. In the past, there have been numerous famous Spanish painters, like Goya, Velázquez, and Picasso, and writers, like García Lorca, Miguel Cervantes, and Lope de Vega. Today there are a growing number of recognized Latin American and Central American authors, like Gabriel García Marquez and Pulitzer Prize–winning Oscar Hijuelos, who are contributing to contemporary literature. Although they have been generally neglected or treated in a distorted fashion in the popular media, Latinos are today being more thoughtfully portrayed in such films as *La Bamba, Stand and Deliver, American Me,* and *Born in East L.A.*

■ NATIVE AMERICANS AND LEISURE PURSUITS

A third major minority population in the United States consists of American Indians—frequently referred to as Native Americans or first Americans. Straussfeld writes that for centuries, white people have perpetuated two contrasting myths about Native Americans: "In one myth the Indian is idle, heathen, and deficient in every respect. In the other he is a 'noble Savage' whose natural way of life reveals the deficiencies of Anglo-American society.[46]

To illustrate, much of America's folklore and published literature contains references to the "noble red man"—as in the novels of James Fenimore Cooper, or the radio and television character of Tonto, the Lone Ranger's faithful companion. A famous author and naturalist, Ernest Thompson Seton, founded a popular organization called Woodcraft Indians and a Woodcraft League near Santa Fe, New Mexico, in the early 1900s. In contrast to the materialism and treachery he found in white civilization, Seton wrote glowingly of the Indian's character:

> Whereas the redman believed in many gods, he accepted "one Supreme Spirit." The redman revered his body and his parents, and he respected "the sacredness of property" such that theft was unknown. . . . For the redman, the "noblest of virtues was courage," and he never feared death. . . . [47]

Despite this widely shared view, American Indians have also been depicted in popular American culture as bloodthirsty, cruel, and treacherous. In pulp magazines, cheap novels, television, and movies, the ongoing war between settlers or U.S. soldiers and savage Apaches has been a staple of childhood play and adult entertainment. For many years the genocidal slogan, "the only good Indian is a dead Indian," justified efforts to exterminate the various Indian tribes in the United States, if not by deliberate starvation or economic policy, then by crushing their culture and forcing them to assimilate. Deloria and Cadwalader wrote:

> In language that today makes one cringe, the Indian Rights Association in 1885 said that "the Indian as a savage member of a tribal organization cannot survive, ought not to survive the aggressions of civilization." These friends of the Indian believed that only assimilation could save the Indian from extermination. Many of them also believed in the superiority of the white man's way of life.[48]

There were consistent efforts to wipe out Indian culture by banning religious dances and other ceremonials as primitive and degrading. Various tribes were doomed to live on barren reservations; widespread illiteracy, disease, and alcohol became commonplaces of Indian life. In recent years, with a growing sense of militant pride, many tribes have strongly reaffirmed their heritage, disclaimed early treaties that exploited or manipulated them, and revived their ancient languages and traditions. A number of Indian tribes have successfully sued local and other governmental units to recover their rights to large land areas in eastern states, salmon and steelhead fishing rights in the Pacific Northwest, and water rights elsewhere.

Native Americans in Sports and Outdoor Recreation

When the first English settlers came to North American shores, they found tribes of the Algonquin nation playing games similar to modern soccer and field hockey. The most distinctive of all the North American Indian games was *lacrosse,* a ball game played with sticks netted on one end with strips of deer or squirrel skin. Baker describes lacrosse, which became a popular school and college sport for many white Americans, as: "a 'little war,' a mock military struggle in which warrior athletes tested their courage, endurance, and skill. The game was surrounded with religious ceremonies designed to obtain the favor of the gods who supposedly bestowed health and fertility on victorious tribes."[49]

In modern times, a number of native Americans became outstanding athletes. Of these the most famous was Jim Thorpe, a brilliant track star and football player. When Thorpe won the decathlon in the 1912 Olympics at Stockholm, King Gustav called him the "world's greatest athlete." Thorpe is credited with the success of the early National Football League; he was the first big-name athlete to play professional football, and the first president of the American Professional Football Association, later to become the NFL. It is generally recognized that the new league started from ground zero with Thorpe and grew into a billion-dollar industry.

Another influence of American Indians on the nation's leisure has been in the realm of outdoor recreation—hunting and fishing, woodcraft, and forest survival skills. These became an important part of the organized play of many American boys and girls and also proved to be a source of revenue for Indian tribes that were able to use their lands and streams to serve hunting and fishing parties of white visitors. A number of tribes operate tourist shops and concessions in national parks and forests, where they sell and display their craft objects, perform ritual dances that are modified for the white visitors, and gain income in other ways.

⏩ TO THE POINT

With the recent revival of interest in native cultures and traditions, other Indian art forms have also gained popularity among whites. For example, the American Indian Dance Theater, founded in Colorado Springs, Colorado, in 1987, has toured in the United States and abroad with great success. The company presents versions of dances performed by eighteen of the nation's 430 recognized Indian tribes, chiefly from the Southwest and the northern plains—the Zuni Rainbow dance, the Buffalo dance, the Hoop dance, the Eagle dance, and Shawl dances for women. Unlike the primitive war dances depicted in western movies, the dance theater's works embody traditional art, music, history, and religion. They are authentic and respectful and have aroused great critical acclaim.

The dance company's success reflects the overall resurgence of interest in Indian culture in recent decades. Today, large pow-wows (three- or four-day gatherings) are held regularly around the country, particularly in the western states, with less stress on single tribes and more on the Indian people as a group. Such festivals or jamborees include both traditional dance, music, folk arts, and ceremonials, and other works that are developed today based on past themes and styles. Linked to this revival has been a growing trade in Indian arts and crafts—Kachina dolls, Navajo rugs, Zuni pottery, and other artifacts—with large-scale American Indian trade shows that are held in major exhibition halls around the country.

A unique development over the past two decades has been the sponsorship of high-stakes Bingo games for outsiders on many Indian reservations. Because of their right of self-government on reservations, Indians initiated these games early in the 1980s. In 1982, although some states attempted to control or limit Indian Bingo, the federal appellate courts ruled that if a state allowed any Bingo gambling—and forty-two states did—it had no authority to control it on Indian reservations. By 1985, the practice had spread to at least eighty-five reservations in eighteen states, ranging from Maine's Penobscots to North Carolina's Cherokees and California's Morongos. With huge jackpots that attract thousands of white visitors, these games provide a major source of income that can be used to build and staff health and day-care centers, provide college scholarships for reservation youth, and meet other needs. Based on their success with Bingo games, a number of tribes have gone ahead to develop large gambling casinos and in some cases diversified tourist attractions based on Native American themes.

Meanwhile, what of the leisure pursuits of Native Americans themselves? There has been limited research on recreation on Indian reservations, although a number of Vista programs sought to develop this, along with needed social services, during the

1960s and 1970s. In an article on the Arapaho tribe on the Wind River Reservation in Wyoming, Swick describes such social problems as widespread unemployment and a heavy reliance on drinking and gambling as leisure activities.[50] Approximately 30 to 40 percent of the children on the reservation are born with fetal alcohol syndrome. Despite these social pathologies, traditional ceremonies continue to be held by the Arapaho tribespeople, and basketball thrives in the local high school gymnasium and community center.

In terms of off-reservation leisure, Carol Pancner and Maureen McDonough of Michigan State University, with a grant from the U.S. Forest Service, carried out a study of Native Americans living in the Chicago metropolitan area.[51] They found that many of their leisure pursuits were similar to those of the population at large—including picnicking and driving for pleasure—but with a much higher emphasis on team sports, including baseball, volleyball, and basketball. About three-fourths of those studied reported taking part in Indian pow-pows during the year and engaging in such traditional pursuits as tribal dancing, beadwork and other crafts, and storytelling.

A final aspect of the role of Native Americans in contemporary culture has to do with the way their image is presented in current films and television programs. Strenuous efforts have been made to eliminate the distorted and bloodthirsty portraits of the past and to have more honest and realistic treatment of Indians—played, whenever possible, by actual Native Americans. Similarly, in the fall of 1991, a number of Native American activists demanded that baseball fans stop their parodying of Indian customs (wearing headdresses, waving tomahawks, and mimicking Indian warwhoops and chants) during the World Series battle between the Atlanta Braves and the Minnesota Twins—and, beyond that, that college and professional teams stop calling their sports teams by such names as Braves, Indians, Chiefs, and Redskins.

■ ASIAN AMERICANS AND LEISURE

A fourth racial or ethnic subgroup to be considered involves Asian Americans. This overall population has lived in the United States since the last century, when Chinese were imported to work on railroad gangs and Japanese were brought to Hawaii and the West Coast as cheap farm labor. Following a period in which they were not permitted to emigrate to the United States, in recent years there has been an immense influx of new residents from varied Eastern countries—Thais, Vietnamese, Filipinos, Koreans, Indians, Cambodians, Japanese, and Chinese.

Unlike the earlier waves of immigration, these newcomers differ widely in terms of their education and professional status. Many are investors and businesspeople who quickly purchase properties or businesses, or work hard and are able to build new enterprises through mutual cooperation. Howard Chua-Eoan writes that, as Asians bring vitality and a renewed sense of purpose to the American West in particular, one must ask: "Just as Europeans took the region from Native Americans, is the West being won all over again by Korean entrepreneurs, Japanese financiers, Indian doctors, Filipino nurses, Vietnamese restaurateurs and Chinese engineers?"[52]

9TH ANNUAL
AMERICAN INDIAN
ARTS FESTIVAL
OCTOBER 10, 11 & 12 11AM TO 6PM

JURIED SHOW & SALE
* Spectacular Aerial Dance Atop A 100 Foot Pole!
* "Dance of the Mother Earth"!   * World Famous Hoop Dancer!
* Alligator Wrestling!   * Live Wolves Show!
* 40 Tribal Nations   * 100 Native Artists & Performers!
* Continuous Performances!   * American Indian Foods!

Coupon
Admit one child 12 or under **Free**
with a paid adult at full admission price!
*** OR ***
Receive **$1 OFF** adult admission!
With this AD!

This offer good for Oct. 1992. May not be combined with
any other offer or promotional discount.

**RANKOKUS INDIAN
RESERVATION**
Westampton Twp.
Burlington County, NJ
(609) 261-4747

Adults: $6.00
Seniors &
Children: $3.00
Group Rates!
No Pets or Videos Please!
(cameras are allowed)

DIRECTIONS
From Philadelphia & South Jersey: take Route 295 North to Exit 45 A. Follow signs to Reservation.(3/4 of a mile on right)
From Trenton & North Jersey: take Route 295 South to Exit 45 A. Follow signs to Reservation. (3/4 of a mile on right)

FIGURE 5.1
Example of Native American art show and festival

The stories of Asian success in America are impressive; the East has replaced Europe as the leading foreign source of U.S. engineers, doctors, and technical workers. From 1975 to 1985, the number of full-time Asian faculty members in United States colleges nearly doubled and the number of capable Asian students in universities skyrocketed, so that a number of top schools felt compelled to establish quotas limiting the number admitted each year, in order to maintain racial balance among students.

However, this picture is deceptive. Not all Asian-American students are super-achievers; many of them are only average, and they suffer from excessive pressure to excel. A study of Asian-American youth by the U.S. Department of Health and Human Services showed that the suicide rate among Chinese Americans aged fifteen to twenty-four was nearly 37 percent higher than the national average; among Japanese-American youth, it was 54 percent higher. Beyond that, many new immigrants meet ethnic hostility. Korean merchants are threatened by black militants, Vietnamese shrimp fishermen are fired at off the Louisiana coast, and newcomers from Southeast Asia, such as Cambodians and the Hmong, find great difficulty in getting jobs, learning English, and surviving in urban ghettos.

There is evidence that the tide of immigration from Asia has resulted in a wave of crimes by youth gangs who practice extortion on Asian merchants, operate gambling rings, manage imported prostitutes, and engage in almost random violence.[53] To a degree, this is understandable in the light of the history of Asian immigrants in America. Distrustful of the police and the courts, many early Chinese settlers joined *triads* (Chinese secret societies) and *tongs* (self-help associations) in major cities, which governed the operation and protection of gambling, drug trafficking, and other crimes, but which also had a degree of standing and legitimacy in the Asian community. However, many of the new immigrants are not willing to be controlled by the tongs. They often have difficulty speaking English, are failing in school, and are recruited to join gangs when they are as young as fourteen. They see the

> easy money and exciting life of the gangs as a sharp, pleasant contrast to that of their parents, both frequently working two or three low-paying jobs in restaurants, laundries or garment sweatshops. . . . There are flashy cars, [and] available women and guns [are] stashed in communal gang apartments.[54]

Stimulated by the lurid and exciting portrayal of gangsters in popular Chinese movies and videotapes, for many young Asians crime represents an attractive way of life—in a sense, an exciting game or sport. School for them represents a dead end, and they feel that no matter how they attempt to assimilate they will always be perceived as racially different and will not be accepted by the larger society. However, gang youth represent only one segment of the Asian-American community. By far the greater number are moving steadily toward integration in American life, and leisure represents one of the channels for this development.

In a comprehensive article on Asian Americans in the United States, *Time* describes the pursuits that different groups are enjoying in California: Filipino cheerleaders in Daly City; Japanese tennis players in San Francisco; Cambodian soccer players in Long Beach; and Korean girls in a beauty contest in Los Angeles.[55] Asian-

American athletes like tennis champion Michael Chang and Olympic gold-medal winner, figure skater Kristi Yamaguchi, have become increasingly visible. From a reverse perspective, millions of Americans have become enthusiasts of varied forms of Eastern exercise and martial arts disciplines, ranging from *yoga* and *tai chi chuan* to *karate* and *kung fu*. Similarly, in 1991, Atlantic City casinos introduced such traditional Chinese gambling games as *pai gow* and *sic bo,* hoping to appeal to regular gamblers and to attract more Asian bettors.

The role of Asian Americans in American culture has often been marked by distortion in the popular media of entertainment. Often the images of Orientals in magazines and movies are deliberately manipulated to conform to national policy and public concerns. For example, Dr. Fu Manchu, a brilliant but diabolical villain, appeared in the period around World War I, when Asian workers were seen as a threat to native labor, and the term *The Yellow Peril* became popular. When more severe immigration restriction laws were passed and the threat of the Yellow Peril passed, detective Charlie Chan (actually played by a white actor in yellowface), became a hero in movie thrillers. Today, Chen writes, as Americans have come to resent Japanese economic domination, including Japanese purchase of American real estate, industries, and even sports teams and resorts, the Japanese gang leader in the "Teen-Age Mutant Ninja Turtles" is portrayed as a demonic and bestial character.[56]

In terms of popular literature, a number of best-selling novels, including works by Pearl Buck and James Michener, have improved public understanding of Asian Americans. Recently, several writers of Chinese and Japanese descent, including Gus Lee, Maxine Hong Kingston, Amy Tan, and Gish Jen have written successful novels and collections of short stories, which tell the stories of Asian Americans' transition from being first-generation foreigners in a strange and different culture, to becoming "ordinary" Americans in their second and third generations here.

■ THE LIVES OF WHITE ETHNICS

Finally, although this chapter has focused on four major groups of racial or ethnic populations that are nonwhite (recognizing that many Hispanic Americans have strains of African or Indian ancestry), it should also deal with the leisure lives of "ethnic" Americans of varied national backgrounds. Each such group, when it came to America, brought with it unique folk characteristics. For example, Malpezzi and Clements describe nine aspects of the lives of Italian Americans who migrated to the United States in the late nineteenth and early twentieth centuries—their conversation; life-cycle customs; calendars of holidays and celebrations; supernaturalism; folk medicine; recreation and games; stories and storytelling practices; drama, music, and dance; and "foodways."[57]

They go on to describe such traditional games as *bocce* and *mora,* wedding customs, and the informal but effective systems of health and life insurance that Italian Americans established through community clubs. Obviously, to the degree that such ethnic groups have assimilated into the larger American culture by intermarriage and by living in communities that have no particular ethnic character, their lives have generally become indistinguishable from the typical ones of the overall society. However, when clusters of families from a given nationality continue to live together, generation after generation, they tend to retain customs and traditions of the past.

Although much of the old snobbery is gone, ethnic identity continues to be linked to social class exclusiveness in American life, and to serve as a bar to acceptance in clubs, resorts, or other aspects of leisure involvement. This was illustrated in the experience of an outstanding figure-skating couple, Rocky Marval and Calla Urbanski—he a truck driver, she a cocktail waitress—who represented America at the 1992 Winter Olympics in France. There was a time, Marval remembers, when he could not be admitted to the best skating clubs in Philadelphia and Wilmington. His real name is Rocco Marvaldi, and his family has been in the meatpacking business for years. When he was ten, the Marvaldis applied for membership in skating clubs in Philadelphia and Wilmington, but were promptly rejected.

> "They were social clubs," Marval said. "If you weren't in their social circles, if you weren't white Anglo-Saxon Protestant, you weren't accepted in."
>
> That is partly the reason he now skates under the name Marval. "A little less ethnic," he said.[58]

Gradually, such patterns of social class and ethnic snobbery have declined in America. At the same time, many young white Americans—particularly those of lower-class background who live in disadvantaged urban neighborhoods—continue to display resentment of other racial minorities. Often this stems from fear of economic displacement in the tightening job world, or from ethnocentric resistance to "outsiders." Particularly among members of white gangs in fringe neighborhoods where other forms of constructive play are lacking, racial disputes offer a break from boredom and represent an ugly kind of play. The commander of a Philadelphia community intervention task force comments: "They pick fights, they drink, they fight, they destroy property. They go out looking to start racial incidents." Black or Hispanic families that move into neighborhoods where such gangs exist are likely to be harassed—to have their windows smashed, their tires flattened, threats whispered in their ears.

In some high schools throughout the nation, white students have responded to the establishment of ethnic minority student clubs by forming their own "European-American" clubs—designed to promote the "educational and social advancement of European-American students."

For all groups, recreation programs offer a means of overcoming racial antagonism and promoting positive relationships among ethnic factions in American society. Many public recreation and park agencies have been active in this respect, sponsoring intercultural festivals, workshops, and celebrations, or offering programs that encourage good-will and develop pride and self-understanding among minority-group members.

However, such programs must be carefully designed, with the input of diverse ethnic representatives, social agencies, churches, and political and special-interest groups. Sharon Washington writes:

It is essential to have a balanced representation of people of color and whites to provide an equitable starting place for planning and negotiation. Programs that reflect local values and interests may elicit greater involvement [and] networking within the community can provide a wealth of information, resources, and creativity that can benefit the parks and recreation program and the community.[59]

■ SUMMARY

Racial or ethnic identity has been a major influence on the leisure of Americans. Originally, such groups as African Americans or Hispanic Americans were often barred from community recreation opportunities by legal restrictions or community custom. In time, these barriers were overcome, and today leisure activities provide a channel for careers and substantial revenues, as in the case of sports and entertainment opportunities for blacks, or outdoor recreation, tourism, and gambling for American Indians. However, racial tensions and varied forms of conflict and discrimination continue to exist throughout the society and represent a critical area of concern for leisure-service managers and civic officials.

■ QUESTIONS FOR DISCUSSION

1. Contrast the white, Anglo-Saxon, Protestant dominance of American society and culture with the melting pot ideals. How did they differ and what did they have in common? Summarize the contemporary arguments on both sides of the multicultural dispute affecting American education practices.
2. Clearly, many of the leisure interests and involvements of African Americans differ from those of the overall white population. What, in your view, is responsible for these differences? Explain the "ethnicity" and "marginality" arguments and assess their relevance with respect to race-based cultural differences today.
3. How have stereotyped and prejudiced images of racial and ethnic minorities appeared in television, movies, and literature in the past—and what are some of the positive changes that have occurred in these forms of popular culture recently? Include references to all minorities (African Americans, Hispanics, Native Americans, and Asian Americans) in your discussion.
4. How have sports in particular represented both a positive and negative form of leisure involvement for American blacks? Provide an overview of past and current developments.
5. We tend to treat each minority population as a single, homogeneous entity, although each may comprise an extremely varied and complex group, in terms of national origins, social class, economic status, or degree of assimilation. Discuss this point in terms of its leisure implications for one of the major minority groups described in this chapter.

■ NOTES

1. RAVITCH, D. 1990. Multiculturalism: E pluribus plures. *The American Scholar* (Jan.):339.

2. ROSE, P. 1964. *They and we: Racial and ethnic relations in the United States.* New York: Random House, pp. 7–8.

3. HESS, B., E. MARKSON, and P. STEIN. 1988. *Sociology.* New York: Macmillan, p. 249.

4. *Ibid.,* p. 250.

5. FURNAS, J. C. 1969. *The Americans: A social history of the United States, 1587–1914.* New York: G. P. Putnam's Sons, p. 612.

6. *See* KRAUS, M. 1966. *Immigration, the American mosaic.* New York: Van Nostrand, pp. 9–10.

7. ROSALDO, R. 1990. A campus forum on multiculturalism. *New York Times* (Dec. 9): E–5.

8. YUHILL, J. M. 1991. Let's tell the story of all America's cultures. *Philadelphia Inquirer* (June 30): 7–E.

9. RAVITCH, *op. cit.,* p. 338.

10. ECK, D. 1992. Old Glory flies over many religions. *Philadelphia Inquirer* (July 4): A–7.

11. MEYER, H. D., and C. K. BRIGHTBILL. 1964. *Community recreation: A guide to its organization.* New York: Prentice-Hall, p. 67.

12. BUTLER, G. 1959. *Introduction to community recreation.* New York: McGraw-Hill, p. 59.

13. BEHR, P. 1986. Study: Doors are open but top jobs are closed to blacks. *Philadelphia Inquirer* (May 27): B–1.

14. KAUFMAN, M. 1991. Nursing home bias is cited. *Philadelphia Inquirer* (Oct.13): B–1.

15. GOODMAN, H. 1991. Racism in justice is cited. *Philadelphia Inquirer* (June 20): B–1.

16. For a detailed analysis of the problem, see HACKER, A. 1992. *Two nations: Black and white, separate, hostile, unequal.* New York: Charles Scribner's Sons.

17. Public notice of U.S. Department of Justice and U.S. Health, Inc. 1989. *Philadelphia Inquirer* (May 20): 4–A. See also SKORNECK, C. 1992. A program to remedy bias. *Associated Press* (Jan. 3).

18. ST. GEORGE, C. 1992. Challenging a Mardi Gras tradition. *Philadelphia Inquirer* (Jan. 19): 1–A.

19. *Outdoor recreation for America.* 1962. Report to the President and Congress by the Outdoor Recreation Resources Review Commission. Washington, DC: U.S. Government Printing Office, Vol. I, p. 28.

20. SHORT, J. F., and F. L. STRODTBECK. 1965. *Group process and gang delinquency.* Chicago: University of Chicago Press, pp. 36–53.

21. KRAUS, R. 1968. *Public recreation and the Negro.* New York: Center for Urban Education, pp. 36–79.

22. FRAZIER, E. F. 1957, 1962. *Black Bourgeoisie.* New York: Collier.

23. STAMPS, S. M., and M. B. STAMPS. 1985. Race, class and leisure activities of urban residents. *Journal of Leisure Research* 17, 1: 40–55.

24. WOODARD, M. 1988. Class, regionality, and leisure among urban black Americans: The post–civil rights era. *Journal of Leisure Research* 20, 2: 87–105.

25. DWYER, J., and P. GOBSTER. 1992. Recreation opportunity and cultural diversity. *Parks and Recreation* (Sept.): 22–31.

26. HENDERSON, K., and L. BEDINI. 1992. NRPA Leisure Research Symposium. *Parks and Recreation* (Jan.): 16, 19–21.

27. HUTCHISON, R. 1988. A critique of race, ethnicity and social class in recent leisure-recreation research. *Journal of Leisure Research* 20, 1: 15.

28. WEST, P. C. 1989. Urban regional parks and black minorities: Subculture, marginality, and interracial relations in park use in the Detroit metropolitan area. *Leisure Sciences* 11: 11–28.

29. ASHE, ARTHUR. 1988. Taking the hard road with black athletes. *New York Times* (Nov.13): S–11.

30. RADER, B. G. 1983. *American sports from the age of folk games to the age of spectators.* Englewood Cliffs, NJ: Prentice-Hall, p. 95.

31. WIGGINS, D. 1991. The involvement of black athletes in intercollegiate sports at predominantly white university campuses, 1890–1972. *Research Quarterly for Exercise and Sport*. 62, 2 (Spring): 167.

32. WILL, G. 1991. Basketball, the team game that can be practiced alone, has its birthday. *Philadelphia Inquirer* (Dec. 20): 18–A.

33. ROSELLINI, L. 1987. Strike one and you're out. *U.S. News and World Report* (July 27): 53.

34. MACNOW, G. 1992. Progress slow for blacks in NFL. *Philadelphia Inquirer* (Jan. 14): 3–D.

35. KRAUS, R., S. C. HILSENDAGER, and B. DIXON. 1992. *History of the dance in art and education*. Englewood Cliffs, NJ: Prentice-Hall, pp. 250–252.

36. DONN, J. 1992. 'Cosby' desensitizes whites, study says. *Philadelphia Inquirer* (April 28): C–1.

37. O'CONNOR, J. 1991. Blacks on TV: Scrambled signals. *New York Times* (Oct. 27): 2–1.

38. PARKS, F. C. 1990. Is the recreation industry color blind? *Parks and Recreation* (Dec.): 43.

39. GONZALEZ, R. A. 1990. Hispanic history is U.S. history, too. *Philadelphia Inquirer* (March 8): 19–A.

40. ABREU, J. 1987. Leisure programming for Hispanics. *Parks and Recreation* (Dec.): 52–54.

41. MOORE, J. 1978. *Home boys: Gangs, drugs and prison in the barrios of Los Angeles*. Philadelphia: Temple University Press.

42. SIMCOX, D., and R. PFISTER. 1990. *Hispanic values and behavior relating to outdoor recreation and the forest environment*. Riverside, CA: U.S. Forest Service.

43. SIMCOX, D., R. PFISTER, and R. HODGSON. 1989. *Communicating with users of the Angeles National Forest, Report no. 1*. Riverside CA: U.S. Forest Service.

44. CHAVEZ, D. 1992. *Ethnic group activities: A survey of Los Angeles residents*. Riverside, CA: U.S. Forest Service, Recreation Research Update (October).

45. WOLF, E. 1992. Reaching Latinos in Santa Monica. *Parks and Recreation* (Sept.): 10.

46. STRAUSSFELD, D. 1984. In *The aggressions of civilization: Federal Indian policy since the 1880s*, ed. S. Cadwalader and V. Deloria. Philadelphia: Temple University Press, p. 20.

47. MECHLING, J. 1985. In *Meaningful play, playful meaning*, ed. G. A. Fine. Chicago: Human Kinetics, p. 50.

48. CADWALADER, S., and V. DELORIA, eds. 1984. *The aggressions of civilization: Federal Indian policy since the 1880s*. Philadelphia: Temple University Press, p. xii and jacket.

49. BAKER, W. J. 1988. *Sports in the Western world*. Urbana and Chicago: University of Illinois Press, p. 71.

50. SWICK, T. 1991. In the land of cowboys and Indians. *New York Times* (June 16): 6–H.

51. PANCNER, C., and M. McDONOUGH. *Use of urban recreation resources by Native Americans*. Michigan State University and U.S. Forest Service Experiment Station in Chicago, n.d.

52. CHUA-EOAN, H. 1990. Strangers in paradise. *Time* (April 9): 32.

53. A tide of Asian immigration brings a wave of gang crime. *New York Times* (Jan. 5, 1991): p. 20.

54. *Ibid.*

55. CHUA-EOAN, *op. cit.*, pp. 34–35.

56. CHEN, G. 1991. Challenging the Asian illusion. *New York Times* (Aug. 11): H–11.

57. MALPEZZI, F., and W. M. CLEMENTS. 1992. *Italian-American folklore*. New York: August House.

58. LONGMAN, J. 1992. Skating pair defies skeptics. *Philadelphia Inquirer* (Feb. 9): C–9.

59. WASHINGTON, S. J. 1990. Provision of leisure services: To people of color. *Journal of Physical Education, Recreation and Dance* (Oct.): 38.

6 Gender, Sex, and Leisure Life-Styles

What are little boys made of?
What are little boys made of?
Frogs and snails, and puppy dogs' tails,
That's what little boys are made of.

What are little girls made of?
What are little girls made of?
Sugar and spice, and everything nice,
That's what little girls are made of.

ANONYMOUS

A second major demographic influence that affects leisure in modern American society is gender, seen both as a biological identity and as a set of attitudes, values, and behaviors. Just as in the case of race and ethnicity, leisure provides a prism through which to examine gender-related issues in contemporary community life. This chapter examines the degree to which the constraints that were imposed on girls and women in various areas of daily life—education, careers, social and political affairs—also limited their participation in leisure in the past. It reviews the progress they have made in recent years, and goes on to discuss the special place of leisure in the lives of men, of lesbians and gays, and finally the role of sex as a form of popular recreation.

■ MEANINGS OF *SEX* AND *GENDER*

The terms *sex* and *gender* are often used in ambiguous and contradictory ways. Schur suggests that true sex roles *are* biological and can only be played by members of one biological sex—roles such as wet nurse or sperm donor. On the other hand, the word *gender* should be used to refer to

> the sociocultural and physiological shaping, patterns, and evaluating of female and male behavior. According to this usage, most "sex roles" are, strictly speaking, "gender roles."[1]

Extending this discussion, one's biological membership in one sex or another—male or female—customarily results in gender identification within a system of normative behavior that society has developed through the years. One's gender role is not established at birth

> but is built up cumulatively through experiences encountered and transacted—through casual and unplanned learning, through explicit instruction and inculcation. In brief, a gender role is established in much the same way as is a native language.[2]

Throughout history, the gender roles of women have been subordinated to those of men in varied spheres of life activity—education, careers, political, and family circumstances. The French novelist and philosopher, Simone de Beauvoir, points out that legislators, priests, philosophers, and scientists have all argued that the subordinate position of women is willed in heaven and advantageous on earth:

> Since ancient times, satirists and moralists have delighted in showing up the weaknesses of women. . . . For instance, the Roman law limiting the rights of women cited "the imbecility, the instability of the sex," just when the weakening of family ties seemed to threaten the interest of male heirs.[3]

She goes on to point out that in the sixteenth century, St. Augustine stated that "woman is a creature neither decisive nor constant," and Clement of Alexandria wrote, "Every woman ought to be filled with shame at the thought of being a woman." Nor were such attitudes confined to Western cultures. The Confucian Marriage Manual held that typical female behaviors were "indocility, discontent, slander, jealousy, and silliness," and Napoleon Bonaparte summed up the feelings of his age:

> Nature intended women to be our slaves. They are our property, we are not theirs. They belong to us, just as a tree that bears fruit belongs to a gardener. What an insane idea to demand equality for women . . . they are nothing but machines for producing children.[4]

Despite such views, in some societies women did hold positions of prestige and honor, and their status has fluctuated through the ages. The ancient Egyptians had women as deities and rulers, as did the Greeks and Romans. Elizabeth I of England, Catherine the Great of Russia, and, most recently, Indira Ghandi of India, Golda Meier of Israel, and Margaret Thatcher of Great Britain were all powerful national leaders. Anthropologists suggest that in the early periods of humankind's existence, women had relatively equal work and influence. During later agricultural eras, when families were tied to farms, males came to have a higher degree of dominance; in the modern industrial period, with women becoming more economically independent, they have gained a fuller degree of social equality.[5]

Jean Schroedel points out that women during the colonial period in America had the same rights as men to own land, enter occupations, marry whomever they wished, and vote if they met the property qualifications. However, after the Revolutionary War, the British legal theory—that husband and wife were one person and that women therefore had no legal standing—gained credence. Schroedel writes:

> Within twenty years only white men could vote in any part of the United States. Women were also beginning to be excluded from professions such as law and medicine, which they had previously practiced. This trend culminated in an 1873 Supreme Court decision upholding the right of a state to exclude women from the legal profession because "the natural and proper timidity and delicacy which belongs to the female sex evidently unfits it for many of the occupations of civil life."[6]

Sexual Vulnerability

Application of English common law in the United States ultimately meant that husbands had control of wives' persons, beatings included, control also of their children and all of a wife's property at marriage unless protected by a previously created trust, as well as numerous other restrictions. The assumption that women were "timid" and "delicate" did not apply to working-class women, who labored up to sixteen hours a day, while their wealthier sisters led lives of enforced idleness in the home or were restricted to the function of supervising servants. Indeed, despite the great concern about "protecting" women during the nineteenth century, slave and lower-class women led sexually vulnerable lives at all times.

During the Industrial Revolution, prostitution became inevitable for many poor women who were drawn into sexual commerce because of their vulnerability or domestic disaster. Thrown on their own resources, young widows and country girls in the city faced desperate economic choices because most women's work paid too poorly to provide decent food, clothing, and shelter. Larkin points out that such women often became part of a huge network that ranged from elaborate and expensive "parlor houses" to more numerous and moderately priced houses, and, at the lowest level, "broken and dissipated" women who walked the streets or haunted dockside grogshops.[7]

■ IMPACT OF THE FEMINIST MOVEMENT

In America, there were two important waves of the women's liberation movement: (1) the first, with roots in the abolition and temperance movements, claimed the Married Women's Property Acts of the 1860s as its first success, and then went on to achieve passage of the Nineteenth Amendment, which granted women suffrage, in 1920; and (2) the modern era of the movement, which began in the early 1960s, when many women who had gained a degree of independence by working during World War II and volunteering in the civil rights and anti-Vietnam War movements became activists in women's causes.[8] Authors like Betty Friedan, Kate Millett, and Germaine Greer sought to establish the intellectual respectability of feminism by presenting a new theory of unisexism, both as a conceptual explanation of human personality and as a program for action. Millett wrote in her influential book, *Sexual Politics,* that it was doubtful that there were

> any significant inherent differences between male and female beyond the biogenital ones we already know. Conditioning runs in a circle of self-perpetuation and self-fulfilling prophecy.[9]

During the early years of the renewed feminist movement, talk of inborn differences in the behavior of men and women became unfashionable, even taboo. Many of the differences—such as male domination of fields like architecture and engineering—were the direct result of social conditioning or environmental pressures, rather than inherent differences between the sexes, it was argued. Gorman writes:

> Women did the vast majority of society's childrearing because few other options were available to them. Once sexism was abolished, so the argument ran, the world would become a perfectly equitable, androgynous place, aside from a few anatomical details.[10]

It was recognized that, in terms of personality, women were usually more intuitive, sensitive, and nurturing, while men were less emotional but better able to perform tasks like reading maps or thinking in three dimensions. However, feminist writers argued that differences in mental abilities, emotional makeup, or even physical skills were the product of past centuries of conditioning. Anthropologist Helen Fisher wrote:

> for two million years, women carried around children and have been the nurturers. That's probably why tests show they are both more verbal and more attuned to nonverbal cues. Men, on the other hand, tend to have superior mathematical and visual-spatial skills because they roamed long distances from the campsite, had to scheme ways to trap prey and then had to find their way back.[11]

Other scientists supported the view that gender traits have been conditioned over time by cultural practices. If men are less adept at recognizing emotions, it is a "trained incompetence," according to Harvard psychologist Ronald Levant. Young boys were told to ignore pain and not to cry, a carryover from the need for them to separate from their mothers, learn to fight, and ultimately engage in hand-to-hand warfare. Many men, says Levant, recognize their emotions only through symptoms like a physical buzz or tightness in the throat.[12]

Following this period, however, biologists, psychologists, and other social and behavioral scientists began to document significant differences between males and females that appeared to be innate, rather than culturally induced. At birth, the skeletons of girl babies are slightly more mature than those of boys, while boys pass girls in this respect by the end of the first year. At the age of two, boys begin to show signs of greater aggressiveness. At three, a female edge in verbal ability disappears, but returns by ten or eleven. Boys show superiority in spatial skills at the age of eight or so, and at ten or eleven start outperforming girls in mathematics.

During adolescence, girls fall behind in body strength, spatial skills, and mathematics, while gaining superiority in verbal skills. Conceding these differences between the sexes, some investigators continue to develop evidence that many behavioral differences are the result of conditioning of boys and girls.

Typically, Harvard psychologist Carol Gilligan points out, on same-sex teams in grade-school sports, when a boy is injured he is removed from the field and the game continues. Among girls, when a teammate is injured, the game stops. Gilligan has noted the phenomenon of young girls in the preadolescent years who are confident and outspoken, but who, on entering the teen years, become less certain, bury their knowledge, experience self-doubt, and even panic in affirming their views. They are "confident" at eleven, "confused" at sixteen.[13]

⮕ TO THE POINT

Childhood play has a significant role in gender acculturation. Some differences in play behavior would appear to be instinctive, or genetically rooted. Lionel Tiger, for example, writes of the separation of the sexes and contrasting behavior among male and female primates, such as monkeys and chimpanzees:

> Sexual differences appear early. Female infants have no contacts with adult males, but are groomed more frequently by and with adult females. More than twice as often as female infants, male infants are threatened and chased by adults. Male play is more active and noisy. The most absorbing and important juvenile activity is play. . . .
>
> Female juveniles engage in dominance interaction less frequently than males. Large juveniles almost always play in groups of one sex; large female juveniles rarely play for more than a few minutes with large male juveniles.[14]

Such observations underline the importance of play in the gender acculturation of the sexes. In the past, it was taken for granted that parents or nursery-school teachers would help little boys and girls learn their "proper" gender roles. Little boys would be given guns and bows and arrows and encouraged to play at vigorous and combative games. Little girls were given dolls, sewing kits, and cooking equipment. Such childhood play emphases seem, however, to reflect children's choices as well as adult encouragement. In play laboratories, young boys appear to spontaneously favor sports cars and Lincoln logs, while girls are drawn more to domestic toys like dolls and kitchen equipment. Gorman writes:

. . . another generation of parents discovered that, despite their best efforts to give baseballs to their daughters and sewing kits to their sons, girls still flocked to dollhouses while boys clambered into tree forts. Perhaps nature is more important than nurture after all.[15]

■ LEISURE IN THE LIVES OF WOMEN

We turn now to a more direct examination of leisure in the lives of women. As was shown in Chapters 3 and 4, women were historically limited by the stereotyped view of them as fragile and sensitive, and by the prudery of the times that placed respectable women on a pedestal.

The Middletown studies found that during the early decades of the twentieth century, most middle- or upper-class women tended to do volunteer community work, patronize the arts and cultural activities, or engage in other leisure pursuits. Lower-class women, whether or not they had paid employment, usually had heavy home-making responsibilities with only occasional breaks for sociability with other women. Kathy Peiss writes:

> Women had to fit their entertainment into their work rather than around it. Washing the laundry, supervising children at play, or shopping at the local market, women might find a few moments to socialize with neighbors. . . . Given the task-oriented nature of their [daily lives] married women's leisure was intermittent, snatched between household chores. . . . [16]

In a study of the lives of farm women, Henderson and Rannells found that their dominant memories were of hard work with relatively little free time, but that they had experienced feelings of pleasure, satisfaction, and self-fulfillment from having contributed to their families' survival:

> The work of the women on the farm provided social interaction whether it was with the family, spouse, neighborhood or community church members. . . . To adhere to the strong work ethic, women often used household obligations as a way to fulfill leisure needs. For example, corn-husking, maple sugar gathering, harvesting, quilting parties and other sewing tasks provided women with [the] opportunity to socialize with other women and get out of the isolation of their homes.[17]

Growing Leisure Opportunities

During the nineteenth century, Peiss points out, there was an essentially masculine "public order" that kept women out of most commercially provided social activities and settings. Saloons, for example, primarily served men, who used them not only for drinking and socializing, but also as informal employment agencies and for union and political meetings. Women were not welcome in such settings.[18]

In time, other forms of commercially sponsored amusement became open to women. The legitimate theater began to provide a more wholesome setting that women might attend, along with other more respectable types of music halls—in contrast with vaudeville and burlesque theaters, which were considered disreputable kinds of entertainment. A new "Sunday-School" circuit of entertainment developed, which guaranteed circumspect language and subject matter, to encourage respectable family attendance. Middle-class women sought the regulation of public commercial amusements, and became more active in volunteer leadership in Girl Scouts, Camp Fire Girls, 4-H Clubs, and religiously sponsored youth organizations that promoted morally acceptable forms of leisure.

During much of this period, girls and women were given far less support in terms of organized recreation programs and were regarded as inferior to boys and men, in terms of their leisure interests and group capabilities. A 1953 publication of the National Recreation Association described the "problems" faced by leaders of female recreation groups:

> It is usually more difficult to lead girls' groups than boys' groups. They need more personal attention, more help in getting started and more encouragement to keep going. Girls do not respond to highly organized competitive activities as well as boys do. They respond better to small group organization where individual interest is developed into individual achievement. Strange as it may seem, many girls need help in accepting with pride their role as women and an appreciation of the special responsibilities which will be theirs because they are women.[19]

An early study of leisure in community life was conducted in Westchester County, New York, in the mid-1930s. It examined the work and free-time patterns of eight different population groups—laborers, white collar workers, high school and college students, professional and executive personnel, housewives, and the unemployed. Housewives were found to have the most leisure (9.2 hours per day) and laborers the least (5.7 hours), based on the principle that women's unpaid tasks in the home, such as cooking, cleaning, or child care, should not be regarded as work.[20]

A half-century later, Susan Shaw examined sixty married couples in Canada, and found that men had significantly more leisure time than their wives on weekends, with only minor differences during the week. Reluctance to regard unpaid housework as "real" work also affected the analysis in Shaw's study. She writes:

> since paid employment is recognized as "work" and is restricted to particular working hours for most people, men have considerable access to leisure during their "non-work" hours, and especially during weekends. Unpaid work, on the other hand, is often "hidden," is not restricted to particular days or times . . . and is thus more likely to impede access to leisure independent of the day of the week.[21]

John Shank explored the lives of professional women, both married and single, in their twenties and thirties, who lived under severe time pressures and had little discretionary time. For them, leisure satisfaction—when they were able to achieve it—was most directly associated with the sense of relaxation and recuperation that it was able to provide from the stress and strain of their daily lives. For these women with heavy work schedules and children and homes to care for:

> leisure was conceptualized as a time for self-directed activity that would result in feelings of renewal, revitalization and stability. It was a time for self-nurturance. Regardless of the form, whether jogging or sewing, [it] became the "glue" or "mortar" that held their lives in a balanced state. Having an aspect of her life, a "space" devoted to herself

alone . . . contributed to [a respondent's] feeling "whole," "centered," and "individu-ated."[22]

STUDIES OF GENDER-INFLUENCED LEISURE VALUES AND BEHAVIORS

As indicated before, play is an important factor in gender acculturation for many children. For example, boys might typically play at being a doctor or a pilot, while girls would expect to be nurses or stewardesses (later called flight attendants). The issue of job status was explored by Allison and Duncan, who studied two kinds of women, professional and blue-collar, to determine their leisure values and behaviors. They found that professional or high-status career women tended to get a feeling of satisfaction, immersion in the activity, and personal reward from their work, while women in lower-level jobs did not achieve the same kinds of emotional values and sought them in leisure.[23]

Other research studies have examined the degree to which leisure activities were commonly regarded as masculine or feminine. Kenneth Gruber had male and female college students rate a list of leisure pursuits according to their perceived masculinity or femininity. Activities identified as masculine generally involved a degree of com-petition and physical contact or risk, including such pursuits as auto racing, wrestling, pole vaulting, handball, and skydiving. Feminine activities included cook-ing, interior decorating, ballet, sewing, knitting, and embroidery. So-called neutral activities, suitable for both sexes, included archery, golf, bowling, tennis, swimming, and bridge.[24]

In a related study, Gentry and Doering examined the sex-role orientations of two hundred male and female college students to determine how their choice of leisure pursuits related to their degree of masculinity, femininity, or androgyny (having a high degree of both masculine and feminine traits; see page 141). They found dis-tinct differences between male and female students in their leisure choices, with the androgynous respondents tending to be much more active overall in their leisure than the other two groups.[25]

Elizabeth Hirschman investigated the relationship between one's gender role and one's motivations for selecting leisure activities. She found that the three leisure motives found to be strongly related to having absorbing leisure experiences *(Fun and Pleasure, Escape from Reality,* and *Deep Involvement)* were most strongly associ-ated with the androgynous sex role. On the other hand, motives that were linked to high levels of masculinity, such as *Competitiveness, Alertness,* and *Perfection,* were neg-atively associated with having deeply absorbing leisure experiences.[26]

WOMEN IN SPORTS

Clearly one of the key areas of leisure involvement in which girls and women were deprived of equal opportunity for participation in the past was sports. Why was this the case?

Simply stated, the sports field, with its emphasis on power, strength, and courage, has historically been viewed as a masculine domain. Sabo and Pantopinto describe football as a critical channel for boys' gender-identity development. Many of the meanings that coaches attached to football revolved around such themes as:

> . . . distinctions between boys and men, physical size and strength, avoidance of femi-
> nine activities and values, toughness, aggressiveness, violence and emotional self-con-
> trol. Sometimes the coach's masculine counsels were overt: "Football is the closest thing
> to war you boys will ever experience. It's your chance to find out what manhood is all
> about."[27]

In reviewing their past experiences in sports, adult men agreed that football helped them achieve success in later life. Football had been a realistic training for the business world. A law student remembered his coach's emphasis on hard work and competition: ". . . he taught us benefits we'll carry for the rest of our lives. We have to learn to be competitive, because it is a competitive world. You have to be a real tough bastard to get to your goal."[28]

⇒ TO THE POINT

Recognizing such meanings in sport, many women felt that athletics offered an ideal medium through which girls and women might gain in self-confidence and feelings of empowerment. Through sports they might show that they were strong, courageous, and in control of their own lives and bodies. One writer summed it up: "I have long believed that physical fitness is the key to woman's emancipation . . . in marathon races, martial arts, or basketball, women are showing that they are not quitters, nor creatures of inferior potential."[29]

Some feminists stressed the potential value of sports in helping women learn principles of strength, cooperation, and solidarity in other areas of life, and thus to transform politics, business, or family life into less oppressive social constructs. Feminist values applied to sports might, in Bialeschki's words, reveal to each woman her real potential and help her overcome the limitations imposed on her by an arbitrary social code.[30] As late as the 1970s, however, the prejudice against women taking part in active sports in the United States was widespread. Gilbert and Williamson wrote in 1973:

> There is no sharper example of discrimination today than that which operates
> against girls and women who take part in competitive sports, wish to take part, or
> might wish to if society did not scorn such endeavors. No matter what her age,
> education, race, talent, residence or riches, the female's right to play is severely
> restricted. The funds, facilities, coaching, rewards and honors allotted to women
> are greatly inferior to those granted men. In many places absolutely no support is
> given to women's athletics, and females are barred by law, regulation, tradition or
> the hostility of males from sharing athletic resources and pleasures.[31]

Historical Involvement of Women in Sports

Women had not always been excluded from sports participation. In a comprehensive study of female involvement in athletics, Allen Guttmann points out that throughout history, women have rowed, wrestled, swum, boxed, fenced, shot arrows, raced horses, and played various team games. He writes: "There has never been a time when girls and women were wholly excluded from sports and there have certainly been times and places where their involvement was almost as extensive . . . as the men's."[32]

Guttmann cites numerous examples of successful women athletes in the past. From 1884 to the turn of the century, an American woman called Jaguarina defeated many men in broadsword contests. In the 1890s, two Danish women broke a number of cycling records that had been set by their countrymen. Nineteen-year-old Gertrude Ederle became the first woman to swim the English Channel in 1926, beating the records of earlier male swimmers by two hours. However, Guttmann continues, sports were often used as a form of sexually oriented entertainment by upper-class male spectators:

> Italian prostitutes in the fifteenth and sixteenth centuries raced on foot for minor prizes. Male spectators would frequently "trip them and send them sprawling to the ground . . . " an activity considered good sport . . . Throughout nineteenth-century France, working-class women boxed and wrestled, sometimes stripping to the waist and fighting in front of a drunken mob.[33]

Such practices were cited as the reason for excluding women from the first modern Olympics in Athens in 1896; Pierre de Coubertin felt that providing sexual entertainment for men was not the true purpose of sports. Despite such concerns, during the Victorian era many women did take part in varied forms of athletics and outdoor recreation. In mid-nineteenth-century America, women began attending sports events like horse racing, baseball, and other athletic contests, in specially built ladies' stands. Women's schools and colleges introduced gymnastics, dancing, and varied games and exercises; gradually such activities as croquet, tennis, horseback riding, swimming, ice- and roller-skating, and bicycling became popular pastimes.

However, men were not permitted to watch women competing because to be seen "sweating" or engaging in vigorous activity would not be "ladylike." And, invariably, fears were expressed that women might become too "masculine" if they played sports too seriously. Protesting against women's playing cricket, for example, a British newspaper warned in 1881 that women might become: "wide shouldered and deep-voiced . . . with biceps like a blacksmith's. [The writer] pleaded 'Let our women remain women instead of entering their insane physical rivalry with men.'"[34]

Through the early decades of the twentieth century, organized sports for girls and women continued to grow, but at a limited pace. A 1936 study showed that only 17 percent of seventy-seven schools surveyed reported female varsity athletics, although about three-quarters of respondents sponsored playdays or "telegraphic meets" (schools competing at a distance, with "wired" results). A unique development during World War II was the establishment of the All-American Girls Professional

Baseball League in the Midwest, intended to compensate for the impact of the war on baseball.

In many ways, discrimination against girls and women in sports was part of a larger pattern in schools and colleges. Sue Durrant points out that before the 1970s, certain classes or courses of study were limited to males and others to females. Males could often live off campus and did not have closing hours in residential halls, while females were required to live in dormitories with stricter rules. Different dress codes were enforced according to gender, and women's dormitories were supplied with ironing boards and sewing machines, while men's dormitories were given recreational facilities and equipment. Durrant continues:

> In physical education and athletic programs, it was not unusual to find males using new equipment and facilities while females used the "hand-me-downs"; for the boys' teams to have specific team uniforms while the girls used their physical education uniforms; for girls to have their team practices early in the morning or at night while the boys had the use of all facilities immediately after school; or for the college men's teams to travel by bus or airplane while the women's teams went in cars driven by the coaches and players.[35]

■ GROWTH OF WOMEN'S ATHLETICS

Despite the resistance to women's sports cited by Gilbert and Williamson, progress began to be made in this area in the post–World War II period. Stimulated by the feminist movement, girls and women pressed for fuller opportunities; in 1966, the Commission on Intercollegiate Athletics for Women (CIAW) was created by the Division for Girls' and Women's Sport (DGWS) of the American Association for Health, Physical Education and Recreation, to sponsor national championships and sanction women's intercollegiate athletic events. This led to a revolution in women's athletic competition; over the next six years, national championships were established in seven sports: golf, gymnastics, track and field, badminton, swimming, diving, volleyball, and basketball. However, hampered by lack of financial resources, this organization was replaced in 1971 by the Association for Intercollegiate Athletics for Women (AIAW), an organization requiring institutional membership with annual dues.

The women's sports movement was immeasurably aided by the enactment of Title IX, federal legislation in 1972, which prohibited discriminatory practices on racial or gender grounds in schools and colleges that received federal assistance. Over the next decade, the AIAW grew to be the largest intercollegiate athletic governance organization in the nation, with a membership of 973 institutions. Christine Grant writes:

> Colleges and universities increased their offerings of women's sports from 2.5 sports per school for women in 1973 to 6.48 in 1979. . . . In approximately the same time frame, budgets for women's athletic programs grew from 1 percent to about 16 percent of the total athletic budget.[36]

The growth of interest in women's sports was accompanied by increased television coverage of girls' and women's athletics. In the late 1970s and early 1980s, the

Girls' and women's sports today are often highly competitive and physically demanding. Above, women athletes at Washington State University in Pullman play basketball and compete in a track meet. Left, women crew members are coached at Smith College in Massachusetts.

NBC and ESPN networks acquired television rights to women's gymnastics and basketball championships, and there was increased coverage of professional tennis and golf tournaments for women, along with their expanded role in Olympic and other international competitions. However, the 1980s also saw a number of setbacks in organized sports for women. In the summer of 1982, the National Collegiate Athletic Association (NCAA), a powerful, predominantly male organization with major influence over all collegiate sports activities, established a number of Division I championships in women's sports. Chu writes:

> Given the inducement of expenses-paid competitions, few of the major powers in women's sport could resist the NCAA championship format, which required NCAA membership and adherence to its rules. After the loss of an antitrust suit in February 1983, the AIAW all but ceased to exist, having had its responsibilities and membership taken over by the more financially powerfully NCAA.[37]

During the 1980s, women's sports in schools and colleges suffered a number of other setbacks. The percentage of women coaching women's sports teams declined markedly in sports such as basketball, tennis, and volleyball, and in thirty-five mergers of formerly separate male and female athletic departments, only one woman was named to head the combined departments following a merger. A major setback occurred in 1984, when the Supreme Court ruled that Title IX would apply only to a specific education program in which discrimination had occurred, rather than to the entire institution and its other programs. This decision was, however, reversed by the Civil Rights Restoration Act of 1987, which reestablished the original intent of Title IX by making it more broadly applicable to the overall programs of institutions practicing gender-based discrimination.

By the early 1990s, it was apparent that, although considerable progress had been made in the support of women's sports in colleges and universities, there was still a marked disparity between men's and women's programs. A March 1992 survey conducted by the NCAA reported that twice as many men as women participated in college sports. Scholarship expenditures for men averaged $849,000, while those for women athletes were $372,000 per institution, and recruiting expenses for men's athletics averaged $139,000, with $28,000 going to women's programs.[38]

During the 1970s and 1980s many of the old myths regarding the dangers of active sports competition were dispelled. One excuse for discouraging women from taking part in vigorous athletics had been that their "fragile" bodily makeup—particularly their reproductive systems—would be affected. By the late 1970s however, there was considerable evidence that these beliefs were poorly founded.

Specifically, research demonstrated that fears of damage to women's ovaries or breasts through active play were not justified. While girls are more loose-jointed than boys, making them more susceptible to injuries affecting muscles, tendons, and ligaments, such risks can be minimized with proper training. Although cessation of the menstrual cycle may occur among women runners, gymnasts, dancers, or ice skaters with rigorous training schedules, the cycle normally returns with the cessation of heavy work; even pregnant women may safely engage in many activities during the first two trimesters, and with careful supervision, in the third.[39]

Confronting Gender Barriers

Increasingly, girls and women have challenged gender-segregation practices in sports, and in a number of cases have successfully played on formerly all-male teams. Jan Felshin and Carole Oglesby point out that in the post–World War II era, high school girls played in boys' baseball leagues, on high school football teams (chiefly as field-goal kickers), and on mixed teams in field and ice hockey. Writing in 1986, they summed up coeducational sports examples in the New York-New Jersey-Connecticut tristate area:

> In Connecticut high schools last year, 11 girls played on boys' soccer teams, 159 swam on boys' swim teams, and 98 ran on boys' cross-country squads. In New Jersey, boys' ski teams had 125 girls on them. Between 100 and 150 high schools fielded coed teams in cross-country, indoor track, and tennis. An additional 98 high schools had mixed bowling teams, and in golf, 81 did.[40]

In addition to such examples, over the past two decades there has been considerable progress in having girls admitted to community sports teams and leagues that were traditionally all male. In Canada, for example, a twelve-year-old girl fought to be able to play in an all-boy ice hockey league sponsored by the Ontario Hockey Association, taking the case to the Ontario Supreme Court. In the United States, a number of lawsuits sought to compel the Little League youth baseball organization to admit girls to competition. In June 1974, Little League gave in and changed its charter to incorporate girls. However, it also organized a softball league, which, while not officially restricted to girls, serves them primarily. Relatively few girls have joined boys' baseball teams, and in some cases they have been denied access by local independent athletic associations. Where discrimination has been persistent and overt, cases have been taken before commissions on human relations, city councils, and law courts.

Women's Participation in Other Physical Recreation Activities

Apart from their involvement in traditionally male team sports, many girls and women have entered other types of sports and physical recreation activities that were regarded as masculine domains. For example, thousands of women today compete in triathlon competitions that combine swimming, biking, and running—including the famed Ironman Triathlon held in Hawaii, which features a 2.4-mile ocean swim, a 112-mile bicycle ride, and a 26-mile, 385-yard marathon. Of five hundred thousand participants in various triathlons each year, by the mid-1980s, approximately 16 percent of competitors were women. At the 1992 winter Olympics, far more American women competitors than men won gold medals.

Similarly, growing numbers of women have taken up martial arts, studying such defense systems as karate, judo, and kung fu and often earning black belts. Many have taken up flying; for example, Janet Guthrie, the racing car driver who completed the Indianapolis 500 three times and was the first woman competitor at a number of other famous events, earned a private pilot's license at seventeen and performed a number of remarkable flying feats in small planes. In 1991, a woman jockey, Gwen Jocson, achieved fame by completing her apprenticeship as the leading young rider in the country.

■ RESISTANCE TO GIRLS AND WOMEN IN SPORTS

Not surprisingly, the rapid growth of female participation in sports and physical recreation has met strong opposition from many men and male-dominated organizations. Women too express concern about their daughters, fearing that they will lose their femininity and become overly aggressive.

⫸ TO THE POINT

One mother describes her conflict as she watches her daughter, who had once been only marginally interested in athletics, who fumbled the ball and tittered in embarrassment, gradually become a "jock"—earning varsity letters in cross-country, soccer, basketball, and softball. Gradually the mother realizes that participating in sports has transformed her daughter—that she is now a serious, intense competitor. Instead of being a girl who had accepted being told, at home and at school, to be quiet, be still, she is now a young women who is assertive and confident. Although the mother still daydreams of her daughter in a typical feminine role—married to a handsome, well-to-do male professional, having children and an attractive home—she appreciates the change in her personality.

The mother confesses that what has amazed her and made her hold her breath in wonder and hope is both the ideal of sports and the reality of a young girl not afraid to do her best:

> I watch her bringing the ball up the court. We yell encouragement from the stands, though I know she doesn't hear us. Her face is red with exertion, and her body is concentrated on the task. She dribbles, draws the defense to her, passes, runs. A teammate passes the ball back to her. They've beaten the press. She heads toward the hoop. Her father watches her, her sisters watch her, I watch her. And I think, drive, Ann, drive.[41]

The unspoken threat for many parents is the identification of women athletes with lesbianism. Often the charge has economic as well as personal implications for women athletes. Rita Mae Brown, in a novel, *Sudden Death,* gave a fictionalized account of her own relationship with tennis star Martina Navratilova and a general discussion of the problems faced by women on the professional tennis circuit. She writes:

> The lesbian threat cowed the women. Each player over the age of twenty knew what it was like to be regarded as a freak because she liked sports. Lesbianism insinuated itself into the consciousness of women and frightened them. It frightened the lesbians most of all. . . . They didn't want to lose their lucrative product endorsements.[42]

Elizabeth Duff points out that the stakes are high; traditionally, the unwritten contract between professional athletes and sponsors demanded in effect that they promised to be or act heterosexual in exchange for corporate sponsorship. In recent years, as a number of leading women athletes have been identified through palimony lawsuits and extensive press coverage as lesbian, the public has faced this issue and these athletes have maintained their popularity. Nonetheless, it continues to be a controversial matter; Mariah Nelson quotes one sports psychologist as saying: "I receive more questions about the potential danger to a daughter's sexuality than anything else. Parents ask, 'How can I protect my daughter from succumbing to the seduction of athletes?'"[43]

Research into Gender Roles of Athletes

A number of scholars have attempted to investigate this issue by studying the personality traits of female athletes and nonathletes. Kathleen O'Connor and James Webb, for example, examined four groups of female athletic competitors in different sports, and one group of nonathletic female students.[44] They found that the personalities of the athletes differed significantly from nonathletes on four of twelve personality traits—intelligence, radicalism, self-sufficiency, and control. Beyond this finding, the research also showed that there were distinctly different personality traits among the women in the four different sports—basketball, swimming, tennis, and gymnastics.

Another study, by Joan Duda, sought to measure the relationship between goals and actual behavior of male and female undergraduate team athletes.[45] Goal choices, between mastery or social comparison emphases, were influenced by gender; females were less oriented to social comparison-based sports than men were. In a related study, Craig Wrisberg examined the gender-role orientations of male and female coaches in basketball—a masculine-type activity.[46] While male coaches endorsed masculine traits to a greater extent than female coaches did, Wrisberg concluded that the gender endorsements of the two groups were not "appreciably different."

The evidence drawn from these studies is inconclusive, in terms of whether involvement in sport influences the degree of masculine or feminine traits of participants. To the extent that women athletes may have more masculine traits than nonathletes, the possibilities are either that participants are self-selected in that girls and women who have stereotypically "masculine" personality traits to begin with are attracted to sports; *or* that the sports experience and environment itself promotes the individual's "masculine" qualities.

■ WOMEN IN SPORTS CAREERS

In the past, those who worked in sports as athletes, coaches, officials, journalists, or commentators were largely male, just as college and professional sports were largely male. In the late 1980s, Joy Defensi and Linda Koehler pointed out that women have increasingly been finding jobs in sports, athletics, and fitness agencies as public relations, marketing, and program managers. At the same time, they stress that 97 percent of combined (male and female) college athletic programs are governed and managed by men, and that women are consistently underrepresented in high-profile management positions.[47]

As competitors, women have been successful chiefly in such sports as professional golf and tennis. There have been a few relatively unsuccessful attempts to promote professional women's basketball, softball, and other sports and, beyond that, exhibition-type contests like American Gladiator, Roller Ball, or women's wrestling and boxing that have been exploitation gimmicks, rather than legitimate contests.

However, growing numbers of women have entered the sports field as journalists and commentators. Lisa Rubarth points out that the surge of women's athletics following the passage of Title IX led to greater acceptance of women in a formerly male domain, including

> opportunities for women to gain experience covering women's sports and hopefully to move into covering men's sports. It has been easier for women to gain employment as sportswriters and sports information directors covering women's sports, but the entrance into covering men's sports has been hard-fought. And the battle is still not over.[48]

One point of conflict has involved the right of women to obtain access to locker rooms of professional teams to conduct post-game interviews as male reporters routinely do. In a widely publicized case, Lisa Olson, a sports reporter for the *Boston Herald,*

> charged five football players of the just-defeated New England Patriots with sexual harassment for making sexually suggestive and offensive remarks to her when she entered their locker room to conduct a post-game interview. The incident amounted to nothing short of "mind rape," according to Olson.[49]

Following this episode, the team and the five players were fined $25,000 each, and the National Organization of Women called for a boycott of Remington electric shavers because its president, who also owned the Patriots, had ridiculed Olson's complaint.

Male resistance to women having a bigger role in sports is illustrated also in the case of Pam Postema, who had worked for thirteen years as a minor-league baseball umpire before she was released after the 1989 season. Postema had graduated from umpire school in 1977, rated seventeenth in a class of 130, and had progressed steadily through the minors to triple-A ball in the Pacific Coast League. In her last active years, she was chief of her umpiring crew and was selected to work in All-Star Games. However, with her unwillingness to accept a job as supervisor of minor-league umpires in lieu of a promotion to the majors, she was released. In a lawsuit against the organized baseball system, Postema claimed that she had consistently been the victim of sexual harassment and discrimination. Among her charges were that:

> Players and managers "on numerous occasions" called Postema a four-letter slang word for female genitalia. Players and managers repeatedly told her that she should be cooking or cleaning instead of umpiring. One major-league pitcher . . . said that if Postema became a big-league umpire, it would be an affront to God and contrary to the Bible.[50]

Beyond such attacks, Postema was frequently spit on during arguments and had to endure more verbal abuse than male umpires had to face. Occasionally she was kissed on the lips by managers when they brought their starting line-ups to the plate. In her lawsuit, she charged that the baseball establishment knew of such sexual harassment and had encouraged it to keep her from becoming a big-league umpire.

Membership in Private Clubs

As another example of gender-based exclusion, through the years many women have been barred from membership in male-only social clubs and business and service organizations. Because such membership societies often are places where influential people in the community establish friendships and make key business decisions, the inability to be part of them represents an important area of exclusion for business and professional women. A number of cities, including New York, San Francisco, and Washington, have passed antidiscrimination laws that forbid barring individuals from membership on sexual, racial, or religious grounds, unless such clubs are clearly private.

On American university campuses, such prestigious societies as Skull and Bones, the secret enclave at Yale University, and the all-male eating clubs at Princeton have yielded under pressure and opened their doors to women. In the late 1980s, many other service groups, such as Rotary International, Moose, Elks, Lions, and Kiwanis, were compelled by Supreme Court decisions to modify their exclusionary policies. Even today, many leading golf clubs continue to bar women as members; in some cases they force them to apply for membership under their husband's name, or restrict their hours of play during the week.

As a final example of contemporary trends in leisure programming for girls and women, many voluntary organizations that had formerly conformed to the traditional stereotypes of feminine behavior and personality, now have adopted a broader and more needs-oriented programming approach. Typically, Girl Scout and Girls Club programs now deal with such elements as consumer education, career development, health problems like bulimia and anorexia, sex and teenage pregnancy, drug abuse, and other problems of youth. Similarly, the Young Women's Christian Association now offers many classes and workshops that relate to the changing role of women in the job world and family life. More and more adult education classes and support groups focus on problems of divorce and single parenting, home maintenance, investment and financial planning, assertiveness training, stress management, sexual harassment, and other needs of women in contemporary society.

■ MEN AND LEISURE

Although this chapter has focused primarily on women and leisure, any gender-related discussion must also consider the role of men in contemporary culture. Paradoxically, the effort made by women over the last thirty years to press for fuller opportunities and status has also caused men as a group to examine their own situation.

While the assumption has traditionally been that men are the stronger sex, in many respects they are more fragile. About 106 male babies are born for every female; yet throughout life they have a higher mortality rate, so that after fifty, women increasingly outnumber men. Even within the womb, embryonic males suffer from a higher rate of mortality than females. Boys are more susceptible to stress than girls at every age, and suffer more from childhood infections and a number of other serious diseases throughout their adult years.

But what of their lives in society? In recent years, a number of observers have concluded that many men are being devastated psychologically and physically by the American socioeconomic system. More and more men over the last several decades have been caught up in a disturbing spiral of self-destruction, addiction, and homelessness. Andrew Kimbrell writes:

> While suicide rates for women have been stable over the last twenty years, among men—especially white male teenagers—they have increased rapidly. Currently, male teenagers are five times more likely to take their own lives than females. . . . America's young men are also being ravaged by alcohol and drug abuse . . . at three times the rate of women of the same age group. More than two-thirds of all alcoholics are men and 50 percent more men are regular users of illicit drugs than women.[51]

Kimbrell suggests that a sense of hopelessness among America's young men is not surprising; real wages for men under twenty-five have declined over the last twenty years, 60 percent of all high school dropouts are male, and the growth of unemployment and homelessness all contribute to a sense of desperation among many men. How did all this come about? In part, it stems from fundamental changes in societal life-styles. In earlier, more primitive cultures, Lionel Tiger points out that men shared lives of physical stress and danger, felt bonded in their work experiences, and shared easy socialization in taverns and clubs.[52] However, in more recent times, many of these factors no longer exist.

Some writers suggest that the mass media present men with a confusing image of superathletes, superstuds, and superwinners in business—when their real lives are not anything like this. Kimbrell agrees that modern men are entranced by this "simulated masculinity," whereas:

> in real life most men lead powerless, subservient lives in the factory or office—frightened of losing their jobs, mortgaged to the gills, and still feeling responsibility for supporting their families. . . . The disparity between their real lives and the macho images of masculinity perpetrated by the media confuses and confounds many men.[53]

As a result, many men have begun to search for new meanings in life and new ways of defining themselves. Some have been attracted to the philosophy expressed by poet Robert Bly in his best-selling book, *Iron John*.[54] Bly's view is that true masculine authenticity began to decline during the Industrial Revolution when fathers left their sons and went to work in factories. At this time:

> The communion between father and son vanished, the traditional connection, lore passing from father to son. And with it went the masculine identity, the meaning and energy of a man's life, which should be an adventure, an allegory, a question.[55]

When boys were raised by women, according to this view, they were co-opted by a female view of masculinity and could only respond softly to the challenges of modern life. As a means of regaining their lost "maleness," at Bly's "Wild Man" encampments men are encouraged to cry, to shriek, to drum and stamp on the earth, returning symbolically to their earlier selves as cavemen and primitive warriors. Just as the women's movement encouraged women to explore their relationships with their mothers in therapy groups and other support relationships, so men are encouraged to overcome their inarticulateness about their fathers with each other. One critic argues that men must regain a sense of *husbandry,* defined as "a sense of masculine obligation—generating and maintaining stable relationships to one's immediate family and to the earth itself . . . as provider, caretaker, and steward."[56]

Mannis concludes that a rebirth of husbandry can help reawaken the male spirit from alienation and isolation, and heal the spiritual wound that many men now suffer. While not all men are familiar with these ideas, certainly a much greater number of them are looking at the business of being male in a new light. Whereas men's magazines used to present an image of maleness in macho terms of naked women, sports cars, pop culture, and conspicuous consumption, newer publications aimed at male audiences are emphasizing articles on health, psychology, relationships, and children. Increasingly, men are feeling freer to define themselves in their own terms and to admit, for example, that they are not interested in sports. Whitson comments that sports were historically considered invaluable in helping men identify with each other and develop the qualities of judgment, courage, endurance of pain, team play, and leadership that were considered critical in the achievement of manhood.[57] Today, however, these values are less important than they were, and other values—such as sensitivity, tolerance, the ability to express emotion, and even gentleness—are regarded as appropriate for men as they are for women.

At the same time, men can openly enjoy pursuits that were considered questionable for "real" males. For example, they need be less defensive about interest in art, music, theater, and dance; they can take pride in their cooking or home decorating skills, in clothing design or other pursuits that once were regarded as feminine.

Group Associations and Fraternities

Another change that has come about in the social lives and leisure pursuits of men in recent years has to do with their traditional involvement in closed groups—particularly secret societies, lodges, fraternities, and other exclusive orders and clubs. Fraternities on college campuses have long been regarded as an integral part of campus life, featuring sports, dances, drinking, and nostalgic memories of brotherhood that, once established, last through a lifetime.

Today, the fraternity system accomplishes much good. Its members often raise money for charities, work as tutors, and assist in neighborhood social programs. But, in recent years, there has been increasing evidence of the negative role played by many fraternities. Mann writes:

> What, in an earlier age, passed for selective admission standards and spirited frat-house behavior today go by different, more accurate names. At colleges large and small, frater-

nities are accused of violent and vulgar racism, sexism and anti-Semitism. The "innocent hazing" of decades ago has degenerated into poisonings, beatings, burnings and burials. Drunkenness and hedonistic excess are rampant. Gang rape is not uncommon.[58]

The incidents are reported in the nation's press by the hundreds. At Middlebury College in Vermont, the brothers of Delta Upsilon hang a mutilated female mannequin from the balcony during a two-day party; the armless, faceless mannequin drips red paint from its breasts, and a sexual slur is written across its back. Antiblack racism is blatant; on Martin Luther King's birthday, a University of Colorado fraternity distributes a poster of a black woman with the caption "Come Play with Me." At George Washington University, Delta Tau Delta circulates fliers advertising a "White History Week" party as a protest to the observance of an official "Black History Month." Says the flier: "Come Help the Delts Celebrate White History Week! Did you know George Washington was a White Man?"[59]

⟫ TO THE POINT

What does all this have to do with leisure? However such racist attitudes or practices may be viewed by psychologists or sociologists, the reality is that they are a form of fun for the fraternity brothers who share them. Dangerous forms of hazing, such as forcing pledges to drink endlessly as part of initiation (occasionally a pledge dies from choking on his own vomit), or branding pledges with the fraternity's insignia on the bare chest with a red-hot iron (as some black fraternities have done) are all part of the game.

Nowhere has this been more evident than in the way many fraternities regard sex as a form of play activity. With increased national concern about sexual harassment and abuse, one of the most disturbing revelations of the late 1980s was the publicity given to the practice of group sex in fraternity parties, where the "brothers" single out a young girl—often naive or emotionally unstable—ply her with drinks or drugs, and then isolate her in a room where they take turns having sex with her. The practice, which has been widely found in collegiate circles, and which many fraternity members have accepted as a social norm, is called "pulling train," because the men involved line up like freight boxcars, waiting to take their turn. The woman may have passed out, be incoherent, or be caked in her own vomit. She may also be resisting the assault—but it does not matter to the men.[60]

Within the inner circle of fraternity brothers, participating in such acts, enjoying sex shows with prostitutes, or engaging in other forms of sex-oriented play are often viewed as ways of proving their own heterosexuality. Within a new climate of respect for women and disapproval of many of the older standards that governed male behavior, such practices are now challenged, and on many college campuses efforts are made to help both male and female students understand their implications and develop more honest and respectful codes of sexual conduct.

FIGURE 6.1
University of Rhode Island sorority members at a campus candlelight vigil, demanding a
safer campus after a rape was reported at a fraternity party.

At the same time, there have been marked changes in the kinds of organized youth programs that are provided for both boys and girls in contemporary society. During the 1930s and 1940s, for example, it was taken for granted that the sexes would be separated in most such groups, and that boys would be permitted far greater latitude in their leisure behavior than girls. Social class lines were sharply drawn in youth organizations, and racial and religious discrimination was overt.

Today, within major youth-serving organizations, such practices or values have come under attack. The requirements that Boy Scout members must profess belief in religion, must pledge patriotic allegiance, and may not be gay, have all been challenged in recent years. Court decisions have condemned discriminatory practices, and the umbrella fund-raising organizations like United Way that help finance youth programs have barred community agencies that discriminate on the basis of race, color, creed, sex, or national origin.[61]

Apart from legal challenges to discriminatory practices, there is a distinct shift in public thinking about such issues as sexual preferences and life-styles, and sex as a form of leisure activity. In part, this shift is based on a recognition that the principle of there being two distinct gender orientations—masculine and feminine—is no longer an unquestioned verity.

Androgyny in Popular Culture

The concept of *androgyny* (drawn from the Greek *andro* "male" and *gyne* "female") represents both what June Singer refers to as an "archetype," a universal and collective image that has existed for centuries in folklore, myths, and fairy tales, and a contemporary rethinking of social beliefs that arbitrarily separate and define people by their biological identity.[62] Jay Mechling suggests that

> the tendency is to move away from the bipolar approach—that is, one that poses masculinity and femininity as extreme ends of a single dimension—toward a dualistic approach that sees masculinity and femininity as quite separate qualities of self-concept, qualities that can vary independently and appear in every individual. The dualistic approach entertains the possibility of psychological androgyny in persons whose self-concept includes both masculine and feminine desirable traits.[63]

To illustrate, a widely used test of personality, the Bem Sex-Role Inventory (BSRI) identifies a number of traits that have traditionally been regarded as masculine (e.g., "Acts as a leader," "Assertive," and "Self-reliant") and others that are thought of as feminine (e.g., "Compassionate," "Gentle," or "Sensitive to the needs of others") along with other traits that are regarded as neutral—belonging no more to one sex than to the other. Based on the BSRI system, four types of individuals may be identified: (1) *androgynous* persons, whose self-concept is above the median on both masculine and feminine traits; (2) *masculine* persons, whose self-concept is above the median on masculine but below on feminine traits; (3) *feminine* persons, who are above the median on feminine and below on masculine traits; and (4) *undifferentiated* persons, whose self-concept falls below the median on both sets of traits.[64]

Thus, androgyny may be understood as a concept that treats people simply as human beings without arbitrary expectations based on biological gender. What are its implications for the study of leisure values and behavior? Karla Henderson, Deborah Stalnaker, and Glenda Taylor conducted a study of students, staff, and faculty members at a southern university, which explored the relationship between subjects' degree of masculinity or femininity and their perceived patterns of leisure behavior. They found that:

> women with stereotypic feminine and undifferentiated personalities . . . had less interest, felt at unease in participating, were reluctant, had not enjoyed recreation activities in the past. . . .
>
> [The problem of] body image, which included lacking the self-confidence to participate, not feeling good about oneself, not being fit enough, and lacking physical skills to participate, was a significantly greater barrier for feminine and undifferentiated personalities than for the masculine and androgynous individuals.[65]

There are numerous examples of androgynous behavior or personalities within the world of popular culture. For example, a considerable number of both male and female rock stars who appear in television music video are almost indistinguishable with respect to sexual identification, in terms of their appearance, makeup, hairstyles, or costumes. The concept of androgyny may also be illustrated through examples of role reversal—what happens when members of one group move ahead aggressively to play the role that had traditionally been held by members of the other group.

An example may be found in the relatively new custom of women attending shows in which men strip. As *Time* points out, "peeling" in public for pay has long been a familiar form of entertainment, but beginning in the 1970s, in nightclubs large and small across the country and in places that certainly were not feminist strongholds, the men were doing the grinding and bumping, and the women were watching. Some see the phenomenon as a "mockery" or a "liberation" thing; one viewer explains "why he believed women enjoy watching men strip in public, [citing] the 'get back' factor—the thrill that women get from turning the tables on men by treating them as sex objects."[66]

In another example of role reversal, anthropologist William Arens described how football, as a "bastion of male supremacy," with its emphasis on muscle, power, and speed, was symbolically invaded by women—and how men responded:

> In an informal game between females in a Long Island community, the husbands responded by appearing on the sidelines in women's clothes and wigs. The message was clear. If the women were going to act like men, then the men were going to transform themselves into women. These "rituals of rebellion" involving an inversion of sex roles have often been recorded by anthropologists.[67]

The intricate nature of gender identification in leisure pursuits is illustrated in football, marked by a militant, intensely *macho* atmosphere (evidenced in part by the exaggeratedly male uniform: enlarged head and shoulders, a narrow waist, and skintight pants accented by a metal codpiece). Despite, or perhaps made possible by, this overt masculinity, men are permitted by custom to engage in frequent gestures of physical affection, hand-holding, hugging, and bottom-patting.

Still another example of role reversal may be found in the growing interest of many women in pornography. Writing in *Harpers Magazine,* one enthusiast, Sallie Tisdale, characterizes herself as a feminist. She argues that women should have the right to do what men do and—recognizing that one group of feminists opposes all pornography as a form of sexual oppression—she enjoys heterosexual, hard-core, "low-brow" porn.[68]

■ LEISURE AND ALTERNATIVE SEXUAL LIFE-STYLES

Any discussion of sex, gender, and leisure would be incomplete without a consideration of homosexuality. While there remains a powerful degree of disapproval of this form of sexual identification and behavior—particularly within conservative religious denominations—many people now accept the view that homosexuality is not an illness or a crime, but is the life-style of millions of men and women who lead responsible and creative lives within the overall society.

The term *homosexuality* is usually used to describe a close identification or attachment to members of one's own sex, which usually includes both emotional and erotic elements. It may involve a total and exclusive involvement in homosexuality as a life-style, or may exist side by side with heterosexual marriage or relationships. It may also include sexual encounters in which participants do not regard themselves *as* homosexuals, as in prisons where individuals seek the only available sexual outlets as an expedient.

Once fiercely condemned by religious and civil authorities and even punishable by execution, homosexuality has also been an accepted part of human behavior in societies throughout history—present in all cultures and condoned in many of them. For several decades, homosexuality was defined as a form of mental illness in Western society, due in part to the writings of the famous psychoanalyst, Sigmund Freud. Yet, in the mid-1930s, when it became evident that the Nazis sought to exterminate homosexuals, Freud wrote to the mother of a gay man, "Homosexuality is assuredly no advantage, but it is nothing to be ashamed of, no vice, no degradation, it cannot be classified as an illness." Despite this conclusion, many of Freud's followers condemned and ridiculed homosexuality in the decades following World War II, and sought to "cure" it, as aberrant behavior.[69]

Over the past several decades, it was believed that some men in every society—usually between 5 and 10 percent—were drawn to homoerotic pursuits. More recent research suggests that the number is closer to 1 or 2 percent, although a 1989 study by researchers affiliated with the National Academy of Sciences found that 20 percent of American men had had sex with another man at least once.[70] The percentage of homoerotic women is assumed to be smaller, although more women are believed to be bisexual than men. The causes of homosexuality are not known, although many psychologists believe that a distant or punitive father is often linked to male homosexuality. There is increasing evidence that homosexuality may be a matter of genetic heritage, rather than parenting, based on an extensive study of identical twins conducted at Northwestern University and the Boston University School of Medicine. There has also been evidence that "gayness begins in the chromosomes," with research showing that a cluster of brain cells that may guide sexual drives is twice as large in heterosexual males as in homosexual males.[71]

On the other hand, some lesbian activists argue that lesbianism is as much a feminist statement as it is a sexual one. Whatever the origin, in 1976 the American Psychiatric Association agreed that homosexuality was not necessarily related to pathology, other than in one diagnostic category: "persistent and marked distress about one's sexual orientation." Beyond that, psychiatrists tend to agree that sexual orientation is difficult to change, and that change is not intrinsically desirable.

For many years gays were forced to live "in the closet," hiding their orientation for fear of legal or economic reprisal. A major change occurred in American society at the end of the 1960s, when crowds of homosexuals rioted violently following a police raid on the Stonewall Inn, a popular gay bar in New York City. The Gay Liberation Front was formed in New York a few days later, and similar groups throughout the country began preaching "gay pride," lobbying for pro-homosexual candidates and legislation, and establishing a gay press that sprang up almost overnight, all with the same message:

It was time for homosexuals to stop hating themselves; homosexuality was not a disease, a "perversion," or an inferior form of sexuality. . . . Attempts to hide one's true sexual preferences must cease. Gay men and women who pretended that they were straight hindered the struggle for sexual self-determination, perpetuated discriminatory hiring and firing practices, and nourished the seedy underworld of homosexual bars, sexual blackmail, and police shakedowns.[72]

Since that time, homosexuals have made remarkable progress in terms of their legal standing and recognition as a political and social force. Many colleges and universities have authorized gay student organizations that publish materials and hold events freely. Homosexual faculty members are widely employed, and courses in gay studies are part of the movement toward intercultural education.

Continued Resistance to Homosexuality

On several levels, however, resistance to homosexuality continues. Among the major religions, practices vary in terms of permitting practicing male or female homosexuals to be ordained as ministers. In May 1992, the United Methodist Church reviewed the report of a three-year study on various aspects of homosexuality, which recommended that the church change its policy of condemning the practice. However, the legislative committee of the church's governing body refused to support this action.

The Catholic church, which has had numerous homosexual priests and nuns within the church through history, has struggled with this problem, not only because such individuals have violated their vows of celibacy but also because there have been a substantial number of cases of catastrophic lawsuits based on the sexual abuse of children by members of the clergy.[73] The church has continued to strongly affirm its opposition to homosexuality. In a statement sent in June 1992 to U.S. Catholic bishops, the Vatican described homosexuality as an "objective mental disorder," comparing it to mental illness, and affirmed its support for discrimination against gay people in public housing, family health benefits, and the hiring of teachers, coaches, and military personnel.[72] In the same year, considerable opposition was expressed to the use of textbooks and course materials depicting homosexual family relationships favorably, which had been introduced for use in the elementary grades in some states.

Within numerous other areas of public life, homosexuals have made progress, but continue to suffer from overt or hidden discrimination. In the military, the Pentagon ousted over a thousand homosexuals following the Persian Gulf war, including a number of celebrated men and women with outstanding records. In June 1992, a congressional study conducted by the General Accounting Office estimated the cost of replacing such individuals as over $25 million in a single year, and concluded that there was no evidence to support the Pentagon's argument that the ban on gays was necessary to ensure "good order, morale and discipline." Its report said:

Many experts believe that the military's policy is unsupported, unfair and counterproductive; has no validity according to current scientific research and opinion; and appears to be based on the same type of prejudicial suppositions that were used to discriminate against blacks and women before these policies were changed.[74]

In the fall of 1992, gay activists and civil rights supporters struggled against legislative efforts in states such as Oregon and Colorado to limit the civil rights of homosexuals. In the business world, despite laws prohibiting discrimination based on sexual factors, many gay men and women hide their sexual preferences. The clearest evidence of homophobia, the fear and hatred of those who choose to have alternative life-styles, may be found in the growing incidence of "gay bashing." Statistics indicate that deliberate, violent, and unprovoked attacks on homosexuals and lesbians have been steadily rising, as "skinheads" and other prejudiced groups carry out random assaults, often with the expectation that they will not be punished for such crimes.

Gays and Leisure

In the past, many homosexuals and lesbians typically sought out their own bars, resorts, bathhouses, and neighborhoods where they might cluster together and seek each other's company. Gradually, this clustering tendency evolved into what researcher John Lee has called the "institutional completeness" of the gay community—a homosexual second society, a social world that has sprung up in every large city and many smaller ones, involving several million men and women, hundreds of organizations, and billions of dollars' worth of business. Lee writes:

> our gay citizen can clothe himself at gay-oriented clothing stores, have his hair cut by a gay stylist, his spectacles made by a gay optician. He can buy food at a gay bakery, records at a gay phonograph shop, and arrange his travel plans through gay travel agents. . . . Naturally he can drink at gay bars and dance at gay discotheques.[75]

Beyond such services, large cities in particular are likely to offer a host of leisure pursuits specifically geared to serving homosexual individuals, including lesbian radio shows, antique stores and art galleries, motorcycle clubs, and numerous other groups, enterprises, or services. Increasingly, gay themes and characters have been sympathetically presented in television shows and motion pictures. As striking evidence of the invasion of popular culture by homosexuals, in the early 1990s, two comic book superheroes, Marvel Comics' *Northstar,* and DC Comics' *Pied Piper,* came out of the closet and revealed their homosexuality to the reader.

Brenda Pitts points out that the lesbian and gay community has over the past three decades established numerous support, informational, political, and health-oriented groups, but had relatively few leisure-linked organizations, apart from gay bars or clubs. However, she continues, in recent years homosexuals have broadened their leisure activity base by forming a host of recreation clubs, leagues, and centers that function on local, state, national, and even international levels—such as the Gay Olympic Games, which have involved several thousand participants from nineteen countries in seventeen different sports. Pitts conducted a study of over 130 organizations providing organized sports or outdoor recreation activities for primarily gay groups of participants. She found that these groups offered a total of fifty-seven different activities, including camping, bicycling, backpacking, snow skiing, volleyball, swimming, cruises, bowling, sailing, travel, running, mountaineering, and tennis. She concluded:

that the lesbian and gay populations are hard at work developing a broad sport and leisure activity service base of their own [centering] around two influencing elements. First, the failure of the existing leisure-service industry to target and satisfactorily service this population [and] second, the lesbian and gay population's . . . desire to promote strong and healthy life-styles [and] positive role models for its own population.[76]

Travel and tourism represent an important area of leisure involvement for many lesbian and gay individuals. Figure 6.2 shows the cover of a widely distributed publication that describes thousands of gay-oriented resorts, travel services, tours and events, cruises, and other tourist attractions throughout the world.

■ SEX AND LEISURE

We now turn to a final issue that links the elements of gender and leisure—the growing recognition that sex represents a form of play in contemporary society. While many of the classics of world literature and art have portrayed sexual dalliance carried on for pleasure, in the early American colonies such pursuits as adultery or sodomy were punishable as capital offenses, and routine fornication was dealt with by public whipping. However, there is evidence that the colonists had a wide range of sexual

FIGURE 6.2
Cover of a travel and tourism publication oriented to the gay and lesbian market.
SOURCE: Worldwide Gay and Lesbian Guide (1993–1994). Ferrari Publications, Phoenix, Arizona.

interests; Furnas points out that men settlers cohabited with their neighbors' wives, with Indian women, and with animals.[77] As described in Chapter 3, in eighteenth-century New England premarital pregnancy was common; nearly one-third of rural brides were already with child, and bundling (the custom that allowed couples to sleep on the same bed without undressing, and with a board separating them) was widely accepted.

During the nineteenth century in America, there were ambivalent attitudes about sex. Initially, it was accepted that within proper social confines, sexual activity was enjoyable and healthy, and that women as well as men had sex drives. However, with growing religious fervor in the nation, authorities began to preach that sexual "indulgence" produced nervous disorders, and that respectable women were above "carnal passion." While prostitution flourished, ministers and educators warned that sexual entanglements outside of marriage were dangerous to the health and well-being of young men. Toward the end of the nineteenth century, as the birthrate declined, the federal government and the states passed harsh new laws that banned

> the teaching of birth control techniques, the manufacture, sale or use of contraceptive devices, and which prohibited premarital and extramarital sex or "unnatural" sex by married couples. Within marriage or without, mouth-to-genital or anal sex became subject to criminal prosecution, under numerous harsh antisodomy measures . . . life in prison in Georgia, thirty years in Connecticut, and twenty years in [several other states] . . . As for the man or woman who turned to solitary and private masturbation, nineteenth- and early twentieth-century medical authorities [warned] them that they would get skin cancer and become imbeciles.[78]

Gradually, such strictures declined in the twentieth century. A major influence, according to D'Emilio and Freedman, was capitalism, in the sense that the ethic that promoted the purchase of consumer products and encouraged an acceptance of pleasure and self-gratification was easily transferred to the province of sex. Particularly in the middle decades of the century, as birth control methods became more widely available and parental authority declined, sex became perceived more widely as a potential business product. Barbara Ehrenreich writes:

> The consumer culture, more than anything else, undermined the old middle-class values of hard work and self denial and fostered a new ethic of determined hedonism. In addition, advertisers quickly learned to enlist sex itself to sell everything from cars to mouthwash. Along with the sexualization of commerce came an increasing commercialization of sex, best represented by the modern pornography industry. But it was mainstream, legitimate business that made sex an inescapable feature of American mass culture. Faced with a multibillion dollar adversary like this, sexual Puritanism never really had a chance.[79]

In the 1950s, the Kinsey Report demonstrated the tremendous discrepancy that had developed between the moral preachments and laws that had supposedly governed the sexual behavior of Americans and their actual practices. During the 1960s and 1970s varied forms of "aberrant" sexual behavior, such as group sex and "swinging," living together out of marriage, legalized pornography, and other nontraditional pursuits constituted a virtual revolution in sexual morality and public behavior.

Scientific studies of erotic behavior through the emerging discipline of sexology gained momentum, and sexual techniques began to be openly taught in school and college courses of human sexuality. But books and college courses were only one evidence of the American interest in sex. It became a major part of popular entertainment, advertising, and product development, and pornography, with the introduction of videocameras, made it possible to view "adult" films within the safety of one's home. Paradoxically, as sex became an increasingly prominent and visible aspect of leisure, it also began to assume the dimensions of work.

Lewis and Brissett in the late 1960s pointed out that dozens of popular marriage manuals warned the reader *not* to take the subject frivolously, but rather to see sex as something to be worked at and developed, requiring intensive study and practice, including knowledge of physiology and psychology—with overall, the dimensions of a work ethic.[80] Schur agrees, commenting that the modern imperatives of technology and specialized expertise extend into all areas of human life, including sexuality. It is ironical, he writes, that today we can only appreciate and enjoy sex through expert assistance:

> That may be a slight exaggeration, but still it is not far from the truth. The era of doing what comes naturally seems to be over. Research on sexuality no longer collects dust in remote library stacks. Its findings and teachings are widely disseminated—through television documentaries, radio and TV talk shows, mass-marketed survey reports, and sexual advice books, popular magazines and daily newspaper columns.[81]

Clearly, sexual activity—either as participant experience or as a form of spectatorship—has become a major element in contemporary leisure. In 1992, for example, the National Centers for Disease Control reported that seven of ten high school students have had sex by their senior year—with implications for three major public health epidemics: (1) the dramatic increase of pregnancy among teenagers; (2) the growth of sexually transmitted diseases, including newer ones like herpes, papilloma virus, and chlamydia; and (3) the spread of AIDS, the deadly disease that is now posing a worldwide threat. As a result of fear of this incurable infection, the nation's leading sex scholars and therapists agree that the only way of avoiding AIDS is to avoid sexual intercourse, unless it is done cautiously, within stable relationships, with protection (condoms), and without exchange of body fluids.

At a recent conference of the Society for the Scientific Study of Sex, there were reports of a trend *away* from intercourse and *toward* "outercourse," meaning a variety of possibilities for sexual pleasure that excluded coitus.

⮕ TO THE POINT

In the early 1990s, the great basketball star, Wilt Chamberlain, reported in an autobiography that he had had sexual relations with over twenty thousand women during his career. At first this was the subject of amusement and joking on talk shows and in the press, but then comments began to be heard about the risk of sexual disease and specifically AIDS, in such a life-style.

Responsible commentators raised the question of athletes serving as role models, an issue that reappeared when another widely admired basketball star, Earvin "Magic" Johnson, reported that he had HIV, presumably as a result of heterosexual intercourse (see page 236).

The danger of promiscuity and the damage done to society by having increasingly greater numbers of children born to single mothers—many of them still children themselves—underlined the need to develop a fuller sense of responsibility, more accurate knowledge, and sounder personal values among young people, with respect to sex. At one point, the federal government entered the picture with the so-called teenage chastity bill, an amendment to the Public Health Services Act that sought to discourage sexual relations among unmarried young people by urging them to exert self-discipline. However, such efforts have generally been ineffective. Richard Keeling, director of Student Health Services at the University of Virginia, reports that lessons like that of Magic Johnson do not translate into changes in their behavior. Students still think that they can get away with it. They think that they can tell who has HIV, and say that they only sleep with "nice" people. Keeling comments that the reason why so many practice unsafe sex

> has to do with the very confusing world in which we live. We sell products with sex; we use sex in movies, TV, music. Then we tell students, "Just say no." This creates a kind of chaos for them about making their own decisions about sex. . . . Many campuses now run peer education groups to let students build their skills.[82]

Sex as a Political Issue

Finally, issues related to sex and gender have become increasingly politicized in recent years. This became fully evident when the U.S. Senate hearings on the confirmation of Clarence Thomas as a Supreme Court justice were forced to confront sensational charges that he had engaged in sexual harassment practices ten years before—and when the backwash of the hearings had a political impact in the following year's elections.

In the summer of 1992, the seriousness of sexual harassment in the U.S. Navy became evident, following the so-called Tailhook incident, when twenty-six women, many of them Navy officers themselves, reported that they had been forced to run a sexual "gauntlet" of naval aviators who fondled and tore the clothes from them at a convention of Navy officers in Las Vegas, Nevada. Also in 1992, a government-financed study reported that over six hundred thousand women had been raped in a single year; other reports confirmed that there were numerous sexual assaults within the U.S. armed forces during the Persian Gulf war.[83] For the first time, during the last two presidential election campaigns, the private lives of major political figures came under scrutiny, with a number of candidates facing press inquisitions about their sexual dalliances. And, although some members of Congress were identified as homosexuals during the 1980s, their constituents continued to reelect them—an indication that this issue is not as critical a public concern as conservative religious leaders have argued.

■ SUMMARY

In this chapter we have seen that women over the past three decades have overcome many forms of discrimination, including those that limited their participation in varied forms of leisure and social activity. There has been progress in sports, outdoor recreation, and other recreational pursuits, but barriers still exist. We have examined the changing status of men in American society and explored the relationship between androgyny and homosexuality and leisure pursuits. We have studied how gender factors play a major role in influencing leisure values and behavior in the United States, and how sex and erotic forms of play have become increasingly recognized as elements of leisure activity and commercial enterprise, with close linkages to a number of leading national institutions, such as education, health, the armed forces, law enforcement, and political life.

■ QUESTIONS FOR DISCUSSION

1. Historically, women have typically had subservient roles in many areas of community or national life: family and marriage roles, education, careers, and political influence. In what ways has leisure reflected this traditional pattern of discrimination?
2. In what ways have recent studies based on gender differences shown a contrast between men and women, with respect to available discretionary time, leisure interests or relationship between masculine and feminine traits, and recreational pursuits?
3. As in the case of African Americans, women have made major advances within the world of competitive athletics over the past two decades. What values have educators attached to the importance of sports and physical recreation for women, and in what ways have they continued to be limited by discriminatory practices?
4. Just as women have been subject to stereotyping and artificial restrictions in their uses of leisure, so men have been expected to conform to an excessively macho model of masculine behavior. How has this evidenced itself in the upbringing of boys, and in the forms of sexual harassment or exploitation of women found in fraternities or other male-dominated settings? What does the recent case of the Spur Posse, a clique of popular, athletic boys in Lakewood, California, who kept score of the numerous girls they had sex with, have to say about youth attitudes today?
5. In what ways have public attitudes and prevailing policies with respect to homosexuality relaxed in recent years? In education? The military? The religious establishment? How have the perceptions of gays and lesbians changed with respect to leisure, in sports and in the entertainment media? What changes have taken place with respect to organized recreation pursuits of homosexuals?

■ NOTES

1. SCHUR, E. 1988. *The Americanization of sex.* Philadelphia: Temple University Press, pp. 10–11.

2. MONEY, J. 1970. In *Sexuality and man,* ed. M. Calderone. New York: Sex Information and Education Council of United States and Charles Scribner's Sons, p. 8.

3. DE BEAUVOIR, S. 1965. *The second sex.* New York: Bantam, p. xxii.

4. BONAPARTE, N. Cited in Fine, R. 1987. *The forgotten man: Understanding the male psyche.* New York: Haworth, p. 98.

5. FISHER, H. 1988. A primitive prescription for equality. *U.S. News and World Report* (Aug. 8): 57.

6. SCHROEDEL, J. 1985. *Alone in a crowd: Women in the trades tell their story.* Philadelphia: Temple University Press, p. 5.

7. LARKIN, J. 1988. The secret life of a developing country (ours). *American Heritage* (Sept.-Oct.): 61.

8. For a review of this period, see: HENDERSON, K., M. D. BIALESCHKI, S. SHAW, and V. FREYSINGER. 1989. *A leisure of one's own: A feminist perspective on women's leisure.* State College, PA: Venture Publishing.

9. MILLET, K. Cited in Davison, N. 1991. Feminism and sexual harassment. *Society* (May-June): 39.

10. GORMAN, C. 1992. Sizing up the sexes. *Time* (Jan. 20): 42.

11. FISHER, *op. cit.*

12. LEVANT, R. Cited in Gorman, *op. cit.,* p. 44.

13. PROSE, F. 1990. Confident at 11—confused at 16. *New York Times* (Jan. 7): 23.

14. TIGER, L. 1969. *Men in groups.* New York: Random House, Vintage, p. 43.

15. GORMAN, *op. cit.*

16. PEISS, K. 1986. *Cheap amusements: Working women and leisure in turn-of-the-century New York.* Philadelphia: Temple University Press, p. 22.

17. HENDERSON, K., and J. RANNELLS. 1988. Farm women and the meaning of work and leisure: An oral history perspective. *Leisure Sciences* 10: 46.

18. PEISS, K. 1990. Commercial leisure and the "woman question." In *For fun and profit: The transformation of leisure into consumption,* ed. R. Butsch. Philadelphia: Temple University Press, pp. 109–118.

19. DAUNCEY, H. 1953. *Planning for girls in the community recreation program.* New York: National Recreation Association, pp. 8, 16, 20.

20. LUNDBERG, G., M. KOMAROVSKY, and M. A. MCINERNEY. 1958. The amounts and uses of leisure. In *Mass leisure,* ed. E. Larrabee and R. Meyersohn. Glencoe, Ill.: Free Press, pp. 193–198.

21. SHAW, S. 1985. Gender and leisure: Inequality in the distribution of leisure time. *Journal of Leisure Research* 17, 4: 266–282.

22. SHANK, J. 1986. An exploration of leisure in the lives of dual-career women. *Journal of Leisure Research* 19, 4: 312.

23. ALLISON, M. T., and M. C. DUNCAN. 1987. Women, work and leisure: The days of our lives. *Leisure Sciences* 9: 143–162.

24. GRUBER, K. J. 1980. Sex-typing of leisure activities: A current appraisal. *Psychological Reports* 46: 259–265.

25. GENTRY, J., and M. DOERING. 1979. Sex-role orientation and leisure. *Journal of Leisure Research* 11, 2: 102–111.

26. HIRSCHMAN, E. 1984. Leisure motives and sex roles. *Journal of Leisure Research* 16, 3: 209–223.

27. SABO, D., and J. PANTOPINTO. 1990. Football ritual and the social reproduction of masculinity. In *Sport, men and the gender code: Critical feminist perspectives,* ed. M. Messner and D. Sabo. Champaign, IL: Human Kinetics Books, p. 124.

28. *Ibid.*

29. CONNOLLY, O. Cited in Bialeschki, M. D. 1990. The feminist movement and women's participation in physical recreation. *Journal of Physical Education, Recreation and Dance* (Jan.): 47.

30. *Ibid.*

31. GILBERT, B., and N. WILLIAMSON. 1973. Sport is unfair to women. *Sports Illustrated* (May 28): 85.

32. See NELSON, M. B. 1991. Review of Guttmann, A. 1991. *Women's sport: A history.* New York: Columbia University Press. In *Philadelphia Inquirer* (Oct. 27): 3–C.

33. *Ibid.*

34. *Ibid.*

35. DURRANT, S. M. 1992. Title IX—Its power and its limitations. *Journal of Physical Education, Recreation and Dance* (March): 60.

36. GRANT, C. 1989. Recapturing the vision. *Journal of Physical Education, Recreation and Dance* (March): 44.

37. CHU, D. 1989. *The character of American higher education and intercollegiate sport.* Buffalo, NY: State University of New York Press, p. 100.

38. More athletes and more money in men's programs, NCAA says. *Philadelphia Inquirer* (March 12, 1992): D–6. See also FOX, C. 1992. Title IX and athletic administration. *Journal of Physical Education, Recreation and Dance* (March): 48–52.

39. ELLYOTT, J. 1978. The weaker sex? Hah! *Time* (June 26).

40. FELSHIN, J., and C. OGLESBY. 1986. Transcending tradition: Females and males in open competition. *Journal of Physical Education, Recreation and Dance* (March): 45.

41. WHITNEY, M. 1988. Playing to win. *New York Times Magazine* (July 3): 8, 37.

42. See DUFF, E. 1991. Review of Nelson, M. B. 1991. *Are we winning yet? How women are changing sports and sports are changing women.* New York: Random House. *Philadelphia Inquirer* (May 12): 3–F.

43. *Ibid.*

44. O'CONNOR, K., and J. WEBB. 1976. Investigation of personality traits of college female athletes and non-athletes. *The Research Quarterly* 47, 2: 206–208.

45. DUDA, J. 1988. The relationship between goal perspectives, persistence and behavioral intensity among male and female recreational sports participants. *Leisure Sciences* 10: 95–106.

46. WRISBERG, C. 1990. Gender-role orientations of male and female coaches of a masculine-typed sport. *Research Quarterly for Exercise and Sport* 61, 3: 296.

47. DEFENSI, J., and L. KOEHLER. 1989. Sport and fitness management: Opportunities for women. *Journal of Physical Education, Recreation and Dance* (March): 55–56.

48. RUBARTH, L. 1992. Twenty years after Title IX: Women in sports media. *Journal of Physical Education, Recreation and Dance* (March): 53–55.

49. PAUL, E. 1991. Bared buttocks and federal cases: Sexual harassment or harassment of sexuality? *Society* (May-June): 4.

50. Female ex-umpire files sex-discrimination suit. *Philadelphia Inquirer* (Dec. 20, 1991): 1–A.

51. KIMBRELL, A. 1991. A time for men to pull together. *Utne Reader* (May-June): 66.

52. TIGER, *op. cit.,* p. 112.

53. KIMBRELL, *op. cit.*

54. MORROW, L. 1991. The child is father of the man. *Time* (Aug. 19): 52–54.

55. *Ibid.*

56. MANNIS, R. In Kimbrell, *op. cit.,* pp. 70–71.

57. WHITSON, D. 1990. Sport in the social construct of masculinity. In Messner and Sabo, *op. cit.,* p. 21.

58. MANN, F. 1988. Fratricide. *Philadelphia Inquirer Magazine* (Sept. 18): 1.

59. ECENBARGER, W. 1988. The rise and fall of the Greek empire. *Philadelphia Inquirer Magazine* (Sept. 18): 24.

60. SANDAY, P. 1991. *Fraternity gang rape: Sex, brotherhood and privilege.* New York: New York University Press.

61. HINDS, M. 1991. In tests of who can join, Scouts confront identity. *Philadelphia Inquirer* (June 23): 1, 20.

62. SINGER, J. 1976. *Androgyny: Toward a new theory of sexuality.* New York: Anchor, p. 20.

63. MECHLING, J. 1985. The manliness paradox in Seton's ideology. In Fine, G. A. *Meaningful play, playful meaning.* Champaign, IL: Human Kinetics Press, p. 47.

64. *Ibid.,* pp. 47–48.

65. HENDERSON, K., D. STALNAKER, and G. TAYLOR. 1988. The relationship between barriers to recreation and gender-role personality traits for women. *Journal of Leisure Research* 20, 1: 77.

66. GILLIN, B. 1983. Ogling the male stripper as he dances in all his glory. *Time* (Nov. 27): 12–R.

67. ARENS, W. 1974. An anthropologist looks at the rituals of football. *New York Times* (Nov. 16): 16.

68. TISDALE, S. 1992. Talk dirty to me: A woman's taste for pornography. *Harpers Magazine* (Feb.): 37–47.

69. GREENBERG, D. 1988. *The construction of homosexuality*. Chicago: University of Chicago Press. See also LEWES, K. 1990. *The psychoanalytic theory of male homosexuality*. New York: Simon and Schuster.

70. EHRENREICH, B. 1993. Essay: The Gap between gay and straight. *Time* (May 10):76.

71. Born or bred? *Newsweek* (Feb. 24, 1992): 46.

72. HARRIS, M. 1981. *America now: The anthropology of a changing culture*. New York: Touchstone, Simon and Schuster, pp. 98–99.

73. KENNEDY, E. 1990. Homosexual priests and nuns: Two assessments. *Commonweal* (Jan. 26): 56. See also: Vatican supports gay bias. *Philadelphia Inquirer* (July 18, 1992): A–3.

74. GIBBS, N. 1991. Defense: Marching out of the closet. *Time* (Aug. 19): 14.

75. LEE, J., cited in Harris, *op. cit.,* p. 101.

76. PITTS, B. 1988–1989. Beyond the bars: The development of leisure activity management in the lesbian and gay population in America. *Leisure Information Quarterly* 15, 3.

77. FURNAS, J. C. 1969. *The Americans: A social history of the United States, 1587–1914*. New York: G. P. Putnam's Sons.

78. HARRIS, *op. cit.,* pp. 84–85.

79. EHRENREICH, B. 1988. Review of D'Emilio, J., and E. Freedman. 1988. *A history of sexuality in America*. New York: Harper and Row. In *Philadelphia Inquirer* (April 24): 1.

80. LEWIS, L. S., and D. BRISSETT. 1968. Sex as work: A study of avocational counseling. *Medical Aspects of Human Sexuality* (Oct.): 14–25.

81. SCHUR, *op. cit.,* p. 48.

82. Teen-age sex, after Magic. *U.S. News and World Report* (Dec. 16, 1991): 90.

83. Study says 12 million women in nation have been raped. *Richmond, Va. Times-Dispatch* (April 24, 1992): A–3. See also FRAMM, A. 1992. Sexual assaults cited in Gulf. *Philadelphia Inquirer* (July 18): A–3.

7 Leisure, Life-Style, and Social Class

All communities divide themselves into the few and the many. The first are the rich and well-born, the other the mass of the people. . . . The people are turbulent and changing; they seldom judge or determine right. . . . Give, therefore, to the first class a distinct, permanent share in the government. They will check the unsteadiness of the second and, as they cannot receive any advantage by a change, they therefore will ever maintain good government.

ALEXANDER HAMILTON[1]

We turn now to a third major group of influences on leisure, which have to do with social class and social status, and with the different life-style patterns that are influenced by these factors. We will review the place of social class in the early American colonies and through the nineteenth century. This chapter summarizes the findings of sociological studies of the early twentieth century with respect to leisure patterns and behavior, and shows how the emphasis shifted from social class to life-style and status analysis, within an increasingly meritocratic nation. Three socioeconomic groups—the wealthy, the middle class, and the poor—are examined with respect to their present-day leisure involvements. The chapter concludes with a discussion of social policy designed to provide subsidized recreation programs for the disadvantaged.

■ PAST PERSPECTIVES ON LEISURE AND SOCIAL CLASS

As earlier chapters showed, Thorstein Veblen was the first to show how the rich and wealthy in society were traditionally known as the leisure class—in ancient Greece, in feudal Europe, and on through the Industrial Age. *Lord* and *serf, patrician* and *plebian,* and in Marxist terminology, *bourgeoisie* and *proletariat*—such terms defined a unique separation between groups of people that reflected itself in their play.

Certainly, rigid class stratification that evidenced itself in leisure was a powerful force in England during the eighteenth and nineteenth centuries. There, the rising class of successful professionals and businessmen sought to control the free time of the working classes—in part by restricting their use of what formerly had been public properties for outdoor play, and by promoting varied forms of "rational recreation" to improve public morality and channel the play impulse into socially desirable pursuits.

Meanwhile, what of life in the emerging American society? While the early colonists were moved by ideals of democracy and equality, there were marked distinctions between the upper and lower classes. For example, in the expedition that founded Jamestown, Virginia, in 1607, there were many whose names were tagged with *Gent.,* defined in these terms: "Whosoever . . . can live without manual labour, and . . . will bear the port, charge and countenance of a gentleman, he shall be called 'master' . . . and be reported a gentleman ever after."[2]

In early New England, the magistrate was known as Master So-and-So, and his wife was addressed as Madam, where the blacksmith was Goodman Such-and-Such and his wife Goodwife or Goody. Furnas points out that the law courts in Massachusetts Bay enforced class distinctions:

> Convicted of theft, a gentleman was merely fined and deprived of the title Master; his servants, convicted as accessories, were heavily flogged. . . . Nor was a gentleman as likely as a man of the lower orders to be summoned to court if a girl laid her child to him. . . . [3]

Assignment of pews in the meetinghouse or church went by social standing, based on wealth and family status. Having descended from laborers or craftsmen meant that one might not serve as justice of the peace; in York County, Virginia, a tailor was fined for matching his horse against another, "it being contrary to law for a Labourer to make a race, being a sport for gentlemen." Until the late 1700s, the traditional signs of deference before social superiors, such as

> . . . the deep bow, the "courtesy," the doffed cap, lowered head, and averted eyes—had been a part of social relationships in Colonial America. In the 1780s . . . there were still individuals in . . . every grade of society who had grown up when a bow was not an offense to fashion nor . . . a relic of monarchy.[4]

As men and women born on American soil and imbued with democratic ideals traveled westward, transforming frontier outposts into thriving communities, people took pride in being equal. Shaking hands became the accustomed American greeting between men—a gesture that symbolized equality. Yet even within the new environment, both mercantile and planter elites mimicked their English counterparts in practicing a culture of manners that set them above the lower classes. Butsch points out that in the theaters that were built in eastern cities, while they housed all classes under one roof: "the seating reflected the class hierarchy of the community, with elites in boxes, mechanics on benches in the pit (now the orchestra), servants and laborers in the gallery."[5]

As the Industrial Revolution gained momentum through the latter half of the nineteenth century and the beginning of the twentieth, Americans became increasingly aware of social class stratification. While they never approached the degree of class antagonism and militancy found in Europe, there were frequent conflicts—some of them sustained and bloody—between workers and their bosses. Generally, however, Americans accepted the reality of class differences in the society at large. Certainly, in the nation as a whole, with its emphasis on democracy and constitutional process, values reflected the beliefs and life-styles of the rising entrepreneurial class, rather than those of a hereditary aristocracy.

■ SOCIOLOGICAL ANALYSIS OF SOCIAL CLASS

At the end of the nineteenth century and the beginning of the twentieth, sociologists began to take a systematic look at the class structure of American society. The term *class*, as it came to be used, referred to the stratification of a population into status levels based on such factors as family background, occupation, income, and education. An influential sociologist, W. Lloyd Warner, wrote:

> By class is meant two or more orders of people who are believed to be, and are, accordingly ranked by the members of the community, in socially superior and inferior positions. . . . A class society distributes rights and privileges, duties and obligations, unequally among the inferior and superior grades. A system of classes, unlike a system of castes, provides by its own values for movement up and down the social ladder . . . in technical terms, social mobility.[6]

As empirical sociology based on scientific observation and measurement developed, researchers identified variables that could be used to assign individuals or families to predetermined class ranks. Warner, for example, identified six classes in a 1941 study of *Yankee City*, a small New England community:

- *Upper-Upper:* long-term wealthy, old family elite (1.4 percent of total Yankee City population)
- *Lower-Upper:* slightly richer than upper-upper, but with family lineage and money less established (1.6 percent)
- *Upper-Middle:* moderately successful business and professional men and their families, with lineage not important (10.2 percent)
- *Lower-Middle:* small businessmen, schoolteachers, factory foremen; solid church-goers, lodge joiners, good citizens (28.1 percent)
- *Upper-Lower:* respectable laboring people (32.6 percent)
- *Lower-Lower:* "unrespectable" people, often unemployed, in trouble, or on relief (25.2 percent).[7]

While many researchers adopted this system of class ranking, others preferred systems with four or five grades, or methods of ranking, that identified people by employment status, such as "managers, supervisors, workers," or "white collar," "blue collar," and "pink collar" (meaning typical women's occupations).

■ SYSTEMATIC STUDIES OF LEISURE

Beginning in the late 1920s and 1930s, a number of sociological studies examined leisure in its relation to social class or occupational status. The Lynds' analyses of Middletown, for example, depicted the middle-class values that dominated a small midwestern city. Typically, businessmen in Middletown had little interest in culture or the arts. They cared about "getting ahead," and were happy to have their wives undertake social, cultural, or other responsibilities. For workingmen, the tangible realities of automobiles, radios, and other tools for enjoying leisure served as rewards for conscientious work.[8]

A 1934 study of several population groups in Westchester County, New York, found that while they all took part in the same general categories of leisure activity, they varied greatly in the amounts of time they devoted to them and the specific ways in which they pursued the activities. For example, professional and executive men spent much more time than working-class men in activities such as sports, motoring, or club activities, while the latter group engaged more often in radio listening, entertainment, and visiting with family or friends.[9]

Hollingshead's study of *Elmtown's Youth* stressed the importance of social class in the leisure affiliations of young people (see page 49). A later study that specifically analyzed class differences in the uses of leisure was reported by R. Clyde White in 1955. Examining several hundred families in four socioeconomic groups in Cuyahoga County, Ohio, White found that the lower classes used such public leisure facilities as parks and playgrounds, community-chest agencies, and commercial amusements more often than upper-level groups, while the latter made fuller use of libraries and other cultural resources. He noted that there were clear distinctions between lower- and upper-class uses of such leisure facilities as radios, phonographs, television, movies, and taverns. These distinctions grew sharper with age:

... the tendency to choose leisure activities on the grounds of membership in a particular social class begins in adolescence and becomes more pronounced in maturity. ... As people get older and settle into the class to which they belong, they choose leisure activities which are congenial to their class.[10]

Another major study of leisure patterns was reported in 1956 by Alfred C. Clarke, who focused on the role of leisure as part of the life-styles of urban adult males.[11] Identifying five levels along a continuum of occupational prestige, he found that men on the highest prestige level were most frequently involved in cultural pursuits like attending concerts or visiting art galleries, playing bridge, reading for pleasure, or engaging in community-service pursuits. Men on the lowest prestige level were the most frequent participants in activities such as television-watching, going to the zoo or baseball games, spending time in taverns, fishing, driving their cars for pleasure, or playing poker.

■ SHIFT FROM CLASS TO STATUS

Gradually, the emphasis on social class as a focus of community studies was replaced by a new emphasis on status and life-style differences. Reissman pointed out that dependence on rigid class labels was anachronistic in a society that had for so long formally subscribed to a belief in social equality. Instead, the idea of status, he wrote, could be

> translated into American symbols: into personal achievement, into social position in the community, and into a style of life. ... "Status" stays within the grasp of individual control, where "class" is far outside, controlled only by super-individual forces in the social universe.[12]

Other sociologists agreed. Baltzell, for example, wrote that the desire for equality, for being "like everybody else," accounted for the overwhelming majority of Americans responding to Gallup polls in the late 1930s by stating that they were members of the middle class. Only 12 percent indicated that they were either "upper" or "lower" class. In effect, Baltzell wrote, this was like saying that no classes existed.[13] In the post–World War II years, a period marked by national prosperity and optimism, it was widely accepted that America was moving toward a truly egalitarian society. Vance Packard wrote:

> Some months ago, a national periodical proclaimed the fact that the United States had recently achieved the "most truly classless society in history." A few weeks later, a publisher hailed the disappearance of the class system as "the biggest news of our era." Still later, the director of a market-research organization announced his discovery that America was becoming "one vast middle class." ... Whatever else we are, we are certainly the world's most self-proclaimed equalitarian people.[14]

This rank-and-file folklore belief in equality coincided with the economic boom that had made it possible for most Americans to live at a level of comfort not known before. The trend was soon reflected in the study of leisure in society. Max Kaplan suggested that the label of "class" had become increasingly dubious, and that inexpensive travel, the mass media, and general prosperity had brought varied forms of play within the psychological and social reach of almost everyone.[15] Kaplan concluded that in no area of American life more than leisure had the idea of social class become an outmoded concept. Similarly, Nels Anderson commented that class lines had become less strictly drawn in leisure:

> . . . all classes attend the same ball games, the same prize fights, the same night clubs, even the same opera. All listen to the radio and view the same television programs. All attend dances or go to the horse races. The difference is in the money outlay; how much is spent for the fishing outfit, the automobile, the television set, the seat at the opera or the table at the night club.[16]

Life-Style as a Determinant of Status

However, it was difficult to accept the conclusion that social class had disappeared entirely in American life. Instead, it revealed itself in a different form—through the varied life-styles that were directly attached to one's level of status, and through economic capability, which influenced all forms of recreational participation. Writing in *America as a Civilization,* Max Lerner suggested that the "insulation" of the classes was carried on through life in terms of etiquette, reading tastes, courtship and sex habits, marriage and divorce, clubs, lodges, and even churches. In every phase of social life, the badges of belonging separated one class from another:

> To go to the right schools, to attend the right dances and parties, to belong to the right churches, to be accepted in the right social and country clubs, to be a "potentate" in a lodge, to drive the right make and model of car, to wear the right clothes and have the right manners, to have your daughter . . . "introduced" to "society" and presented at the cotillion, to have your son spend his military service in the officer corps and not as a lowly private: these become for their appropriate class members matters not of choice or opportunity but a social necessity.[17]

Similarly, Russell Lynes, in *The Tastemakers,* argued that Americans had surrounded themselves with a variety of status symbols that enabled one to climb up the ladder of social success:

> If we aspire to rise in the world but fail to take on the coloration of the group we aspire to—by failing to discard our old status symbols, friends, club memberships, values, behavior patterns, and acquiring new ones esteemed by the higher group—our chances of success are diminished.[18]

Lynes suggested a system of horizontal social strata marked by life-style values, tastes, and choices that he categorized as "highbrow," "middlebrow" and "lowbrow." To a degree, these coincided with such traditional elements as wealth, education, and occupation, but went beyond them in defining patterns of taste and life-styles that were characteristic on each level.

A number of investigators in the 1950s and 1960s sought to link leisure with life-style by measuring such factors as the degree of autonomy, creativity, vitality, prestige, and gregariousness of subjects and correlating them with their roles as parents and spouses, workers, and participants in community affairs. Based on such research, a number of life-style categories, such as *community-centered* or *home-centered* styles, were identified. A widely read study was David Riesman's *The Lonely Crowd,* which analyzed play and sociability in American society and suggested that there were fundamental *inner-directed* and *outer-directed* personality types that were vividly illustrated in leisure values and behaviors.[19]

In a recent analysis of life-style and leisure in contemporary society, A. J. Veal writes that within current sociological thinking, the concept of status

> links leisure, via life-style, to the wider social order. . . . What then is life-style and how might it be studied? [One definition is] 'the system of values, customs, and habits distinctive to a group.' As such it is indistinguishable from the concept of 'culture.' Indeed the term of 'way of life' is often used interchangeably with both.[20]

Veal summarizes several recent studies of life-style in relation to leisure, pointing out that such research must examine more than the clusters of activity that people engage in, and must embody the broader needs and motivations of groups of subjects. For example, he describes the Vals Typology (VALS standing for Values, Attitudes of Life Styles), a classification system identifying four major types of life-style groups: *Need-driven, Outer-directed, Inner-directed,* and *Combined Inner- and Outer-directed groups.* Within each such overall type, there were distinctive subgroupings, such as "belonger," "emulator," "experimental" or "achiever" styles.

In American society today, a number of life-style contrasts are frequently referred to, including those based on levels of aesthetic taste, political and social beliefs, degree of conformity or individualism, and need for sensation and risk-taking in leisure experiences. However, thus far no single set of empirically measurable variables has been developed that satisfactorily establishes clearly recognizable life-style groups in relation to leisure. The most influential factors continue to be linked to social status and to economic capability.

Meritocracy and the "Power" Elite

Today, members of the socially elite continue to wield power in America's business world and in community life. They gain status by attending the right schools and colleges, belonging to the right clubs, serving on the same boards, and being part of a self-conscious "power" elite in the society. However, this status level is much more open to those who prove their worth through "meritocracy"—the demonstration of personal ability and business, professional, or political accomplishment.

At the same time, there continues to be a self-conscious, exclusive upper-class society that identifies itself with yachts, condominiums in exclusive resorts, polo playing, fox hunting, and zealously guarded memberships in established country clubs.[21] While wealth is necessary to belong to this group, it is not enough by itself. True upper-class status is derived from "old" money and the accomplishment of one's ancestors—as described in the Social Register—along with colleges, clubs, and yacht size. Members of this group busy themselves with raising funds for charities that benefit the arts, medicine, or other social causes through events that have largely replaced the extravagant balls of earlier generations. At the same time, although inherited social status no longer has the unquestioned prestige it once had, successful men and women in the present generation desperately yearn for class. And one way of achieving it, along with the traditional arbiters of money, education, and inherited standing, is through one's leisure life-style.

■ ECONOMIC INFLUENCE ON LEISURE BEHAVIOR

Of all the factors that underlie both social status and life-style identification today, probably the most influential is money. With a price tag placed on all but the most basic free-time experiences, it is impossible to develop a distinctive leisure life-style without considering the effect of money on one's choices.

Today, the popular press and financial periodicals tend to classify people in terms of their annual incomes—usually in three broad groups: the *wealthy*, generally considered to be those with incomes of $80,000 or more a year; the *middle-income*, with incomes of $15,000 or $20,000 a year to approximately $75,000; and the *low-income* or *poor*, with less than $15,000 a year. Obviously, these parameters vary in terms of region and residence, the size of one's family, and the availability of supplementary income or support. Consistently too, the margins of each category continue to rise, based on inflationary trends in the economy.

Leisure and the Wealthy

Who are the rich in American society today? They include a broad spectrum of individuals and families, some with inherited wealth and others with recently amassed possessions. In the early 1990s, it was reported that about 5 percent of the population make more than $100,000 a year; about 1 percent make more than $200,000. Being a millionaire is no longer a rarity; *Fortune* reported that there were fifty-eight American billionaires, at least a thousand worth $100 million, and several tens of thousands who have accumulated at least $10 million.[22]

How does being wealthy affect one's leisure life-style? In the past, it would have meant that one had much *more* free time than others. However, numerous studies have shown that the most successful executives and professionals in American society work long hours, take work home, travel extensively on business, and also assume other nonpaid civic responsibilities. Although they have less discretionary time than those in lower income brackets, the rich tend to use their leisure in more intensive and purposeful forms of play. Often they are highly organized and scheduled, in terms of play, vacations, and entertainment, in contrast to the workingman's pattern of spending relaxed hours at the television set or drinking beer on the porch or at the corner bar.

⫸ TO THE POINT

In terms of settings for leisure, throughout the 1980s and early 1990s, corporate magnates, investment bankers and lawyers, computer and service-industry entrepreneurs have been buying luxury homes that run into the high millions.

Such mega-homes are likely to include exercise centers, complex sound systems or film-viewing rooms, elaborate lighting systems, swimming pools, spas, and other impressive leisure-related features. Unlike the homes of the rich in the past, they tend to be built in developments, often shoehorned into small lots— an example being the Sanctuary, a development of houses costing as much as four or five million dollars, built along a canal near Boca Raton, Florida, on half-acre lots. Such expensive developments are often linked to golf courses, marinas, and other recreational facilities. For example, in the village of Oak Brook, Illinois, a privately developed enclave built in the 1960s included a huge sports center, forest preserve, shopping center, industrial park, and

> a polo club and 12 polo fields, soccer fields, a private air strip that is the home of a glider soaring club, a golf course, a riding academy and riding trails with stables for 300 horses, skeet shooting . . . and, inside the village limits another private golf club, a public course and a lake for canoeing, sailing and skating.[23]

At a less expensive level, many housing developments, including rental apartments, condominiums, and private homes, today offer swimming pools, tennis courts, fitness centers, clubrooms, and similar facilities designed to serve residents and their families. At a more exclusive level, the very rich may own vacation homes in regions like the Platte River Valley in Wyoming, where movie stars and producers rub shoulders with aviation tycoons, ex-presidents, and top corporate executives. Armed guards staff the gate house at the Old Baldy Club to ensure the privacy of its wealthy members as they play golf, fish for trout, and engage in other leisure pursuits.[24]

Closer to home for the rich at all levels are country clubs that cover a broad range of exclusivity and expensiveness. Initially, private clubs that offered golf, tennis, and social companionship for members of America's social elite were developed during the latter decades of the nineteenth century, to provide settings for leisure that were more accessible than the lavish vacation communities of Saratoga Springs, Newport, and Bar Harbor.[25] By 1929, there were fully 4,500 clubs in the United States; the number declined during the Depression and World War II, but revived again in the post-war years. Most country clubs maintained discriminatory membership policies that excluded blacks, Jews, and often members of other, less-favored white ethnic groups. In more recent years, many clubs have been established to serve ethnic and racial-minority members and many other clubs have relaxed their exclusionary policies.

While the wealthy obviously enjoy many of the same leisure interests as the rest of the population, certain activities are clearly recognized as upper-class. These include such pursuits as riding to hounds and English-style equestrian events like horse shows or polo; sailing and deep-sea fishing; and sports such as squash and croquet. As suggested earlier, the wealthy tend to be important patrons of the arts, attending and supporting opera, ballet, symphony concerts, and art exhibits, both as a form of social obligation and as a class-linked pastime.

Withdrawal of the Wealthy

Economist Robert Reich suggests that many successful professionals now belong to a class that he describes as "symbolic analysts." They are people whose jobs consist of analyzing and manipulating symbols—words, numbers, or visual images. Among the most prominent of these, Reich writes, are

> management consultants, lawyers, software and design engineers, research scientists, corporate executives, financial advisers, strategic planners, advertising executives, television and movie producers, and other workers whose titles include terms like *strategy, planning, consultant, policy, resources,* and *engineer.* 26

Increasingly, such individuals no longer live in traditional cities, towns, or suburbs. Instead, they have congregated in suburbs and exurbs where corporate headquarters have been relocated and research parks have been established. Such new residential and business centers often include post-modern office buildings with sophisticated equipment linking them to the rest of the world, hotels with glass-enclosed atriums, upscale shopping plazas, and galleries, theaters, and luxury condominiums. More and more, those who live and work in such environments, according to Reich, are withdrawing their support and psychological linkage from the communities and people around them. A process of privatization has taken place, he writes, with the wealthy dedicating their dollars and energy to their own private environments and services.

> As public parks and playgrounds deteriorate, there is a proliferation of private health clubs, golf clubs, tennis clubs, skating clubs, and every other type of recreational association in which costs are shared among members. Condominiums and the omnipresent residential communities dun their members to undertake work that financially strapped local governments can no longer afford to do well—maintaining roads, mending sidewalks, pruning trees, repairing street lights, cleaning swimming pools, paying for lifeguards and, notably, hiring security guards to protect life and property. 27

Reich makes the case that today's highest earners now inhabit a different land from the rest of America. Linked by jet, modem, fax, satellite, and fiber-optic cable to other commercial and recreational centers of the world, they are less connected with the cities or regions around them. Studies of the charitable contributions of the wealthy show that their giving no longer flows mainly to health, educational, and recreational programs serving the public or the poor, but rather to the places and institutions that serve the rich, including cultural institutions, private hospitals, and elite universities.

■ LEISURE AND MIDDLE-INCOME AMERICANS

We turn now to the lives of those in the middle range of income in American society, consisting of a broad range of blue-collar and white-collar employees, civil service workers, moderately successful professionals, and small business owners.

During much of the 1980s the middle class shrank in numbers, as a result of the disappearance of well-paid jobs in the "smokestack" industries and their replacement by poorly paid service jobs as aides, guards, or fast-food workers. Most new jobs during this period paid less than $7,000 a year, according to the Joint Economic Committee of Congress.[28] Thus, the number of households with annual incomes within a middle-income range declined by 13 percent in a five-year period in the late 1970s and early 1980s. Of those who left the middle class, three-fourths suffered a decline in their standard of living, and one-quarter rose. In middle-class families that *had* gained in income, the most common cause was the entry of wives into the workplace to provide a second family income. By 1990, it was apparent that the gap between the rich and the middle class had grown markedly.

In 1990, *Fortune* provided a series of profiles of middle-class Americans who were representative of varied occupations, family status, and age distribution, with incomes at or near the local medians. The profiles show that the aspirations of these families remain the conventional ones:

> a steady job, a home of one's own, a good education for the kids, a secure retirement, and the pursuit of happiness. But their lives also personify what's different. . . . these Americans are marrying later, having fewer children, retiring earlier, and living longer than did their cohorts of a generation ago.[29]

The *Fortune* sample of middle-income Americans showed the kinds of typical leisure pursuits that represent family interests and moderate-level expenditures: the full range of sports, games, and hobbies, including golfing, car repair and restoration, cruises for single individuals, family camping and travel to theme parks, and similar involvements.

A key factor in describing the leisure of the middle class is that they tend to live chiefly in the suburban communities that surround the central cities and in smaller towns. Their leisure often makes heavy use of public recreation and park facilities like swimming pools, golf courses and tennis courts, arts centers, senior centers, and other programs that may charge fees, but do so at a moderate, self-sustaining level. Major companies like IBM, Johnson and Johnson, and the Xerox Corporation frequently operate recreation programs for their employees and their families. Many members of the middle class belong to moderate-cost country clubs, hunting and fishing clubs, or service organizations, fraternal groups, or churches that sponsor family and youth activities.

Travel and tourism is a major leisure preoccupation of America's middle class. While they may not fly expensive Concordes to Paris, they frequently take inexpensive charter flights or guided tours. Visiting national parks and other popular tourist destinations continues to be a favorite family vacation pastime. Certainly it is the middle class that is the primary target of America's vast entertainment industry, that goes to Las Vegas or Atlantic City to gamble, and that shares hobbies like collecting and trading cards, stamps, or coins. Primarily, those in middle-income brackets attend health and fitness clubs, provide volunteer leadership for Boy Scouts and Girl Scouts and Little League and, in general, pursue a life-style suggestive of Norman Rockwell's paintings of everyday Americans.

■ LEISURE AND LOW-INCOME AMERICANS

Meanwhile, what of low-income Americans? This population extends from those who have regular jobs, are self-supporting, and are close to the border of middle-class Americans, to those who are truly destitute and are described as "poor" or "underclass." In the late 1980s, the U.S. Census Bureau, by including benefits from Medicare and Medicaid, rent subsidies, and food stamps, lowered its estimate of the number of impoverished Americans from 32.4 million to 27.6 million. It also concluded that nearly two-thirds of the nation's minorities are either marginally poor or distinctly in the underclass. Seven million white children and four million black children under the age of fifteen live below the poverty line.

The conventional thinking is that the underclass consists of a core of poor inner-city blacks and Hispanics who are trapped in an unending cycle of joblessness, broken homes, welfare, and, often, drugs. For example, a twenty-year follow-up to the 1968 Kerner Commission report concluded that: "unemployment, poverty, social disorganization, segregation, family disintegration, housing and school deterioration and crime are worse now [than in 1968].[30]

However, some authorities disagree, pointing out that on a number of measures of social progress, inner-city minority group populations have begun to overcome past pathologies. For example, sociologist Christopher Jencks of Northwestern University's Center for Urban Affairs and Policy Research points to statistics showing that the murder rate, the illegitimate birthrate, and the percentage of families on welfare among African Americans all declined significantly during the 1980s.[31]

What of the leisure of lower-income groups? For blue-collar workers in general, a study published by the American Heart Association in 1986 indicated that this population is distinctively different from white-collar workers in terms of life-style factors that have a negative impact on their health. A spokesperson for the Association points out:

> White-collar workers can socialize on the job, and so they're much more comfortable with solitary exercise in their time off, such as running, or even playing tennis. . . . But blue-collar workers want to get together after work. And that usually means group games—the classic ones are bowling and softball—which involve a lot of sitting around, drinking and smoking.[32]

⮕ TO THE POINT

Economic constraints obviously prevent the poor or near-poor from engaging in many of the pursuits enjoyed by those with higher income—entertainment, travel, hobbies, or club memberships. Beyond this, their life-styles tend to involve street-corner groups for both youth and adults, and often rely heavily on the corner bar for sociability and on television for entertainment. Children and youth are largely dependent on voluntary agency programs and on public playgrounds, parks, swimming pools, and ballfields for their organized, socially "desirable" forms of play.

Over the past two decades, as economic pressures have forced many communities to cut back on their social services, urban recreation and park departments have frequently had their budgets slashed and staffs reduced. As a consequence, often buildings and fields are poorly maintained, subject to vandalism and deterioration and to the harassment of fighting gangs, drug dealers, and addicts. Thus, city residents with the greatest need for inexpensive, constructive leisure opportunities often receive the poorest services. Within the overall low-income segment of the population, however, there is a sharp contrast. In many neighborhoods populated by lower middle-class or working-class families, there tends to be considerable support for public recreation and park operations. Parents take pride in local recreation centers, raise funds for them, and provide volunteer leadership or assistance in maintaining facilities and conducting youth sports leagues or other programs.

In poorer and more deteriorated neighborhoods and particularly those populated by disadvantaged racial or ethnic minority groups, programs are often far more limited. There is less of a tradition of volunteerism; facilities are frequently vandalized and recreation staff members terrorized. One solution would be for nonprofit organizations to take up the slack. However, in many cases, such organizations, including religious institutions, moved from central cities to outlying or suburban neighborhoods during the post–World War II decades. Those remaining in impacted inner-city neighborhoods, as in the case of many YMCAs and YWCAs, often are unable to charge registration and membership fees as their wealthier suburban counterparts can, and thus are dependent on government subsidies, grants, or other forms of financial assistance.

The question arises—*should* the government, or society at large, bear a serious responsibility for subsidizing free-time pursuits of the poor? In the past, when recreation was regarded as a reward for having worked well and "idleness" itself was viewed as a social evil, there would have been little support for such a policy. However, any moralistic opposition to providing enriched leisure opportunity for the disadvantaged groups should consider who the poor really are. Miriam Lahey, for example, identifies three special populations that are largely neglected in current social policy: "children living in poverty, the working poor (alarming numbers of whom are without homes and/or medical insurance), and the frail elderly living in the community."[33]

As a therapeutic recreation specialist, Lahey argues that recreation is one of the critical services needed to serve such groups. For example, it could play a key role in identifying and working with at-risk youth or those who live in dysfunctional or abusive home environments, helping them become aware of the broader social environment and develop positive social values and group associations. Robin Kunstler agrees, pointing out that recreation programs carried on in shelters for the children of homeless families help to provide a normalizing experience for youngsters who are separated from the normal, stabilizing influences of school, friends, and play.[34]

In poor inner-city neighborhoods, recreation facilities are often barren, and residents develop their own leisure outlets. Here, in a north Philadelphia neighborhood, a mural on the wall of a local building depicts scenes of everyday life. A small recreation center has been vandalized and gutted; however, the minister of a nearby church is able to attract crowds of children and youth—mostly African-American and Hispanic—to outdoor recreational events. Youngsters meet before a wall where the names of dozens of gang members are painted. The message on the wall says "In memory of Chicano"—a youth killed in a recent gang fight.

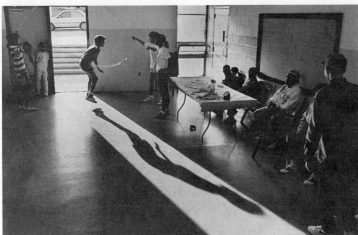

Children in ghetto neighborhoods often have abundant energy and physical talent. Here, inner-city youth in a public recreation center enjoy "Double Dutch"—an intricate form of rope jumping. Below, a boy performs trampoline-like stunts over a discarded mattress in the city's drug "badlands." Lacking accessible public pools, children cool off in the spray from a water hydrant. When they get older, they often seek more exciting and daring leisure outlets.

Today, a number of European nations provide diversified leisure programs specifically designed for unemployed and economically disadvantaged persons. "Social tourism," meaning tourism for the poor, is an example of such services. The travel authority, Arthur Frommer, writes that this

> is a concept known to every prosperous nation other than our own, to every rich continent other than North America, to every major language other than English. . . . Here in America, apart from various fresh-air funds sending underprivileged children to summer camps, not a single major program brings away-from-home vacations to low-income groups.[35]

In Europe, as early as 1956, travel officials and social agency representatives began to meet to bridge the gap between low income and the ability to travel. They formed the Bureau Internationale du Tourisme Sociale, an association of ninety-odd organizations that promote social tourism policies and programs. They work closely with governments, transportation agencies, resorts, labor unions, and philanthropic organizations to provide low-cost travel vacations for the poor as a basic human right.

The Social Role of Leisure

Should leisure be deliberately used or controlled to achieve specific societal outcomes or governmental goals? Clearly it *has* frequently been used in this way in the past, in both domestic and authoritarian societies. Don Dawson points out that the social engineering approach to the management of leisure was vividly illustrated in fascist Italy, where the dictator Benito Mussolini founded the *Dopolavoro,* a government-sponsored leisure-time organization intended to maintain the stability of Italian capitalism, promote healthy family life for workers, and impose a work-oriented discipline on recreational pursuits. Dawson cites de Grazia:

> No longer seen as an "end" in itself, leisure was now construed as a "means" of improving the worker in the national interest, curing the defects of the proletarian character, teaching workers not to kill time, and instructing them in the virtues of self-discipline.[36]

Despite the common understanding that leisure is marked by personal freedom, Dawson points out that neo-Marxist theorists argue that it has traditionally been used to help the working class "adjust" to a subordinate position in capitalist society. He cites Rojek and Frith:

> Leisure relations are held to create the illusion of freedom and self-determination which is the necessary counterbalance to the real subordination of workers in the labor process. . . . Leisure is not really free time at all, but an organization of non-work time that is determined by the relations of capitalist production.[37]

In contrast with this view, which he calls the "reproduction" concept (leisure being used to reproduce or sustain the dominant capitalist ideology and class structure), Dawson presents an alternative "leisure democracy" position, which holds that leisure is substantially independent of the larger political economy. The truth is likely to be a blend of the two positions. Certainly, government and major social institutions seek to reinforce positive social values and promote community stability through leisure facilities and programs. At the same time, the marketing of sports, travel, tourism, and popular entertainment by huge conglomerates with worldwide outlets means that society's leisure is heavily controlled and shaped by powerful business interests that are independent of government control.

Within this framework, how do different social classes view leisure? Dawson suggests that the middle classes tend to see play as a means of achieving discipline, social status, or other purposeful goals, while working-class members value play chiefly as an end in itself. Beyond this, while leisure is subject to class and social status influences and may serve to perpetuate or strengthen differences among socioeconomic groups, it may also help to break them down and provide an area of freedom in the lives of people on every status level.

In conclusion, one may ask—where do we stand with respect to social class in America today? One of the trends in contemporary film-making is to promote the myth that social classes do not really exist and that—master and servant, yuppies and waitresses, millionaires and hookers—we are really all just the same. Critic Benjamin DeMott describes several recently popular movies:

> At their best, Hollywood's new-style "class movies" nod at realities of social distance—and then go on to obfuscate them. At their worst, these films are driven by near-total dedication to a scam—the maddening, dangerous deceit that there are no classes in America.[38]

Vanneman and Cannon suggest that, in the prosperous years following World War II, much of the antagonism that had stemmed from earlier labor disputes diminished; with deadened class consciousness, most Americans tended to regard themselves as middle class. However, it would be a mistake to assume that the society *has* become essentially classless. Vanneman and Cannon urge caution "against too readily accepting any conclusions about the 'end of ideology.' Contemporary American workers do recognize class divisions, and they are not distracted by the many status distinctions that have proliferated in this century.[39]

■ SUMMARY

Despite American ideals of equality and democracy, the nation has had fairly clearly defined levels of social class through its history—and leisure values and pursuits have reflected class differences. Moving from a rigid class-structure approach to life-style analysis, this chapter has presented an overview of three socioeconomic groups—the wealthy, the middle class, and the poor—in terms of their leisure patterns. While some of the sharp differences that have characterized such socioeconomic levels in the past may diminish over time as American life-styles become more homogenized, economic and status factors are likely to continue to influence recreational preferences and access in the future.

■ QUESTIONS FOR DISCUSSION

1. America has often been pictured as a land of equality, where all citizens might be free of the rigid class barriers that characterized European countries. How true was this of the early American colonies and the new republic? How did class differences evidence themselves in leisure pursuits?

2. What were some of the findings of sociological studies of American communities during the early decades of the twentieth century, with respect to who had leisure and how it was used?

3. Why did sociologists shift from a focus on social class, as exemplified in Warner's breakdown of class groupings, to an emphasis on status and life-style patterns? What was the role of leisure both as a means of becoming part of a new meritocratic elite, and as a reward for those who achieved success within it?

4. Contrast the major differences among the three socioeconomic groups identified in this chapter (wealthy, middle-class, and poor), with respect to their leisure values and behaviors.

5. Should government have a strong commitment to serving the poor and the other disadvantaged populations described in the chapter, in terms of subsidizing their leisure involvements? What are the pro and con arguments surrounding this issue?

■ NOTES

1. KAHL, J. A., and K. DAVIS. 1957. *The American class structure*. New York: Rinehart, p. 1.
2. FURNAS, J. C. 1969. *The Americans: A social history of the United States, 1587–1914*. New York: G. P. Putnam's Sons, p. 49.
3. *Ibid.*, p. 62.
4. LARKIN, J. 1988. The secret life of a developing country (ours). *American Heritage* (Sept.-Oct.): 64.
5. BUTSCH, R., ed. 1990. *For fun and profit: The transformation of leisure into consumption*. Philadelphia: Temple University Press, p. 9.
6. WARNER, W. L., and P. S. LUNT. 1941. *The social life of a modern community*. New Haven: Yale University Press, p. 82.
7. KAHL and DAVIS, *op. cit.*, p. 26.
8. LYND, R., and H. LYND. 1937. *Middletown in transition*. New York: Harcourt, Brace, pp. 243–245.
9. LUNDBERG, G., M. KOMAROVSKY, and M. A. McINERNEY. 1958. The amounts and uses of leisure. In *Mass leisure*, ed. E. Larrabee and R.

Meyersohn. Glencoe, IL: Free Press, pp. 173–198.
10. WHITE, R. C. 1955. Social class differences in the uses of leisure. *American Journal of Sociology* 61, 2 (Sept.): 145–150.
11. CLARKE, A. 1956. Leisure and occupational prestige. *American Sociological Review* 21, 3 (June): 301–307.
12. REISSMAN, L. 1959. *Class in American society*. Glencoe, IL: Free Press, pp. 8–9.
13. *Ibid.*, p. 12.
14. PACKARD, V. 1961. *The status seekers*. New York: Pocket Books, p. 2.
15. KAPLAN, M. 1960. *Leisure in America: A social inquiry*. New York: Wiley, p. 92.
16. ANDERSON, N. 1961. *Work and leisure*. New York: Free Press, p. 34.
17. LERNER, M. 1957. *America as a civilization*. New York: Simon and Schuster, pp. 530, 641.
18. LYNES, R. 1949, 1980. *The tastemakers*. New York: Dover, p. 5.
19. RIESMAN, D., with R. DENNEY and N. GLAZER. 1950. *The lonely crowd*. New Haven: Yale University Press.

20. VEAL, A. J. 1989. Leisure, lifestyle and status: A pluralist framework for analysis. *Leisure Studies* 8: 148.
21. O'REILLY, B. 1990. How much does class matter? *Fortune* (July 30): 123.
22. FALTERMAYER, E. 1990. Who are the rich? *Fortune* (Dec. 17): 95.
23. ROBBINS, W. 1966. Houses in a suburb of Chicago offer their originality at a price. *New York Times* (Jan. 9): R–1.
24. COATES, J. 1987. A new paradise: The rich and famous have made Wyoming the place to be. *Philadelphia Inquirer* (June 21): 24–A.
25. GORDON, J. S. 1990. The country club. *American Heritage* (Sept.-Oct.): 75–80.
26. REICH, ROBERT. 1991. Secession of the successful. *New York Times Magazine* (Jan. 20): 42.
27. *Ibid.*, p. 44.
28. KRUGMAN, P. 1992. Business: Disparity and despair. *U.S. News and World Report* (March 23): 54–56.
29. RICHMAN, L. 1990. The new middle class: How it lives. *Fortune* (Aug. 13): 107.
30. The surprising news about the underclass. *U.S. News and World Report* (Jan. 1, 1990): p. 23.
31. *Ibid.*
32. DOYLE, L. 1986. A blue-collar syndrome: More risk of heart illness. *United Press International* (Nov. 17).
33. LAHEY, M. 1991. Serving the new poor: Therapeutic recreation values in hard times. *Therapeutic Recreation Journal* 25, 2: 14–15.
34. KUNSTLER, R. 1991. There but for fortune: A therapeutic recreation perspective on the homeless in America. *Therapeutic Recreation Journal* 25, 2: 23.
35. FROMMER, A. 1986. Paid vacations aimed at the poor. *Philadelphia Inquirer* (Nov. 30): 3–R.
36. DAWSON, D. 1988. Social class in leisure: Reproduction and resistance. *Leisure Sciences* 10: 194–195.
37. *Ibid.*
38. DE MOTT, B. 1991. In Hollywood, class doesn't put up much of a struggle. *New York Times* (Jan. 20): 2—1.
39. VANNEMAN, R., and L. CANNON. 1987. *The American perception of class*. Philadelphia: Temple University Press, p. 128.

8 Leisure and the Life Cycle: Family and Disability Factors

Adult life used to be fairly predictable, and so were theories of aging. It was simple: the older you got, the more you lost—sex drive, memory, brain cells, energy, intelligence. Now psychologists find that Grandma refuses to mind the grandchildren; she and Harry have bought a Winnebago and are camping in Yosemite. Aunt Sarah took up marathon running and local politics at the age of 73. And Uncle Fred retired at 58 from Amalgamated Teabiscuit and Muffins to become a jazz musician. Growing old is not what it used to be.[1]

A key factor that affects leisure values and behavior in American society is one's age or, stated more broadly, the life cycle, extending from infancy and childhood through later maturity and aging. At each stage of development, there are specific tasks that must be mastered as part of healthy physical, emotional, social, and intellectual growth. This chapter outlines the role played by leisure in this process and the challenges that face individuals today in a rapidly changing society. A concluding section of the chapter examines recreation's contribution to family life and the impact of disability on Americans of all ages.

◼ THE AGING PROCESS

Usually when the term *aging* is used, it is assumed that we are speaking of elderly persons or the later stages of life. Actually, age is a neutral concept and applies to all periods of life; from the moment we are conceived, we are aging. Bernice and Dail Neugarten point out that in American society, as in other cultures, age is a key factor in such systems as schooling, the job world, voting and political rights, the criminal justice system, and family life. Even the simplest societies, they write, recognize at least three periods: childhood, adulthood, and old age.

> In more complex societies, a greater number of life periods are differentiated, and transition points are differently timed in different areas of life. In modern America, people are considered adults in the political system when they reach 18 and are given the right to vote; but they are not adults in the family system until they marry and take on the responsibilities of parenthood. Or people may be adult in the family system, but if they are still in school they are not yet adult in the economic system.[2]

In recent years, marked changes have occurred in the definitions of aging and the timing of major life events. Certainly, early retirement and extended life expectancy have changed American life-styles during the later periods of life, compared to the past when most individuals worked until they could no longer. In *The Christian Century,* Wade Roof comments:

> we are no longer very certain to which age group we are referring when we speak of the young, the middle-aged or the old. These are culturally created categories which are easily recast in times of demographic shifts. Baby boomers approaching 40 are not in the same life situations that their parents were at this age: they have stayed in school longer, started work later, married and had children later, and based their families on two incomes. [Thus] the script for each stage of human life keeps getting revised.[3]

◼ THE HUMAN LIFE CYCLE

Despite such changes, for all persons the human life cycle represents a similar process of development, in which varied biological, psychological, and other tasks or milestones are chronologically distributed. Osgood and Howe write:

> Life is portrayed as a progressive unfolding of crises and resolution. Certain psychological tasks must be completed before the individual may move on to other stages. . . . The

psychologic crisis of ego development, which confronts the individual at various life stages, influences personal values; motivations for behavior; the meanings, significance, and satisfactions derived from various activities (including leisure activities); and patterns of life involvement.[4]

A number of behavioral scientists have identified and described the stages of the life cycle, as they understood them. The psychoanalyst Erik Erikson, for example, formulated an eight-stage model showing how human beings develop personal identity through the life span. To simplify its analysis, this chapter suggests a very basic model of the life cycle, consisting of four major periods: childhood, adolescence, adulthood, and aging. At all stages, leisure and recreation play an important role in the individual's development and healthy functioning.

■ LEISURE AVAILABILITY IN THE LIFE CYCLE

There are marked fluctuations in the amount of leisure available to people throughout the life cycle. To illustrate, during the mid-1960s, the Southern California Research Council carried out a study of the amounts and uses of leisure for almost thirteen million residents in its region, based on extensive surveys of all age groups and social classes.[5] Documenting leisure patterns at each life stage, it found that the bulk of time in infancy was spent in self-care or maintenance activity, such as rest, sleep, and eating. In early childhood, play and beginning study activities occur. In later childhood and adolescence, school, self-care, and recreation pursuits dominate time use, with children assuming some chores at home, and adolescents increasingly taking on outside work activities as well. For adults, discretionary time amounted to between twenty-five and fifty hours a week. For the young and the old, it rose to between fifty and seventy hours weekly, with leisure increasing dramatically for retired persons.

More recently, Szwak reported a United Media survey that compared the situations of elderly persons, teenagers, single adults, and childless couples, who had the most free time, with those of traditional, single, and dual-career couples, who had the least.[6] Obviously, such findings involve statistical generalizations, and individuals within each group may differ widely from others in the same category.

We now turn to a detailed discussion of leisure in the lives of the four major age groups. At each point, we must ask: how can leisure be used to fulfill specific needs of growth and development for individuals within this age bracket? Beyond this, what are our societal expectations and values with respect to leisure at each stage?

■ LEISURE, PLAY, AND RECREATION IN CHILDHOOD

Childhood as a chronological period extends from birth through the age of twelve, although the onset of puberty or adolescence may actually occur well before or after that age. It is a time for physical and psychomotor growth and for dealing with such tasks as gaining a sense of self and relating to others, learning responsibility and self-discipline, and developing social, cognitive, and communicative skills.

People of all ages enjoy sports and outdoor recreation today. In Long Beach, California, elderly residents take part enthusiastically in Senior games, while young adults race downhill at the Sugarbush Ski Center in Warren, Vermont. Family camping is popular throughout the nation, as shown here at Lake Powell in Utah.

Apart from study and self-maintenance responsibilities, play fills a major portion of the child's time. It is a phenomenon that appears among various living species and in all human societies. While it is difficult to define play precisely because it takes so many forms, in general, it is regarded as activity that is not serious (that is, not carried out for a deliberate, practical purpose), but that may involve such elements as contest, mimicry and imitation, exploration, problem solving, and humor. A leading psychoanalyst, Bruno Bettelheim, stressed play's importance in the emotional development of children:

> . . . children use play to work through and master quite complex psychological difficulties of the past and present. So valuable is play in this connection that play therapy has become the main avenue for helping young children with their emotional difficulties; it is a "royal road" to the child's conscious and unconscious inner world.[7]

Beyond these values, play contributes to the child's physical and intellectual development, ability to deal with others, perseverance, and confidence. In a detailed review of the values of play experience that have been documented by research, Lynn Barnett emphasized its contribution to the child's cognitive growth, including divergent thinking and problem-solving skills.[8]

As we examine leisure and play in the lives of children today, it is important to recognize the real problems that face many youngsters in contemporary society. For example, while many children grow up in happy and financially secure homes and communities, too many others experience stress from parental abuse or family breakup.

The period of the 1980s represented a "terrible decade for children," according to a report issued in 1991 by the nonprofit Center for the Study of Social Policy. Nationally, there were substantial increases in the percentage of children living in poverty, juveniles who were incarcerated, out-of-wedlock births, violent deaths of teenagers, and the percentage of babies with low birth weights, which often leads to physical and mental impairment.[9]

⇒ TO THE POINT

Beyond such changes, it is apparent that many of America's children have lost their "innocence" in terms of having a harsher and crueler understanding of the adult world. Based on hundreds of interviews with elementary school children, researcher Marie Winn comments: "their testimony about marijuana, sex and pornographic movies on cable television would have deeply shocked parents a decade or two ago. The reticence and shyness once associated with childhood have clearly gone the way of curtsies and pinafores."[10]

Linked to such changes, Winn writes, are profound changes in adult conceptions of childhood itself. In the past, most parents felt obliged to shelter their children from life's ugliness; today, many appear to accept the belief that children must be exposed early to adult experience in order to survive in an increasingly uncontrollable world. The "Age of Protection" has ended; an "Age of Preparation" has set in. Many of the changes came from trends in adult life that necessitated new ways of dealing with children, such as:

the great social upheavals of the late 1960s and early 1970s—the so-called sexual revolution, the drug epidemic, the women's movement, the breakdown of the conventional two-parent family, the spread of psychoanalytic thinking and the proliferation of television. . . . [11]

Role of Parents in Children's Play

Recognizing that children's play can be a positive growth experience and a means of buffering youngsters against such negative influences, it is helpful to examine the role of parents in children's leisure lives. Barnett and Chick point out:

> The most salient force in the young child's environment is the presence and influence of parental models. Play behavior is a dimension of experience and exploration available to most children, but it has been shown that the richness and frequency of play arises from a set of optimal conditions that include the behaviors of parents for identification and modeling. Parents have been shown to exert a strong directing influence on their children's imaginative and cognitive play styles, and, in a more subtle manner, parental attributes and personality traits produce correlates with children's tendency toward playfulness.[12]

Barnett and Chick explored several aspects of the relationship between children's and parents' attitudes toward leisure and satisfaction with leisure, play styles, and interest in specific pursuits. They found that a number of the key factors included the influence of the parent of the opposite sex, the age and even the occupation of parents, and the size and sibling order of the family itself. There were distinct differences in how boys and girls were influenced by parental models. Some of their findings were that:

> (1) Overall, young boys' play styles were more affected by their parents' leisure than young girls' play styles; (2) children's play tended to be influenced more by the parent of the opposite sex, in terms of leisure satisfaction, than the parent of the same sex; (3) sense of humor for both boys and girls is strongly related to mothers' satisfaction with their leisure, but negatively related to fathers' leisure satisfaction; and (4) more playful children tend to be later-born in the family configuration, and playful boys tended to have fewer brothers and more sisters, while playful girls had more brothers.[13]

Based on such research, it is clear that parents play a critical role in helping children develop constructive leisure values and habits of participation. In many situations, however, parents may fail to show interest or may provide a negative model, as in the case of families where parents have problems related to drugs or alcohol or sexual promiscuity. Other problems may be linked to the lack of community resources for healthful recreational pursuits.

On the other hand, some parents who are social "strivers" may attempt to use children's play to compensate for their own lack of success or prestige by having the child become a successful athlete or performer—or may do so to help the youngster embark on a hopefully lucrative career. This may take the course of enrolling children in a relentless schedule of music or ballet classes, figure skating, or other pursuits at an extremely early age. One parent describes how she and her competitive, highly status-conscious friends sought to have their children enter the "fast lane" in infancy:

> we compress their time and pack it with play dates, lessons of all kinds and enriching experiences like camping and skiing. . . . It begins in the first year of life, when infants are enrolled in special gyms . . . [at a] "children's fitness center," where the babies crawled around a padded obstacle course . . . one of the babies started walking at eight months, which caused a stir. "See that!" the mothers whispered to their charges. "Look at Megan, you can do what she does. You just have to be more assertive!"[14]

⯈ TO THE POINT

When André Agassi, now a leading tennis professional, was a newborn infant, his father hung a tennis ball and racquet on a string above his crib, so that as soon as he could focus his eyes, he would follow the ball visually. By the time young André was three, he was hitting topspin drives with consistency, and on his fourth birthday he rallied with twenty-two-year-old Jimmy Connors for fifteen minutes. By his early teens, he was a national tennis prodigy. Other parents have pressured their young children to complete marathons; in April 1972, one-year-old Steve Parsons (actually he was one day short of his second birthday), "ran" a mile around a track in Northfield, Illinois, setting age-group records along the way. Such efforts to promote children's "fitness" at an early age, which have led to the establishment of major chains of franchised tot exercise and fitness centers, are not regarded as really helpful to their normal development. A report of the American Academy of Pediatrics concluded, based on a two-year study of preschool exercise programs, that they did not in any way give children a meaningful head start.

One of America's leading authorities on child-raising, Dr. Benjamin Spock, urges that children not be pushed too hard and—especially—that the emphasis of many parents on fierce competition and "getting ahead" minimizes the importance of cooperation, helpfulness, kindness, lovingness. He writes:

> These latter qualities are the things that we need much more than competitiveness. I'm bothered, for instance, at the way we coach young children in athletics and, even more ludicrous, the interest we focus on superkids. . . . It imposes strains on children. It teaches them that winning is the important thing. We've gone much too far in stressing winning.[15]

Despite the publicity given to such programs, the majority of school-age children have inadequate physical education programs and lack fitness on a number of important measures. Currently, only seventeen states have mandatory physical education, and only a third of all schoolchildren take such classes daily. In many communities, the traditional practice of children playing outdoors after school has largely disappeared. In many homes, they watch television instead; if they live in impacted urban neighborhoods, they are warned to stay indoors where they will be safe.

At the same time that many disadvantaged children lack community resources or adequate programs of constructive play, children in wealthy families are being wooed as a key target audience by major airlines, cruise ships, hotel chains, and theme parks. To promote family travel, airlines publish children's magazines and activity books and offer lounges and other special attractions for children.

A key example of how commercial interests and lack of meaningful parental concern threaten the healthy development of America's children in their leisure may be found in television programming. Studies by the A. C. Nielsen Company show that the average child in the two-to-eleven-year-old age group watches television for over twenty-seven hours a week. While there are a few excellent children's television programs, these have declined in number and are inaccessible in some sections of the country. Dr. Spock points out that the average American child watches eighteen thousand murders on television. He writes:

> we know that every time a child or an adult watches brutality, it desensitizes and brutalizes them to a slight degree. We have by far the highest crime rates in the world in such areas as murders within the family, rape, wife abuse, and child abuse. And yet we're turning out more children this way with this horrible profusion of violence that children watch on television. It's a terrible thing.[16]

In considering the role of children's play, it is important to recognize the work of youth groups such as the Boy Scouts and Girl Scouts, Boys and Girls Clubs, 4-H Clubs, the leading sports leagues, church-sponsored groups, Police Athletic Leagues, Junior Achievement, and a host of other special-interest groups that serve millions of boys and girls with positive and constructive youth programs. These organizations often provide a valuable cross section of outdoor recreation activity and camping, along with arts and creative pursuits, homemaking skills, and leadership training.

■ ADOLESCENTS AND LEISURE

The adolescent or teenage period extends from the onset of puberty, roughly between eleven and fourteen, to the late teen years, when individuals begin to be perceived as young adults. Adolescence is a time when young people must develop a healthy and realistic sense of self and of their sexual identity. They must master the academic challenges in school and college that equip them to function effectively as adults in community life, and the related task of choosing career options and preparing for future employment.

In past centuries, adolescence was not recognized as a separate period of life. Instead, children often assumed adult responsibilities at an early age. However, they began to assume a separate identity in the early twentieth century, as the years of schooling were prolonged and entrance into the work force was postponed. Wartella and Mazzarella point out that teenagers became recognized as a group needing public policy action and intervention at this time, with growing concern about how they spent their time: "concern with children's leisure was part of a list of child-related interests among Progressive reformers. . . . [As high school attendance became the predominant pattern] children became the focus of scientific studies. . . ."[17]

Surveys of major cities documented the ways in which adolescents were spending their time—particularly in such forms of commercial recreation as movies, public dances, poolrooms, and vaudeville and burlesque theaters. By the end of the 1920s, the American public came to realize that adolescents were developing an autonomous and highly commercialized peer-oriented leisure culture. Through the post-war years, fears have increasingly been expressed about youth's involvement with popular music and dance, the burgeoning world of drive-ins and movies, rock-and-roll, teen idols, mall hangouts, the impact of television, and, over the past three decades, involvement with sex, drugs, and alcohol.

It was recognized that the mass media were helping to create a separate teen culture, marked by its own customs and tastes and resistant to the traditional values of adult American society. In time, the generations were so physically segregated by the factors of suburban living, forced school attendance, and after-school work and play that the young spent

> the greater portion of their day in a world dominated by peers, so the mass media ideologically segregated them; youthful language, style of dress, goals, and behavior became more and more foreign to adults—as well as more and more commercialized. . . . teenagers, by erecting barriers of fashion and custom around adolescence, had walled off a secret and potentially antagonistic area of American culture.[18]

This trend was made more vivid and threatening by the youth rebellion of the 1960s and 1970s, when growing numbers of high school and college students resisted parental authority and became increasingly involved in potentially self-destructive leisure pursuits. A 1989 report by the national Parent's Resource Institute for Drug Education, Inc. (PRIDE) reported that alcohol and drug abuse were serious problems in both low-income housing projects and affluent suburbs. Strikingly, both forms of substance abuse were consistently higher for white students than for black—a refutation of popular beliefs.[19] In 1990, a study by the Search Institute for the Lutheran Brotherhood reported that 5 percent of American children commonly attend drinking parties as early as the sixth grade, and as many as 61 percent do so regularly as high school seniors. The study also reported that numerous children lacked adult supervision, watched television extensively, had parents with alcohol and drug problems, and had been physically or sexually abused by adults.[20] A major panel report in 1990 concluded that because of problems related to substance abuse, unplanned pregnancies, venereal disease, and emotional problems, many modern teenagers were "unlikely to attain the high levels of educational achievement required for success in the twenty-first century."[21]

Adolescent Leisure Values and Behavior

Linked to concern about American teenagers, a number of studies have sought to identify and analyze adolescent views of leisure and their own free-time involvements. Douglas Kleiber, Reed Larson, and Mihaly Csikszentmihalyi, for example, studied several thousand accounts of adolescents' reporting on various dimensions of leisure during their daily lives.[22] Based on these reports, they grouped the activities of teens into three major categories: (1) *productive,* such as classwork, studying, jobs, or other productive tasks; (2) *maintenance,* including eating, personal care, transportation, chores and errands, and rest and napping; and (3) *leisure,* including socializing, sports and games, television watching, nonschool reading, arts and hobbies, and other freetime pursuits.

Within the third category of involvement, the researchers identified two basic kinds of leisure. The first, which they called "relaxed leisure," involved such free-time activities as socializing, watching television, reading, and listening to music—pursuits that provided pleasure without making high personal demands of participants. The second form of leisure they called "transitional." It includes activities that require a degree of effort and demand, such as sports and games, crafts, and hobbies. These more structured pastimes, they concluded, serve adolescents as preparation for more serious adult roles. At a stage in their development when young people are often bored and disinterested in responsibilities placed on them by adults

> these transitional activities would appear to provide a bridge. They offer the experience of freedom and intrinsic motivation within highly structured systems of participation, systems that require discipline and engage an adolescent in a world of symbols and knowledge outside the self [and lay] a groundwork for experiencing enjoyment in more obligatory adult activities.[23]

In 1993, Linda Caldwell reviewed more recent research by Douglas Kleiber, Reed Larson, Kenneth Mobily, and others, which examined such issues as: (1) positive and negative influences on adolescent leisure; (2) typical activities engaged in by adolescents; (3) barriers to participation; and (4) developmental contributions of sport.[24]

Sanford Dornbusch, Director of the Stanford University Center for the Study of Families, Children and Youth, points out that, while peer influence among adolescents is powerful, there is no single, dominant peer culture or value system in America: "Instead . . . researchers have found multiple peer cultures that support the diversity of adolescent values and behavior. . . . Indeed, the variation in values among adolescents was as great as the variation between adults and youths."[25]

➤ TO THE POINT

Within a culture that has transformed leisure into a profit-seeking industry, adolescents represent a huge market for business, spending an estimated $83 billion a year on their personal needs. They are a prime target for the marketing of travel opportunities, fast foods, rock music concerts and other forms of entertainment, cars, clothes, and a host of other leisure-oriented products and services. They congregate by the thousands at spring breaks at Florida or Texas beachside resorts, and flock through shopping malls, attending video-game arcades and movie theaters, or simply "cruising."

On the other hand, particularly in disadvantaged urban neighborhoods, lacking financial resources or the opportunity for organized, constructive recreation, many teenagers simply "hang out," committing vandalism and break-ins, randomly assaulting strangers driving or walking through their neighborhoods, or engaging in other casual forms of delinquency. When asked why and how such incidents occur, teenagers often complain that they have "nothing to do"—that life is boring, and that they just want to "chill out" with their friends. James Calloway points out that a significant number of today's youth are overstimulated by the mass media, spiritually empty, and emotionally isolated from needed support systems: "[They] show less emotion, devalue life and are lonely, fearful and anxious. They seek life-threatening adventures and events which excite and stir their human spirit. Lesser challenges will not do."[26]

In the effort to combat such problems, varied youth-serving organizations strive to acculturate youth to societal values and expectations, expose them to varied environments and educational experiences, and use challenging physical pursuits as a way of diverting their aggressive or hostile drives. In such settings, recreation often serves as a "threshold" activity that helps to bring neighborhood youth through the doors of the agency, where they may then be involved in academic tutoring and counseling, drug and alcohol prevention and treatment programs, job training and career counseling services, and other types of assistance designed to overcome the effects of the constricting ghetto environment.

■ LEISURE DURING THE ADULT YEARS

We now move into a consideration of leisure during the adult years, including both early adulthood, which is generally considered to be the period between twenty and the mid-thirties, and the so-called mid-life years, from the late thirties to the early sixties. Authorities identify a number of key developmental tasks or challenges that confront all persons during the adult life course. Many of these tasks, Osgood and Howe suggest, are

> related to the psychological need to establish intimacy. The urge to merge generally culminates in marriage, settling down, buying a home, and starting a family . . . as primary developmental tasks of young adulthood. Much of the leisure in this late phase of young adulthood is centered around the marriage, carving out the roles of the wife and husband.[27]

Beyond such needs, young adults also face the task of developing economic independence, assuming civic and community roles, and in the broadest sense continuing to develop as fully rounded persons. For young men and women who attend college, much leisure involvement centers around campus pursuits, such as dormitory parties and friendships, participating in intramural sports or attending sports events, going to dances, listening to music, membership in sororities and fraternities, and other social, political, and literary activities.

For young adults who do not attend college, commercially sponsored agencies such as health spas or racquetball clubs, singles bars or clubs, rock concerts, and other forms of entertainment provide sociability. In addition, churches and synagogues, employee recreation programs, and public recreation and park departments also provide opportunities for sports and social recreation. Many of the pursuits that young people engage in at this stage of life represent a continuation of interests first developed during childhood and adolescence. For example, McGuire, Dottavio, and O'Leary found that 70 percent of all outdoor recreation activities enjoyed by older adults were first engaged in before the age of twenty-one.[28] Similarly, Scott and Willits confirmed strong continuity from adolescence through the adult years in five major types of leisure activities, including socializing and intellectual pursuits, involvement in formal organizations, and artistic or creative pursuits.[29]

The values of young adults have shifted markedly over the past three decades. The 1960s and early 1970s were a time when many young people held idealistic views of life, devalued work, and committed themselves to social programs. By contrast, the late 1970s and 1980s, the period of the Yuppies, marked a return to work values in that making money and achieving career success were widely shared goals, within an atmosphere of selfishness and narcissistic behavior. As shown in Table 8.1, college students shifted many of their attitudes from liberal or socially minded positions to more conservative stances during this period. In the late 1980s, a growing number of young people began to return to earlier altruistic values, in many cases committing themselves to environmental or community-service programs. Alan Deutschman writes that members of the new "baby-buster" generation are nothing like the workaholic yuppies who preceded them:

These are the Employees Who Can Say No, a novel breed that won't be easily manipulated into workaholism by the traditional lures—money, title, security, and ladder climbing. . . . [They] insist on getting satisfaction from their jobs but refuse to make personal sacrifices for the sake of the corporation. Their attitude: Other interests—leisure, family, life-style, the pursuit of experience—are as important as work.[30]

TABLE 8.1
Shifting social values of college students, as shown by survey of over two hundred thousand American college students by the University of California at Los Angeles and the American Council on Education.

Statements of Social Values	Fall 1976	Fall 1986
	Agree strongly or somewhat	
Marijuana should be legalized	48.9%	21.3%
It is important to have laws prohibiting homosexual relationships	47.0	52.2
The death penalty should be abolished	32.6	25.4
	Think it essential or very important	
To promote racial understanding	35.8	27.2
To be very well off financially	53.1	73.2
To be involved in environmental cleanup	27.7	15.9
To develop a philosophy of life	60.8	40.6

SOURCE: *New York Times*, January 18, 1987, p. 30.

For many young adults who postpone marriage and family commitments, this period of life represents the opportunity for advanced education and career development, and a time for relatively free spending and enjoyment of leisure. Economist Fabian Linden comments, "This longer period of financially independent young adulthood amounts to an economic, social, and psychological revolution." Many young singles are able to indulge in "the 'me-me-me purchasing cycle' of chic clothes, cars, cruises, and other luxuries. But the free-spending ways halt after they marry, have children, and begin worrying about paying for cribs, condos, and colleges."[31]

For young adults who marry and begin to raise families, leisure begins to center around children, in terms of membership in Parent-Teacher Associations or serving as volunteer leaders or coaches in youth groups and leagues. Often recreation is carried on close to home, in backyard games and picnics; travel, when it occurs, is aimed at national or state parks or family-oriented theme parks, rather than popular singles destinations or cruises.

Contrary to the assumption that active recreation automatically drops off through the decades of adulthood, Rodney Warnick cites research findings showing that both the 25-to-34-year-old and the 35-to-44-year-old segments of the adult population have higher participation rates in a number of outdoor recreation activities than the younger cohorts of adults aged 18 to 24.

> [P]articipation rates were higher for 24- to 34-year-olds than for 18- to 24-year-olds in such activities as bicycling, swimming, fresh water fishing, salt water fishing, hiking, cross-country skiing, health club membership. . . . This trend carried over to the . . . middle-aged adult segment in activities such as salt water fishing, health club membership, and travel. . . . These changes appear to have occurred in the 1980s. In fact, for probably the first time, evidence now exists that participation rates are higher among older adults, particularly the middle-aged adults, than young adults in a wide variety of activities. . . .[32]

■ MIDDLE AGE

Osgood and Howe describe the mid-life period as the "establishment phase" of the life cycle, in which individuals make significant life investments and commitments, settle down, move ahead in a work career, assume increasing responsibility in civic organizations, and become "culture bearers" to the next generation. Now that life is "half over," many men and women reexamine their career goals and family status from a new time perspective, and it is not uncommon to make major life changes at this point.

For Americans, people in the middle decades of life are commonly thought of as the baby boomers—born in the two decades after World War II, between 1946 and the mid-1960s. Seventy-five million strong, they packed the maternity wards as infants, the classrooms as children, and the campuses, employment lines, and mortgage markets as young adults. Although in many ways the baby boomers define the contemporary culture, standing out in sharp contrast to the smaller generations that preceded and followed them, they also represent a highly diverse generation, in terms of personal values, career success, and life-styles.

In terms of demographic characteristics, the baby-boom generation differs from those who preceded them in that a lower percentage are married and a higher percentage are divorced or have never married. They are better educated and have fewer children, but are unlikely to be able to "catch up" to their parents in terms of real income or net worth. But, as they approach the preretirement years, research indicates that most mid-life Americans are satisfied with their life situation. According to the American Board of Family Practice, an organization of thirty-seven thousand family physicians, the majority of Americans view the ages of forty-six through sixty-five very positively, as a time for becoming closer to their spouses, children, and friends: "for most men, middle age is a period of settling and reconciling personal and occupational goals. For most women it is a period of greater independence and freedom."[33]

There was little support for the notion that mid-life was a time of crisis or personal anguish, or for the widespread belief that men discard their wives and begin driving fancy sports cars when they enter middle age. For many middle-aged men and women, however, this period does represent a time when they seek to recapture their youth, in terms of nostalgia—attending concerts by seventy-year-old singers who were pop idols when they were young, or indulging the fantasy of playing baseball with other men in their forties and fifties, at so-called Dream Weeks at training camps with former star athletes.

■ LEISURE AND THE ELDERLY

In the late 1980s, the American Association of Retired Persons reported that those sixty-five or older numbered over twenty-nine million in the United States. This represented over 12 percent of the nation's population, a steadily growing number that is expected to increase each decade until, in the third decade of the twenty-first century, the elderly will represent 20 percent of the population.

Our views about growing old are sharply contradictory. On the one hand, many individuals look forward eagerly to retirement and being able to lead independent, relaxed lives. On the other hand, the elderly are often denigrated in society; to be old has frequently meant to be isolated, no longer a contributing member of the community, ill or disabled, and economically vulnerable.

In general, elderly persons in the United States are more satisfied with life than their counterparts in such other industrialized nations as Japan and Germany, according to a 1993 poll conducted by the Louis Harris organization for the Commonwealth Fund. Apart from serious concern about the cost of medical care, they are significantly more contented, active, and independent than older persons in these other societies.

⫸ TO THE POINT

The reality is that aging is a complex phenomenon that varies greatly from person to person. Actually, there are three or more stages of aging, ranging from those who are healthy, mobile, independent, and optimistic, to those who have

serious problems of health and/or locomotion and are unable to live independently. Aging is generally regarded as a physiological development, with a
gradual slowing of biological functions and breakdown of body systems, along
with progressive disabilities of the heart and nervous system, and decline of
vision and hearing. However, aging clearly has social and psychological components as well, and the degree to which individuals are able to remain active
and involved with friends, family, and enjoyable life-style pursuits may greatly
influence the rate of physical aging. Robert Butler, former head of the National
Institute on Aging, points out that apart from such factors as brain disease,
cancer, or other kinds of serious illness over which one may have limited control, the difference in one's functional aging often comes down to personal and
psychological factors. He writes:

> People who are actively involved in life will seem younger than people who are
> emotionally and physically sedentary. People who are productive stay healthy,
> and if you remain healthy you're more apt to be productive. . . . Whether it's paid
> or unpaid work there have to be opportunities to keep people active. . . . [34]

In a study of the effect of retirement from work, Jonathan Long points out that
the conventional wisdom is that the loss of paid employment causes severe distress to
many elderly persons. He summarizes his research findings:

> Apart from the family, work was the aspect cited most frequently by respondents as an
> important aspect of their lives prior to retirement (39 percent). Yet there was still a
> majority who did not think to mention it, and when asked after retirement what they
> missed about work, many (28 percent) said there was nothing. . . . As an indication of
> the extent of their continued attachment to work in retirement, respondents were asked
> whether they would like their old jobs back if they had the opportunity. Almost two-
> thirds decided that they would not. . . . [35]

Continuing Education and Volunteerism

For many elderly persons, leisure provides the opportunity to enrich their lives and
diversify their interests. Their new free-time pursuits may take many forms.
Hundreds of colleges and universities offer specially designed summer programs for
older persons through the Elderhostel movement, which serves thousands of mature
students in short-term courses throughout the United States and abroad. Campus
housing and faculty resources provide inexpensive packaged programs covering a
wide range of educational and cultural subjects. In some cases, entirely independent
programs for elderly persons have been established, and in others they are served
side by side with younger students.

Another major form of productive retirement activity for elderly persons consists
of volunteering. Hundreds of thousands of individuals in their senior years provide
regular assistance in hospitals, community centers, organizations like the Salvation
Army, the American Red Cross, Foster Grandparents, and the Service Corps of
Retired Executives. Defined as unpaid work within the context of a formal organiza-

tion or voluntary association, volunteering is frequently conceptualized as a satisfactory substitute for work, fulfilling most of the functions that paid work does and, in addition, constituting a service to society. Based on a study of elderly volunteers, Niska Cohen-Mansfield identifies their key motivations:

> The most frequent (53 percent) attribution for motivation to volunteer is an ideological and philanthropic one: to perform a service to society, to help others, and to fulfill a citizenship duty. The other main attributions in order of frequency were: filling time (18.3 percent) and finding interest in the volunteering activity (14.8 percent).[36]

Beyond these motivations, other studies have shown that elderly persons gain a sense of recognition and self-worth through volunteer work, and that it provides a structure in their lives as well as social contacts that compensate for lack of other group involvement. In addition to continuing education and volunteerism, the leisure lives of elderly persons include a broad range of recreation pursuits similar to those engaged in by younger individuals. These may be enjoyed in mixed groups of people of all ages, in senior centers and Golden Age clubs, or in recreation centers in retirement communities.

As an example, one of the largest retirement communities in the nation, Sun City in Arizona, operates a network of recreation centers that house sports, arts and crafts, hobbies, and other pursuits, with over 140 chartered clubs in varied leisure activities. In California, Laguna Hills offers its residents over forty-five different pastimes, ranging from aerobics, art, billiards, bocce, bowling, calligraphy, and cards, to stamp collecting, swimming, table tennis, tennis, a therapy pool, weaving, and woodworking.

A major thrust in leisure programming for elderly persons today involves active sports leagues and tournaments. Typically, many cities sponsor softball leagues for those sixty or older. In some cases, they may schedule tennis tournaments in which the combined ages of players on a doubles team must be at least 140 or 150 years. A unique example of such sports programming is the North Carolina Senior Games program (NCSG, Inc.). Formed in 1981, NCSG is a year-round health promotion program for adults fifty-five and older. In a typical year in the mid-1980s, it sponsored over two hundred sanctioned games, with several thousand participants taking part in over forty different events, including basketball shooting, cycling, bowling, croquet, track and field, golf, horseshoes, softball throw, spin casting, swimming, and tennis.

Importance of Leisure in Healthy Aging

Apart from the pleasure and social satisfaction that varied leisure pursuits may provide for elderly persons, recreation can clearly contribute to healthy aging in several major respects. In a detailed study of the psychological benefits of participation in leisure pursuits, Tinsley, Teaff, and Colbs identified eight important areas of value for the elderly. These were: (1) *self-expression,* the creative use of one's talents; (2) *companionship* with others; (3) a sense of *power,* involving one's ability to deal effectively with social situations; (4) *security,* based on activities being carried out in safe and familiar settings; (5) *compensation,* satisfying the need for new or unusual experiences that may make up for other losses or gaps in the individual's life; (6) *service* to others; (7) intellectual and cultural *stimulation;* and (8) *solitude,* involving the person's ability to spend time alone comfortably.[37]

A final important value of active recreation for elderly persons has to do with maintaining health and fitness. Numerous studies have shown that even moderate physical exercise can make a significant contribution to the health of aged persons. One cardiologist suggests that physical activity for older persons should include four basic elements: (1) relaxation; (2) endurance exercises to condition the heart, lungs, and circulation; (3) muscle-strengthening exercises; and (4) stretching exercises to improve joint mobility and reduce the aches and pains that may accompany aging. Physiologist William Evans of the Tufts University Center on Aging states: "There is no group in our population that can benefit more from exercise than senior citizens. For a young person, exercise can increase physical function by perhaps 10 percent. But in an old person you can increase it by 50 percent."[38]

Beyond the consideration of the leisure values and interests of major age groups, it is important to recognize two other factors that influence the course of healthy development through the life cycle. These involve the family itself, along with problems of physical or mental disability that affect many millions of American individuals.

■ LEISURE AND THE FAMILY

It is tempting to sentimentalize the American family in terms of the images of loving mothers and fathers and their mischievous but obedient children that appeared in popular television series during the 1950s and 1960s. However, the reality is that the American family today represents a far more complex and diversified picture than this. The incidence of divorce, unmarried pregnancy, child abuse, drug-addicted parents and infants—as well as the pressures of having both parents working, the lack of adequate day-care programs, and increasing numbers of latchkey children—all have contributed to the problems facing families in contemporary American society. Studies have shown that children who are alone at home for eleven or more hours a week after school are twice as likely to abuse alcohol, tobacco, or marijuana as are supervised youngsters. In the late 1980s, two-thirds of all school-age children had working mothers. Since United States employers, unlike those in most other industrialized countries, are not required to provide maternity leave, many infants now go into group care when they are only a few weeks old. And, although the number of children spending their time in day-care or preschool programs has doubled in recent years, the number of organized day-care facilities is still insufficient to meet the demand.

Within this context, how can leisure and recreation help in the solution of the problems that many American families face today? There has long been a widely shared belief that "the family that prays together stays together." This belief is now often changed to "the family that plays together stays together." Dennis Orthner and Jay Mancini point out that the research literature consistently shows that husbands and wives who share leisure time together in joint activities tend to be much more satisfied with their marriages than those who do not. They write:

> The value that shared leisure experience can have for families has been widely acknowledged. One study found that men and women ranked companionship highest on a list of nine goals of marriage. In another study, a national sample ranked such things as liking the same kinds of activities as more important to marital success than having children or financial security.
>
> By the 1980s, desire for companionship reached almost universal proportions. When asked about their primary leisure objectives, a national sample of adults listed "spending time with your family" and "companionship" as their two most common objectives.[39]

Other surveys during the 1980s showed that 82 percent of parents said that children gave them their greatest satisfaction in life, and that participation in sports and recreation within the family unit ranked second only to television-watching as a common family activity. Laura Szwak cites research findings that show that one of the common characteristics of healthy, functioning families is "'doing things together.' According to the survey, joint leisure time was an important element in promoting high quality marital and family life."[40]

Szwak also cites Nationwide Recreation Survey findings showing that households with children account for the bulk of the American public's outdoor recreation participation. While parents with younger children did more passive, nonstructured activities such as walking and going to zoos, fairs, and nearby parks and recreation areas, those with older children were involved heavily as coaches of youth teams, or in many cases sharing pursuits like hunting or fishing with them.

In 1991, the Gallup Poll conducted a study that asked a national sample of employed adults whether, if they were offered a job that had significantly higher pay and prestige—but that would require considerable time away from their families—they would take it. Only 8 percent said they would take the job without reservations; 59 percent said they would turn it down; 32 percent said that they would accept it with some reservations.[41] Clearly, many Americans recognize that shared leisure time represents an important factor in assuring happy family life.

PROVISION OF FAMILY LEISURE PROGRAMS

Many different types of leisure-service organizations provide recreational opportunities designed specifically for family groups. These include public recreation and park agencies, Ys and other nonprofit organizations, employee and armed forces recreation programs, and religious groups. Various denominational organizations and individual churches in particular emphasize recreational family programming, both as an alternative to less desirable play and to strengthen family ties and encourage involvement in other church functions.

TO THE POINT

As an example, the Church of Jesus Christ of Latter-Day Saints (Mormons) has been particularly active in sponsoring family recreation as part of its religious creed. Clark Thorstenson points out that the church, from its beginnings in the early 1800s, has emphasized wholesome leisure involvement to promote family cohesiveness and moral values. He writes:

> As a result, family-centered sports, dance, song, theater, and reunions are regularly conducted in thousands of centers throughout the world as a means of providing spiritual, social and physical outlets for its members. . . . Church organizations sponsor family oriented sports competitions such as basketball, volleyball, soccer, tennis, golf, and softball during weekends and on Saturdays.[42]

In addition, Mormons often purchase mountain land or other suitable property for outdoor recreation for church members. Throughout the year, Monday evenings are set aside for family nights, for families to share varied hobbies and leisure pursuits. The church publishes a 346-page *Family Resource Manual,* including guidelines and examples for taking part in games, sports, and aquatics, cultural and social pursuits, and other forms of family enrichment activities.

As a contrasting example of growing concern with family leisure, numerous commercial recreation businesses have packaged their attractions to appeal more directly to family units. To illustrate, in the mid-1980s, the ski industry throughout the country began to recognize that, with growing numbers of families with young children, the number of single adult skiers was declining, and that the overall rate of participation was suffering. A number of major ski resorts in New England, the Midwest, and the West have now initiated strategies to appeal to family participation. These include free lift tickets on weekdays for children; on-site nurseries and day-care programs for younger children; other sports and entertainment facilities, including video game rooms; family transportation and lodging packages; and other marketing strategies to appeal to family units.

Varied gambling businesses, including major casinos in Las Vegas and Atlantic City and riverboat casinos on midwestern rivers, have also sought to picture themselves as centers of family entertainment and have advertised a "wholesome" atmosphere and diversified family recreation activities in an effort to draw a wider set of players. As an extreme illustration, three major casino companies announced in March 1992 that they were planning to build a $2 billion "family entertainment and casino mega-center" in Chicago, a sign that the financially strapped city might turn to casino gambling to create badly needed jobs. To be built on a confined area of 100 acres, it was anticipated that the proposed complex would create twenty thousand permanent casino and theme-park jobs. Johnston writes: "Besides gambling, the proposed complex would have a sports and performing arts arena. There would be carnival rides, ice skating, bowling, seasonal fairs, food emporiums and various attractions for children and families, the companies said."[43]

What this plan raised as an issue, of course, was whether the concept of family recreation could legitimately embrace any sort of activity or whether it should be restricted to socially and morally desirable activities that promote healthy family interaction and relationships.

■ LEISURE AND DISABILITY

A final issue to be considered in this chapter has to do with the impact of disability on the leisure needs of individuals throughout their life span and in family contexts. The term *disability* is used to describe a significant, continuing form of physical or mental impairment that substantially limits the ability to participate in one or more major life activities, such as education, pursuing a career, living independently, or the enjoyment of leisure. It has been estimated that forty-three million persons in the United States today—of all ages, races, and socioeconomic backgrounds—are significantly disabled. In Canada, a national Health and Disability Survey in the mid-1980s reported that about 2.8 million Canadian adults and children were disabled. When one recognizes that for each disabled individual there is usually a family unit that is affected both emotionally and financially by the disability, the true impact of this problem is clear.

For example, Zeigler points out that when a spouse is brain-injured as a result of an accident:

> Roles within the family are quickly, and often permanently changed. The injured partner is normally unable to carry out his or her responsibilities and duties. The uninjured spouse must frequently assume singular responsibility for a variety of tasks: household management, parenting, maintenance of an income, visiting and/or caring for the injured spouse, decision making, and dealing with the health care and social service system.[44]

Similarly, Ralph Smith sums up the psychological and logistical effects on families who have children with physical disabilities: (1) disabled children are more homebound and parent-dependent than able-bodied children of comparable ages, resulting in many constraints on their parents; (2) parental free time and extra-familial social contacts may be reduced; and (3) overall family leisure pursuits may be limited or shaped to conform to the needs of disabled children.[45]

As children with disabilities move into adolescence and adulthood, their problems related to the constructive and pleasurable use of leisure become more severe. Even those children who have had relatively good social relationships with other youngsters tend to become more isolated in the teen years. For adults, the reality is that a high proportion of disabled men and women are unable to find paid employment. A study conducted by the General Accounting Office of the federal government shows that, although an estimated 10 to 15 percent of the nation's disabled workers might be able to work, fewer than 1 percent of those who receive job training actually do return to work.[46] In a systematic study of several hundred adults with physical disabilities living in the greater Delaware Valley region of the United States, Kinney and Coyle found that only one in five were employed on a full-time basis. Many led "remarkably lonely and isolated" lives. Kinney and Coyle write:

> Leisure activity participation is characterized by solitary and sedentary passive entertainment. Among the top five favorite leisure activities, only one . . . requires any exertion, and only one . . . requires interaction with other humans. Community involvement also is reflective of isolation. Nearly half . . . cannot identify more than three accessible leisure, sport or cultural facilities in the community.[47]

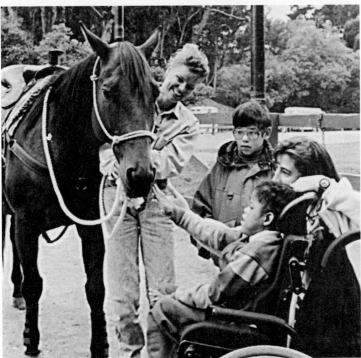

Long neglected in terms of leisure participation, today physically and mentally disabled persons are increasingly finding opportunities to participate in community-sponsored recreation. Left, the San Francisco Recreation Center for the Handicapped (RCH, Inc.) provides a wide range of services for all age groups; here, participants enjoy gardening and horseback riding. Below, Long Beach, California, offers social programs and adapted sports for disabled youth.

IIII➡ TO THE POINT

In recent years, research has documented the contribution of physical recreation to health on a number of levels, including the maintenance of cardiovascular fitness, controlling obesity, and helping to prevent heart attacks or strokes. However, regular exercise is also invaluable in promoting neuromuscular fitness and in preventing arthritis and degenerative bone conditions among older persons. Men with active jobs are less likely to develop colon cancer than those with more sedentary work, and active, athletic women cut their risk of breast and uterine cancer by half, and of diabetes by two-thirds. Obviously, while exercise can be taken as medicine—that is, as a prescribed daily routine—it is far more enjoyable and likely to be continued regularly in the form of sports, swimming, jogging, or other recreational pursuits carried on within a social environment.

However, there is more to health than physical fitness or the absence of disease. The modern concept of "wellness" implies that an individual is functioning fully and happily in a number of spheres of life, including family and social life, play, and work; it includes physical, emotional, and social components. Studies have shown that during the mainstream years of twenty to fifty, those who are happiest and best adjusted are active participants in varied forms of life activity. Iso-Ahola and Weissinger conclude that:

> Empirical research leaves little doubt that intrinsically motivated leisure is positively and significantly related to psychological/mental health. That is, those who are in control of their leisure lives . . . and have feelings of engagement in and commitment to leisure activities [and] experiences are psychologically healthier than those who are not in control of their leisure lives and do not have [such] feelings of engagement and commitment.[48]

For all these reasons, constructive and enjoyable leisure activity represents a critical element in the lives of disabled persons, just as it does with the nondisabled population. However, it has another, broader purpose for disabled individuals—to promote their integration within the larger society. For many centuries, persons with serious mental or physical disabilities tended to be hidden away by their families or imprisoned in custodial institutions that prevented them from reaching their true potential or leading any sort of normal lives. Even when society, over the past several decades, came to recognize their capabilities and to provide special services for them—including residential, educational, and leisure programs—these tended to be structured on a segregated basis. Leandra Bedini writes that society's attitudes toward people with mental disabilities, for example, are

> based on the assumption that they cannot make choices by themselves. Segregation has encouraged the participants' dependence and the community's condescension and pity. . . . [Even] the label of "special" as in "special populations," the term commonly used to identify the segregated recreation programs for people with disabilities, is very detrimental to the normalization process.[49]

Joanne Decker suggests that the real need is not simply to provide access to community facilities or other leisure resources through segregated programs designed for disabled persons as a separate concern. Instead, she writes:

> The issue is the disabled person's need to become a full participant in community life. Disabled persons may live in a deinstitutionalized community facility, attend work or school, and still have minimal contact with nondisabled persons. Recreation activities in community settings do not assure integration; they simply lay the foundation for a sense of belonging—the key to both integration and community.[50]

In the 1970s, a number of major pieces of federal legislation were enacted to ensure the rights of disabled persons in society. They included laws such as the Education of All Handicapped Children Act (1975), the Amateur Sports Act (1978), and the more recent Americans with Disabilities Act (1990), which mandated fuller opportunities for disabled persons within community and educational settings. Today, many community-based programs provide integrated participation with nondisabled persons. Schleien, Heyne, Rynder, and McAvoy describe one such example in a Jewish Community Center in St. Paul, Minnesota, which integrates several dozen youngsters with disabilities with their nondisabled peers each year in a full range of social and recreational activities. They gathered comprehensive evidence showing that these children and youth gained "competencies in swimming, gymnastics, camping, basketball, karate and video game skills, among others. Through these programs, social interaction skills and friendships were also developed by the children with disabilities [going] beyond involvement in programs at the JCC."[51]

Such programs serve to illustrate the value of recreation and leisure for disabled persons of all ages in American society. Today, freed of many of the limiting stereotypes of the past, many individuals with serious impairments are able to accomplish feats that never would have been thought possible. Individuals in wheelchairs race in marathons, engage in tennis and a variety of other sports, and literally climb mountains. Blind individuals ski, and others who are quadriplegic paint with brushes strapped to their foreheads. Such examples illustrate the potential values of leisure for a major segment of the American population.

■ SUMMARY

This chapter has provided an overview of the role of leisure experience through the life span, within the family setting, and in the context of personal disability. At each stage of life, play and recreation may meet important personal and social needs and contribute to the individual's physical health and social and cognitive development. Unfortunately, there is a severe inequity in the provision of leisure opportunity—particularly for children and youth. While some are given a wealth of play experiences and constantly stimulated and encouraged, others suffer from environments that lack resources and healthy models of leisure involvement. When the family cannot or does not provide such opportunities, schools and community leisure-service agencies have an obligation to offer them. At the other end of the life span, it has become increasingly clear that for the elderly, rich leisure involvements are a critical part of satisfaction with one's life and with healthy aging. The chapter concludes with a discussion of the special role of leisure services for persons with disabilities, both as part of the treatment or rehabilitation process, and as part of integrated living in the community.

■ QUESTIONS FOR DISCUSSION

1. Identify and discuss the importance of leisure and recreation within the human life cycle, as part of the developmental process described by Osgood and Howe.
2. What are the special roles of leisure and play in the lives of children? How can play be a positive force for healthy development or, as a less desirable possibility, be a negative influence in their lives? What are the roles of parents within this process?
3. This chapter describes two types of leisure pursuits among adolescents today: transitional and relaxed. Give examples of each, and identify their contribution and the kinds of settings in which they may be found. In your experience, what are some of the major hazards that teenagers face in contemporary society, with respect to their uses of leisure?
4. Describe the transition that adults undergo as they enter the mid-life period, in terms of other time pressures and demands, the increased availability of leisure, and new opportunities for personal growth.
5. What are the specific contributions that the positive and constructive use of leisure can make to family life? As part of this discussion, describe the impact that having a seriously disabled or ill family member has on other members of the family, and how leisure can become a helpful tool in meeting the needs of this individual and his/her siblings and parents.

■ NOTES

1. TAVRIS, C. 1987. Old age is not what it used to be. *New York Times, The Good Health Magazine* (Sept. 7): 24.
2. NEUGARTEN, B., and D. NEUGARTEN. 1987. The changing meaning of age. *Psychology Today* (May): 29.
3. ROOF, W. 1990. The spirit of the elderculture. *The Christian Century* (May 16): 529.
4. OSGOOD, N., and C. HOWE. 1984. Psychological aspects of aging. *Society and Leisure* 7, 1: 176.
5. *The challenge of leisure: A Southern California case study.* 1967. Claremont, CA: Southern California Council and Pomona College.
6. SZWAK, L. 1988. Leisure and the changing American family. *Journal of Physical Education, Recreation and Dance* (April): 28.
7. BETTELHEIM, B. 1987. The importance of play. *Atlantic Monthly* (March): 35.
8. BARNETT, L. 1990. Developmental benefits of play for children. *Journal of Leisure Research* 22, 2: 138–153.
9. Study: For children and teens, the 1980s were a 'terrible decade.' *Washington Post* (Feb. 1, 1991), n. p.
10. WINN, M. 1983. The loss of childhood. *New York Times Magazine* (May 8): 18.
11. *Ibid.*

12. BARNETT, L., and G. CHICK. 1986. Chips off the ol' block: Parents' leisure and their children's play. *Journal of Leisure Research* 18, 4: 266–267.

13. *Ibid.*, pp. 278–279.

14. DAVIDSON, S. 1988. Kids in the fast lane. *New York Times* (Oct. 16): 52.

15. SPOCK, B. 1986. Don't push your kids too hard. *U.S. News and World Report* (Oct. 27): 64.

16. *Ibid.*

17. WARTELLA, E., and S. MAZZARELLA. 1990. A historical comparison of children's use of leisure time. In *For fun and profit: The transformation of leisure into consumption,* ed. R. Butsch. Philadelphia: Temple University Press, p. 174.

18. *Ibid.*, p. 187.

19. MORRIS, D. 1989. Survey: White students more apt to use drugs. *Philadelphia Inquirer* (Dec. 19): 2–A.

20. NELSON, W. D. 1990. Study finds 6th graders at booze parties. *Associated Press* (Oct. 17).

21. BARRINGER, F. 1990. What *is* youth coming to? The trouble with kids depends on which kids. *New York Times* (Aug. 9): E–1, E–5.

22. KLEIBER, D., R. LARSON, and M. CSIKSZENTMIHALYI. 1986. The experience of leisure in childhood. *Journal of Leisure Research* 18, 3: 169–176.

23. *Ibid.*, p. 175.

24. CALDWELL, L. 1993. Research on adolescents and leisure activities: Research update. *Parks and Recreation* (March): 19–23.

25. DORNBUSCH, S. 1989. The sociology of adolescence. *Annual Review of Sociology* 15: 249.

26. CALLOWAY, J. 1991. Leisure and youth: Make the connection. *Parks and Recreation* (Nov.): 57.

27. OSGOOD and HOWE, *op. cit.*, p. 184.

28. MCGUIRE, F., F. D. DOTTAVIO, and J. O'LEARY. 1987. The relationship of early life experience to late life leisure involvement. *Leisure Sciences* 9: 255.

29. SCOTT, D., and F. WILLITS. 1989. Adolescent and adult leisure patterns: A 37-year follow-up study. *Leisure Sciences* 11: 323–335.

30. DEUTSCHMAN, A. 1990. What 25-year-olds want. *Fortune* (Aug. 27): 42.

31. RICHMAN, L. 1990. The new middle class: How it lives. *Fortune* (Aug. 13): 108.

32. WARNICK, R. 1987. Recreation and leisure participation patterns among the adult middle-aged market from 1975 to 1984. *Journal of Physical Education, Recreation and Dance* (Oct.): 49.

33. DETJEN, J. 1990. Study finds midlife isn't crisis time. *Philadelphia Inquirer* (Jan.23): 1–A.

34. Today's senior citizens, pioneers of new golden era. *U.S. News and World Report* (Jan.2, 1984): 52.

35. LONG, J. 1987. Continuity as a basis for change: Leisure and male retirement. *Leisure Studies* 6, 1 (Jan.): 59.

36. COHEN-MANSFIELD, N. 1989. Employment and volunteering roles for the elderly. *Journal of Leisure Research* 21, 2: 215.

37. TINSLEY, H. E., J. D. TEAFF, and S. COLBS. n.d. *The need satisfying properties of leisure activities for the elderly.* Southern Illinois University and Andrus Foundation, pp. 2–3.

38. EVANS, W., as cited in *Time* (Feb. 22, 1988): 79.

39. ORTHNER, D., and J. MANCINI. 1990. Leisure impacts on family interaction and cohesion. *Journal of Leisure Research* 22, 2: 126.

40. SZWAK, L., *op. cit.*, p. 27.

41. Family values: Gallup poll. *Philadelphia Inquirer* (Dec. 2, 1991): D–1.

42. THORSTENSON, C. 1984. The Mormon commitment to family recreation. *Journal of Physical Education, Recreation and Dance* (Oct.): 50.

43. JOHNSTON, D. 1992. Casino complex proposed for Chicago. *Philadelphia Inquirer* (March 25): 3.

44. ZEIGLER, E. 1987. Spouses of persons who are brain-injured: Overlooked victims. *Journal of Rehabilitation* (Jan.-March): 50–51.

45. SMITH, R. 1986. Physically disabled children and parental time use. *Journal of Leisure Research* 18, 4: 284–299.

46. SPEARS, G. 1988. Study: Few disabled go back to job. *Philadelphia Inquirer* (Feb. 23): 7–B.

47. KINNEY, W. B., and C. P. COYLE. 1989. *Predictors of quality of life among physically disabled adults.* Philadelphia: Temple University and U.S. Department of Education, p. 11.

48. Iso-Ahola, S., and E. Weissinger. 1984. Leisure and well-being: Is there a connection? *Parks and Recreation* (June): 41.

49. Bedini, L. 1990. Separate but equal? Segregated programming for people with disabilities. *Journal of Physical Education, Recreation and Dance* (Oct.): 40.

50. Decker, J. 1987. A social process: Integrating people with disabilities into community recreation. *Journal of Physical Education, Recreation and Dance* (April): 50.

51. Schleien, S., L. Heyne, J. Rynder, and L. McAvoy. 1990. Equity and excellence: Serving all children in community recreation. *Journal of Physical Education, Recreation and Dance* (Oct.): 45.

PART THREE

Popular Pursuits in American Life

9 Outdoor Recreation, Travel, and Tourism

Tourism is forecasted to be the largest business activity in the world by the turn of the century. It is the largest source of foreign exchange earnings for many countries of the world. . . . Yet, tourism is much more than a business. While many people travel to conduct business, sell services and products, and exchange information, most people travel to fulfill personal needs. They travel to refresh, revitalize, or enrich their lives. They travel to relax, learn, and escape routine. . . . Today, many people perceive their vacation and leisure time as a necessity for a healthy, fulfilling life.[1]

Two of the most popular uses of leisure today are outdoor recreation and travel and tourism. In many ways, these pursuits overlap. Although outdoor recreation may be enjoyed close to home, it often requires travel to distant locations where skiing, white-water rafting, hunting, and similar pastimes are available. Similarly, although tourism may involve trips to cities or stays at luxurious resorts, it also may incorporate various outdoor pursuits or the exploration of unique natural environments. Both outdoor recreation and tourism may run the gamut from safe and relatively passive forms of spectator activity to challenging and even high-risk pursuits. Taken together, they comprise a major, multibillion-dollar sector of the leisure market today, appealing to all age groups and socioeconomic classes.

■ MEANING OF OUTDOOR RECREATION

On the face of it, the term *outdoor recreation* applies to any form of play that is carried on in the outdoors, such as strolling through a park, playing basketball in a school yard, or attending a band concert in a city square. However, a stricter definition would suggest that outdoor recreation consists primarily of activities that depend on the natural environment, such as camping, nature photography, scuba diving, and similar pursuits.

How popular are such uses of leisure? The Statistical Abstract of the United States reported that the number of visits to all units of the National Park System, which had risen steadily in the post–World War II era, climbed to over 280 million visits in the late 1980s. At the same time, there were over 260 million visits to sites operated by the National Forest System, and many millions of other visits to facilities of the Fish and Wildlife Service, the Bureau of Land Management, the Bureau of Reclamation, and the Tennessee Valley Authority. In 1990, there were over 720 million visitors to state park and recreation areas as well.

Of the approximately 4.6 billion outdoor recreation trips Americans take each year, about 50 percent are taken to participate in wildland activities, such as camping, canoeing, fishing, hunting, and hiking. A comprehensive profile of a wide range of outdoor pastimes enjoyed by Americans in the mid-1980s is shown in Table 9.1.

Motivations Underlying Wilderness Recreation

From the time of the earliest settlements, Americans have enjoyed hunting and fishing in wilderness settings—partly for food, but also as a traditional form of play. In the mid-1800s, as growing numbers of well-to-do easterners began to engage in outdoor play in such regions as the remote Adirondack Mountains, the view was widely shared that nature was the "dwelling place of God," offering cures for both physical and spiritual woes. Writers spoke of finding God in nature:

> The wilderness is one great tongue, speaking constantly to our hearts; inciting to knowledge of ourselves and to love of the Supreme Maker, Benefactor, Father. . . . Here, with the grand forest for our worshipping temple, our hearts expanding, our thoughts rising unfettered, we behold Him, face to face.[2]

TABLE 9.1
Outdoor recreation participation profile

Activity	Percent of Population Participating One or More Times Annually	Median Number of Days of Participation Annually by Those People Who Participate
Land-based activities		
Sightseeing	46.9	12
Picnicking	46.2	6
Walking for pleasure	41.3	29
Driving for pleasure	38.4	19
Nature study/photography	36.2	13
Developed camping	34.9	7
Day hiking	23.8	5
Primitive camping	14.2	5
Other hunting	11.8	9
Backpacking	10.4	4
Big-game hunting	9.9	7
Driving ORVs	9.2	10
Horseback riding	8.6	2
Water-base activities		
Swimming outdoors	50.3	17
Warm water & saltwater fishing	30.9	10
Motorboating	22.2	7
Cold-water fishing	16.7	7
Waterskiing	12.9	4
Canoeing/kayaking	13.9	2
Sailing	7.5	2
Snow and ice-based activities		
Downhill skiing	9.8	4
Sledding	9.3	3
Cross-country skiing	6.5	4
Ice skating	6.0	2
Snowmobiling	2.7	3

SOURCE: 1985–1987 Public Area Recreation Visitor Study (PARVS), compiled by Outdoor Recreation and Wilderness Assessment Group, Athens, Georgia, based on thirty-six thousand visitor contacts at 290 sites.

Others have concluded that Americans' interest in the outdoors in the present day stems from our long and rich history of exploring the wilderness, and that it is linked to the nation's popular folklore about the exploits of loggers, hunters, cowboys, and pioneers crossing the land. La Page and Ranney describe this fascination with America's wilderness as an integral part of our common culture, writing:

> One of the most powerful sources of this country's essential cultural fiber clearly is in the land. The roots of the new nation and its people became the forests and rivers, the deserts and mountains, and the challenges and inspirations they presented, not the ruins of ancient civilizations most other cultures look to for ancestral continuity. Thus, America developed a different attitude and identity.[3]

It was to satisfy this interest that Congress created the National Wilderness Preservation System in 1964, with an initial nine million acres that provided places that were untrammeled and unmodified by the human hand, settings that were dangerous, unpredictable, and wild. McAvoy and Dustin point out that such areas offer us the opportunity to resurrect the feeling of the frontier, to live simply, and to meet challenges to our safety, through courage and self-reliance.[4]

While outdoor recreation in wilderness settings is a valuable personal experience linked to patriotic values and historical perspective, it also represents an important economic function. Greer points out that outdoor recreation involves a variety of leisure-oriented products

> such as camping paraphernalia, outdoor sports equipment, and clothing, as well as a bewildering array of trail bikes, four-wheel-drive vehicles, and snowmobiles. There are also transportation, tours, lodging, and dining intended for outdoor recreationists. The profitable production and sale of these recreational goods and services requires the existence of certain kinds of physical settings and an elaborate infrastructure of roads, trails, ski runs, and campsites. [5]

Realistically, much outdoor recreation does not take place in remote wilderness settings. Instead, it may be enjoyed in a neighborhood park, a nature center, or a heavily used beach or lake close to a crowded urban environment. A major conclusion of the Outdoor Recreation Resources Review Commission in 1962 was that many urban dwellers are at a distance from available wilderness areas, and that there is a continuing need to establish more parks and other areas close to the crowded metropolitan regions of the country. As a consequence, a number of National Seashores and Recreation Areas have been established close to large cities, particularly along the east and west coasts.

■ OVERVIEW OF MAJOR PURSUITS: HUNTING AND FISHING

We now turn to a direct examination of several of the most popular types of outdoor recreation pursuits enjoyed by Americans today, beginning with hunting and fishing. Table 9.2 summarizes statistics of involvement in these two activities.

Outdoor adventure and wilderness exploration are favorite leisure pursuits of many Americans. Above, a party of white-water rafters plunges down the Gully River in West Virginia, while Woodswomen, Inc., a Minnesota organization, sponsors numerous workshops, courses, and outings in outdoor recreation activities for girls and women. Below, the National Outdoor Leadership School, in Lander, Wyoming, trains leaders in a host of wilderness activities, including rock-climbing and mountain back-packing.

TABLE 9.2
Participation in hunting and fishing: 1985

Type of Fishing	Number (millions)	Type of Hunting	Number (millions)
Total: All fishing	46.3	Total: All hunting	16.6
All freshwater fishing	39.6	Big game	12.5
Freshwater, except Great Lakes	38.4	Small game	10.8
Great Lakes	3.7	Migratory bird	5.0
Saltwater	13.9	Other animals	2.8

SOURCE: *Statistical Abstract of the United States.* 1990. Washington, DC: U.S. Department of Commerce, Bureau of the Census, p. 234.
NOTE: Includes persons sixteen years old and over, who fished or hunted at all during year. Numbers add up to more than total, since some sportspersons engaged in more than one form of activity.

Fishing as Outdoor Recreation

By 1990, the number of fishing licenses sold each year rose to 36.9 million and the number of hunting licenses to 29.7 million. Of the two pursuits, fishing is more readily accessible; it can be carried on in many different settings—in local streams, ponds, and lakes, along ocean beaches, or from private or commercial fishing craft. In a study of urban youth who fish, Dargitz explored the influence of such factors as race, gender, residence, and angling socialization (family interest) among several hundred teenage students in a midwestern city. He found that

> gender appears to be a more important factor in angling socialization than either race or residence. . . . Children who have anglers in their households are more likely to engage in fishing more frequently and are more likely to enjoy angling as a leisure activity than are children who do not have anglers in their households. Because males are more likely to enjoy angling than are females, teenage boys are more active within the urban context.[6]

With respect to race, Dargitz cites earlier research showing that fishing was one of the few outdoor recreation pursuits for which African Americans ventured out of their home communities to any significant degree. His study found that race was not a factor that influenced teenagers' decisions with respect to places to fish. However, it *was* a factor with respect to eating fish that are caught; a higher percentage of black anglers ate their catch taken from both nonpolluted and polluted waters—a finding that Dargitz attributes to a subcultural or ethnic pattern of associating fishing with obtaining table fare, rather than considering it simply as a leisure pursuit.

At a more expensive level, growing numbers of fisherman enjoy their hobby at private trout- or bass-fishing preserves, such as New York's Eldred Preserve, tucked away in the Catskill Mountains, where typical rates are $50 per boat for four hours, and where trophy fish may be kept for a per-pound charge. Another example of the commercialization of sport fishing may be found in the popular bass-fishing competitions that are held today around the country. Major tournaments sponsored by organizations like the Bass Anglers Sportsman Society (B.A.S.S.) offer prizes amounting to hundreds of thousands of dollars. Taylor writes:

> For the consistent winners . . . the prize money is secondary to a wealth of sponsorship and endorsement deals from boat, motor and tackle manufacturers eager to reach a $2 billion-plus market of 20 million bass fishermen. Syndicated television shows have given the best fishermen widespread recognition, along with six-figure incomes. Izaak Walton's "calm, quiet, innocent recreation" is no longer "a reward to itself."[7]

Big-money bass tournaments are complicated, tightly run affairs, with rules governing the boats, equipment, timing, and reporting of catches. High-powered bass boats are equipped with sophisticated gear: foot-controlled electric trolling motors, gauges to measure the acid-base balance of the water, its temperature, and clarity, and depth recorders and liquid crystal screens that help locate fish.

Hunting as Outdoor Recreation

A second popular form of outdoor recreation includes both big-game and small-game hunting. Originally a source of food, hunting is still enjoyed for this purpose in many regions and rural areas, although it is primarily a leisure activity.

Although in the past some species were decimated or even destroyed by overhunting, today nature restocks its shelves each year with the creatures killed by hunters—50 million mourning doves, 28 million quail, 102 thousand elk, a thousand wolves, 750 bison, and miscellaneous goats, wolverines, and musk oxen—plus uncounted numbers of deer, which today have assumed pest status in many regions. Hunting is a peer-group activity participated in primarily by males. O'Leary, Behrens-Tepper, McGuire, and Dottavio describe the nature of the young hunter's introduction to the sport as a form of socialization into masculine society:

> a parent, close relative, or other responsible adult [acts] in the role of teacher and, not incidentally, transmitter of the hunting culture. It is perhaps not only this intimate interaction with an older hunting companion that causes hunting to persist into adult life, but also the implied rite of passage.[8]

Although city dwellers may think of hunters as simple country folk, demographically today's hunters are relatively well educated and drawn from a range of occupations and status levels. Hunting technology, like fishing technique, has become increasingly complex, with so-called prey acquisition systems that include scents and wildlife calls to attract game, infrared binoculars, "bionic earphones" to sharpen hearing, and trail monitors that record animals passing by in a particular location. A growing number of private clubs and lodges own or lease land—much of it from timber companies—for hunting preserves. In some western states like Montana and South Dakota, livestock ranchers have turned to operating shooting preserves for game ranging from geese and pheasants to antelope and bison.

The most serious objections to hunting practices today come from animal-rights activists who condemn hunting as a cruel and barbaric "sport." They are outraged by the practice of allowing hunters to shoot animals—ranging from otters to grizzly bears, whistling swans to bighorn sheep—on national wildlife refuges, tracts of prime habitat maintained by the U.S. Fish and Wildlife Service.

Organized outdoor recreation has become a major industry, with packaged tours and guide services for hunting, fishing, wilderness travel, and boating expeditions. Here, Rio Parissmina Lodge, on the Caribbean coast of Costa Rica, attracts many North Americans in search of superb tarpon and snook fishing. Above, the Allagash Guide Service in Allagash, Maine, serves bear or moose hunters with bow, primitive firearm, rifle, or camera. Winterhawk Outfitters, in Silt, Colorado, offers a variety of trail rides, fishing, photography, and sightseeing experiences.

⟹ TO THE POINT

Cleveland Amory, founder and president of the Fund for Animals, extends the case against hunting, pointing out that millions of animals and birds are crippled each year and die painful, lingering deaths. Beyond this, in a recent year, 177 people were killed and 1,719 injured by hunters, including many innocent bystanders walking in the woods or on their own property. Responding to the argument that hunters are the prime revenue source for protecting nonendangered wildlife, because they pay over $500 million a year for licenses, duck stamps, and excise taxes, Amory says:

> The bloodthirsty nuts claim they provide a service for the environment. Nonsense! A hunter goes into the woods to kill something, period . . . [and to] brag about his exploits or have a bearskin rug in his den. Hunting is an antiquated expression of macho self-aggrandizement, with no place in a civilized society.[9]

On the other hand, many hunters claim that hunting represents an important spiritual experience for them. Columnist Darrell Sifford encouraged readers to debate the views of a psychiatrist who had told him that hunting had significant meaning in his life. One reader wrote that the pressure of his work life made hunting both an escape and a reminder that there is "man's time and God's time." Groping his way through the woods or up a mountainside before dawn tells him that there is a cycle of life that doesn't need him or his petty comings and goings:

> The ebb and flow of the seasons, of life and death, moved by a cosmic force that has nothing to do with taxes, dioxin . . . movers, shakers, politics or most things important to human beings. . . . Hunting reminds me of that. I must dig through the crust of civilization and recapture the basic skills of my ancestors. . . . I touch a world where we've all—or at least most of us—forgotten how to cope, where we survive by our ability to take our sustenance from the wild state. It helps me put my daily world in better perspective.[10]

Although a number of state legislatures have begun to impose new curbs on hunting practices, it seems unlikely that animal activists will succeed in barring hunting as a popular leisure pursuit. It represents a tradition in many families and communities that will not be easily overthrown, and is linked to powerful national organizations like the National Rifle Association. As evidence of the economic implications of both hunting and fishing, major sports and outdoor recreation shows are held throughout the country, presenting demonstrations of sporting equipment, competitions, and other displays (see Figure 9.1).

Water-Based Recreation

One of the most attractive and popular forms of outdoor recreation involves water-based play. Rivers, ponds, lakes, reservoirs, and ocean areas all provide settings for a wide range of pursuits that include swimming, surfing, scuba diving, sailing, canoeing, waterskiing, and motorboating. In the mid-1970s, Ditton, Goodale, and

FIGURE 9.1
Advertisement for hunting
and fishing show

Johnsen studied a five-county area in Wisconsin in order to identify clusters of water-based recreationists to assist in government resource planning efforts. They examined participation frequencies for eight activities (fishing, sailing, waterskiing, motorboating, swimming, duck hunting, picnicking, and camping), and studied the interaction of these activity choices with such factors as age, level of education, and occupation. Based on their findings, they identified eight different clusters of participants who were attracted to different types of water-based environments—a useful tool in outdoor recreation planning.[11]

Similarly, John Heywood explored the relationships among different types of river recreation groups, in terms of their activity choices and the characteristics of their social groups. He identified a set of thirty-six different motivations for engaging in water-based recreation and found that these were linked to streams with different types of flow characteristics. White-water rafting, for example, at one level— that of relaxed floating down a gentle stream in inner tubes or on rubber inflatables—is likely to appeal to teenagers, family groups, or others seeking casual fun. On the other hand, white-water rafting down powerful streams with turbulent rapids may attract individuals who seek excitement and adventure.[12]

Boating as such is an immensely popular activity; the number of recreational boats of all kinds owned by Americans rose from 8.8 million in 1970 to 16 million in 1990. Varied forms of water play have also expanded. For example, scuba diving has become a $1 billion industry, according to the Diving Equipment Manufacturers Association, which reports that there are about 2.5 million scuba divers in the United States, with several hundred thousand new divers being certified each year. Sailing and competitive rowing tend to be elite sports, often appealing to young men and women who encounter them in yacht clubs and colleges. However, all forms of boating have grown in popularity over the last three decades, with approximately sixty million people who go boating at least a few times a year, as of the late 1980s. As an example of the economic impact of boating in a single state, Stoll, Bergstrom, and Jones reported that the recreational boating industry employed approximately 10,220 people in Texas in a recent year, with total revenues of over $610 million.[13]

As a final example of water-based recreation, surfing has long been a popular pastime of tanned, long-haired youth, particularly along the California coastline. Celebrated in movies and popular records, surfing represented a hedonistic life-style that flourished in the 1960s, when the quintessential surfer was a casual dude who lived for the moment. As surfing, like other leisure pursuits, has become increasingly commercialized, major beer, soft-drink, and other companies have used it as a focus of life-style marketing aimed at affluent young adults. Airlines and automobile companies today sponsor professional surfing tours and competitions, with television coverage and hundreds of thousands of dollars in prizes. In 1991, the Association of Surfing Professionals World Tour offered prizes totaling $2.2 million, and packaged surfing with beach volleyball and waterskiing in popular television shows.

At another level, surfing has become available to millions of Americans who do not live near the ocean through the introduction of wave pools, which use one of several engineering methods to send a surge of water several feet high from one end of the pool to the other at regular intervals. In a number of cases, such pools have been made part of complex water-play parks that include diving platforms, waterfalls, body flumes, and slides that provide exciting fun for family groups. Increasingly, pool designers have developed so-called leisure pools, which have sloping "beaches" leading into shallow water, with free-form shapes, lighting, and landscaping that give them the aura of tropical beaches—rather than traditional rectangular pools suited for instruction or for lap swimming.

■ OTHER COMMERCIALIZED ACTIVITIES: SNOWSKIING AND BIKING

Two other examples of outdoor recreation activities that have become highly commercialized leisure pursuits over the past three decades are snowskiing and biking. When it first became a popular pastime, snowskiing was a relatively simple sport, with close-to-home slopes, natural snow, inexpensive equipment, and simple rope tows. But as skiing became more popular in the 1960s and 1970s and hundreds of ski centers opened up around the United States, more elaborate and expensive equipment became necessary. Resorts from California to Maine, often with multimillion-dollar vacation-home complexes, conference centers, and upscale shopping and restaurant facilities, appealed to well-to-do singles and young families; in the 1980s, skiing became a $7 billion industry. However, changing demographics (with aging baby boomers and more young families unable to afford the cost of ski vacations), increased competition, concern about environmental problems, and disappointing weather conditions all led to a crisis in the industry, with many marginally profitable centers going out of business in the late 1980s.[14]

At the same time that it has undergone an economic recession, skiing has flourished as a spectator sport. Ski stars have become celebrities in Europe and America—and along with their increased exposure, have gained rich endorsement money and performance contracts with ski equipment companies. And, as the sport has become more of a spectacle, the nature of ski competitions has changed, with "hot-dog" skiers devising daredevil, high-flying stunts. For the average participant, however, skiing remains an exciting and challenging sport. For many, cross-country skiing serves both as an ideal fitness activity and as a safer form of winter play.

A second popular leisure pursuit that has been heavily commercialized in recent years is bicycling. In the mid-1970s, the A. C. Nielsen Company, a leading market-research firm, reported that bicycling was second only to swimming as a participant activity, with over sixty-five million participants each year. At that time and in the early 1980s, the lean touring cycles popularly known as 10-speeds accounted for 80 percent of United States bicycle sales. But in the late 1980s, a growing boom in biking interest—due in part to joggers who were frustrated with sore knees and ankles—led to a new kind of vehicle, the mountain bike. A crossbreed of rugged utility and European racing technology, these tough, practically maintenance-free cycles, also known as all-terrain bikes, make use of high-tech alloys, tubing, and lugs borrowed from the aerospace industry for lightweight strength. They feature flat handlebars for upright seating and thick tires that handle sand, gravel, and rough slopes as easily as pavement. It was reported in 1991 that sales of bikes had climbed by as much as 30 percent in one year, with mountain bikes representing over half of those sold.[15]

Conflicts Between Environmentalists and Recreationists

As bicycling has become a more fashionable sport, as many as fourteen million Americans from eight to eighty enjoy trail-riding in wilderness settings. But there is a dark side to this trend. Sandra Blakeslee writes:

> Many hikers and equestrians, who are being asked to share their favorite trails with mountain bikers, are putting up a stiff fight. They say that the bikers are eroding mountain trails, shattering the peace and quiet of wilderness retreats and careening down hills at speeds that endanger the safety of other trail users.[16]

This dispute is part of a much larger conflict between those who are concerned about protecting the natural environment and a diversified group of outdoor recreationists who are using off-road vehicles, as well as an ongoing conflict between different groups of recreationists themselves. Bernard Mergen points out that recreational travel has become a huge, complex industry, involving a great variety of vehicles: "the manufacture and sale of pickup trucks, motor homes, vans, off-road vehicles, snowmobiles, trail bikes, motorcycles, motorboats, and airplanes have increased enormously. Bicycles, sailboats, canoes, gliders, and balloons have also pro-liferated."[17]

As an example of the popularity of such forms of outdoor recreation, the use of off-road vehicles on Bureau of Land Management properties rose from 19.4 million visits in 1982 to 63 million in 1990. But by the mid-1980s, public opposition to the use of all-terrain vehicles had grown dramatically in many areas of the country. Many property owners in rural areas have been disturbed by the use of vehicles that destroy property, cause land erosion, create high noise levels, and are used for illegal hunting of deer. In some cases, booby traps have been placed in wooded rural areas, with hidden pits and pointed oak poles implanted in them, and with fishing line, chains, baling wire, and steel hooks hung at eye level to catch riders. Additionally, a number of state park and environmental departments have passed regulations to prohibit the use of ATVs on public roads, or on state forest or game lands. This represents only one of the areas in which authorities are concerned about the impact of invasive vehicles on wildlife, the natural environment, and other outdoor recreationists. Riders of jet skis, for example, have been described as "motorcycle gangs on the water," as they race at speeds of over forty miles an hour, are involved in frequent accidents, and harass other recreationists on the nation's lakes and rivers.

Beyond such problems, there are numerous other examples of conflicts between different groups of outdoor recreationists. Jackson and Wong document several studies that show marked differences in leisure motivations and outdoor behaviors that pit cross-country skiers and snowmobilers against each other:

> Cross-country skiers prefer self-propelled, low-impact activities which reflect their desire for solitude, tranquility and a relatively undisturbed natural environment. Snowmobilers prefer machine-oriented and extractive activities which provide an outlet for adventurousness and sociability.[18]

Similar disagreements have been found between adherents of motorboating and canoeing, trail-biking and hiking, boating and fishing, and other outdoor pastimes. In part, the frictions stem from overcrowding, with many natural attractions experiencing what has been called "greenlock." Everywhere, *Time Magazine* reports,

> authorities are having to ration the outdoors with lotteries, permits and reservations for everything from biking to hiking. . . . [For example] the U.S. Forest Service, which administers the Salmon and other prime Idaho rivers, grants just 1,100 permits to rafting parties annually. They are chosen by lottery from more than 11,000 applicants.[19]

▐▶ TO THE POINT

Ticketron reservations for campsites at Yosemite go on sale eight weeks in advance, and are snapped up in less than five minutes. Even bicyclists planning to pedal Canyonlands National Park's Island in the Sky trail in Utah must apply at least two weeks ahead. In part, the problem is one of commercial interests dominating the nation's natural resources. For example, most of the twenty-two thousand slots for riding the Colorado River through the Grand Canyon go to commercial companies; individual applicants face a minimum waiting time of three to five years. Beyond this, some of the most valued national treasures, unique for their natural wonders, have been outfitted with overly civilized amenities. Yosemite's Ahwahnee Hotel offers guests cozy rooms equipped with television sets and minibars; visitors can patronize a pizza parlor, a gourmet deli, a one-hour photo service, an automatic bank machine, and a gift shop filled with items with the Yosemite logo.

Critics of such arrangements cite the warning of Horace Albright, first civilian superintendent of Yellowstone and second director of the Park Service:

> Oppose with all your strength and power all proposals to penetrate your wilderness regions with motorways and other symbols of modern mechanization. Keep large sections of primitive country free from the influence of destructive civilization. Keep those bits of primitive America for those who seek peace and rest in the silent place . . . remember, once opened, they can never be wholly restored to primeval charm and grandeur. . . . Park usefulness and popularity should not be measured in terms of mere numbers of visitors. Some precious park areas can easily be destroyed by the concentration of too many visitors. We should be interested in the quality of park patronage, not in the quantity.[20]

Within the spectrum of conflicting leisure pursuits in heavily crowded outdoor settings, what values should be given priority? Robert Manning points out that wilderness visitors are not homogeneous populations, but have value systems that cover a wide and often conflicting range. Often activity choices are dictated by age and family life-cycle factors, with camping activities shifting through each stage of the life cycle. For example, from a Pacific Northwest study, it was determined that

> combination campers (those who participated in both wilderness and automobile camping) were found to generally represent the early stages of the family life cycle, automobile campers represented the middle and postretirement stages, and wilderness camping families represented those just beginning their families and those in the contracting stage of the family life cycle.[21]

As a way of dealing with such diversified interests and needs, a number of classification or zoning systems for recreation areas have been proposed through the years. Typically, these suggest six or seven types of zones, ranging from "wilderness" to "intensive-use" areas. Ultimately, since they are responsible for administering major outdoor recreation resources and dealing with the public that uses them, Leo McAvoy argues that members of the park and recreation profession should assume fuller leadership for environmental stewardship. He points out that too often recreation managers wind up battling with environmental advocates, with whom they should be allied.[22]

McAvoy urges park and recreation professionals to adopt an environment ethic that will serve as the basis for making policy decisions and choices in resource planning and program development. Such an ethic would not only establish a code of behavior, but would also assign priority to educating the public with respect to environmental stewardship, and to developing political advocacy for needed policies and practices.

■ ADVENTURE RECREATION

Much of the appeal of outdoor recreation stems from the degree of risk it entails, as men and women pit themselves against the challenges that are inherent in the wilderness environment or are found in certain forms of vigorous and dangerous activity (see Table 9.3).

Today, such activities are often categorized as forms of "risk" recreation, although they may have sharply different emphases. Some adventure programs are concerned with character development and may be used, in the form of survival training, with such diverse groups as business executives, military personnel, and disturbed or delinquent adolescents to strengthen their positive self-concepts, leadership skills, and modes of interaction with others. Most adventure activities, however, are not undertaken as part of such educational or therapeutic programs, but are simply part of the spectrum of outdoor play. Activities such as mountain climbing, ski jumping, and hang gliding satisfy the craving that some people have to experience danger and challenge. Alan Ewert and Steve Hollenshorst describe adventure recreation as: "A variety of self-initiated activities utilizing an interaction with the natural environment, that contain elements of real or apparent danger, in which the outcome, while uncertain, can be influenced by the participant and circumstances."[23]

It is worth noting that many girls and women have become involved in varied forms of risk recreation, including all-female rock-climbing groups, white-water rafting trips, and wilderness exploration outings, partly because they perceive these as forms of self-empowerment. Indeed, Bialeschki points out that as long ago as the late 1800s, many women took part in dangerous expeditions and mountain-climbing adventures and were a large part of the membership of the Sierra Club and the Alpine Club of Canada.[24]

TABLE 9.3
Killer sports: Death rates of outdoor recreation activities

Activity	Deaths per 100,000 Participants
Mountain climbing	599.0
Hang gliding	114.0
Parachuting	24.0
Snowmobiling	13.0
Mountain hiking	6.4
Scuba diving	2.9
Boating	2.7
Alpine ski racing	2.5
Waterskiing	0.3
Downhill skiing	0.1

SOURCE: National Safety Council; based on fatalities reported during the five-year period preceding 1987. See *U.S. News and World Report,* January 15, 1990, p. 67.

Fascination with danger is not limited to participation in traditional forms of outdoor recreation. Many spectator events, such as stock-car racing, air shows, and other contests that have the constant risk of deadly accidents appeal to huge audiences. In some cases, specific forms of risk-recreation may develop cults of enthusiasts, such as a unique group of hang gliders in Hawaii at Makapuu Point, atop a 1,200-foot sheer cliff at the east end of the island of Oahu, who died one after another in gliding accidents in the mid-1970s.

In the search for new challenges, outdoor recreationists have evolved new forms of traditional pursuits. For example, mountain climbing has given rise to such variations as ice-climbing on frozen waterfalls; bouldering, which involves climbing short, extremely difficult grades; and trekking, a combination of long-distance hiking and different varieties of mountaineering. More and more, risk activities are being commercially packaged and marketed to the public at large. For example, in the early 1990s, a modified form of skydiving was introduced to the United States, as the Australian sport of bungee-jumping—leaping from a cliff or a bridge while attached to a long rubber cable—caught the public's fancy.

There are numerous other examples of fads or stunts that people engage in as forms of exciting play that have a serious risk of death or injury. Some simply represent an extension or variation of a familiar pursuit. For example, roller-skating has given rise to in-line skates—similar to ice skates on wheels. These high-speed, tricky devices have evolved into a $150 million industry—and have caused a rising number of serious fractures, sprains, and contusions, as racers speed along, often without protective padding or helmets. Participants in other risky outdoor pursuits include boaters who drink and race their craft wildly, tourists who ignore natural dangers such as bubbling hot springs or crocodiles in shallow rivers, and entrants in snake-sacking contests, who gather diamondback rattlesnakes as part of fund-raising drives.

Such forms of play, which involve deliberate flirting with danger, may in their most extreme forms become almost suicidal. Psychiatrist Paul Haun labeled them "pathological play," citing such pursuits as Russian Roulette as games that might have immediately fatal consequences.[25] Regularly, brief items appear in newspapers giving details of children and youth who lose their lives playing chicken on the highway (two cars race toward each other, with the first to veer away labeled as "chicken"), riding on the underside of elevators in housing projects, or taking part in other daredevil stunts that appeal to youth gangs. Giant roller coasters, which are actually much less dangerous, but are designed to create fear, thrive on the element of danger and tragedy. When a major accident occurs at an amusement park, attendance climbs dramatically.[26]

⏵ TO THE POINT

What accounts for this human fascination with risk, danger, and violence? One theory of play suggests that a common drive underlying much leisure activity consists of the personal need to experience competence or mastery in overcoming challenges that go beyond the sober realities of everyday life. Stainbrook writes: "So much of life has become sedentary, inhibiting action; thrill-seeking expresses an almost desperate need for assertive mastery of something."[27]

A psychology professor at Johns Hopkins University, Marvin Zuckerman, points out that boredom often leads people to engage in such thrill-seeking activities as risky forms of play, adulterous sex, the use of drugs or alcohol, and even physical aggression. Zuckerman has designed a "sensation-seeking" scale designed to show the extent to which different individuals need such forms of excitement and seek higher levels of stimulation in everything from commodities-market speculation to skydiving.[28] University of Wisconsin psychologist Frank Farley suggests that the society itself promotes such behavior. He calls America a "type-T" nation—"the 'T' stands for thrill seekers—in which creative risk takers comprise as much as 20 percent of the general public. 'They are the great experimenters of life,' asserts Farley. 'They break the rules.'"[29]

Within a more analytical framework, Stephen Lyng describes a model of voluntary risk-taking behavior that he calls "edgework," based on his own involvement as a "jump" pilot for a local skydiving center, including a five-year study of a group of skydivers. He writes:

> edgeworkers typically seek to define the limits of performance for a particular object or form. One category of edgework involves efforts to discover the performance limits of certain types of technology, as when test pilots take their airplanes "to the outside of the envelope" . . . or when race-car drivers push their cars to their mechanical limits.[30]

Lyng found that participants in different forms of edgework claimed that the experience produced a sense of "self-realization," "self-actualization," or "self-determination." Clearly, risk-takers were not suicidal; they experienced considerable fear in the early stages of an "adventure," but also felt that their experiences led to a sense of hyperreality—being much more vivid and real than other, day-to-day activities. However, his concept applies chiefly to risk-takers who are highly skilled, who attempt to control the circumstances of their involvement by getting as close as possible to the "edge" without going over it. They are not typically interested in gambling or other forms of thrill-seeking danger that they cannot control to a degree.

The "No-Rescue" Proposal

Some authorities have suggested that "no-rescue" wilderness areas should be established, where those seeking high adventure might come fully to grips with the possibility of life-or-death challenges. Initially, historian Roderick Nash suggested the establishment of five categories of wilderness, including one category described as

> "remote, rugged, and dangerous; expedition level skills, no trails, signs, patrols, or search-and-rescue." He proposed a no-rescue wilderness as an area of land in a national park, forest or preserve where the government would be prohibited from conducting search-and-rescue operations.[31]

Nash's proposal led to a spirited debate. Those in favor of the no-rescue idea argued that, from a philosophical perspective, such wilderness areas would symbolize the last stronghold of individual freedom and responsibility in an increasingly regulated and bureaucratic world. Opponents to the proposal retorted that it would be inhumane to abandon people who had overestimated their own abilities or were the victims of unforeseen catastrophes. Don Peterson summarizes the negative views, pointing out that inevitably, if persons like important government officials, pregnant women, or the very old and frail sought rescue, it would be very difficult to ignore them—and thus the policy would be discriminatory.[32]

■ NEEDS OF URBAN RESIDENTS

Although outdoor recreation is frequently thought of in terms of remote wilderness areas or federal and state parks, approximately 80 percent of the nation's population lives in metropolitan areas. As described earlier, to meet their needs most cities and surrounding suburban communities today have park and recreation departments that operate sports facilities, pools, nature centers, marinas, and other leisure facilities.

Even in ghetto areas of large cities, residents may engage in varied forms of nature-oriented play, including pigeon-raising on tenement rooftops, picnicking and even overnight camping in large urban parks, and visiting natural history museums, botanical gardens, and zoos that increasingly provide accurate replicas of natural settings. At the same time, it is a reality that many poorer urban residents are unable to afford more than the most limited exposure to such outdoor experiences. Only a few cities have established arrangements through which children from city slums are able to visit suburban or rural homes for a week or two each summer. Thus, the barriers to diversified leisure opportunity based on socioeconomic factors are vividly illustrated within the realm of outdoor recreation.

■ TOURISM: A MAJOR INDUSTRY

Closely linked to outdoor recreation as a form of leisure activity is travel and tourism. The term *travel* usually describes trips extending over a minimum period of time, such as one day with an overnight stay, or trips covering a distance of 100 miles or more. *Tourism* represents that portion of travel that is carried on for personal reasons such as pleasure-seeking, visiting new environments, family reunions, or other leisure-related purposes, as opposed to purely practical functions. In the mid-1980s, John Hunt pointed out that tourism had become a major business enterprise in the United States and throughout the world:

> Tourism creates immense business activity. It accounts for 6 to 7 percent of the Gross National Product and ranks as the third largest retail industry in terms of sales and the second largest private employer in the United States. Estimates generated by the U.S. Travel Data Center indicate that Americans made total travel expenditures of $234 billion on trips of 100 miles or more from home in 1984. Nearly 93 percent of this was spent on travel in the United States. . . . [Expenditures] generated 4.7 million jobs with a payroll of $50.9 billion.[33]

TABLE 9.4

Selected trip characteristics for U.S. travelers: 1983–1990. Table shows number of trips, in millions.

Characteristic	1983	1988	1990
Total	540.9	656.1	661.1
Purpose			
Visit friends and relatives	181.9	213.8	246.0
Other pleasure	189.6	241.5	214.5
Business or convention	103.6	155.6	155.6
Other	65.8	45.2	45.0
Mode of transport			
Auto, truck, recreational vehicles	396.1	472.6	483.9
Airplane	116.2	154.6	144.9
Other	28.6	28.9	32.3
Vacation trip	307.8	396.2	422.3
Weekend trip	225.5	271.7	280.0

SOURCE: U.S. Travel Data Center, Washington, DC, Annual National Travel Survey

The growth and extent of tourism are illustrated in Table 9.4, which describes the characteristics of travel in America during the 1980s.

There are five essential interrelated elements in tourism: the people who travel, transportation to and from destinations, accommodations and related facilities, information and travel arrangements, and attractions. The motivations for tourism are varied. Most people travel to meet personal needs—to revitalize or enrich their lives, to relax, to escape routine, or to learn about different environments. Based on these motivations, some authorities suggest that there are four different styles of tourism: (1) educational, cultural, and historical, involving cultural awareness and enrichment; (2) sightseeing, which focuses on spectacular, beautiful, or unusual scenery or natural phenomena; (3) relaxation and hedonism, which emphasizes simple pleasure as a focus of travel; and (4) adventure, in which the tourist seeks out experiences that provide a challenge and often a physical risk.

From a scholarly perspective, many of the key elements of tourism may be directly related to academic studies and research. For example, tourist motivations may be studied in psychology departments; host-guest relationships in anthropology; environmental impacts in ecology or natural science; tourist marketing in business education; tourist planning and development in urban and regional planning; rural tourism in agriculture; legal aspects in departments or schools of law; and tourist agency management in departments of park and recreation management. The tourist experience itself has been conceptualized as a form of performed art, as Judith Adler points out in the *American Journal of Sociology*. She writes:

> Travel has been written about and consciously practiced as an art for almost five centuries. . . . The travel writings of Laurence Sterne and of Rousseau, for example, inspired emulative "sentimental" journeys in the late eighteenth century. Later, many travelers overtly gave themselves and their journeys such labels as "romantic," "picturesque," "philosophical," "curious," and "sentimental."[34]

Tourism may involve a wide variety of individual or group purposes. A trip to Washington, D.C., may center about an emotional visit to the Vietnam War Memorial to mourn a family loss. Third-generation Americans may make an excursion to the Statue of Liberty or to Ellis Island, where their immigrant grandparents first set foot on this country's soil. Motivations for tourism may also include hedonistic purposes, like visiting Las Vegas or Atlantic City to enjoy casino-based gambling and entertainment. A single leisure interest, such as sports, accounts for many trips each year; millions typically travel to sports events and major tournaments.

Roughing It vs. Luxury Tourism

Some tourist travel is rough and ready, with a minimum of personal comfort. Over five thousand guides, outfitters, and travel agents now offer or arrange packaged trips to locations that were almost impossible to reach in past years. It is possible to travel by horse, bicycle, dogsled, or one's own two feet, and to opt for primitive camping and total immersion in native cultures.

On the other hand, many travelers prefer the comfort of ocean cruises. During the 1980s, major cruise companies built huge new ocean liners that were far more than simply vehicles to get from one country to another, but instead evolved into floating amusement parks, health spas, nightclubs, and classrooms. The growth of ocean cruising has been spectacular, climbing from half a million Americans who took cruises in 1970, to 1.5 million in 1982, to a record four million in 1991. Booth writes:

> There's a cruise ship for virtually every taste and pocketbook—122 based in North America alone—from megaliners with more than 2,600 passengers to small exploration-type vessels for fewer than 100. The 250 passengers now taking the full round-the-world cruise on Cunard's QE2 paid as much as $126,900 for their staterooms and luxurious life-style, but the rich aren't alone on the high seas. About 40 percent of today's cruise passengers earn $20,000 to $39,000 a year and a three-day cruise in the Bahamas can cost as little as $500 to $800 for two.[35]

Cultural Tourism and Group Tours

In contrast to purely pleasure-oriented tourism, many travelers today are shunning all-play vacations for archaeological digs, research expeditions, horticultural field trips, and other learning excursions concerned with finding out about the arts, history, science, and culture of different countries. In many cases, they are part of group tours—a popular phenomenon in modern-day tourism. Molly Schuchat analyzed such tours from an ethnographic perspective, pointing out that Americans often join tours to be guided by experts, meet counterparts and unfold their own personal identities, and learn how to be travelers within an organized and relatively safe framework. Industry experts agree that people move in tour groups for safety and assistance, and to get more for their money—often within a limited period of time. Schuchat writes:

Tourist motivations and modes of travel vary widely. Above, visitors examine jewelry and other craft articles made by Native American artists in the pueblos surrounding Santa Fe, New Mexico, and a Pueblo Indian girl takes part in feast day ceremonies as others watch. Left and below, tourists enjoy a luxurious cruise to Mexico offered by Royal Caribbean Cruise, Ltd.

Tour groups offer a delimited and defined testing ground for the resolution of identity crises. They are often used by individuals recently bereaved by death or divorce. Sometimes the group tour will provide support for a return to places previously visited with a loved one—or only known of through a loved one.[36]

Nostalgic tourism often is based on Americans who wish to explore or relive their personal past or interesting elements of the nation's history. This is made possible by the establishment of museums, restoration villages, or other tourist attractions that show buildings, occupations, ethnic customs, costumes, and life-styles of earlier periods of history. Probably the best known example of historic preservation is Colonial Williamsburg—a depiction of what life was like in a colonial Virginia village. Recently, social critics have begun to challenge such reconstructions, claiming that they lack any sense of reality or historic continuity and instead are often detached, remote, and essentially lifeless. They comment:

> Williamsburg is a fantasy in which the more pleasing aspects of colonial life are meticulously evoked, with the omission of smells, flies, pigs, dirt and slave quarters. [It is] history homogenized, cleaned up, and expurgated . . . an entirely artificial recreation of an imaginary past.[37]

Such criticism was stimulated by ferment in the historical museum field in the 1960s and 1970s, when grassroots museums sprang up around the United States to preserve and commemorate local heritage. In some cases, black community residents joined forces to save and maintain the slave cabins, "shotgun" houses, little frame churches, and one-room schoolhouses that tell the story of African Americans in the past. Museums and historical collections provide a broader perspective on blacks in America. Washington, D.C., publishes an extensive list of tours and attractions highlighting African-American history in the nation's capital, extending back in time to the role of Benjamin Banneker, a black mathematician who assisted Pierre L'Enfant in designing the city.

Native Americans represent a major element of tourist interest, with hundreds of attractions on Indian reservations that involve traditional ceremonies, rituals, and the display of dance and other customs, drawing many visitors.

Once discouraged and even forbidden by the federal Bureau of Indian Affairs, today these ceremonies, which blend religion, respect for nature, and community harmony, are increasingly finding their place as a national treasure. Due to concern that such religious rituals may be affected by the presence of too many tourists, tribal authorities try to regulate the number of spectators, although outsiders may attend most traditional events, provided that they maintain a respectful attitude.

In general, the trend in museums, celebrations, festivals, and other cultural and historical tourist attractions is to provide a more accurate picture of America's past than textbooks and movies have traditionally done. For example, the familiar idea that heroic white male settlers brought civilization to a savage wilderness is now viewed as distorted and, in many cases, racist and sexist. Recent historical research shows that the early West was a place of pitiless struggle involving not only courageous white men but many other human types: Indian chiefs and black newspapermen, society women and prostitutes, fur trappers and squaws. More than half the people who traveled west to search for gold and silver found nothing and went home—if they went home at all—nearly destitute. There was suffering and oppression, of women, of those who were black, Asian, or Hispanic, and of Indians, who were cheated and massacred wholesale.[38]

As part of cultural tourism, many museums have diversified their holdings and developed new appeals for the traveling public. For example, the famous federal penitentiary at San Quentin, California, has transformed an abandoned building into a museum designed to appeal to tourists. It features a rich and diverse history that makes use of old uniforms, photographs, a scale model of a gas chamber, a ball and chain, home-made weapons, depictions of a famous group escape, and other elements of life behind the bars.

Patriotic sites, military battlefields, buildings, and events provide the basis for other tourist attractions around the nation. Even the Vietnam Veterans Memorial, a long wall of black marble with the names of thousands of victims of this conflict, has proven to have such a powerful degree of public interest that four fiberglass replicas of it have been constructed and are touring the country, staying in different communities for set periods of time. People continue to have a strong reaction to these traveling walls. They leave flags, letters, poems, flowers, and Father's Day cards at them, and they touch the names lightly and cry.

In many cases, special events or traditional customs draw huge crowds to given cities. Examples include the World Series, the Super Bowl, the Indianapolis 500, Mardi Gras in New Orleans, and Cheyenne Frontier Days in Wyoming—events that appeal strongly to vacationists. Even natural catastrophes may help create tourist Meccas, as in the case of Mount Saint Helens, whose massive eruption led to hundreds of thousands of travelers who travel to Washington State each year to marvel over the devastation it wrought.

While "cultural" tourism may provide valuable insights into the lives of other people, it may also represent a form of exploitation. When the countries that are visited are markedly poorer than the tourist-generating nation, leisure travel may involve callous indifference to the misery of the people who are being observed. Research in tourist settings in the Caribbean has shown that usually native residents hold only the most unskilled and poorly paid service jobs, with little income going directly to the local economies. Adler points out that much tourist development in the Third World

> has been concerned with the deformation of native cultures as they become staged for commercial consumption and misrepresented through the distorting lens of marketing imagery [and with] nationalists in tourist-receiving countries [becoming] particularly sensitive to . . . perpetuation of a racist or colonialist vision.[39]

⮞ TO THE POINT

One of the less savory aspects of such exploitation as an aspect of tourism has to do with travelers who seek forms of hedonistic play or entertainment that are not readily available in their own nation. For example, one of the most famous tourist attractions in India has traditionally been the Hindu temple complex at Khajuraho, a small, isolated town in the central Indian state of Madhya Pradesh. The temples are embellished with thousands of sculptures of gods and goddesses, spirits, men, women, and animals in an infinite number of sexual postures. Niloufer points out that in contemporary, puritanical India, where journals and movies are highly censored, this art is damned as pornography, but permitted to exist and to provide a major tourist attraction because of its legitimate religious origins and because it represents one of India's major cultural and economic resources.[40]

In a more contemporary vein, tourism in present-day Thailand is heavily based on sex, with many thousands of visitors, particularly from other Asian nations, who come to the country because of its readily available prostitutes—particularly child prostitutes. As a consequence, Thailand is suffering from an epidemic of AIDS; in 1993 it was reported that 60 percent of Japanese men who had contracted AIDS through sex with women had caught it on overseas "sex tours" to Thailand, South Korea, and Taiwan. Typically, before Cuba was taken over by Fidel Castro, Havana and other Cuban cities were used as "sin" playgrounds by many American tourists, who went there for commercialized sex, drugs, and gambling that were not easily available in the United States.

A related type of attraction involves so-called sleaze tourism—travel in search of more dubious aspects of American culture. Travelers by the millions seek out curious sites each year through "scandal tours" that visit such places as: "Bonnie and Clyde's death car; where JFK met Judith Campbell Exner; directions to Pete Rose's bookie's joint; where they ambushed John Dillinger; where Huey Long was shot; where Nixon's dog Checkers is buried . . ."[41]

■ ECONOMIC ROLE OF TOURISM

As this chapter has shown, tourism represents a huge and growing source of income for many states, regions, and nations. In Baltimore, Maryland, for example, the creation of a critical mass of attractions in the city's Inner Harbor increased the amount of annual tourist spending to a total of $400 million. With the construction or reconstruction of numerous hotels and the addition of new retail and entertainment facilities, over thirty thousand new jobs have been created. Beyond such statistical benefits, the Inner Harbor developments led to a change in the psychological attitudes of Baltimore residents toward their own city: "Prior to the 'renaissance,' Baltimoreans had been disdainful of their city, and sarcastic comments were the rule rather than the exception. After the success of the revitalization program the citizens of the city turned into frank and unashamed 'boosters.'"[42]

Economic benefits similar to those gained in Baltimore may be found in many other cities. While obviously the jobs provided by tourism are critically important in bolstering local economies, in some cases tourism has expanded so greatly that states have begun to discourage tourists, just as they have discouraged new residents. On the

1. Respect the frailty of the earth.
2. Leave only footprints. Take only photographs.
3. Educate yourself about geography, customs, manners, and cultures.
4. Respect the privacy and dignity of others.
5. Do not buy products from endangered plants or animals.
6. Follow designated trails.
7. Learn about and support conservation-oriented programs and organizations.
8. Whenever possible, walk or use enviro-sound transportation.
9. Patronize hotels, resorts, airlines, tour operators who advance energy and enviro-conservation, water and air quality, recycling ...
10. Ask your Asta Travel [agent] to identify those organizations that subscribe to Asta enviro-guidelines.

FIGURE 9.2
Ten commandments of the American Society of Travel Agents

international scene, a typical example is the village of St. Napa on the island of Cyprus, which has been overwhelmed by crowds of Scandinavian, German, and British sun-seekers. The effect of tourism on St. Napa has been to turn its beaches into topless playgrounds and its picturesque old neighborhoods into a garish tourist ghetto of discotheques, souvenir shops, fast-food places, and pubs—totally altering the quality of life for year-round residents.

Growing sensitivity of both outdoor recreation professionals and those involved in tourism is displayed in Figure 9.2, which presents guidelines for minimizing the impact of pleasure travel on the natural environment.

■ THEME PARKS: THE DISNEY PHENOMENON

No discussion of contemporary tourism would be complete without considering the role of theme parks, which represent a major type of family-oriented travel attraction. Theme parks had their origin in American amusement parks, which flourished in the late nineteenth century and the early decades of the twentieth. Often built in combination with transportation facilities, such as trolley-car lines or excursion boats, amusement parks usually combined several different types of entertainment—roller coasters and other "thrill" rides, midways with varied game booths, funhouses, "freak" shows, and restaurants and beer gardens.

Some of the more famous amusement parks, like New York's Coney Island, had large, impressive structures with fantastic or futuristic architecture similar to buildings designed for major world's fairs at the time. Others featured fire-and-rescue panoramas, pygmy tribe "villages," haunted houses, or rides through frightening environments.

During the years before and after World War II, amusement parks gradually became more tawdry and run-down, with forms of entertainment that were no longer family-oriented. As attendance declined and properties were sold for other real-estate uses, many parks were closed. Then, in the mid-1950s, a new kind of attraction—the theme park—appeared on the American scene. The first major theme park was Disneyland, established in Anaheim, California, in 1955. Disney's formula was to provide a carefully designed, wholesome, and appealing environment geared to meet family values, with an astute combination of essentially passive recreational experiences—rides through imaginatively designed and technologically clever environments and entertainment featuring the Disney cast of characters.

During the 1960s and 1970s, numerous other theme parks appeared, usually with central themes or images drawn from children's literature, history, or exotic environments or forms of adventure. Among the most successful were the Bally Corporation's Six Flags chain, Busch Entertainment's Dark Continent, Olde Country, Silver Dollar City, and The Great Escape, and Marriott's Great America chain. Some parks, with a variety of rides, water-play facilities, and children's play areas, are participatory in nature; others provide essentially passive or spectator-type entertainment.

Not content with its early successes, Disney added the Disney World complex in Orlando, Florida, in the 1970s and then the Epcot Center (an acronym for Experimental Prototype Community of Tomorrow), an $800 million, 260-acre development consisting of two portions: (1) Future World, with corporate pavilions primarily concerned with technology; and (2) the World Showcase, with international pavilions showing tourist attractions of various nations around the world—all connected to Disney World's Magic Kingdom by a monorail. In the late 1980s, the Florida complex was expanded with the addition of Disney-MGM Studios, featuring the Great Movie Ride, a tram trip through cinematic wonders, a Backstage Studio Tour of Disney's television and movie-production facilities, and other inside looks at the world of movie "magic."

⫸ TO THE POINT

In the 1990s, the Disney theme park operations continue to expand, with a 470-acre Disneyland Resort in California, a mega-project costing an estimated three billion dollars, six times the size of the original Disneyland. Its new Westcot Center, modeled after the futuristic Epcot Center in Florida, is expected to create 27,900 jobs and generate about $2.4 billion annually. Beyond these domestic ventures, Disney has also expanded on the international scene, with new parks in Japan and France, built with cooperative planning and licensing arrangements with business groups in those nations. The Euro Disneyland, which opened near Paris in 1992, met angry criticism from French intellectuals and social critics, who saw it as evidence of American "cultural colonialism." George Will writes:

> French intellectuals are calling Euro Disneyland "a cultural Chernobyl" and a "terrifying giant step toward world homogenization" and a "horror made of cardboard, plastic and appalling colors, a construction of hardened chewing gum and idiotic folklore taken straight out of comic books written for obese Americans."[43]

Popular Florida theme parks offer varied attractions that appeal especially to family patrons. Visitors to Silver Springs come face to face with giraffes (left) and, at a Wildlife Outpost (above), a bald eagle, hawk, black bear, western cougar, and other native animals. Below, Cypress Gardens features a spectacular water-ski show, beautiful gardens, and other entertainment.

Despite such reactions and initially disappointing attendance, the spectacular Disney park, built on 4,800 acres with six huge hotels and a championship golf course at a total cost of $4 billion, is expected to be a financial success—in part because it will facilitate the marketing of thousands of Disney-licensed products throughout Europe in the years ahead. The complex network of Disney entertainment ventures, of which tourism is only one part, clearly illustrates the domination of a major portion of American leisure by powerful conglomerates. The Disney empire, in addition to its theme parks (which include numerous hotels, restaurants, shops, and other profitable enterprises) encompasses a huge movie studio, which, in the late 1980s, ranked as the top American filmmaker, with a 30 percent share of all U.S. box-office revenues. The Disney television channel has been the fastest growing pay-TV service in the United States, and the company has expanded its Disney Store chain into a 100-shop operation, along with a successful direct-mail catalogue aimed at home buyers of Disney-related products.

Beyond its financial successes, however, the Disney entertainment operations have had a profound impact on American culture in other respects. Recognizing that the Disney parks draw more visitors annually than any other American attraction, and that they have become "total destination resorts" without rival, directors of museums of every kind are using their principles to attract, involve, and educate the public. Writing in *The Futurist,* Margaret King points out that the Disney-pioneered approach to theming has become

> a standard and model for all large-scale exhibit installations. . . . Although often dismissed as mere entertainment, the theme park has generated an ever-widening circle of influence, ranging from town planning and historical preservation to building architecture, mall design and merchandising. Its impact extends further to video- and computer-assisted education, home and office decor, exhibit design, and crowd management.[44]

With their innovative applications of technology to design, construction, and entertainment, Disney's "Imagineers" have widely influenced the nation's cultural landscape, bridging the gap between art and science, in

> the arts of audioanimatronics; applications of computers to problems in communication and exhibition; new uses of videodiscs, electronics and fiber optics; the remaking of historic artifacts as "surrogate objects" by advanced engineering; the melding of space-age with neotraditional forms and functions . . .[45]

■ SUMMARY

Taken as a whole, outdoor recreation, travel, and tourism in the United States represent a unique and diversified sector of leisure involvement. Outdoor recreation relies in part on a love of the land and its traditions, and on enjoyment of nature-centered pursuits, along with many opportunities for adventurous forms of play. Tourism is based on sophisticated planning and marketing that probes the wishes and needs of the public and blends past and future, fantasy and reality together in complex commercial attractions. Despite their differences, outdoor recreation and tourism are often linked, as people travel to picturesque destinations to fish, hunt, ski, or explore new environments. For the middle- and upper-classes, they offer appealing diversion, excitement, cultural and educational enrichment, and the thrill of seeing new regions and landmarks. For the poor, they are realistically limited to only the most basic kinds of experiences.

■ QUESTIONS FOR DISCUSSION

1. Discuss outdoor recreation as a major type of leisure activity, in terms of the degree of freedom and personal choice it offers, the values obtained from it, and the motivations of participants. Refer to specific forms of outdoor play as illustrations.

2. How significant is outdoor recreation as a form of economic enterprise? What are examples of major areas of spending and economic benefit? What are some of the negative aspects of highly attractive and successful outdoor recreation operations for local residents or the environment?

3. Some forms of outdoor recreation are controversial, such as those mentioned in this chapter: hunting, use of off-road vehicles, or high-risk activities. Select any one of these and identify its positive and negative aspects, along with appropriate policies for constructive management in publicly owned parks and forests.

4. Tourism may be carried on with several different kinds of styles and motivations, such as "comfort," "cultural," "nostalgic," "adventure," or "hedonistic" emphases. Give examples of each of these, and show how they may be marketed with respect to different demographic characteristics of potential travelers (age, education, gender, or social class and life-style factors).

5. A theme park may be seen as an ideal type of tourist attraction, particularly for families, or as an artificial, essentially passive form of packaged entertainment. In your view, what accounts for the success of theme parks? Do you agree with the criticism cited of the new Disney park in France?

■ NOTES

1. HUNT, J. D. 1986. Tourism comes of age in the 1980s. *Parks and Recreation* (Oct.): 31.
2. STREET, A. B., cited in P. G. Terrie. 1985. *Forever wild: Environmental aesthetics and the Adirondack forest preserve.* Philadelphia: Temple University Press.
3. LA PAGE, L. F., and S. R. RANNEY. 1988. America's wilderness: The heart and soul of culture. *Parks and Recreation* (July): 24.
4. MCAVOY, L., and D. DUSTIN. 1989. Resurrecting the frontier. *Trends* (Third Quarter): 42.
5. GREER, L. S. 1990. The U.S. Forest Service and the postwar commodification of outdoor recreation. In *For fun and profit: The transformation of leisure into consumption,* ed. R. Butsch. Philadelphia: Temple University Press, p. 152.

6. DARGITZ, R. 1988. Angling activity of urban youth: Factors associated with fishing in a metropolitan context. *Journal of Leisure Research* 20, 3: 192.

7. TAYLOR, N. 1985. Fishing for bass and bucks. *New York Times Magazine* (July 28): 27.

8. O'LEARY, J., J. BEHRENS-TEPPER, F. MCGUIRE, and F. D. DOTTAVIO. 1987. Age of first hunting experience: Results from a nationwide recreation survey. *Leisure Sciences* 9: 225.

9. AMORY, C. 1990. "They are bloodthirsty nuts." *U.S. News and World Report* (Feb. 19): 4.

10. SIFFORD, D. 1983. It's not the quarry or the trophy that moves these hunters. *Philadelphia Inquirer* (Nov. 3): 3–D.

11. DITTON, R. B., T. L. GOODALE, and P. JOHNSEN. 1975. A cluster analysis of activity, frequency and environment variables to identify water-based recreation types. *Journal of Leisure Research* 7, 4: 282–295.

12. HEYWOOD, J. L. 1987. Experience preferences of participants in different types of river recreation groups. *Journal of Leisure Research* 10, 1: 1–12.

13. STOLL, J., J. BERGSTROM, and L. JONES. 1988. Recreational boating and its economic impact in Texas. *Leisure Sciences* 10: 51–67.

14. STERN, R. 1991. Downhill bracer. *Forbes* (May 27): 57.

15. CASTRO, J. 1991. Sporting goods: Rock and roll. *Time* (Aug. 19): 42.

16. BLAKESLEE, S. 1990. Mountain biking high. *New York Times Magazine* (Oct. 7): 15.

17. MERGEN, B. 1989. Leisure vehicles, pleasure boats, and aircraft. In *Handbook of American popular culture,* ed. M. T. Inge. Westport, CN: Greenwood, 2nd ed., p. 615.

18. JACKSON, E. L., and R. WONG. 1982. Perceived conflict between urban cross-country skiers and snowmobilers. *Journal of Leisure Research* 14, 1: 47.

19. REED, J. D. 1990. Take a number to take a hike. *Time* (July 23): 64.

20. ALBRIGHT, H., quoted in R. Reinhold. 1990. Environmentalists seek to run Yosemite business. *New York Times* (Sept. 23): 30.

21. MANNING, R. E. 1985. Diversity in a democracy: Expanding the recreation opportunity spectrum. *Leisure Sciences* 7, 4: 378.

22. MCAVOY, L. 1990. An environmental ethic for parks and recreation. *Parks and Recreation* (Sept.): 89–92.

23. EWERT, A., and S. HOLLENSHORST. 1989. Testing the adventure model: Empirical support for a model of risk recreation participation. *Journal of Leisure Research* 21, 2: 124–125.

24. See MITTEN, D. 1992. Empowering girls and women in the outdoors. *Journal of Physical Education, Recreation and Dance* (Feb.): 56–60. See also BIALESCHKI, M. D. 1992. We said, "Why not?"—A historical perspective on women's outdoor pursuits. *Journal of Physical Education, Recreation and Dance* (Feb.): 52–55.

25. HAUN, P. 1964. Recreation: A medical viewpoint. In *Recreation: A medical viewpoint,* ed. E. Avedon. New York: Teachers College, Columbia, Bureau of Publications.

26. DEWOLF, R. 1984. Tragedy: Great for the gate. *Philadelphia Daily News* (May 16): 51.

27. STAINBROOK, E., quoted in P. Axthelm. 1974. The thrill seekers. *Reader's Digest* (Nov.): 217.

28. ZUCKERMAN, M. 1978. The search for high sensation. *Psychology Today* (Dec.): 38.

29. SKRYCKI, C. 1987. Are you a type-T personality? *U.S. News and World Report* (Jan. 26): 60.

30. LYNG, S. 1990. A social psychological analysis of voluntary risk-taking. *American Journal of Sociology* 95, 4: 858.

31. NASH, R., cited in R. Harwell. 1987. A 'no-rescue' wilderness experience: What are the implications? *Parks and Recreation* (June): 34.

32. PETERSON, D. 1987. Look ma, no hands! Here's what's wrong with no rescue-wilderness. *Parks and Recreation* (June): 40.

33. HUNT, J. D., *op. cit.*

34. ADLER, J. 1989. Travel as performed art. *American Journal of Sociology* 94, 6 (May): 1372.

35. BOOTH, C. 1992. Against the tide. *Time* (Feb. 17): 54.

36. SCHUCHAT, M. 1983. Comforts of group tours. *Annals of Tourism Research* 10: 469.

37. BENSON, S., S. BRIER, and R. ROSENZWEIG. (eds.) 1986. *Presenting the past: Essays on history and the public.* Philadelphia: Temple University Press, p. 155.

38. BERNSTEIN, R. 1990. Unsettling the old west. *New York Times Magazine* (March 18): 34.

39. ADLER, *op. cit.*, p. 1384.

40. NILOUFER, I. 1983. Tourism at Khajuraho: An Indian enigma. *Annals of Tourism Research* 10: 75–92.

41. Travelog: Sleaze tourism. 1991. *Modern Maturity* (April-May): 16.

42. MILLSPAUGH, M. L. 1990. Leisure and tourism: Economic strategy. *World Leisure and Recreation* (Summer): 13.

43. WILL, G. 1992. Euro Disneyland near Paris means progress is possible—even in Europe. *Philadelphia Inquirer* (April 16): A–18.

44. KING, M. 1991. The theme park experience: What museums can learn from Mickey Mouse. *The Futurist* (Nov.-Dec.): 24.

45. *Ibid.*, p. 27.

10 Sports in American Life

In the end, you always get back to this, back to the game itself. The extraordinary appeal of baseball, its astonishing hold on vast adult sections of this nation, may be disparaged, deplored, dismissed or accounted for with dozens of simple or intellectual explanations. But in the last analysis, it is not the spectacle of the game, not its unplanned aesthetics, not the self-identification nor the hero-worship, not the capitalistic aspects of the sport nor the democratic aspects, not its pleasant summer setting nor home-town pride which make baseball so popular. It is the game itself.[1]

In November 1991, when one of America's favorite athletes, Earvin "Magic" Johnson, professional basketball player with the Los Angeles Lakers, informed a crowded press conference that he had become infected with HIV, the virus that leads to AIDS, a stunned nation reacted as if a national leader had been assassinated. Immediately, more attention was focused on the AIDS crisis than had happened in all the preceding years. A newspaper sports columnist wrote: "We've always been the fun-and-games section of the daily paper. Now we're dealing with real life."

From any perspective, it must be recognized that sports represent far more than trivial amusement or children's play in American society. Any enterprise that involves hundreds of billions of dollars in equipment and facilities, personnel costs, admissions charges, television fees, and other forms of expenditure must be based on more than superficial appeal. Of all types of leisure involvement, it seems likely that sports command the highest degree of personal interest and emotional involvement—both for those who participate actively in them and those who are part of a vast army of fans of school, college, and professional teams.

■ THE APPEAL OF SPORTS

Sports represent almost a religion today, in terms of the public's worship of leading athletes as folk heroes. Sports are closely linked to such social phenomena as politics, warfare, and big business, and citizens see their cities' reputations rise or fall depending on the fortunes of their professional teams. Alumni of colleges and universities contribute to athletic support and follow their schools' teams avidly throughout their lifetimes.

What makes sports so uniquely appealing in contemporary society? It has been argued that they represent the modern equivalent of hand-to-hand combat and that, since modern civilization has reduced the physical hazards that face humans, they offer a way of meeting the atavistic need to test oneself in battle. The sense of fellowship that comes from being part of a team, the praise and admiration of others, and the sheer pleasure of performing physical feats are all part of the complex appeal of athletics.

At the same time, it must be recognized that sports in American life have negative as well as positive qualities. Athletes are often exploited in schools and colleges, and sports are often brutal and sadistic, leading to more violence than they channel away harmlessly. Yet, without question, sports represent a major leisure pursuit for millions of boys and girls, men and women. This chapter explores this reality, as well as a number of the key issues that surround the place of sports in American society.

Sports Defined

Hess, Markson, and Stein characterize sports as: (1) activities with clear performance standards; (2) involving competition through physical exertion; (3) governed by norms defining role relationship; (4) typically performed by members of organized groups; (5) with the goal of achieving a reward; (6) through the defeat of other participants.[2]

In a briefer definition, Allen Guttmann suggests that there are three essential features that distinguish sports from other related activities, such as games or fitness pursuits. These are that sports are physical activities demanding exertion and skill; that they involve a contest or competition; and that they have both formal rules and informal standards of etiquette and fair play.[3] The term *athletics* is often used synonymously with *sports,* but tends to be applied more often to organized team sports on school, college, and professional levels, than to individual lifetime sports like golf, tennis, and skiing.

Although sports are obviously an important form of free-time activity, in many ways they do not conform to the traditional view of leisure. Rather than relaxed activity carried on within a context of casual free choice, sports are often highly structured, purposeful, and disciplined, with elaborate rules and rich rewards. At the same time, sports represent an important social institution, recognized as such not only in the United States but around the world. A Polish sociologist, Zbigniew Krawczyk, wrote in 1980:

> The complex character of sport as a social phenomenon has [long] been emphasized in scientific literature. . . . historians have revealed sport's connections with health, hygiene, physical efficiency and with education of the young generation. They emphasized its affinity to myth, religion, art and politics, entertainment and games, but at the same time with man's work. The first sociologists who took an interest in sport [like Florian Znaniecki] shared this opinion with the historians. . . . [4]

■ STATISTICS OF SPORTS INVOLVEMENT

Based on a survey of ten thousand households drawn from a national sample, the *Statistical Abstract of the United States* reported the most popular sports activities engaged in at least once a year by Americans over the age of seven (see Table 10.1).

Some forms of sport, such as baseball, ice hockey, and football are primarily masculine in participation and interest, while others are geared to feminine interests, and still others are gender-neutral. In terms of age levels, many active sports are most popular during the teenage or young adult years, although some games and active outdoor pursuits actually increase in participation among those in older age brackets (see page 187). With respect to income level, participation is usually highest for those in the $35,000 to $49,999 income brackets, although sports such as golf, soccer, downhill skiing, and tennis have their highest rate of involvement in the over-$50,000 bracket.

TABLE 10.1
Percentages of involvement in popular sports

Activity	Percentage	Activity	Percentage
Swimming	32.8	Tennis	8.0
Basketball	19.7	Baseball	6.2
Bowling	17.5	Football	5.7
Golf	10.5	Skiing (downhill)	5.7
Volleyball	10.1	Racquetball	4.3
Softball	9.5	Soccer	4.0

SOURCE: *Statistical Abstract of the United States,* 1990. Washington, DC: U.S. Department of Commerce, Bureau of the Census, p. 231.

⟫→ TO THE POINT

Most recreational sports have gained in participation over the past two decades. For example, amateur softball play increased from 16 million participants in 1970 to 30 million in 1980 and 41 million in 1990; golf play rose from 11.2 million in 1970 to 15.1 million in 1980 and 27.8 million in 1990. In terms of attendance at college and professional sports events, the number of spectators has risen steadily as well. Major league baseball admissions increased from 43.7 million in 1980 to 55.5 million in 1990; National Basketball Association totals from 10.6 to 18.8 million; the National Football League from 14.0 to 17.6 million.[5]

In secondary schools during the early and mid-1980s, there were more than 923,000 boys playing on eleven-man football teams in over 13,000 schools. Other statistics of high-school play included: ". . . the next three highest participatory sports for boys were basketball (514,000 participants in nearly 17,000 schools), outdoor track and field (475,000 participants in 14,400 schools) and baseball (410,000 participants in more than 13,000 schools)."[6]

Basketball topped the list of participatory sports for girls, with nearly 402,000 playing on teams in nearly 16,500 schools. Other top sports for girls were: ". . . outdoor track and field, with more than 355,000 girls in nearly 14,000 schools; volleyball with nearly 270,000 girls in 13,900 schools; and fast pitch softball, with 189,000 participants in 7,500 schools."[7]

In addition to school, college, and professional leagues, millions of sports participants are served by municipal, county, or special-district recreation and park departments, nonprofit youth organizations (many of which focus on a single sport, such as Little League or Biddy Basketball), industrial sports leagues, country clubs, and military recreation services. In general, the management of sports events, the setting of standards and rules for play, and similar functions are carried out by national organizations that govern competition and promote instructional programs for youth.

George Sage summed up the scope of organized sports in American life:

> The unmistakable societal preoccupation with sports is illustrated by the fact that some 30 million boys and girls are involved in youth sport programs each year, 6.5 million adolescents participate on interscholastic teams annually, over 250,000 intercollegiate athletes compete in NCAA- and NAIA-sponsored events each year, professional sports teams have multiplied at a bewildering rate in the past 25 years, and thousands of hours of sports are broadcast into home television sets each year. . . . It is not an exaggeration, then, to say that sport has assumed a central role in the lives of millions of participants and hundreds of millions of spectators.[8]

As an indication of the economic impact of sports in the United States, the purchase of all forms of sporting goods rose from $16.6 billion in 1980 to a projected $45 billion in 1991. Athletic clothing and footwear alone totaled expenditures of over $17 billion in 1990.

■ HISTORICAL PERSPECTIVES ON SPORTS

William Baker points out that almost every sport in the modern world is a refinement of physical contests originating in ancient and medieval times. Evolved from primitive hunting and warring pursuits necessary for survival, competitive athletics took the form of religious rituals in early pre-Christian cultures. These societies, he writes, developed precise standards of status, age, and gender for participants in their various cultic games:

> Slaves and "barbarian" foreigners were excluded from the Greek athletic festivals; on the other hand, only slaves and criminals were forced into the Roman gladiatorial arenas. . . . Later in medieval Europe, tournaments, jousts, and court tennis were reserved by law for feudal kings and aristocrats, while only peasants customarily played football, quoits, and stick-and-ball games.[9]

In the Middle Ages, peasant games like bowls were taken from rough grounds and rainy outdoors into the homes of the nobility and transformed into new games like "shovel-board" (shuffleboard) and billiards, played on a tabletop. A number of different sports were traditionally played on religious holidays such as Christmas and Easter during the Middle Ages and the Renaissance. As evidence of the historical linkage of religion and sport, in Mexico and other Central American countries, ball games were played with specific ceremonial purposes in stone courtyards that were part of temple complexes.

However, during much of this period sports were also condemned by religious authorities in Europe or had an unsavory reputation because of their linkage with gambling and drinking. Rader describes the metropolitan "sporting fraternity" of the late nineteenth century:

> The saloon keepers especially courted those interested in politics, sport, and gambling. There, the two extremes of society—young "dissolute" men of some means and the workingmen—could meet to review the latest sport gossip, schedule sporting events, and take bets. . . . Without ties to wives or traditional homes, many [bachelors] sought friendship and excitement at the brothels, gambling halls, billiard rooms, cockpits, boxing rings, or the race tracks.[10]

In time team sports gained respectability in England and America as the concept of "muscular Christianity" entered the literature and began to be heard in religious sermons. Churches, YMCAs, and educators all encouraged sports as a means of achieving physical fitness and self-discipline and as an alternative to other forms of dissipation in play. Gradually, sports became dominated by commercial interests, and the manufacture of sporting goods evolved into a successful industry. Hardy writes:

> through their involvement with such nascent governing bodies as the National League, the Intercollegiate Football Association, and the United States Lawn Tennis Association, sporting goods firms helped turn informal activities into commodities of fun and spectacle. This collaboration set the foundation for an even larger sports industry: an interlocking network of the rules committees, trade associations, manufacturers, and professional groups that have heavily influenced both the range and styles of sports in America.[11]

The decade of the 1920s marked a spectacular growth of interest in sports in America, with the building of huge stadiums and expansion of college and professional competition. Star athletes became national heroes in baseball, boxing, golf, and football. Behind these public idols were shrewd promoters and managers, along with a host of sports journalists and broadcasters who helped to popularize them. In newspapers and magazines, on radio, and even in motion pictures, the heroic feats of athletes were celebrated.

Sports as Folk Religion

Today, so popular are college and professional sports that many scholars have concluded that they have become America's newest folk religion. One such observer, Professor Charles Prebish of Pennsylvania State University's religious studies program, states:

> For growing numbers of Americans, sport religion has become a more appropriate expression of personal religiosity than Christianity, Judaism or any of the traditional religions. [Prebish cited] terms that athletes and sportswriters regularly use: *faith, ritual, ultimate, dedicated, sacrifice, peace, commitment, spirit*.[12]

Similarly, James Mathiesen, professor of sociology at Wheaton College, an evangelical school in Illinois, comments that the collegiate bowl games and professional football's Super Bowl spectacular are "in fact, a ritual expression . . . communicating a secular religion of the American dream. If I were to show a visitor to the United States a single, recurring event which has come to characterize folk religion, the Super Bowl would be it.[13]

He goes on to point out that the Super Bowl is strategically located in the calendar year as part of a sequence of religious and lay holidays—Thanksgiving, Hanukkah, Christmas, New Year's Day, and others—along with an array of sports and games that provide entertainment and ritualistic celebration. "What is sacred and what is secular?" Mathiesen asks. "Does it matter for most Americans?"

Russell Chandler points out that football is often used as a metaphor for religious faith. He describes how, thirty-five years ago, a young Texas Baptist, Jarrell McCracken, wrote and recorded a script that equated football with *The Game of Life*. In the record, which led to a multimillion-dollar music and publishing business:

> Jesus was the head coach and "Average Christian" was the quarterback. The bottom line of the sermonizing allegory was that if Christians followed their heavenly blockers and skirted the evil defenders, they made it safely to the big end zone in the sky. . . . More recently, a country singer recorded a hit song that pleaded: "Drop kick me, Jesus, through the goal posts of life."[14]

Over the past several years, numerous athletes have attested their religious faith through membership in the Fellowship of Christian Athletes. Other influential groups include Sports Ambassadors and Athletes in Action, an element within the Campus Crusade for Christ organization. One writer points out that the resurgence of evangelical sects brought with it a return to the "Social Darwinism" of the athletic arena. "Jesus the teacher had become Christ the competitor."[15] Professional football teams hold prayer circles on the field, and the Chicago Bulls publicly prayed the Lord's Prayer after winning the NBA playoffs. Today there are numerous "chaplains" who accompany individual and team competitors—in tennis, golf, and stock-car racing. Several Christian liberal arts schools and Bible colleges provide courses to train sport evangelists, including one Los Angeles college with a four-year degree in sports ministry.

At the same time, one physical education administrator, Shirl Hoffman, warns that Christian theology is dominated by "radicalism of grace—the first shall be last and the last, first. . . ." He continues:

> We must be careful not to delude ourselves into thinking that God in any way cares about the outcome of a game. Those who feel that God especially cherishes winners— or that a win somehow glorifies him more than a loss—have theologically reduced God to a spectator who sits on the sidelines caught up in the [outcome] of the contest.[16]

Although one may question the actual religious character of organized sport, it clearly represents a significant form of ritual in American life. Kendall Blanchard points out that collective rituals have six primary properties: repetition, acting, stylization, order, evocative presentational style or staging, and a collective dimension or social message.[17] Sports, with their singing of the national anthem, presentation of players and coaches, formal handshakes, organized cheering, and sacrificial moments (when players are injured and carried off the field), are clearly secular rituals. Often their staging is spectacular. At the 1992 Winter Olympics in Albertville, France, the two-hour opening ceremony included a choreographed exhibition of performance art:

> Eight military jets swooped overhead, their vapor trails the color of the Olympic rings. A ball of fire ran up a guy wire to light the Olympic flame. Jugglers appeared from giant alpine horns. Twenty acrobats attached to bungee cords put on a gracefully hypnotic routine of slow, solemn tumbling and soaring Peter Pan leaps. . . . As large balloons drifted from their heads, men paraded on stilts. Eight puppet dancers performed on raised platforms. . . . Drummers hung like wind chimes from a crane. High-wire artists climbed cables while dressed as court jesters . . . Trampoline artists tumbled in costumes resembling full-body condoms.[18]

The Role of Spectators

In a recent book on the sports fan through history, Allen Guttmann tells how thousands of spectators cheered gladiatorial contests and chariot races in ancient Rome, and how different classes viewed sports events during the medieval and Renaissance periods in Europe. He points out that respectable middle-class members avoided most sporting events until the mid-nineteenth century, when private clubs, schools, and colleges began conducting rowing, track, and cricket and football matches, and safe and comfortable stands and stadiums began to be built.[19] Contrary to the neo-Marxist view of modern sports as an exploitative division of labor between active athletes and passive spectators, sports fans frequently are active in supporting their teams—sometimes through hooliganism and rioting.

Sport as spectacle. Swimming is uniquely America's most popular outdoor pastime and also a major competitive sport. Here, the 1990 U.S. Olympic Festival is held at the University of Minnesota's Aquatic Center—an outstanding facility operated by the Department of Recreational Sports in the University's Student Affairs program. Around the arena, banners publicize the names of corporate sponsors of the U.S. swim team; overhead, a "blimp" is anchored to televise races from above.

▐▶ TO THE POINT

A unique example of the emotional investment that many spectators make in their favorite teams was cited several years ago when a group of physicians carried out an inquiry into the habits of British soccer crowds. They found that many middle-aged, industrious men who were normally models of behavior at work and at home turned into violent and abusive fans at soccer matches; there were numerous reported cases of husbands coming home after a losing game and beating their wives severely. So excited do many American sports fans become that heart attacks have become increasingly frequent at college and professional football games.

Beyond such traumatic outcomes, many fans become so involved with their teams that they visit them at spring practice, travel with them to distant games, and wear special costumes or adopt special cheers to root them to victory. An example is the Hogettes, a band of middle-aged, paunchy, bald businessmen and professionals who wear outrageous wigs, too-tight dresses, and molded rubber hog snouts over their noses while cheering wildly from seats behind the Washington Redskins professional football team's bench. In Cleveland, a group of masked, dog-faced fans inhabit an end-zone section they call the Dog Pound, where they bark and toss dog biscuits onto the field.

However, sports represent far more than entertainment or light amusement. Instead, they are played for heavy stakes; the serious implications of sports were revealed vividly in a number of feature stories on the front page of the sports section of the *New York Times* on a Sunday in the mid-1960s. Headline after headline described the following events:

- Five people were killed and four injured—including both driver and spectators—at a Sebring, Florida, auto race.
- Two major league baseball pitchers, Sandy Koufax and Don Drysdale, were involved in a contract holdout that was depicted as a struggle against "slavery"—with players being treated like chattel, without the freedom to meaningfully negotiate their own contracts.
- Several horses and riders were injured, tumbling over each other in falls at the Grand National Steeplechase in England.
- In the United States, a federal grand jury investigated death threats by a crime syndicate to force a heavyweight championship fight; meanwhile, a title fight buildup was exposed as "just a charade."[20]

Political Role of Sports

In a number of European nations during the period of growing nationalism and imperialism in the latter half of the nineteenth century, sports were closely linked to military training and patriotic indoctrination. It was at this time that the first international sports contests were held between teams drawn from both bourgeois and aristocratic classes of European nations, while at the same time sports were used as a form of social control by channeling workers' energies and leisure time into sports imbued with such values as obedience, self-discipline, and teamwork.

In discussing the linkage of sports and political ideology, John Hoberman points out that in twentieth-century fascist and communist regimes, sports heroes were idealized, and political, military, and industrial workers all were depicted symbolically as athletic supermen. Grandiose and spectacular sports festivals were used for nationalistic purposes, with mass athletic demonstrations that displayed thousands of bodies in choreographed displays and athletic feats. In Nazi Germany, the SS ideal of manhood was represented as a disciplined, perfectly formed, aggressive athlete, symbolized by Reinhard Heydrich, who had risen through the SS ranks to become head of the Gestapo at thirty-two—a tall and athletic man who had "a passion for all forms of sport; he was a fencer, a horseman, a pilot, a skier and modern pentathlon competitor; he was also SS inspector for physical training."[21]

In the Soviet Union, heroes of the Communist society were depicted as athletic supermen within a number of spheres: the Stakhanovites, or work-athletes, who accomplished brilliant feats in industry; the heroes of the stratosphere and Arctic expeditions; and workers driving underground shafts for the new Moscow subway. Hoberman points out that a common slogan on factory walls was: "Every Sportsman Should Be a Shock-Worker, Every Shock-Worker— A Sportsman."

In Communist China, national leader Mao Ze-dong sought to bolster the cult of his own athleticism by making a legendary swim down the Yangtze River in 1966. Mao supposedly covered a distance of about ten miles in sixty-five minutes—about the speed of a world-class racing shell—a mythic act requiring a remarkable leap of faith on the part of the Chinese public. Not surprisingly, it was not challenged.

For three decades, Iron Curtain countries like the Soviet Union, East Germany, and Romania subsidized their Olympic athletes generously, establishing elite schools (sometimes described as ruthless "sports factories") that selected children at an early age and groomed them intensively for world-class competition. The most advanced training methods, including both psychological conditioning and the use of steroids, were consistently employed. The United States, which did not provide comparable support for its athletes, was frequently humiliated during this period. Only with the collapse of the Communist regimes in the Eastern bloc and with America's providing fuller support and using professional athletes on its teams was international competition made more equal.

At this time, in the late 1980s and early 1990s, the emphasis in international sport shifted from ideological and political goals to commercial ones. The United States Olympic effort became increasingly dominated by business sponsors of teams, lucrative television contracts, and star athletes making millions of dollars in advertising testimonials for running shoes, soft drinks, breakfast cereals, and other products. With the end of the Cold War, professional basketball and hockey teams in the United States began to sign star athletes from the former Soviet bloc, and basketball and football leagues were established in Europe.

Military Aura of Sport

Despite the shift in emphasis from political to commercial goals, sports continued to be linked with the military in ways that were vividly shown in the brief war with Iraq in the winter and spring of 1991. For years, football has shared such terms as *bomb* and *blitz* with airborne warfare. As the United States and its allies waged air war against Iraq, the action was described in football metaphors. President Bush accused Saddam Hussein of a diplomatic "stiff-arm" and U.S. pilots returning from sorties against Baghdad compared the war to sport: "It was just like a big football game," said one. "It was like a football game where the defense never showed up," said another. "It was like a midget volleyball team taking on the San Francisco 49ers," said one commentator.[22]

There were strange sounds on a Sunday afternoon as the television networks broadcast play-by-play accounts of both war and football:

There's going to have to be a hair-trigger defense throughout. . . . This battle is being fought in the trenches. . . . Their forces were able to target the attack. . . . They were both intercepted. . . .[23]

One announcer said that, with the power and accuracy of a cruise missile, you could shoot it in Boston and put it between goal posts at RFK Stadium in Washington, D.C. When the war came to a sudden end, it was with deception worthy of football—a mock landing of thousands of Marines, use of British Bedouins disguised as Arab shepherds, phantom tanks made of fabric stretched over metal frames, and finally an "end-around" drive into the western flank of Iraq forces that was the crushing conclusion to battle.

■ ROLE OF SPORTS IN AMERICAN EDUCATION

Initially, sports and physical training were used in a number of European nations to produce healthy and patriotic citizens. It was widely believed that athletics were helpful in developing traits of aggressiveness and leadership that were essential in both the business world and military life. When American schools and colleges began to encourage team sports, it was assumed that sportsmanship, loyalty, unselfishness, integrity, and other desirable personal traits would be enhanced among student athletes.

In recent years, however, behavioral scientists have challenged these assumptions and found them wanting. Susan Greendorfer reviewed the literature on the outcomes of sport and found limited evidence supporting the view that sport helped athletes achieve upward mobility. She found that athletes tend to

> enter college with poorer academic background, receive lower grades, and have a relatively low probability of receiving an education or graduating compared to nonathletic peers. This is particularly true if they were on scholarship, were admitted with special consideration, or were in revenue-producing sports.[24]

She also summarized a number of recent studies showing that there was no proof that sports promote sharing, honesty, and altruism in children and youth. To the contrary, research suggested that competitive athletics tended to undermine prosocial behaviors, a finding reported by several studies of youth sports. Nash, for example, maintains that excessive pressure from parents and coaches may be responsible for a number of physical and psychological ailments in youth athletes—particularly when intense training and competition lead to injury, illness, or burnout.[25] Hellstedt acknowledges that many children gain from competitive sports play by having fun, making friends, and learning or improving skills. However, he cites three areas of negative outcomes, including low self-esteem, aggression, and excessive anxiety.[26] Similarly, Gelfand and Hartmann present data from several studies showing that in both laboratory and natural settings, strongly competitive athletic games lead to increased aggression and hostility in children.[27]

Despite such findings, there is a widely accepted belief that sports *do* contribute significantly to the lives of young athletes. In a discussion of the efforts being made

I **Personal Enjoyment**	II **Personal Growth**	III **Social Harmony**	IV **Social Change**

Enjoyment/fun
Flow
	Physical health
	  cardiovascular
	  muscular strength
	  muscular endurance
	  flexibility
	  bone structure
	  weight management
	Psychological well-being
	  anxiety reduction
	  depression reduction
		Socialization
		Intergroup relations
		Community
		  integration	

FIGURE 10.1

Types of outcomes derived from sport

SOURCE: Wankel, L., and B. Berger. 1990. The psychological and social benefits of sport and physical activity. *Journal of Leisure Research, 22,* 2: 167–182.

to retain high school athletics in cities where school budgets had been cut sharply, Frank Lawlor points out that the vast majority of teenage competitors never get headlines, championships, or scholarships, but play simply for the love of the game. He continues:

> Surveys, in particular a broad 1989 study commissioned by the Women's Sports Foundation, show that high school athletes in almost every racial, social, and geographical category do better on standardized tests than nonathletes, achieve more in the classroom, and are more active in their communities when they leave school.[28]

As an example, he cites a study by the Minnesota State High School Athletic Association that showed that nonathletes in that state had an overall grade-point average of 2.39, while one-sport athletes had 2.61 and two-sport athletes had 2.82.

Wankel and Berger developed a systematic four-part model of what are commonly regarded as the primary values of sport and physical activity (see Figure 10.1). Within each of these categories, they concluded that it was not possible to say that sport is automatically "good" or "bad," or that it routinely achieves certain outcomes. Instead, competitive athletics have the potential for achieving positive and negative outcomes, depending on the conditions under which they are carried on.

Frey and Massengale point out that the values associated with school and college sports reflect virtues that are generally approved in American society: striving for excellence, achievement, humility, loyalty, self-control, respect for authority, self-discipline, and deferred gratification. However, they conclude that, although athletic administrators profess to operate according to the goals and values of a participatory amateur sports model, in reality they are heavily influenced by professionalized sports practices. As a result the structure of modern school sports at all levels does not permit the implementation of the values traditionally associated with athletics. Goal displacement has taken place. Building character and enhancing education have been replaced as guiding values by the desire for profit, power, prestige, notoriety, visibility, community support, and organizational survival.[29]

Beyond this, Frey and Massengale argue that school sports are so entrenched, so "paranoid" about the edge in competition, so dependent on external constituencies, so enamored of their position of power and prestige that serious attempts to restructure the system would be vehemently resisted. How did this situation come about, and what are its implications?

■ BACKGROUND OF INTERCOLLEGIATE SPORTS

As earlier chapters have shown, many American colleges and universities began to support sports clubs and intercollegiate competition in the second half of the nineteenth century. College deans and presidents felt that athletics, particularly football, were invaluable in building the visibility, enrollment, and reputation of their institutions. Rader writes:

> Even the older, more prestigious institutions of the Northeast turned to football as a means of recruiting students. . . . [They] also found that football developed an alumni loyalty that was far more profound than fond memories of chapels, classrooms, pranks, or professors. "You do not remember whether Thorpwright was valedictorian or not," wrote a young college alumnus in 1890, "but you can never forget that glorious run of his in the football game."[30]

However, almost from the outset, there was severe criticism of the growing emphasis on collegiate sports, particularly football. In 1883 the Harvard Committee on Athletics declared that football was "no longer governed by a manly spirit of fair play" and had become dominated by "a spirit of sharpers and roughs." At the turn of the century, Woodrow Wilson, then president of Princeton University, said, "So far as colleges go, the sideshows have swallowed up the circus, and we in the main tent do not know what is going on." In 1929, in a report on *American College Athletics,* the Carnegie Foundation for the Advancement of Teaching spoke of:

> demoralization of the college and of academic work, dishonesty, betting and gambling, professionalism, recruiting and subsidizing, the employment and payment of the wrong kind of men as coaches, the evil effects of college athletics upon school athletics, the roughness and brutality of football, extravagant expenditures of money and the general corruption of youth by the monster of athleticism.[31]

College basketball became the nation's most scandal-ridden sport when New York City became the hub of big-time college basketball during the 1930s and 1940s, with Madison Square Garden hosting major tournaments and bringing in the top teams from around the country. But, Rader writes:

disaster struck. In 1951 New York District Attorney Frank Hogan revealed that thirty-two players from seven colleges, including players from the strongest teams in the nation, had been involved in fixing point spreads. The Garden was not only the mecca of college basketball; it was the "clearinghouse" for New York's sports gambling establishment.[32]

With the criminal prosecution of athletes and gamblers, New York's preeminence in college basketball declined, and state universities throughout the country began to fill the vacuum left by Madison Square Garden's discontinuance of big-time double-headers. In the 1960s and 1970s, they built over eighty huge new fieldhouses, many seating over ten thousand spectators, scheduled major intersectional tournaments, and intensified recruitment of star prospects. Basketball soon rivaled football for its flagrant violation of the rules of intercollegiate sport. In 1952, federal judge Saul Streit condemned the University of Kentucky as the acme of "commercialism and overemphasis," citing "covert subsidization of players, ruthless exploitation of athletes, cribbing at examinations, illegal recruiting and the most flagrant abuse of the athletic scholarship."[33]

Through the 1970s and 1980s, the abuses of college sports continued to be widely publicized. A study conducted by the American Council on Education cited such practices of overzealous coaches, alumni, or athletic "boosters" as:

> Altering high school transcripts; threatening to bomb the home of a high school principal who refused to alter transcripts; changing admission test scores; offering jobs to parents or other relatives of a prospect; firing from a state job the father of a prospect who enrolled elsewhere than the state's university; promising one package of financial aid and delivering another; tipping or otherwise paying athletes who perform particularly well on a given occasion.[34]

Coaches like Bear Bryant of the University of Alabama had their own private fleet of planes to assist in scouting and signing football prospects and were paid salaries that far exceeded the presidents of their institutions. Andre and James report numerous examples of the hypocritical treatment of athletes:

> Although Moses Malone had a C average in high school, he received scholarship offers from over 300 colleges and universities. None of the schools could match the $3 million contract offered by the Utah Stars; Malone went directly to the American Basketball Association. After Chris Washburn failed to answer a single question correctly on his verbal Scholastic Aptitude Test, he was recruited by 150 universities. . . . At the end of Marcus Dupree's freshman year [at the University of Oklahoma] the university showed its appreciation by honoring him with an award for "excellence in scholarship and athletics." At the time, Dupree had a C− average.[35]

There was little surprise or shock when the Washington Redskins' defensive end, Dexter Manley, was shown to have attended Oklahoma State University for four years without receiving a degree or having learned to read. One of the schools most frequently cited for its violations of athletic policy was the University of Nevada at Las Vegas, where it was almost impossible to control players' contact with professional gamblers. Their lives were not like those of other students:

> Like student athletes at many other schools, UNLV's players often arrive on campus with severe reading problems, poor study skills and swollen egos. They practice as much

as four hours a day, seven days a week, and miss 30 to 40 days of classes because of road games. During their absence, notetakers are hired to attend class for them. All players are required to attend a two-hour study hall after practice, but some are so exhausted they can barely keep their eyes open.[36]

College athletes in high-pressure programs are often coddled and managed to the point that they make few decisions for themselves, and fail to develop needed qualities of judgment and responsibility. Academic difficulties are only part of the problem of many athletes. Often the corruption and exploitation that are found in many high-pressure college sports programs are reflected in the off-the-field behavior of team members. Over two dozen University of Colorado players were arrested in a recent three-year period, on charges ranging from trespassing, assault, and burglary to rape.[37] Within a few weeks at the University of Oklahoma in 1989, a young woman was gang-raped in the athletic dormitory, one football player shot another, and the star quarterback (who had been featured in anti-drug television announcements) was arrested for selling cocaine.[38]

Influence on High School Sports

The roots of big-time college sports reach down into the high school systems of many states, as talented young athletes are groomed for college stardom. The secondary-school mania for athletic glory is illustrated in Odessa, Texas, where the football team plays home games in a $6.7 million stadium, while academic departments struggle with inadequate budgets. As depicted by H. G. Bissinger, a Pulitzer Prize–winning journalist, Odessa's passion for its gridiron heroes in their pursuit of state championships is typical of other secondary schools in Texas, a state ranking thirty-fifth in the nation in expenditures per pupil, and forty-sixth in average SAT scores. Bissinger shows how interscholastic football reinforces an otherwise antiquated social order in a racially divided town that was, at the time of his writing, known as "Murder Capital, U.S.A." He writes:

> Female students vie for a place on the Bepettes, where they are assigned to play the role of "geisha girls" for male student football players. A once great black running back sidelined by a serious knee injury suddenly plunges from heroic stature to the ignominy of being, in the words of one of the Panther coaches, "just another dumb nigger."[39]

Throughout the country, there is tremendous pressure to recruit talented high school basketball players. Thousands of leading athletes attend summer basketball camps sponsored by athletic shoe manufacturers or other entrepreneurs or coaches, where they play against the best in the land and are seen by college coaches and recruiters. Blue-chip players look for the right combination of perks, ranging from free equipment to all-expense-paid trips, at such camps.

Policing College Sports

The task of enforcing amateur athletic standards in colleges and universities belongs to the National Collegiate Athletic Association (NCAA), which has sought for decades to crack down on recruitment and other athletic abuses. The NCAA is an immensely wealthy organization with an operating budget of $168 million in a recent year, derived chiefly from television contracts, ticket sales, and government grants. Charged with enforcing amateur athletic policies at 847 institutions of higher learning, it has a small and poorly trained enforcement staff, and spends more on public relations than it does on investigations. Penalties are meted out by an NCAA panel, the "infractions committee," based on highly complicated rules and lacking in precise application.[40]

In 1983, the NCAA voted at its national convention to adopt Proposition 48, requiring athletes to score a combined minimum of 700 out of a possible 1600 points on Scholastic Aptitude Tests—the equivalent of a generous D. Athletes who failed to reach the 700 mark might be "partial qualifiers"—eligible for a full athletic scholarship, but forbidden to practice with the team or suit up for a game until they had passed some eight courses. In 1985, the NCAA Presidents Commission urged a set of reforms to strengthen the role of the association, which had historically been dominated by athletic directors and coaches. At the instigation of 213 college presidents who attended the meeting, NCAA delegates voted overwhelmingly to apply more severe penalties to schools that chronically broke its rules and to give presidents more authority over athletic budgets. In 1989, NCAA rules governing academic eligibility were tightened with a new Proposition 42, and a number of college coaches denounced the association for its actions by claiming that the new, higher admission standards were aimed at black athletes, to prevent them from "dominating" college sports.[41]

Many top athletes with poor academic records and test scores typically take the route of attending two-year colleges with strong sports programs, where they are able to overcome their academic deficiencies and become eligible to transfer to major four-year colleges. Recently, legislators in half a dozen states introduced legislation to establish more rigorous guidelines for NCAA investigative and enforcement procedures.[42]

Priorities in College Sports

Underlying it all is the influence of television, which has sharply increased the revenues going to major colleges with winning records in football and basketball, particularly those playing in bowl games or key tournaments. With coaches' jobs depending on winning, many take the position that they are more likely to be fired for losing records than for violations of NCAA rules. The paradox is that the assumption that all colleges are getting rich from sports is a myth.

> Robert Atwell, president of the American Council on Education [states] "They are not." In fact, most universities lose money on their athletic programs. "Over 90 percent of the schools in [big-time college sports] are in deficit budgets," says Frank Windegger, athletic director at Texas Christian University.[43]

⫸ **TO THE POINT**

A growing number of educators and sports authorities say that the hypocrisy of college big-time sports would be ended if institutions simply admitted that they were not being represented by students, and if a fully professional model of intercollegiate athletics were adopted, with hired athletes, paid for their work but not required to attend classes, playing for them. D. C. Myers comments that athletics and universities are really two separate enterprises with little in common, and should be judged by separate criteria:

> It is significant that team uniforms are never embossed with the official seal of a university, which represents its authority to grant degrees; instead they are adorned with a special insignia of the team's own. For college sports, the university is not an educational institution at all: it is merely a locus, a means of coordinating the different aspects of the sporting enterprise.[44]

What is ironic is that the public at large does not seem to care about the scandals and corruption that have afflicted school and college athletics. At the same time, it is also ironic that financial support is being increasingly withdrawn from the low-visibility sports, such as wrestling, fencing, or crew, which do not draw huge audiences or public interest, but which clearly represent amateur participation for its own sake. As an example, in February 1992, Cornell University announced over $600,000 in athletic department budget cuts, which would eliminate entirely four sports (men's and women's gymnastics and fencing), and would force four other non-revenue programs (nationally ranked men's and women's equestrian polo, men's lightweight football, and men's squash) to depend entirely on their own fund-raising.[45] Similarly, in a number of rowing programs across the country, including the University of California at Los Angeles, the University of Wisconsin, Yale, and Amherst, crew competition was either abandoned or reduced in financial support. Yet it is widely agreed that such sports are invaluable in terms of meeting the true educational goals of character development, fitness, preparation of lifetime leisure skills, and socialization. Beyond this, they are invariably far less expensive than the big-name sports. A university professor did a study during the budget-cutting process that showed "that Wisconsin spent an average of $45,000 a year on each football player, $30,000 on each women's basketball player, $17,000 on each tennis player and $400 on each rower. Only the men's rowers won a national championship."[46]

■ PUBLIC SPORTS VALUES

Apart from the misuse of sports within schools and colleges, one must ask what support the public at large gives to the values of competitive sports—or, rather, what kinds of values they demonstrate as fans or as parents of young athletes.

First, there is an inherent contradiction in the notion that sports are intended to teach fair play, honesty, and good sportsmanship—at the same time that winning is accepted as an overriding goal of competition. For example, in basketball, it is taken for granted that fouls, which are violations of the rules of the game, are a useful strategic tool. Giving a "good" foul, using a rough play to intimidate an opponent, or deliberately fouling a player to force him or her to shoot the foul shot, is an accepted part of the game.

The principle of winning at all costs can be so strong that fans often use unsportsmanlike conduct to help their teams win. Football fans deliberately create a tremendous volume of noise so the opposing team's players will not be able to hear their quarterback's signals. Basketball fans sitting behind a glass backboard often wave their arms, jump up and down, and scream to distract opponents who are attempting foul shots. Attempts are made to intimidate opposing players, coaches, and even officials. There have been numerous examples of parents of youngsters playing in youth baseball, hockey, and football games threatening, assaulting, and even shooting officials who made "bad calls." Beyond such incidents, the urge to win is often so overpowering that athletes themselves lose sight of what should be the legitimate personal goals of sport, with tragic consequences.

Two examples of frustrated athletes deliberately injuring themselves at the point of losing in a sports event occurred in the late 1980s. In one, a North Carolina State distance runner jumped off a fifty-foot-high bridge after being forced to drop out of the ten-thousand-meter event at an NCAA outdoor track and field championship. She suffered a serious spinal injury. In a similar incident, a Tennessee high school football player, upset by a close loss in a state playoff game, sprinted several feet and butted headfirst into a brick wall outside the locker room. He broke his neck and severed his spinal cord, suffering quadriplegia.

■ VIOLENCE IN SPORTS

One of the arguments frequently used to justify aggressive team sports is that they are believed to channel off hostility harmlessly, through a psychological mechanism known as catharsis or displacement. However, research studies have found that college athletes in combative sports frequently have a marked increase in hostility, rather than a decrease, during competition. Beyond this, violent play is clearly part of the appeal of many sports for spectators, as in ice hockey, where frequent fistfights among players occur.

Football is probably the most violent game, in terms of the number and seriousness of the injuries that regularly occur. In 1905, before the days of protective padding and hard helmets, twenty-three deaths occurred from football in a single year, and the game was on the verge of being abolished. Since then, although far fewer deaths occur, crippling injuries are frequent; studies have shown that two-thirds of National Football League players who competed after 1970 had some form of serious, debilitating injury when they retired. An actuarial study of 1,800 players who had spent at least five years in the league between 1921 and 1959 found that the life expectancy of this group was sixty-two years—twelve years below the national average for men.[47]

While such statistics are disturbing enough, there is considerable evidence that competitive team sports whip fans into a frenzy, leading to fights in stands, attacks on officials, and major riots resulting in multiple deaths. For example, at the Asian Games in December 1966, pitched battles occurred between Korean and Thai athletes, with fans breaking down gates, climbing walls, assaulting players and officials, and stamping other spectators to death. In 1969, a disputed match between El Salvador and Honduras led to a brief war, known as the Soccer War, in which thousands were killed or injured.

Curiously, the supposedly "civilized" British appear to be the most violent sports fans, in terms of precipitating bloody soccer confrontations. In June 1985, 38 spectators were killed and 437 wounded by an English assault against Italian fans at a soccer match between Liverpool of England and Juventus of Italy, held in Brussels, Belgium. In April 1989, over 90 people were killed and more than 180 others injured when soccer fans caused a stampede at a match in the English city of Sheffield. Despite international sanctions against British soccer fans, violent rioting continued in the 1990s, when hundreds of them clashed with Italian police at a World Cup final in Cagliari, Italy. Again and again, similar episodes have occurred, with West Germans and Yugoslavs battling in Milan, Italy, and English fans attacking West Germans after a World Cup loss. Dean writes: "There is a consensus among sociologists . . . that sports violence is increasing . . . from Beijing to Tiger Stadium, from Seoul to the Montreal Forum, acid, bricks, seats, urine, rocks, pipe bombs, firecrackers and feces are being tossed."[48]

Numerous learned papers and scholarly hypotheses have been offered to explain the causes that degrade friendly rivalry and turn it into confrontation. One group of sociologists suggests that sports violence is characteristic of social systems, with teams representing communities of subordinate ethnic minorities more likely to be violent than others. Others argue that sports violence has become a legitimate expression of masculine aggression among youthful peers—linked to a feeling of hopelessness stemming from poor economic prospects and limited job opportunities in drab housing environments. Sports riots are often stimulated by the media and the advance publicity that elevates simple sporting events into spectacles of intercity passions.[49]

A major precipitating cause of violence at spectator sports is drinking by fans. In an effort to control such problems, some stadium officials have banned or limited tailgating parties, stopped serving beer after halftime intermissions at games, and prevented spectators from bringing liquor into the stands. However, they are invariably reluctant to give up the revenue that comes from beer advertising on radio and television sports broadcasts.

■ SPORT AS COMMERCIAL ENTERPRISE

Everything that has been discussed in this chapter—sport as popular pastime, international sports competition, and school and college athletics—is rooted in the fact that sports represent a universally popular form of diversion that is heavily marketed to the public at large. The immense salaries paid to professional athletes illustrate the point. For example, in 1990, over one-third of approximately 750 major league baseball players were paid over $1 million a year—this during a period of serious economic recession. By 1992, they were being paid an average of a million dollars a year. Salaries or prizes for winning tournaments are only part of the income of pro-

TABLE 10.2
Highest-paid athletes in 1991 (figures in millions of dollars)

Name	Sport	Salary/Winnings	Other	Total
Evander Holyfield	Boxing	60.0	0.5	60.5
Mike Tyson	Boxing	30.0	1.5	31.5
Michael Jordan	Basketball	2.8	13.2	16.0
George Foreman	Boxing	14.0	0.5	14.5
Ayrton Senna	Auto racing	12.0	1.0	13.0
Alain Prost	Auto racing	10.0	1.0	11.0
Razor Ruddock	Boxing	10.0	0.2	10.2
Arnold Palmer	Golf	0.3	9.0	9.3
Nigel Mansell	Auto racing	8.0	1.0	9.0
Jack Nicklaus	Golf	0.5	8.0	8.5
Larry Bird	Basketball	7.4	0.5	7.9
Monica Seles	Tennis	1.6	6.0	7.6

SOURCE: Some big names at the bank. *Philadelphia Inquirer* (August 6, 1991): C–1.

fessional athletes. Advertising endorsements and related business ventures provide substantial revenue as well (see Table 10.2).

A major source of revenue for teams and players comes from television contracts for broadcasting games, and fees for commercial advertising. Richard Zoglin points out that television coverage has contributed immensely to the popularity of sports by making it possible for the public to find some sort of athletic competition in progress at almost any hour of the day or night. At the same time, television has entailed a sort of Faustian bargain in its impact on the packaging of sports. Zoglin writes:

> TV is a double-edged sword for colleges. Media exposure brings national attention and dollars into the coffers. But it also stretches out games and seasons, wreaks havoc with schedules and helps boost the importance of sports at the expense of academics. . . . The lure of lucrative TV contracts also contributes to a win-at-all-costs mentality that can lead to recruitment scandals and other abuses. . . . [50]

The initial coverage of sports by television was modest. Limited to the small screen, it tended to emphasize such indoor sports as wrestling, prizefighting, and the Roller Derby, which became highly theatricalized spectacles, rather than genuine sports contests. The later era of sports coverage, beginning in the 1970s, featured extensive television contracts for team sports, with new cable networks and superstations employing transmission satellites. With many more games and dramatically increased revenues, television influenced both the players and the audiences. Rader writes:

> The moguls of sports quickly began to package their games so that they would be even more appealing to television. To obtain a larger share of the new largesse, athletes organized unions, held strikes, and sought assistance in the court system. The battle of the networks expedited the professionalization of the amateur sports of college basketball and football, of track and field, and of school sports.[51]

At the same time, by overwhelming the viewer with excessive images and leading fans to expect only the best, television undermined the essential appeal of sports and their ability to truly release people from the boredom of daily life. Rader sums up its impact:

> With its enormous power to magnify and distort images, to reach every hamlet in the nation with events from anywhere in the world, and to pour millions of additional dollars into sports, television . . . has sacrificed much of the unique drama of sports to the requirements of entertainment. . . . [It] has swamped viewers with too many seasons, too many games, too many teams, and too many big plays. Such a flood of sensations has diluted the poignancy and potency of the sporting experience.[52]

The trend continued through the early 1990s, as television coverage of sports became increasingly lavish and expensive. When CBS covered the Winter Olympics in 1960, the rights to broadcast the games cost $50,000. For the 1992 Winter Olympics, CBS paid $243 million—with twice as many commercial announcements as any preceding Winter Olympics had. Broadcasting a single sports event, the professional football Super Bowl in 1991, brought ABC about $43 million in advertising revenues, with a single half-minute of network time costing $800,000.

Two sharply contrasting kinds of criticism have been leveled at the commercial sports establishment in the United States. On the one hand, writing in *Forbes Magazine,* Alster argues that in many ways major league sports are "socialistic." Citing the degree to which team owners are limited by such processes as binding arbitration, salary caps, and draft procedures that give the teams with the poorest records first crack at the young talent coming out of high school and college each year. Alster writes:

> Imagine an industry where employers surrender the right to set the salaries of workers with three or more years of service. . . . Now imagine that only a handful of enterprises in this industry are prosperous, with an ever-growing number running in the red. Finally, imagine a system where the rules are changed again and again to penalize the successful competitors in hopes that the weaker enterprises can stay in business. The industry we're talking about is, of course, major league baseball, an enterprise that has much in common with socialist bureaucracy.[53]

On the other hand, writing from a socialist/feminist perspective, Catherine Bray claims that the interests of the owners of sports franchises, television networks, advertisers, and the print media are all served by the provision of professional sports to large segments of the public. She writes:

> North American sport culture is dominated by professional sport, which is governed by the need for profit. . . . [It] is not, for instance, provided completely free by the state, or by benevolent rulers in the capitalist economy. The need for profit in a consumer economy results in an emphasis on paid spectatorship rather than free recreational participation which does not produce a profit.[54]

There is growing evidence that professional sports teams are heading for harder times, with new free-agent rulings permitting athletes to initiate bidding wars that result in multi-year contracts for several million dollars a year—in some cases for players who are little more than average. McCarroll points out that baseball in particular is beginning to strike out financially:

After years of booming ticket sales, record profits and lucrative television contracts, major league baseball has fallen into a slump. Stadium attendance is flat, payrolls are climbing, and revenues are on the decline. . . . There are even rumors of one or two franchises going bankrupt within the next few years.[55]

Entrepreneurial Sports Ventures

Despite such warning signs, it seems clear that college and professional teams will continue to represent a major form of sports enterprise in the years ahead. At the same time, there are numerous other examples of athletics being marketed to the public at large through innovative products and services. For example, while gambling on sports is illegal in most states, dispensing information on gambling is not. Thus, throughout the country, dozens of "tout" services that make use of the 900 lines for telephone advice on sports gambling (with names such as "Rolls-Royce selection" or "Diamond-studded play") have become a multimillion-dollar industry.

An immensely popular sideline for many athletes is selling their baseball-card rights to trading-card companies. In the 1950s, the value of baseball cards was in the dreams and visions of youth as they traded cards and completed collections of their favorite players and teams. By the late 1980s, baseball-card collecting had ballooned into a $50 million industry. Linked to card collecting are sports memorabilia shows, where fans and their children buy and sell autographs, publications, gloves, bats, and other baseball-connected items. Under the licensing agreements signed in the early 1990s by the Major League Baseball Players Association, every big-leaguer—from top stars to raw rookies—earned thousands of dollars from the sale of cards, figurines, and the like. Indeed, it was reported in 1993 that college merchandising of their names, insignia, and colors for sports equipment and clothing had been growing by 25 to 30 percent a year, and had reached 1.5 billion dollars in sales in 1992. Increasingly, chains of stores selling sports products are operated on a franchise basis by famous ex-athletes or coaches. In some cases, they feature Ticketron ticket booths for sports events, electronic message boards flashing updated scores, and guest appearances by star players.

Major league teams have a host of moneymaking resources beyond admissions and television revenues. Their stadiums usually have skyboxes that are rented to corporations for as much as $100,000 or more a year. In addition, they make substantial profits from concessions for refreshments, from parking fees, and from other entrepreneurial ventures, including required preseason ticket sales for regular season-ticket holders. Within each type of sport marketed to the public at large, new kinds of technology and sophisticated tailoring of the product are at work.

An example of how sports have been commercialized is tennis. Once a relatively exclusive amateur sport linked to elite country clubs, tennis has now become a big-money game controlled by the interlocking directorate of agents, promoters, and television producers. Played throughout the year on an international circuit, tennis tournaments are being regularly televised. They have led to the emergence of teenage stars who receive millions of dollars under guarantee arrangements—often illicit— simply for appearing at tournaments, and who display temper tantrums and other forms of loutish behavior that would be permitted in few other sports. In an account of the professional tennis circuit over a one-year period, John Feinstein reveals the less glamorous side of the sport, such as the incidence of anorexia among leading women players who seek to be slender and attractive in order to be marketable and the conflicts among agents who represent both players and tournaments. Nor is racism dead in professional tennis, a nearly all-white sport. Feinstein gives an example:

> Zena Garrison, who is black, began 1990 as the fourth-ranked woman player in the world, but did not have an endorsement contract for shoes or clothing. Fourteen-year-old Jennifer Capriati, the sensation of women's tennis, began the season unranked but had an endorsement contract worth $3.5 million.[56]

■ REEXAMINING SPORTS VALUES

Despite the negative aspects of sports that have been described in this chapter, they continue to represent a tremendously popular and appealing form of leisure pursuit for great numbers of Americans young and old. Why is this the case?

Sports clearly satisfy human urges to meet challenges, compete with others, master skills, release emotions, join with others in team efforts, and develop personal fitness. They may be experienced at any level of intensity, from relatively relaxed, informal play for the weekend golfer, bowler, or volleyball player, to highly skilled and strongly motivated competition by amateur or professional athletes.

Over the past three decades, a number of parents, teachers, coaches, and leading athletes have sought to change the face of youth sports, giving it a simpler, more inclusive, and psychologically positive character. Youth sports associations have striven to reform practices in youth sports, promoting more responsible coaching and stressing desirable values and outcomes. For example, the American Alliance for Health, Physical Education, Recreation and Dance has published a bill of rights for young athletes (see Figure 10.2).

    I Right to participate in sports
   II Right to participate at a level commensurate with each child's maturity and ability
  III Right to have qualified adult leadership
  IV Right to play as a child and not as an adult
   V Right of children to share in the leadership and decision making of their sport participation
  VI Right to participate in a safe and healthy environment
 VII Right to proper preparation for participation in sports
VIII Right to an equal opportunity to strive for success
  IX Right to be treated with dignity
   X Right to have fun in sports

FIGURE 10.2
Bill of rights for young athletes
SOURCE: Martens, R., and V. Seefeldt, eds. 1979. *Guidelines for Children's Sports.* Washington, DC: American Alliance for Health, Physical Education, Recreation and Dance.

Although the major team sports get the bulk of publicity, most actual participation by American adults is in so-called lifetime sports like tennis and golf. Once regarded as an elite, country-club pastime, tennis is now played by all groups in society. Hundreds of future champions are groomed in the famous Bollettieri tennis complex in Bradenton, Florida, left. Inner-city youth now learn to play tennis at the Arthur Ashe Youth Tennis Center in Philadelphia and similar centers around the country, and hundreds of wheelchair-bound youth enjoy tournament competition as well.

Research studies have shown that it is possible to influence the values of young athletes in positive directions, in terms of fair play, honesty, and playing for fun, through changes in league formats and the screening and preparation of coaches.[57] Increasing efforts are being made to ensure that all players receive fair amounts of playing time, and that teams are balanced properly in terms of skilled players. Some community recreation departments and youth sports organizations today offer two kinds of leagues: one for highly motivated and skilled players, and another for youngsters who wish simply to enjoy games and are not primarily motivated by the need to win.

▶ TO THE POINT

In some communities, school systems have deliberately adopted policies with respect to extracurricular activities that would ensure mass participation. In the town of Plainfield, Indiana, for example, with minor exceptions no middle-school student can be cut from a club or team because of lack of skill: "The uncoordinated can be on the football team. The unmusical can be in the band. Anyone at all can be a cheerleader or serve on the student council. A mediocre speller can represent the school in a spelling bee."[58]

Beyond this policy, all members of teams and clubs are exposed to high expectations and a strong work ethic, which encourages them to work hard to improve and perform well. However, the emphasis is on teamwork and the group experience. The school's basic philosophy is that it is more important to use the sports program as a way of getting as many youngsters as possible to gain from involvement and feel connected to school, than to serve the outstanding few.

Research on Youth Motivations in Sport

Over the past two decades, a number of youth sports have exploded in popularity. The number of children playing on United States Soccer Federation youth division teams, for example, grew from slightly over 100 thousand in 1975 to more than 1.5 million in 1989. The number of girls on softball teams more than doubled from 1980 to 1990, growing from about 306 thousand to over 638 thousand. However, many children start with a burst of optimism and enthusiasm, but then quit within a few years. In part, the problem is that they are plunged into organized sports at too early a point, in terms of physical or emotional readiness. For example, in the Pop Warner League, the largest organized youth football league in the country, seven-year-olds play tackle in full gear. Gina Kolata writes:

> Many pediatricians and other sports experts believe that children should not play regulation games on full-size fields until they are at least nine or ten. Until that time, they should be learning basic skills, such as kicking a soccer ball or hitting a tethered-T-ball. Or they should play modified games that allow everyone on a team to have adequate playing time.[59]

National youth sports and fitness programs are often sponsored by major American corporations. Left, Olympic decathlon champion Rafer Johnson helps direct Hershey youth fitness activities; the Hershey Corporation's National Track and Field Youth Program involves over 2,900 communities and nearly 350,000 children. Plainfield, Indiana, Middle School students compete in football and swimming (below).

⏩ TO THE POINT

A leading authority on youth sports, Vern Seefeldt, director of the Institute for the Study of Youth Sports at Michigan State University, points out that as soon as children become involved in adult models of games, skill development falls to practically zero. Children, he says, need to be in situations "where their participation and ability to learn skills are maximized. In an adult game, you try to throw the ball so the batter can't hit it or kick the ball where it can't be retrieved. With kids, you need to do just the opposite."[60]

In a major study of ten thousand students in eleven American cities that was sponsored by the Athletic Footware Association, it was found that even among the most dedicated athletes, winning took a back seat to self-improvement and competition. When asked to select the single most important reason for playing their best school sport, "to win" ranked in seventh place among boys and tenth place among girls. The five most important reasons cited by all youngsters were: (1) to have fun; (2) to improve my skills; (3) to stay in shape; (4) to do something I'm good at; and (5) for the excitement of competition. On the other hand, the reasons for stopping participation in a sport were: (1) I lost interest; (2) I was not having fun; (3) it took too much time; (4) coach was a poor teacher; and (5) too much pressure and worry.[61]

In many communities, parents take the lead in conducting youth sports leagues, and do an excellent job of volunteer coaching and officiating, fund-raising for equipment and maintenance, and giving other forms of supplementary program assistance to public recreation and park agencies. In Philadelphia, for example, dozens of athletic associations in the city's northeast area sponsor baseball, softball, basketball, soccer, and other leagues for thousands of children. In some cases, they design, build, and maintain fields, or remodel indoor facilities; in so doing, they help to maintain the character and stability of their neighborhoods. Infield writes:

> This kind of private enterprise on public property is a regular occurrence in Northeast Philadelphia. And that says a lot about the role of athletics in the community. . . .. In many ways the clubs *are* the Northeast, the tie that binds in a region of 410,000 people, nearly the size of Pittsburgh. No other institution cuts across so many ethnic, religious and social boundaries, nor offers a comparable arena for people to meet each other.[62]

Beyond its contribution to neighborhood life, parental involvement in youth sports often becomes an important part of the tie between parents and children. Tom Brokaw, the NBC anchor, comments that, in his family's life, sports were not solely a father's province. His wife, liberated from her 1950s confinement to cheerleading, became a tennis player, skier, backpacker, and marathoner, and shared the role of family athletic model. He writes that, as parents, he and his wife sought to find the right balance between encouragement, perspective, and pride.

> It wasn't always easy. When one daughter's team won a volleyball championship, I wanted to cry. When the players kept their emotions in check, so did I. That same daughter set the school shot put record when she was 16. I was thrilled—my daughter

the shot putter. . . . When another daughter won her school's award for the most inspi-
rational athlete, she publicly thanked me for encouraging her. It was at once a proud,
touching and embarrassing moment.[63]

Brokaw described another parent, a father who had dreams of his son—a better-
than-average athlete but no star—breaking out of the pack and achieving glory.
Going into the final lap of the two-mile relay, his team was about five yards behind.
As the son took the baton for the anchor leg . . .

his father came to his feet and begin to shout, calmly at first, "Go, big boy, go!" The
boy was running stronger than we had ever seen him. He took the lead. I stopped
watching the race, however, because I was transfixed by the sight of his father. By now
he was standing on his seat, pumping his right hand in the air, his face a deep red, tears
running down his cheek as he cried out, "Go, big boy, go!" over and over.[64]

Brokaw commented that the father's investment in the outcome seemed excessive.
Yet it typified the emotional feelings that many Americans have about sports, and
this, in the final analysis, must be what underlies their deep involvement in it.

⫸ TO THE POINT

For some, sports may provide a means of social mobility—particularly for
those who come from disadvantaged backgrounds. An example may be found
in the biography of Willie E. Gary, an African-American youngster who was
one of eleven children in a migrant farm worker family. Only five-feet-seven,
he applied at several Florida colleges in the late 1960s, hoping to win a football
scholarship—but found no takers until he used his last few dollars for a bus to
Shaw University, a black institution in North Carolina. He found

no spots there, but he hung around, sleeping on a couch, eating handout meals
and voluntarily cleaning up the locker room. They made him water boy, until the
day he subbed for an injured player and won a spot on the team—and an athletic
scholarship. Now one of the most successful malpractice and personal injury
lawyers in the South, the 44-year-old Mr. Gary announced . . . that he would give
Shaw $10 million over the next five years. It is the largest gift ever for the histori-
cally black school. Mr. Gary, who is chairman of the university's board, called it
"a very small payment on the very big debt I owe Shaw."[65]

Despite all the negatives then, sports somehow have a magical quality about
them, tied to dreams of glory and fame.

William Allman writes of sporting events as a way of rising above life's ambiguities; sports represent an all-out assault on everyday life's compromises and uncertain-
ties. In sports, there is always a final accounting, and there is the image of the hero.
He describes the great basketball star, Michael Jordan, saying that in his miraculous
leaps, Jordan typifies the willing suspension of disbelief that we bring to sports. It is
a yearning to be removed from earthly complications and to experience a world
made perfect and, in Jordan's case, played to perfection. Allman continues:

Perhaps the best player in the history of the sport, he seems as reverent and respectful of his amazing abilities as we are. Jordan is precisely what we love about sports. He defies gravity as much as he defies the tyranny of everyday life. For the moment, he is flying. For the moment, we are transported to a world free of sticky ends, compromises and complications. We watch him leap, hoping he will never come down.[66]

Ultimately, the secret appeal of sports can never be measured by statistics of play or by empirical research that examines their economic, physical, or social outcomes. Instead, it is a matter of emotion, of being part of a game that has been passed down through the centuries, taking its shape from all those who have run the bases through the years. The distinguished philosopher Jacques Barzun comments that whoever wants to know the heart and soul of America should do it by learning about baseball and about

the wonderful purging of the passions that we all experienced in the fall of 1951, the despair groaned out over the fate of the Dodgers, from whom the league pennant was snatched at the last minute [a loss that gives us] some idea of what Greek tragedy was like. . . .[67]

Finally, there is the tribute to baseball of A. Bartlett Giamatti, who left the presidency of Yale University to become the commissioner of major league baseball. Giamatti engaged in a protracted struggle to bar Pete Rose, a convicted tax evader and gambler on sports, from organized baseball. Shortly after this was accomplished, he died suddenly. Years before, he had written:

It breaks your heart. It is designed to break your heart. The game begins in the spring, when everything else begins again, and it blossoms in the summer, filling the afternoons and evenings, and then as soon as the chill rains come, it stops and leaves you to face the fall alone. You count on it, rely on it to buffer the passage of time, to keep the memory of sunshine and high skies alive, and then just when the days are all twilight, when you need it most, it stops. . . . Of course, there are those who learn after the first few times. They grow out of sports. And there are others who were born with the wisdom to know that nothing lasts. They are the truly tough among us, the ones who can live without illusion, or without even the hope of illusion. I am not that grown-up or up-to-date. I am a simpler creature, tied to more primitive patterns and cycles. I need to think something lasts forever, and it might as well be that state of being that is a game; it might as well be that, in a green field, in the sun.[68]

■ SUMMARY

This chapter outlines the scope of sports participation in the leisure of Americans today, in terms of both active play and spectatorship. It explores the history of competitive games and presents sport both as a form of folk religion and from an international, political perspective. The values of athletic competition are examined, along with the abuses in many school and college sports. Guidelines for the constructive use of sports with children and youth are considered, and the chapter concludes with an acknowledgement of the important social and emotional meanings that sports hold for millions of people today.

■ QUESTIONS FOR DISCUSSION

1. What accounts for the immense popularity of sports in American society—in terms of both participation and spectator activity? In human terms, why are sports so appealing?

2. We often hear the expression "But it's just a kid's game." But why do sports deserve to be considered far more than just trivial amusement? In terms of historical background, economic impact, or other factors, why should sports be regarded as an important social institution and a relevant subject for scholarly inquiry?

3. The history of college competitive athletics is one of steady growth, but also of serious abuses and attempts to control and govern that have often failed. What are some of the most negative aspects of present-day collegiate sports? How would you respond to the suggestion some authorities have made, that sports in colleges should be divorced from the academic enterprise, with team members frankly being regarded as professional employees and not being expected to attend classes or earn degrees?

4. Recent research shows that a high percentage of younger children who initially take part in such sports as baseball, hockey, basketball, and soccer quit organized teams in the preteen or early adolescent years. Why is this so, and what could be done to reverse it? Which forms of sport offer the greatest potential and most positive benefits for lifelong participation?

5. What are some of the most obvious impacts of television on college and professional sports, both positive and negative? In what other ways have sports emerged as a major form of commercial activity in present-day America?

■ NOTES

1. ANGELL, R. 1984. Baseball the perfect game. *New York Times* (Apr. 1): 8–E.

2. HESS, B., E. MARKSON, and P. STEIN. 1988. *Sociology.* New York: Macmillan, pp. 571–572.

3. GUTTMANN, A. 1988. *A whole new ball game: An interpretation of American sports.* Chapel Hill, NC: University of North Carolina Press.

4. KRAWCZYK, K. 1980. Sport in culture. *International Review of Sport Sociology,* 15, 3: 7.

5. *Statistical Abstract of the United States,* 1990, p. 229, and 1992, p. 239. Washington, DC: U.S. Department of Commerce, Bureau of the Census.

6. Traditional sports far outpace lifetime sports in U.S. high schools. *Report by National Federation of State High School Associations* at National Conference on Youth Fitness (June 8, 1984).

7. *Ibid.*

8. SAGE, G. 1988. Sport, culture and society. *Journal of Physical Education, Recreation and Dance* (Aug.): 34.

9. BAKER, W. J. 1988. *Sports in the Western world.* Urbana and Chicago: University of Illinois Press, p. 1.

10. RADER, B. 1983. *American sports from the age of folk games to the age of spectators.* Englewood Cliffs, NJ: Prentice-Hall, p. 32.

11. HARDY, S. 1990. Adopted by all the leading clubs: Sporting goods and the shaping of leisure. In *For fun and profit: The transformation of leisure into consumption,* ed. R. Butsch. Philadelphia: Temple University Press, p. 72.

12. PREBISH, C. In Chandler, R. 1987. Are sports becoming America's new folk religion? *Philadelphia Inquirer* (Jan.3): 1–C, 5–C.

13. MATHIESEN, J. In Chandler, *op. cit.,* p. 5–C.

14. *Ibid.*

15. MATHIESEN, J. 1992. From muscular Christians to jocks for Jesus. *Christian Century* (Jan. 1–3): 1–2.

16. HOFFMAN, S. In Chandler, *op. cit.,* p. 5–C.

17. BLANCHARD, K. 1988. Sport and ritual—a conceptual dilemma. *Journal of Physical Education, Recreation and Dance* (Nov.-Dec.): 48.

18. LONGMAN, J. 1992. New light on Olympics torch begins with a surreal ceremony. *Philadelphia Inquirer* (Feb. 9): A–1.

19. GUTTMANN, A. 1986. *Sports spectators.* New York: Columbia University Press.

20. See Sunday Sports Section, *New York Times* (March 27, 1966).

21. HOBERMAN, J. 1984. *Sports and political ideology.* Austin, TX: University of Texas Press, p. 100.

22. CAPUZZO, MIKE. 1991. Think of it as a football game with no referee. *Philadelphia Inquirer* (Jan. 19): 1–D.

23. GUNTHER, M. 1991. The sounds of T.V. on a strange day. *Philadelphia Inquirer* (Jan. 21): 3–E.

24. GREENDORFER, S. 1987. Psych-social correlates of organized physical activity. *Journal of Physical Education, Recreation and Dance* (Sept.): 59.

25. NASH, H. 1987. Elite child-athletes: How much does victory cost? *The Physician and Sportsmedicine* 15, 8: 129–133.

26. HELLSTEDT, J. 1988. Kids, parents, and sport: Some questions and answers. *The Physician and Sportsmedicine* 16, 4: 59–71.

27. GELFAND, D., and D. HARTMANN. 1982. Some detrimental effects of competitive sports on children's behavior. In *Children in Sport,* ed. Magill et al. Champaign, IL: Human Kinetics Press, pp. 196–203.

28. LAWLOR, F. 1993. Two cities that saved sports. *Philadelphia Inquirer* (May 2):D-1, D-6.

29. FREY, J., and J. MASSENGALE. 1988. American school sports: Enhancing social values through restructuring. *Journal of Physical Education, Recreation and Dance* (Aug.): 40.

30. RADER, *op. cit.,* p. 76.

31. MAEROFF, G. 1991. Big-time sports don't belong in college. *New York Times* (Dec. 15): 14–E.

32. RADER, *op. cit.,* p. 276.

33. CALLAHAN, T. 1989. You do it until you get caught. *Time* (Jan. 9): 43.

34. CHU, D. 1989. *The character of American higher education and intercollegiate sport.* Buffalo, NY: State University of New York Press, pp. 8–9.

35. ANDRE, J., and D. JAMES. 1991. *Rethinking college athletics.* Philadelphia, PA: Temple University Press, p. 23.

36. GUP, T. 1989. Foul! *Time* (Apr. 3): 57.

37. *Ibid.,* p. 55.

38. MYERS, D. C. 1990. Why college sport? *Commentary* (Dec.): 48.

39. HUNT, H. 1990. Review of H. G. Bissinger, *Friday night lights: A town, a team, and a dream.* New York: Addison-Wesley. In *Philadelphia Inquirer* (Sept. 30): 1–C.

40. JOHNSON, C. 1992. The rules of the game. *U.S. News and World Report* (Apr. 13): 60–62.

41. MYERS, *op. cit.,* p. 50.

42. JOHNSON, C. 1992. De-fense against the NCAA. *U.S. News and World Report* (Jan. 13): 25.

43. MYERS, *op. cit.,* p. 50.

44. *Ibid.,* p. 49.

45. Athletes opposing decision to cancel at least four sports. *New York Times* (Feb. 9, 1992): 52.

46. PUCIN, D. 1991. Will cuts ground the crews? *Philadelphia Inquirer* (May 10): 6–C.

47. WEISMAN, J. 1992. Pro football—the maiming game. *The Nation* (Jan. 27): 84.

48. DEAN, P. 1990. Bloody Sundays: Experts try to find reason for increasing fan violence around world. *Los Angeles Times* (Oct. 15): E-1, E-6.

49. TWOMEY, S. 1985. The spread of soccer violence. *Philadelphia Inquirer* (June 2): C–1.

50. ZOGLIN, R. 1990. The great T.V. takeover: Billion-dollar fees and ever-expanding coverage are reshaping American sports. *Time* (Mar. 26): 66.

51. RADER, B. 1984. *In its own image: How television has transformed sports.* New York: Free Press, Macmillan, p. 5.

52. *Ibid.*

53. ALSTER, N. 1991. Major league socialism. *Forbes* (May 27): 138.

54. BRAY, C. 1988. Sport and social change: Socialist feminist theory. *Journal of Physical Education, Recreation and Dance* (Aug.): 50.

55. McCARROLL, T. 1992. A whole new ball game. *Time* (June 22): 63.

56. GOLDSTEIN, S. 1991. Review of J. Feinstein, *Hard Courts*. New York: Random House. In *Philadelphia Inquirer* (Oct. 27): 3–C.

57. WANDZILAK, T., G. POTTER, and C. ANSORGE. 1985. Reevaluating a sports basketball program. *Journal of Physical Education, Recreation and Dance* (Oct.): 21.

58. LEO, J. 1991. On society: Two cheers for Plainfield. *U.S. News and World Report* (Oct.23): 19.

59. KOLATA, G. 1992. A parent's guide to kids' sports. *New York Times Good Health Magazine* (Apr. 26): 15.

60. SEEFELDT, V., cited in Kolata, *op. cit.*, p. 46.

61. EWING, M., and V. SEEFELDT. 1991. *American youth and sports participation*. N. Palm Beach, FL: Athletic Footwear Association and Michigan State University.

62. INFIELD, T. 1985. Where sports reign; clubs pinch-hit for the city. *Philadelphia Inquirer* (May 1): B–1.

63. BROKAW, T. 1991. Of fathers and children and sports. *New York Times* (June 16): S–9.

64. *Ibid.*

65. Mater love. *New York Times* (Feb. 9, 1992): E–7.

66. ALLMAN, W. 1991. Liftoff: Rising above the ordinary ambiguities. *U.S. News and World Report* (June 10): 10.

67. BARZUN, J. 1984. Reveling in the levels of the game. *New York Times* (Apr. 1): 8–E.

68. GIAMATTI, A. B. 1984. The green fields of the mind. *New York Times* (Apr. 1): 8–E.

11 Arts and Entertainment in Popular Culture

The explosion in public participation in the arts and attendance at arts events has been a phenomenon of modern American life. Clearly, the arts have struck a deep and sensitive chord in literally millions of Americans. When probed to say in their own words what makes the arts unique, people say that they are a reflection of life, that they are an important outlet to express something of meaning, that they give a real spiritual lift and a memorable time.

But what emerges more than any other fact from this survey [Louis Harris Poll on the Arts] is the size of the audience for and participants in the arts. The arts in America in the 1980s have truly become a mass proposition. People have learned that you don't have to be an elitist to appreciate music, ethnic dance, painting, or sculpture, or to play a musical instrument seriously.[1]

We turn now to a third major form of leisure involvement, commonly referred to as arts and entertainment. This broad heading includes such varied forms of active participation or spectatorship as painting, drawing, and sculpture; music, drama, and dance; the literary arts; and the electronic media: radio, television, and motion pictures. These pursuits comprise a major portion of the free-time activity of Americans. Arts and entertainment have traditionally been considered to fall along a spectrum of taste, ranging from "elite" to "vernacular," or "lowbrow," forms of expression. Today, such distinctions continue to exist, although there is a vast middle ground of popular culture that all Americans enjoy.

■ MEANING OF *ART*

The term *art* is used ambiguously in modern society. In the broadest sense, it refers to any advanced skill or craft, such as the "arts" of trout fly-tying, of cookery, and of persuasion. The term may also refer to different categories of creative activity, such as "the performing arts" or "visual arts." In its narrowest meaning, "fine arts" describes creative processes or products such as painting, drawings, prints, or sculpture.[2]

Throughout history, the various arts have been presented at different levels of aesthetic worth and linked to different social classes. During the Middle Ages and the Renaissance, for example, the common folk or peasantry sang robust folk songs, played crude instruments, and performed simple country dances, while members of the nobility patronized court composers and orchestras and learned more complex dances that ultimately led to the creation of ballet as an aristocratic art form.

In the modern era, this distinction between art of the common people and of the upper classes is generally portrayed as a distinction between "elite" or "highbrow" forms of art, and "vernacular" or "lowbrow" forms. The term *entertainment* usually implies that a play, a movie, or a book is not regarded as a serious piece of artistic expression, but intended chiefly for easy enjoyment. For example, the English novelist, Graham Greene, who was highly respected by literary critics, referred to his mystery or adventure novels as entertainments. Today, classical music, opera, or serious painting would usually be thought of as elite forms, while rock and roll, rap music, and soap operas on television would be seen as vernacular art, or entertainment. Dwight MacDonald describes the two contrasting forms as "high" culture and "mass" culture, and writes:

> The historical reasons for the growth of Mass Culture since the early 1800s are well known. Political democracy and popular education broke down the old upper-class monopoly of culture. Business enterprise found a profitable market in the cultural demands of the newly awakened masses, and the advance of technology made possible the cheap production of books, periodicals, pictures, music, and furniture, in sufficient quantities to satisfy this market. Modern technology also created new media such as the movies and television, which are especially well adapted to mass manufacture and distribution.[3]

During the late nineteenth and early twentieth centuries, the influential upper classes founded art museums and conservatories, symphony orchestras and halls, opera and ballet companies; read books written by serious writers; attended professional theater performances; and generally supported these forms of elite creative activity. At the same time, as MacDonald suggests, a huge and diversified body of cultural products and experiences became available for the public at large, appealing to a less demanding level of popular taste.

Growth in the arts was striking after World War II. Over a three-decade period, the number of American symphony orchestras more than doubled, from about six hundred to over fourteen hundred, and the sale of records and musical instruments increased by over 850 percent. Numerous community art centers were built to house the fine and performing arts, ranging from New York City's $142 million Lincoln Center for the Performing Arts to smaller centers in hundreds of other communities.

By the late 1980s, attendance at varied kinds of artistic events had grown dramatically throughout the United States. During the period between the mid-1970s and mid-1980s, attendance at live performances of plays, musical comedies, and other forms of theater rose from 53 percent of the adult population to 67 percent—up to 116 million people a year. Those attending live musical performances by popular singers, bands, and rock groups increased over the decade from 46 percent to 60 percent, a total of 104 million attendees. Attendance at live performances of classical or symphonic music, ballet, modern or ethnic dance, and opera and musical theater also rose sharply.

A detailed analysis of participation in specialized forms of artistic and cultural pursuits in the mid-1980s is shown in Table 11.1, based on a survey conducted for the National Endowment for the Arts. It shows the impact of such factors as age, gender, race, income and education, on involvement in the arts.

In addition to attendance at cultural events, the number of Americans taking part directly in varied forms of artistic pursuits increased steadily during the 1970s and 1980s, as shown in Table 11.2.

■ VALUES OF ARTISTIC EXPERIENCE

Both for those who engage in creative leisure pursuits directly and for those who form the audience for the arts, such activities have the following important values:

1.   The arts provide beauty in our lives—not necessarily in the sense of attractive, harmonious, or beautifully designed objects or works, but rather in terms of their emotional impact and depth, and the vision they provide of the world.

2.   In a world dominated by the mass media, marked by conformity of beliefs and behavior, the arts provide an opportunity for people to develop their individual talents and make unique personal statements in one or another area of aesthetic performance.

3.   In a world that tends to value material accomplishment and competition for external goals, the arts provide an opportunity—not always realized—to be deeply immersed in an experience for its own sake.

TABLE 11.1

Participation rates for arts performances and leisure activities, 1985: Percentage of population eighteen years old and over who participated at least once in each activity, in the twelve months prior to the survey.

Characteristic	Attended performance at least once					Visited at least once— art museum or gallery	Read— novel, short stories poetry, or plays
	Jazz	Classical Music	Opera	Musical	Ballet		
Average	10	13	3	17	4	22	56
18–24 years old	14	11	2	15	4	22	57
35–44 years old	10	16	4	21	6	27	62
55–64 years old	5	11	3	18	4	19	50
75 years old and over	1	10	1	8	2	10	48
Male	10	11	2	15	3	21	48
Female	9	14	3	19	5	23	63
White	9	14	3	18	5	23	58
Black	13	6	1	9	2	11	44
Other races	8	15	4	13	5	24	50
Household income, 1985							
$5,000–9,999	7	7	1	8	2	12	43
$15,000–24,999	8	11	2	12	4	19	53
$50,000 and over	19	30	8	37	11	45	77
Education							
Grade school	1	3	1	3	1	4	23
High school graduate	7	7	1	12	2	14	52
College graduate	18	29	6	34	9	45	78
Graduate school	24	41	11	40	15	56	80

Source: *Statistical Abstract of the United States,* 1990. Washington, DC: U.S. Department of Commerce, Bureau of the Census, p. 235.

4.   Unlike sports or vigorous outdoor recreation, the arts are easily adaptable to persons of all ages and at all levels of physical capability—including those who are physically or mentally disabled. From a therapeutic perspective, artistic expression often provides a valuable form of emotional release and may constitute a specific treatment modality.

5.   Although audiences for the arts may be deeply affected by viewing paintings, sculpture, or theater pieces, or by hearing symphonies or chamber music, artistic involvement is particularly rewarding for those who participate actively and creatively. Robert Henri, the art critic, wrote several decades ago:

> Art, when really understood, is the province of every human being. . . . When the artist is alive in any person . . . he becomes an inventive, searching, daring, self-expressive creature. He becomes interesting to other people. The world would stagnate without him—and the world would be beautiful with him. He does not have to be a painter or sculptor to be an artist. He can work in any medium.[4]

TABLE 11.2

Amateur artistry: Percentage of American adults engaging at least occasionally in creative activities

Activity	1975	1987
Take pictures	19%	51%
Do needlepoint or weaving	39	41
Play a musical instrument	18	30
Paint, draw, or etch	22	27
Write stories or poems	13	24
Do ballet or modern dance	9	23
Sing in a choral group	11	22
Do folk or ethnic dance	5	15
Make pottery or ceramics	8	14
Sculpt	5	8

SOURCE: National Research Center for the Arts, March 1990.

6.   Finally, art in all its forms represents a way of perceiving the world—either literally, as in a poem, short story, novel, or painting, or symbolically, as in the work of many modern artists or composers.

⫸ TO THE POINT

The urge to create and to perform is almost overwhelming in many people. A unique and shattering example was found in a Nazi concentration camp in World War II—the Czech ghetto camp of Terezin, where the Nazis sequestered professional musicians, artists, and actors before shipping them to Auschwitz gas chambers. Members of Terezin's *Freizeitgestaltung* (Administration of Free Time Activities) were allowed to be full-time artists:

> They could—and did, with a feverish intensity—practice, compose, train choirs, give piano lessons to their children, form string quartets and cabaret bands, and stage operas. Verdi's great *Requiem* was repeated many times with trained opera singers and a 150-voice chorus. At least one encore performance required an entirely new chorus, however; in the interim, members had been shipped to Auschwitz.[5]

Community Programs in the Arts

In simpler terms, artistic involvement can be a relaxing, "fun" kind of activity, appealing at any age level. Working in a studio or a play rehearsal is a social experience, involving cooperation and the blending of joint efforts, and often leading to the excitement of an exhibit or performance before an audience. A strong case may be made that community recreation programs often provide more extensive opportunities in the arts than the public schools do. Since the 1950s, emphasis on science and mathematics and cost-cutting curriculum slashes have sharply reduced many school-based programs in the arts. Conn writes:

Particularly in areas where there had been major cutbacks in arts programs in schools, there was a real hunger for entry-level education in instrumental music, voice, dance, painting, ceramics, sculpture, and sometimes film and video. The early enrolees were children, but recreation departments soon got used to the long lines of adults waiting to sign up for classes for themselves *and* their children.[6]

In city after city, from Tulsa, Oklahoma, to Raleigh, North Carolina, and Miami, Florida, to Portland, Oregon, cities have established community arts centers with capable instructors, exhibitions, and performing groups that bring varied forms of art to the public at large. Community arts festivals including folk music, jazz, story-telling, ballet, modern, and ethnic dance, and theater productions have become popular across the country, and the field of arts administration has become a recognized discipline and area of special training today.

There are essentially four different types of artistic or creative activity that may be enjoyed in leisure. These are: the visual arts, the performing arts, electronic entertainment, and the literary arts.

■ VISUAL ARTS

The term *visual arts* refers specifically to the arts that are meant to be seen, such as graphic forms of expression like painting, drawing, or print making, or plastic arts like sculpture or ceramics. They may be approached at varied levels, from finger painting, simple crafts, and sketching for very young children, to portrait and landscape painting for adults.

Public recreation departments usually offer arts and crafts as a staple of playground, day camp, or adult leisure programs—sometimes with an extensive battery of classes and clubs that use community-center or school facilities. Weaving, work with clay, nature crafts, and jewelry, and metalworking may be approached on different levels of expertise and may extend to such useful projects as dressmaking, sewing, and similar activities. Many public departments operate arts centers with workshops, exhibition galleries, and ties to community organizations concerned with the arts.

In addition, many private schools, summer camps, and arts organizations also sponsor extensive programs in the visual arts. For example, Dillman's Sand Lake Lodge, a privately operated resort and workshop in Lac du Flambeau, Wisconsin, offers a year-round series of classes and special programs in the arts, directed by nationally known artists and crafts experts. Both at its scenic lakeside environment at Lac du Flambeau and at other winter workshops in Illinois and Wisconsin, the school offers family-vacation formats, corporate seminars and retreats, and group tours of the region, with a huge variety of subjects: watercolor, portrait and figure painting; nature, animal, and portrait photography; maritime seascapes and landscape photography; intaglio carving on gems and glass; porcelain and floral painting; calligraphy; quilting; printmaking; and a variety of other hobbies and workshops. Reflecting the expanded interest in handmade crafts, dozens of huge craft fairs are held today around the United States, and the field itself, according to *Trade Show Week* Magazine, comprises a $3 billion retail industry.

Community-sponsored arts programs serve millions of children, youth, and adults throughout America. At Riverside Park, in Vero Beach, Florida, the Children's Theatre offers children's drama classes (above) and both amateur and professional performances. Left and below, Vero Beach's Center for the Arts schedules numerous classes in sculpture, portrait and watercolor painting, and other art media.

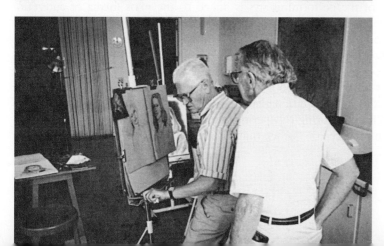

As such forms of creative expression gain both popularity and critical esteem, the historic separation of art into "high" art and "low" art—the one considered serious, worthy of public support, and the other cheap, lacking in taste, is breaking down. Over the past twenty-five years, with the emergence of so-called pop art, which makes use of found objects or images drawn from comics, advertising symbols, packaging, or other cultural artifacts, popular culture has invaded the museum world and become part of the serious art spectrum. Indeed, Edward Sozanski writes:

> one could argue that the term "high art" is invalid, that art should not be defined as "high" or "low" but as either unique or mass-produced, and, within these categories, as good or bad. . . . The dichotomy between "high" and "low" developed with the rise of the mass media and the creation of elitist organizations such as symphony orchestras and art museums. Unique works such as paintings became the province of the moneyed class, while the working class made do with multiples and disposable images—prints, newspapers and magazines.[7]

Sozanski goes on to suggest that the distinction between "high" and "popular" art was sharpened by the development of movies, radio, and television, as "mass culture" forms. However, he writes, it is a distinction between the exclusive and the commonplace, between the expensive and the affordable, not between intrinsically superior and inferior ways of making art. The ultimate truth is that all art proceeds from life, and that the twentieth-century artists who incorporated mass-produced images and common objects into art—pasting newspaper headlines onto collages, using comic-book panels as paintings, depicting Campbell Soup cans or multiple images of Marilyn Monroe or the American flag, or installing vertical electronic message boards that blink continuously in red—are affirming this connection.

■ PERFORMING ARTS

The performing arts—music, drama, and dance—are important elements in popular leisure. Just as in the visual arts, they may be approached on different levels of intensity or artistic quality. They may be enjoyed as leisure activity by young children in simple rhythmic or musical experiences, creative dramatics, or beginning ballet classes. On the other hand, adults may take classes in playing instruments, musical theory, or choral music, or may join performing groups on an amateur or professional basis. Each of the performing arts is linked to the mass media of entertainment—either in popular forms like soap opera, musical comedy, dance, or rock and roll or rap music, on the professional stage or in television and motion pictures.

Audience involvement in the performing arts has generally risen over the past several decades, although in some cases there have been declines in attendance and financial pressures have constricted some forms of performing activity (see Table 11.3). These statistics reflect the remarkable growth in numbers of opera companies and symphony orchestras during this period—but also the fact that they are primarily "college," "community" or "other than professional," which means essentially amateur in nature.

The performing arts are heavily supported by colleges and universities and by culturally minded civic organizations throughout the United States and Canada. The Krannert Center for the Performing Arts at the University of Illinois presents an Illinois Opera Theatre performance of *Madame Butterfly,* Kabuki-style, above. The Ottawa, Canada, Ballet (left) is a respected ballet company; below, students learn modern dance technique at Randolph-Macon College in Virginia.

TABLE 11.3
Performing arts: Selected data for 1970–1988 (receipts, expenditures, income, and attendance in millions).

Activity	1970	1975	1980	1985	1988
Legitimate theater	62	59	67	31	31
Broadway shows, new productions					
Playing weeks	1,047	1,101	1,541	1,062	1,114
Gross box office receipts	53.3	57.4	143.4	208.8	253.4
Road shows					
Playing weeks	1,024	799	1,351	993	893
Box office receipts	48.0	50.9	181.2	225.9	222.9
Opera companies	648	807	986	1,123	1,250
Major	35	54	109	168	187
Expenditures	36.5	(NA)	133.6	256.5	352.3
Total performances	4,779	6,428	9,391	10,642	12,361
Symphony orchestras	1,441	1,463	1,572	1,572	1,572
College	298	300	385	371	350
Community	1,019	1,003	926	946	903
Major	28	29	32	30	36
Concerts	6,599	14,171	22,229	19,969	17,774
Attendance	12.7	18.3	22.6	23.7	23.6
Earned income	43.1	70.9	141.2	250.7	328.2
Contributed income	30.2	53.6	105.1	184.7	228.9

SOURCE: *Statistical Abstract of the United States,* 1990, p. 236.
NOTE: NA means not available.

Music as Recreation

Turning now to the separate forms of performing art, music represents a major leisure interest of millions of Americans, in terms of either making or listening to music. Music may be approached informally, as part of family recreation in the home, although the old tradition of families gathering around a piano and singing as a regular form of family "togetherness" clearly has declined through the years. However, in many other ways, music continues as a recreational experience. Children and youth join various types of musical groups, such as rock bands, marching bands, choral groups, church choirs, and similar aggregations; they enjoy Christmas caroling, singing around a camp fire, or playing guitars for folksinging.

Many public recreation departments sponsor varied forms of musical activity for children and youth, offering instrumental instruction, classes in musical theory, and different types of performing groups. Some sponsor summer music camps or schools, while others assist opera companies, chamber music societies, and similar organizations in finding facilities and promoting their performances with the public at large.

Audience Involvement

In addition to attendance at musical performances of all kinds, a key measure of the popularity of music as entertainment consists of purchase of phonograph records, compact discs, and prerecorded cassettes. Between 1975 and 1991, the number of unit shipments of various forms of recorded music rose from 531 million units to 801 million units annually, with total manufacturer's value that rose from $2.3 billion to $7.8 billion in the later year.

The immense sums of money involved in the public's enjoyment of music is further illustrated by the money earned by individual performers and groups within the popular music field, such as Michael Jackson, the Rolling Stones, the Grateful Dead, and others. Madonna, the bleached-blonde pop star, is the president and sole owner of a multimillion-dollar corporate organization that in peak season has hundreds of employees and operates through half a dozen entities. In 1990, *Forbes Magazine* reported that Madonna had earned $125 million over a four-year period.

Marketing Practices in the Music Industry

However, the overwhelming popularity of youth-oriented musical products is accompanied by a number of critical abuses, which show how the public's leisure is often shaped and manipulated by commercial interests. For example, a recently published book, *Hit Men: Power Brokers and Fast Money Inside the Music Business,* shows how popular music is corrupted by its "schlockmeisters," or independent producers.[8] Shady business practices of these key figures, who are hired by the major record labels to promote priority releases, include a widespread system of "payola" to disc jockeys, including payment of cash and sometimes cocaine, to play records. Charges of links to the Mafia, trafficking in drugs, fraud, and racketeering have been leveled against some of the promoters who help records achieve popularity among American youth.

Another abuse has been the recently exposed practice of having "hit" singers or groups being given credit for work that was not really their own. A scandal occurred when the National Academy of Recording Arts and Sciences stripped pop duo Milli Vanilli of its Grammy award as best new artist for 1990, because the two Milli performers hadn't sung a note on the band's debut album. Instead, they had simply lip-synched words sung by others on the album—a practice common on television and in music videos, where sound tracks are usually pretaped before visual taping or "live" performances. Similar charges were leveled in 1992 against the popular New Kids on the Block; their producer revealed that 80 percent of the material on their four albums had been masked with vocals by better singers, while the "kids" simply lip-synched their music on "live" concert tours.

Social Impact of Rock and Rap

Apart from the way in which merchandise is marketed to the young and the techniques that are used to create it, the chief concern with much of popular music today is its message for young people. Initially, much of the adult concern about rock and roll had to do with its sexual imagery and linkage with drugs and violence.

The world of heavy-metal bands encompasses more than entertaining sound. Instead, it is a life-style initiated by veteran bands like Judas Priest, AC/DC, and Iron Maiden. There are also numerous subcategories known as "speed metal," "thrash," "glam," "metal-funk," and other groups that seek to outdo each other with louder and faster sound. They are embellished by hair spray, clothed in animal skins, accessorized by chains and other bikeresque hardware, covered with tattoos and often semi-nude—and they are featured in fan magazines with names like *Rip, Screamer, Mean Street, Thrust, Metal Maniacs,* and *Metal Head*. Often today's rock bands are deliberately violent, crude, and unrelentingly sexist and racist. Queenan writes that for the cover of their hugely successful debut album, *Appetite for Destruction,* Guns 'N Roses selected a painting of a sinister robotic figure towering over a

> ravished female with her undergarments around her knees. The album, whose leitmotifs were violent sex, drug abuse, alcoholism and insanity, featured lyrics like "Tied up, tied down, up against the wall/be my rubber/made baby/An' we can do it all." The record sold 14 million copies.[9]

In the early 1990s, rap music (a fast-talking, highly rhythmic form of pop entertainment) was identified by a large-scale research study in several major cities as the only form of communication that ghetto youth were really responsive to—the best way of reaching them with a social message.[10] What was the message that rap groups were delivering to their most committed fans, African-American youth? While some of it is simply light, entertaining, and amusing, much of it consists of an angry, racist, violent sermon. One critic writes that rap songs deliver a constant obscene onslaught about "bitches, whores and brutal sex." Women seem to exist merely to be picked up, used, abused, and quickly discarded. One group, N.W.A. (Niggers with Attitude) teaches its audience that "all ladies are bitches . . . money-hungry, scandalous, groupie whores," and that "If you got a gang . . . the bitch'll let you rape her."

⇒ TO THE POINT

The term *rap terrorism* is increasingly applied to many of the most popular groups. N.W.A. urges general violence:

> " . . . you gotta commit murder in the first degree and manslaughter . . . my appetite for destruction . . . is tremendous." Another major rapper, Ice Cube, pleads for violence against Jews "to get rid of that devil. Real simple. Put a bullet in his temple. 'Cause you can't be a nigger for life crew with a white Jew telling you what to do."[11]

In Ice Cube's album, *Death Certificate,* Koreans are threatened: "Pay attention to the black fist or we'll burn your store right down to a crisp." Sister Souljah urges the death of white police, and rapper Chuck D's video depicts an armed paramilitary force on a war mission that poisons a white senator and blows up a governor's car. Columnist John Leo protests against the argument that efforts to control rap groups constitute censorship or deprivation of artistic freedom. It is not, he says, simply a matter of obscene or bawdy language that shocks bluenoses. Instead, it is about the degradation of women, packaged and beamed to kids as popular entertainment—sold freely in stores and featured on the airwaves.[12] It is more than a coincidence that, in December 1992, as racist, neo-Nazi skinhead youth in Germany began to commit violent beatings and arson in a concerted assault against Turkish families and other foreigners living in Germany, several German rap groups were making records urging the killing and rape of "outsiders."

As the society spends billions of dollars to produce and consume such tawdry and destructive forms of musical entertainment, other valuable forms of musical expression are being starved for financial support. For example, throughout the 1980s, a deepening economic crunch forced many orchestras to cut back on their seasons, reduce pay scales for musicians, and restrict their repertoire in other ways. In the early 1990s, twenty-eight of the nation's largest symphony orchestras reported serious budget crises; many were forced to reduce their operations significantly.[13]

As reported earlier, public school programs in the arts have also been sharply curtailed; only nine states today mandate arts curricula for all high school students. In Los Angeles County, 30 percent fewer juniors and seniors take music courses than in the 1950s. Yet a recent College Entrance Board study

> found that students who took more than four years of music and arts scored 34 points higher on verbal SATs and 18 points better on math SATs than those who took music for less than one year. At the University of California at Los Angeles, a study of students served by the . . . County's Artist-in-Residence program found improvement in reading, writing, and speaking skills, social studies, science and math.[14]

While American educators have largely lost sight of the connection between the arts and other areas of academic development, both Japan and Germany, countries noted for their high level of academic achievement and business success, require education in the arts for all students from kindergarten through high school.

■ DRAMA AS LEISURE ACTIVITY

The theater has had a long and rich tradition in American culture, ranging from the first struggling touring companies in the New England and Middle Atlantic colonies to a full blossoming of a native American theater in the twentieth century. Since World War II, in Broadway's Times Square district—traditionally the heart of American drama—many theaters have been abandoned because of rising costs of production, crime, and unstable real estate values.[15]

However, the theater itself is far from dead in America. Many college and university towns have established cultural complexes with repertory companies that put on the works of Shakespeare, Ibsen, and other classical writers, along with new plays by native playwrights. In 1992, Barbara Janowitz, director of management services for the Theater Communications Group, the umbrella organization for the nation's non-profit companies, commented:

Despite all the negative implications of the recession, strong leadership and sophisticated management skills [in the nation's theaters] have been truly impressive. This, as
well as an outstanding commitment on the part of theater trustees, will see the theaters
through these difficult years.[16]

Many companies throughout the country are persuading the public that
theatergoing is an exciting activity by presenting first-rate classical and modern plays
in high-quality productions. A leading example was found in the work of Joseph
Papp, a social activist and artistic visionary who first became famous for producing
free Shakespeare works in New York City's Central Park. Papp's innovative
approaches to theater won three Pulitzer Prizes and numerous other critics' awards,
nurtured many new playwrights and performers, and resulted in works like *A Chorus
Line* and *That Championship Season* that established records for performance or
were successfully transferred to commercial theater venues. William Henry comments that Papp's genius was that he saw no reason for an intellectual chasm
between a learned elite and the masses. Born in a poor, non-English-speaking household of immigrant parents, his vital legacy was neither his shows nor his institutions,
but his audiences:

He . . . introduced impoverished ghetto students to the classics, cherished minorities
and the dispossessed among writers and performers. He always saw himself as a bel-
ligerent radical. Yet his passion was a deeply conservative idea that art, culture and tradition should form a central force in the life of every human being.[17]

Given the pressures under which theater must operate today, the artistic directors
of nonprofit regional and community theaters throughout the United States must
become skilled businessmen and businesswomen. To deal with such problems,
Hilary De Vries writes, the work of stage directors

is less and less about artistry and more and more about managing a business venture in
which the needs of actors, playwrights and directors may at times be secondary.
Regional theaters are no longer tiny pioneering stages. Most are multimillion dollar
institutions with hefty subscriber lists, extensive boards of directors, large administrative
staffs, impressive budgets—and, too often, impressive deficits.[18]

Apart from professional forms of theater, a second important aspect of drama as a
form of leisure is that it offers a major opportunity for creative self-expression in
amateur theater performance. Among the programs that may be offered by
public recreation and park departments, voluntary youth agencies, schools, and colleges are the following: (1) the use of dramatic play in regular recreation programs,
including charades, pantomime, puppetry, storytelling, pantomime, dramatic
games, and other unstructured and creative acting experiences; (2) amateur theatrical programs, including school plays for youth and one-act plays or drama festivals
for local performing groups, in some cases linked to historical pageants or civic
celebrations; (3) children's theater programs, in which they receive instruction
in acting and stagecraft and put on formal drama productions; and (4) the specialized use of drama as a therapeutic technique with mentally or physically disabled
persons.

■ DANCE IN RECREATION

Dance has two primary aspects as a form of leisure activity: as a social pastime and as a stage art. As a social activity it ranges from the more formal kinds of ballroom dance that are taught in private academies to the children of the well-to-do, to swing, disco, and rock-and-roll dance performed more widely in clubs and other recreational settings. Ballroom dancing is done at school proms and teen parties, on cruise ships, and in many other leisure settings. Linked to the popular music of the time, it is often featured in movies and on television, and represents a traditional pastime that renews itself with each successive generation. Folk, square, and country dancing are also popular forms of social dance, carried on throughout the country.

Beyond its social role in leisure, dance also is a concert art form. Its best-known form is ballet, originally a classical court dance in Renaissance Italy and France that was popularized in America by George Balanchine of the New York City Ballet. Today, there are a number of highly regarded companies in major cities such as Boston, Atlanta, Houston, and San Francisco, while numerous smaller companies enjoy public support in regional settings. An essentially aristocratic art form, ballet tends to be patronized by the well-to-do in American communities. Dance has traditionally had the aura of being a feminine art. Balanchine himself perpetuated this stereotype, speaking of ballet as " . . . a purely female thing; it is a woman—a garden of beautiful flowers, and the man is the gardener." Despite this reputation, many leading choreographers and performers are male, and ballet has come to be recognized as an androgynous art form—not to be labeled for one sex or the other.

A second important form of concert dance is modern dance, a movement that stemmed from the rebellion of Isadora Duncan, Ruth St. Denis, and Ted Shawn against the classical ballet during the early 1900s, and was brought to maturity by Martha Graham, Doris Humphrey, Merce Cunningham, and other choreographers and teachers during the middle decades of the twentieth century. Modern dance represents the more exploratory, avant-garde form of art dance that tends to be taught more widely than ballet in the schools and colleges of the nation.

Performance Art

While dance as an art form is a nonverbal activity, it is often used to communicate symbols or feelings. In this context, it is closest to a new form of creative expression known as performance art. This consists of avant-garde movement presentations that have strong links to other contemporary art forms, including speech, gesture, use of a wide range of objects, nudity or partial nudity, and other elements. Stephan Salisbury describes the performance of Karen Finley, a leading artist in this medium:

> . . . she shed most of her clothing during the course of her performance, smeared her body with chocolate and sprinkled it with alfalfa sprouts and glitter. The performance created an unholy mess. At first, the audience laughed, amused to see an adult playing with food the way kids are told never, never to do. But as Finley's multiple monologues continued, as she became infused with the personae of an abused woman, an alcoholic woman, a dying AIDS victim, the mess became emblematic of the mess American society has made of whole segments of the population. The laughter stopped.[19]

A whole new opportunity for profit opened up when motion pictures began to be released for home viewing in the form of videocassettes, after their profitability in movie house runs declined.

From the outset, American motion pictures both reflected the image that the nation had of itself and helped to shape its cultural values and behavior. In the gangster films of the 1930s, stars like Jimmy Cagney and Pat O'Brien epitomized the nation's rejection of Prohibition and its fascination with violence and big-city mobsters like Al Capone or roaming bank robbers like John Dillinger. American attitudes toward racial minority groups underwent a transition in the decades following World War II, as described in Chapter 5, with the superficial stereotyping of African Americans gradually shifting to a more honest and sympathetic presentation of black life in the United States.

⬛⮕ TO THE POINT

The treatment of women in films also paralleled the influence of feminism, with women increasingly being shown in roles of strong career women, union organizers, detectives, and other forceful parts. At the same time, some critics suggest that current films paint a deliberately negative picture of independent women. Susan Faludi, for example, writes that in typical movies of the 1980s

> women were set against women; women's anger at their social circumstances was depoliticized and displayed as personal depression instead; and women's lives were framed as morality tales in which the "good mother" wins and the independent woman gets punished.[22]

Faludi concludes that Hollywood producers were deliberately reinforcing a backlash response to feminism; American women were depicted as unhappy because they were too free; their liberation had denied them marriage and motherhood. In top-grossing films, she writes, women are either subservient, bland housewives, voiceless "babes," or mannish female villains, child-hating shrews, or homicidal career women. Opposed to this tendency, the early 1990s saw a number of successful women directors making films for the first time on a wide range of themes. Women directors are no longer limited by the notion that they are only capable of making delicate little films, and are increasingly able to influence Hollywood moviemaking.

Gradually, films are dealing with the issue of homosexuality with more honesty and frankness. For years, homosexual characters in movies were portrayed as creepy misfits or campy caricatures—marginal, dubious people. However, in a number of films in the late 1980s and early 1990s, gay and lesbian relationships were portrayed more sympathetically. There was an uproar of protest in 1992, when the film *Basic Instinct* presented lesbian and bisexual women as man-hating murderers, and protests were launched by gay activists' groups against this and other films that have presented homosexuals in a distorted light.

At the same time that such pressures are being exerted, some of the controls on the portrayal of explicit sexual behavior on the screen have been relaxed. Since 1968, the Motion Picture Association of America had used a rating system that attached the X category to films that were in its view too overtly sexual. However, in the early 1990s, the Motion Picture Association removed the X category from its rating system, replacing it with an NC-17 category (no children under 17 allowed). *The Christian Century* commented on this change:

> By replacing the X category with the NC-17, the MPAA now offers directors a "respectable" category for their excesses. The restraint is removed. [Directors determined to present overtly sexual material] are now able to stand in the back of the room and harass the teacher with impunity. Freedom and responsibility should remain in tension. In eliminating the pejorative X rating, the industry has decided that responsibility is less important than freedom.[23]

A final important point about American moviemaking today is its growing international influence. There is increasing domination of worldwide film, television, and home-video markets by American producers. In Europe, where movie attendance is one-third that of the United States, American films account for nearly three-quarters of all box-office gross receipts. The box-office boom in Europe for United States entertainment products began in the early 1980s, when state-run television industries made room for private networks. Starved for programming content, these new channels began running American movies and language-dubbed television shows, which proved popular and created a larger audience for Hollywood products. Today, the export of entertainment yields an $8 billion trade surplus annually to the American economy. However, some critics wonder what Europeans must think of the America that is depicted: a relentlessly unfolding series of rapes, murders, shootings, and car chases. Ross Baker comments that Europeans do not get to see the positive side of American life—the ideals of the American Revolution, the progress of the civil rights movement, or the image we have of ourselves as a beacon of freedom in the world. Instead, he writes: "We have exported our culture quite successfully but it is a culture that shows only the seamy underside of American society and offers little or no evidence that an alternative exists."[24]

■ TELEVISION AND POPULAR LEISURE

The newest and most powerful medium of popular entertainment in the United States is clearly television. The growth of this form of home-based leisure activity has been spectacular. By 1990, over 98 percent of American homes had television sets, and over 59 percent of these subscribed to cable television. In the mid-1980s television watching in the average home reached a new high of almost seven hours a day.

A study by United Media Enterprises concluded that television served chiefly as a backdrop for other family activities, and that it seemed not to erode basic family and community concerns as much as it coexisted with them. In effect, the report concluded that television had become "the new American hearth—a center for family activities, conversation and companionship." It explained:

Far from creating a generation of television zombies, the tube showed almost no ability to deflect Americans from other favorite pursuits around the house. Frequent adult watchers seem to be as home-centered as those who watch very little TV. Avid TV viewers read to their children and engage in family chats, possibly because the prime evening viewing hours coincide with time usually set aside for family activities.[25]

Twenty years ago, when students went to college, television sets were found chiefly in dormitory lounges, rather than in individual rooms. However, by the early 1990s, the new generation of college students, who had grown up on *Sesame Street,* then moved on to MTV, the youth-oriented music video program, took television sets to college with them as a matter of course. Todd Gitlin, professor of sociology at the University of California at Berkeley, comments:

> TV is their collective dream machine, their temple, their sense of being members of a nation. It's as if they're carrying their pews with them. They've always watched "LA Law." They can't imagine a world without it. It's normal. College is one episode in this unfolding normality.[26]

A 1991 survey by Roper College Track, a market research service, found that college students watched television an average of eighteen hours a week, with the most popular programs including soap operas and late-night talk and comedy shows. At the same time, a number of students were critical of television's role in their lives. "TV's turning us into a mush nation," said one college senior. A freshman agreed, "Nothing's on, and they all sit around watching it. TV destroyed the American family. Adults come home from work and watch TV. It cuts off communication."

Another widely shared leisure pursuit among children and youth is video games. *U.S. News and World Report* commented in the early 1980s that America had become a "stay-at-home society," with a flurry of electronic products—videogames, videocassette recorders, big-screen TVs, color cameras, and home computers—all filling the nation's leisure. It stated:

> The appetite for videogames seems boundless. Estimates are that sales this year will more than double, to $3 billion, as popular arcade games become available in cartridges for use on home TVs. In Washington, D.C., one retail chain sold a truckload of 3,000 Pac-Man cartridges, at $30 each, in 24 hours. . . . Some 2 million videocassette recorders are expected to be sold this year, up from fewer than 1.4 million last year.[27]

Through the late 1980s and early 1990s, the video game market proliferated, with companies like Nintendo and Sega designing a whole host of games with richer color, clearer sound, faster action, and more sophisticated play. By 1992, Nintendo controlled an estimated 85 percent of the almost $5-billion-a-year video game market, with thirty million families caught up in its successively more expensive and complex systems.

Impact of Television on Children and Youth

Almost from the beginning, adult concern has been expressed about the impact of television watching on children and youth. In the mid-1980s, it was argued that many of the educational programs for children, like "Captain Kangaroo," had disappeared, and that highly acclaimed programs offered by the Public Broadcasting System, such as "Sesame Street," were unavailable in many areas of the country. In May 1993, a former children's television executive for ABC reported that the number of educational programs offered by the three major networks, which had totaled eleven hours a week in 1980, now involved less than one hour a week.[28] Instead, the major networks were offering chiefly vacuous cartoon programs in prime children's television time. The more serious criticism is that many children have become hooked on television. Richard Zoglin writes of the six-year-old TV addict:

> He watches in the morning before he goes off to school, plops himself in front of the set as soon as he gets home in the afternoon and gets another dose to calm down before he goes to bed at night. He wears Bart Simpson T-shirts, nags Mom to buy him Teenage Mutant Ninja Turtles toys and spends hours glued to his Nintendo. His teachers says he is restless and combative in class. What's more, he's having trouble reading.[29]

⮞ TO THE POINT

A 1982 study by the National Institute of Mental Health concluded that "violence on television does lead to aggressive behavior by children and teenagers who watch the programs." The National Coalition on Television Violence, a citizens' group, reported "a recent deluge of high-action, violent cartoon shows." The coalition's psychiatrist head concluded, "We can only pump so much violence into our people before we explode." In 1992, an article published in the *Journal of the American Medical Association* concluded that childhood exposure to television violence was at the heart of the nation's 100 percent increase in violent crime and the doubling of homicides since television was introduced. And, in 1993, despite assurances by the Motion Picture Association of America that video stores did not allow children to rent videos that contained clearly adult depictions of sex or violence, a field test conducted by *U.S. News and World Report* found that many children ages ten to fourteen *were* able to rent such films.

In response to such concerns, in the same year the three major television networks, ABC, CBS, and NBC, agreed on standards governing television violence that would result in toning down excessive or overly shocking scenes and would use greater care when portraying children as the victims of violence, and in children's programming generally.[30] However, some critics maintain that television is simply part of a total environment—including movies, rock music, and other media—that is drenched in sex and violence. Columnist Charles Krauthammer documents a quadrupling of rapes in thirty years, the random shootings of children in our cities, and the soaring rates of teenage pregnancy and suicide. He asks:

> What happened to innocence? . . . The signs of decay produce a general puzzlement. How did we get to such a pass? How? Well, culture has consequences. Life imitates art. Is it so hard to make a connection between culture and society? Most people fervently

believe in the connection between good art and the good society. . . . And yet the corollary—if good art can elevate, then bad art can degrade—is a proposition they refuse to grasp.[31]

■ LITERARY FORMS OF LEISURE

We turn now to a fourth major category of leisure involvement within the spectrum of arts and entertainment—literary leisure. While many informal kinds of play may deal with words as such—telling jokes, puzzles, storytelling, solving crossword puzzles and anagrams—literary leisure consists primarily of reading and writing in the full range of books, magazines, and newspapers that present fiction, nonfiction, criticism, and poetry to all age groups in the society.

Although it has been widely predicted that reading will disappear as a popular pastime under the impact of more visual, easy-to-comprehend communications media, over the past two decades the sale of books has continued to rise steadily. The total number of hardbound and softcover books sold rose from 1.5 billion in 1975 to 1.8 billion in 1980 and 2.2 billion in 1988, with total consumer expenditures on books rising from $4.9 to $18.4 billion over this period. Nor has this trend been limited to adults; the number of children's books published has more than doubled to well above five thousand yearly, and sales have more than quadrupled.

The growing interest in reading is demonstrated by the growth of major book chains, with huge supermarkets offering every type of book. Companies like Waldenbooks, Dalton, and Crown have opened such outlets in suburban malls throughout the country; in many cases, they are designed to be everything a typical mall store is not, with gentle lighting, wooden shelves, armchairs, and even coffee bars, intended to make them "browser-friendly."

In addition to more sophisticated merchandising at the point of sales, the book publishing industry has become more highly competitive in the effort to generate books that will hit the best-seller lists and return sizable revenues. Publishers are constantly on the lookout for books on controversial or timely topics that may bring free advertising through interviews on talk shows like "Oprah Winfrey," "Donahue," "Geraldo," and the network morning shows. Books picked as a main selection by the Book-of-the-Month Club or the Literary Guild have a marked edge in sales performance, and such factors as cover design, strategic timing of release, and putting authors "on the road" from city to city all are part of making best-sellers.

Poetry is also an important part of the literary use of leisure, and has undergone a period of unprecedented expansion in terms of publishing and reading habits. Never before have so many new books of poetry been published, so many anthologies or literary magazines or other forms of criticism of contemporary poetry. Congress and twenty-five states now have official poets laureate, and there are numerous grants for poets, including foundation fellowships, prizes, and subsidized retreats.[32] However, the audience for poetry today is narrower than it was in the past, when a broader cross-section of the public read verse. It consists chiefly of teachers, students, editors, and publishers. An exception to this conclusion is the vogue of poetry readings, both in bookstores that feature authors of many different types and in neighborhood bars or coffeehouses. Open-microphone sessions and poetry competitions for cash prizes attract a young crowd, who enjoy hearing the spoken word, sometimes linked with projected video images.

Other specialized publications that satisfy leisure reading interests include a huge variety of magazines and newspapers. Although such popular weekly magazines as the *Saturday Evening Post, Colliers,* and *Liberty* went out of existence after World War II, the overall number of magazines of all types rose from about 9,500 in 1970 to over 11,500 in the late 1980s.

A unique type of periodical is the comic magazine, which, beginning in the late 1930s and early 1940s, has continued as a popular form of entertainment. Despite their name, most comic books are not humorous; instead, they involve a huge range of subject matter, including Superman-type comics, crime, adventure, Western, horror, science-fiction, and romance subjects. Great literary classics have been translated into comics, and Bible Comics have been used to tell religious messages; others preach anti-drug sermons, urge teenage chastity, or deliver other social content. Collectors prize early copies of such magazines as *Superman, Batman,* and *Captain Marvel,* and mint-condition copies of the top magazines may sell for as much as $40,000 or $50,000 at international art auctions. Increasingly, comics have become recognized as a significant segment of today's literary scene, and are the subject of panel meetings at conferences of the American Booksellers Association. Although they were originally aimed at children, they now are read heavily by adults.

■ ARTS, ENTERTAINMENT, AND THE ECONOMY

During the past three decades, the arts and entertainment have become an immensely lucrative sector of the American economy. This trend may be illustrated in three ways: through the huge salaries that are paid to leading entertainers; the merging of giant, multibillion-dollar corporations in communication and entertainment conglomerates; and the packaging and merchandising of a great variety of products linked to entertainment as a source of additional profits.

�III➡ TO THE POINT

For example, *Forbes Magazine* reported in 1990 that numerous entertainers, including talk-show hosts, singers, producers and directors, rock bands, and actors and actresses, were earning sums in excess of $40 million or more a year. Rarely does such income stem from a single source. Bill Cosby, for example, writes books, does comedy acts, produces television shows, and makes jazz records. He is also one of America's favorite product spokespersons in television advertising.

As an example of huge entertainment conglomerates today, in 1991 media giant Time Inc., after buying Warner Communications in a $9 billion stock-for-stock deal, merged with Japan's Toshiba and C. Itoh in an ocean-spanning film and television venture. The resulting venture, called Time Warner Entertainment, has the following major components: motion picture and television studios; the nation's largest record company; twenty-four publications, with *Time Magazine* as the flagship; cable television, with some 5.5 million basic subscribers, including Home Box Office, the nation's largest pay-television programmer; and a major hardcover and paperback book publishing enterprise. Other huge entertainment empires include megacompanies that operate motion picture studios, record companies, television networks, sports teams and arenas, ski resorts, cruise lines, and similar providers of mass leisure.

Product licensing provides another illustration of how arts and entertainment have been commodified in America. Typically, hundreds of sports heroes, popular entertainers, and cartoon characters as diverse as Michael Jordan and Garfield the Cat are used to sell sporting goods, toys and games, health and beauty aids, food, beverages, apparel, and accessories. Overall, the licensing industry has grown from $11 billion in retail sales in the early 1980s to over $66 billion in the early 1990s, with over ten thousand licensed names and images in the United States.

■ COMMODIFICATION OF LEISURE

Taken altogether, the conversion of arts and entertainment into a gigantic, profitable commodity illuminates the extent to which we have abandoned the notion of leisure as a relaxed form of personal escape and self-definition. With high-powered, sophisticated advertising and marketing techniques, huge corporations play a major role in influencing our choice of leisure activities—the sports and games we play, the toys we give our children, the films and television we watch, the books we read, and the destinations we travel to. Several decades ago, the psychotherapist Erich Fromm pointed out that Americans had increasingly become dominated by a consumer mentality. As consumers, he wrote, we are manipulated and sold products we do not really need or understand. Marketing techniques have transformed ordinary people into passive, alienated consumers of leisure goods and services that are thrust on us, and that we are brainwashed into accepting as necessary.[33]

Recently, other sociologists have commented that the relatively new discipline of social archaeology shows how material objects and mass-produced services influence and manipulate popular culture and social values. Driven by such institutions of the modern economy as marketing, advertising, and easy credit, people tend to become obsessively concerned with the purchase of goods and services, at the expense of their relations with other people or having genuine experiences in their leisure.

Beyond this effect, an inescapable corollary of the commodification and mass marketing of leisure is that so many of the artifacts of arts and entertainment, such as books, magazines, films, and television are produced by the few for the many. Bernard Miege, in *The Capitalization of Cultural Production,* points out that in capitalist society, creative workers who are employed in cultural, profit-making enterprises "are for the most part paid on a royalty basis rather than by wages. This has the effect of greatly rewarding a few 'stars' while condemning the majority of creators to near poverty or to work outside of the industry."[34]

In the United States, the reality is that within each area of the arts, the fact that we mass-produce objects like phonograph records, television shows, and movie cassettes to entertain millions of people means that only a tiny percentage of artists, actors, musicians, or other performers can be professionally employed. Inevitably, the mass of people who seek to perform in the arts must do so as amateurs—in their leisure.

Values Expressed in Popular Entertainment

Given the concentration of policy-making in the mass media of communication and entertainment in a relatively small number of individuals, it is instructive to examine the fundamental values that are expressed in sitcoms, soap operas, television dramas, and other forms of popular culture. A prime illustration lies in the contrast between "The Andy Griffith Show" of the 1960s and its counterpart of the late 1980s and early 1990s, "The Simpsons." In the first show, one of the top ten programs in all eight of its prime-time seasons, the little town of Mayberry, North Carolina, provided a sense of stability, family affection, and decency. Sheriff Andy did not wear a gun; he relied on persuasion, conversation, and one-on-one dialogue to bring up his young son, Opie.

In contrast, Homer Simpson, father of the family, is known to his boss as "Bonehead," constantly bickers with his wife and, after his son gets beaten by a bully, he advises him: "Never say anything unless you're sure everyone feels exactly the same way." Bart, the smart-mouthed, mischievous, bristle-headed boy, constantly exchanges insults with his parents, and the show as a whole shamelessly panders to a kid's-eye view of the world. Parents give stupid advice, school is a bore, and Bart shows his affection for sister Lisa as a "sniveling toad, egg-sucker and butt-kisser!" Overnight, this half-hour cartoon show emerged as a breakaway ratings hit, a merchandising phenomenon, and, among its fanatical followers, a viewing experience verging on the religious.[35]

The Griffith story reassures us that small-town American values are still the best, and that family members can all love and respect each other. In contrast, Bart Simpson and his siblings show an extraordinary disdain for family values. While it is obviously a satire, youthful reviewers who are asked to pinpoint the appeal of the Simpson clan say that they like it because this dysfunctional family is so "real."

In the fall of 1992, as the nation approached a key presidential election, *Time* pointed out that television had become the arena where American myths competed, and where political factions sought to use popular entertainment as a means of winning votes. A few months before, Vice President Dan Quayle had made a speech criticizing the sitcom "Murphy Brown" for depicting unwed motherhood in a sympathetic light. He linked this program sequence with the breakdown of American family values and with the mass rioting in Los Angeles that had occurred shortly before. When attacked by numerous artistic and feminist groups for his apparent assault on single mothers, Quayle responded with a follow-up attack on the cultural "elite" of Hollywood and television who, in his view, scorned and brainwashed the American public. In turn, at the September Emmy awards, Quayle was ridiculed by a number of comics, actors, and television producers. In the opening program of the fall "Murphy Brown," the show's star, Candice Bergen, bitterly rebuked Quayle for his tactics. At the same time, other leading television series continued to feature plot lines that dealt with the crumbling economy, race riots, the rights of homosexuals, and similar politically sensitive issues.

Some media critics claimed that current movies and television shows *did* systematically disparage such values as patriotism, religious faith, and marital fidelity—and that millions of Americans now saw the entertainment industry as an alien, corrupting force. Columnist John Leo saw the conflict in values as a continuation of the effort of the "liberation" movement of the 1960s to discredit traditional institutions.[36] Movie critic Michael Medved documented Quayle's attack on the cultural elite in his book, *Hollywood vs. America: Popular Culture and the War on Traditional Values.*[37]

Time questioned the legitimacy of the new attack on the movie and television industry:

> Republican politicians think they can rack up political points by attacking shows that are watched and loved by millions. A Hollywood community that produced the most conservative President of the century has, it is alleged, come under almost total domination by a clique of liberals. Is it all just political posturing? Or has television really crossed the line from entertainment to advocacy?[38]

How valid is the argument that television and movies promote antisocial values and criminal behavior? It might be argued that much of the violence and criminality shown on television stems from real life—as in the accounts of a mother trying to have the mother of her daughter's chief competitor for cheerleading honors assassinated, or a teenage girl shooting the wife of her middle-aged lover. Yet it may also be argued that television helps to publicize such events and to make them so familiar in popular culture that they seem natural and normal behavior. Beyond this, it is clear that the *methods* of commercial television have clearly influenced the nature of political discourse in modern America. The picture tube has become a vital tool in political campaigning—as illustrated by Ross Perot's becoming a viable presidential candidate in 1992 by buying substantial television time and hiring an army of volunteer coordinators throughout the nation. Today, candidates use cleverly designed advertisements, sound-bites, speeches, and carefully packaged meetings with constituents to enhance their own images and destroy those of their opponents. In effect, the candidate becomes a show, and the electorate finally makes its choice, not by buying an advertised product but by pulling the "right" voting lever.

Christopher Lasch, the social historian who wrote *The Culture of Narcissism,* concludes that the development of an entertainment-oriented economy has had even broader effects on American life—the "enormous trivialization" of cultural goods. The public's desire for drama, escape, and fantasy means that everything becomes entertainment: news, political events, cultural analysis. He writes: "The most significant thing about the process is that it abolishes all cultural distinctions, good and bad, high and low. It all becomes the same, and therefore all equally evanescent and ultimately meaningless."[39]

■ POLITICS AND FEDERAL SUPPORT OF THE ARTS

A final key factor with respect to the place of the arts in American life stems from the fact that, while popular arts are immensely profitable and have generous financial support, the so-called elite arts of classical music, serious drama, ballet, and modern dance must struggle to maintain themselves on shoestring budgets. Unlike most of the other nations in the Western world, which provide relatively generous subsidies to the arts through federal, provincial, and local grants and sponsorship of cultural centers, the United States has long had a history of ignoring or starving them.

In the 1930s, when the federal government gave strong support to the performing, visual, and literary arts as part of its effort to sustain public morale, enrich national culture, and provide employment, it was soon attacked as encouraging left-wing propaganda. In the Cold War period that followed World War II, such programs were sharply reduced, although the U.S. State Department assisted international tours of music, dance, and theater companies. Then, in 1964, the National Arts and Cultural Development Act established a National Council on the Arts within the Executive Office of the President. A year later, the Arts and Humanities Act of 1965 established a National Foundation on the Arts and Humanities, with separate endowment programs and advisory bodies for the arts and the humanities. The National Endowment for the Arts was empowered to provide funds to non-profit organizations and to state and other public organizations and individuals to assist artistic and cultural productions that encouraged American creativity and professional excellence.

During the years that followed, approximately $170 million each year was given to the arts through federal grants, contributing significantly to grass-roots arts activities and major institutions alike. However, this sum was markedly below that given by the states ($273 million in 1991), or by private corporate business, which contributed over $630 million a year in the late 1980s to assist music, drama, dance, fine arts, public television, and other cultural pursuits. The level of support for the arts given by the federal government was also considerably below the amounts spent by the German, French, and Japanese governments. John Rockwell, a *New York Times* art critic, commented that, seen from a European perspective, America's neglect of the arts was galling:

> the largesse the Germans lavish on their theaters and museums and concert halls is legendary. . . . French cultural subvention represents a truly regal extension of the royal patronage of the Old Regime, a feeling that politicians win glory in the eyes of history for the artistic legacies they leave behind. . . . Europe's politicians, for all their pomposity and vainglory, care enough about culture to support it as a necessity of life. Ours defame the arts by paying earnest attention to laughable philistines concerned only about the publicity they may reap by attacking "obscenity."[40]

The early 1990s illustrated Rockwell's point, as the National Endowment for the Arts came under angry political attacks for funding exhibits and performances that dealt with homoerotic and sadomasochistic themes—photographic exhibits by Andres Serrano and Robert Mapplethorpe, performance art by Annie Sprinkle, and other avant-garde work denounced by Senator Jesse Helms of North Carolina and fellow conservative Congressional critics and members of the religious right. Following a period of controversy, John Frohnmayer, chairman of the National Endowment, was forced to resign. He was replaced by an acting chief who promptly rejected a number of proposals that had been recommended for support by peer advisory panels. Many arts organizations withdrew proposals or plans to submit new ones, rather than yield to artistic censorship, and several members of review panels refused to serve under the new review policies.

Although the "godless perversion" charge that had been leveled against some of the more controversial works that had been funded was the apparent reason for the attack on the National Endowment for the Arts, underlying it appeared to be strong opposition to government's playing any significant role at all in the support of arts institutions—arguing that if the arts could not justify themselves through public support, they had no right to exist. Other critics charged that grants were slanted toward "liberal" causes. A conservative think tank, the Heritage Foundation, opposed renewed funding for the Corporation for Public Broadcasting, claiming that it had a "left-wing" tilt. Others opposed the documentaries funded by the Independent Television Service, an agency funded by Congress in 1988 to bring more minority voices into public broadcasting, criticizing its productions that dealt with racial concerns in the United States.

In response, those arguing for government support point out that in America's uniquely pluralistic democracy, art should spring from a wide variety of artists and flow to a diverse audience of people all exploring their own cultural heritages. They claim that art is a nation's most precious heritage, and artists, like scholars and scientists, need special protection from the rigors of the free market—along with a climate that encourages freedom of thought, imagination, and inquiry.

In 1992, a large-scale survey of the American public showed that a majority of citizens believe that federal tax dollars should be spent to support the arts, without artistic censorship. Louis Harris reported that:

> 60 percent of those polled in the East and South supported federal arts funding, followed closely by the West and Midwest and by large majorities in all demographic segments. It is striking that all regions of the country, all strata of education, all races and all income levels support federal funding of the arts. Clearly, the dominant feeling in this country is in favor of continued federal assistance to the arts.[41]

■ SUMMARY

The four major types of aesthetic involvement and spectatorship are the visual, or fine arts; the performing arts, such as music, drama, and dance; the mass media of communication and entertainment; and the literary uses of leisure. The social impact of television and such musical forms as rock and rap are part of the concern about the present level of popular taste and the growth of violence and crime, particularly among the young. While the claim of supposed societal degradation caused by the "cultural elite" is debatable, the issue of the support of the arts by federal subsidy has become a key political issue that is likely to continue in the years ahead.

■ QUESTIONS FOR DISCUSSION

1. Traditionally, we have accepted the idea that there are two major levels of artistic presentations: elite, or highbrow, art, and popular, or lowbrow, art. Can you make a case that this distinction has been lessened, and that there is instead a continuum of artistic taste, with many forms of expression that comprise mass culture and appeal to all classes and taste levels?

2. What are the varied types of sponsorship under which the arts are presented in leisure contexts, in American communities? Refer to specific kinds of expression, such as graphic, performing, or literary art, in your discussion.

3. In recent years, there has been considerable criticism of such elements in popular culture as the sexist and racist elements in rap and rock music and the flagrant violence found in movies and television. How serious are these concerns, and how might the nation deal with them without resorting to censorship that abridges constitutional rights of free expression?

4. Reading represents a major form of leisure activity, but is threatened, in the view of many authorities, by visual forms of entertainment that are more directly appealing and easier to comprehend. Is this a legitimate concern? How might parents and educational leaders respond to it?

5. Government subsidy of the fine arts and other cultural forms in the United States has been episodic and at a much lower level than in European nations. What has accounted for this unwillingness to nurture creative expression in America, and what is the rationale of conservative legislators and religious leaders who seek to eliminate or sharply reduce such subsidies? What is your position on this matter?

■ NOTES

1. HARRIS, L. 1987. *Inside America.* New York: Vintage, Random House, p. 163.

2. FEIBLEMAN, J. 1949. *Aesthetics: A study of the fine arts in theory and practice.* New York: Duell, Sloan and Pearce, p. 302.

3. MACDONALD, D. 1957. A theory of mass culture. In *Mass culture,* eds. D. M. White and B. Rosenberg. Glencoe, IL: Free Press, p. 59.

4. HENRI, R. 1923. *The art spirit.* Philadelphia: Lippincott, p. 5.

5. VALDES, L. 1991. The artists of Terezin led lives of creativity despite captivity. *Philadelphia Inquirer* (Nov. 4): 8–E.

6. CONN, B. 1988. Arts in the mainstream: Recreation gives arts new focus. *Parks and Recreation* (June): 26.

7. SOZANSKI, E. 1990. Culture and contemporary art. *Philadelphia Inquirer* (Oct. 21): 1–H.

8. DANNEN, F. 1990. *Hit men: Power brokers and fast money inside the music business.* New York: Random House.

9. QUEENAN, J. 1991. Misfit metalheads. *Time* (Sept.30): 83.

10. SAMUEL, T. 1992. Young urban blacks a study in alienation. *Philadelphia Inquirer* (May 28): A–1.

11. KLEIN, M. 1992. Rappers chant a refrain of hate. *Philadelphia Inquirer* (May 8): A–19.
12. LEO, J. 1990. Polluting our popular culture. *U.S. News and World Report* (July 2): 15.
13. GOUGIS, M. 1992. Orchestras feel squeeze of recession. *Associated Press Dispatch* (Feb. 1).
14. HORN, M. 1992. Looking for a renaissance: The campaign to revive education in the arts. *U.S. News and World Report* (Mar. 30): 52.
15. DISCH, R. 1991. The death of Broadway. *The Atlantic* (Mar.): 92.
16. JANOWITZ, B., quoted in Ridley, C. A. 1992. Beyond present gloom, future belongs to the bold. *Philadelphia Inquirer* (Apr. 6): C–3.
17. HENRY, W. 1991. A showman of the people. *Time* (Nov. 11): 99.
18. DE VRIES, HILLARY. 1991. It's a tough job, but somebody's got to want it. *New York Times* (Aug. 18): 1–H.
19. SALISBURY, S. 1990. An unsettling kind of art. *Philadelphia Inquirer* (July 9): I–1.
20. BROWNE, D. 1991. Pop radio suffers a midlife crisis. *New York Times* (July 28): 2-1, 2-8.
21. BAGDIKIAN, B. 1992. Pop radio. *The Nation* (Apr. 13): 473, 488.
22. FALUDI, S. 1991. The fatal detractions by Hollywood. *Philadelphia Inquirer* (Nov. 12): E–1.
23. NC-17 rating removes restraints on filmmakers. *The Christian Century* (Oct. 10, 1990): 891.
24. BAKER, R. K. 1992. The face of America overseas comes through a tube darkly. *Philadelphia Inquirer* (Mar. 1): E–7.
25. Living: TV as the new fireplace. *Time* (Dec. 27, 1982): 70.
26. GITLIN, TODD, quoted in Rimer, S. 1991. Television becomes basic furniture in college students' ivory towers. *New York Times* (Oct. 27): 8.
27. Now, it's the "stay-at-home society." *U.S. News and World Report* (June 28, 1982): 64.
28. SCANLAN, C. 1993. Children's television: Quantity, not quality. *Philadelphia Inquirer* (May 2): D–3.
29. ZOGLIN, R. 1990. Is TV ruining our children? *Time* (Oct. 15): 75.
30. DUSTON, D. 1992. Three networks agree to standards governing violence on television. *Associated Press* (Dec. 12).
31. KRAUTHAMMER, C. 1990. Yes, good art can elevate society—and degrading art has its equivalent effect. *Philadelphia Inquirer* (Oct. 30): 10–A.
32. GIOIA, D. 1991. Can poetry matter? *The Atlantic* (May): 94.
33. FROMM, E. 1955. *The sane society.* New York: Fawcett, pp. 124–215.
34. MIEGE, B. 1989. *The capitalization of cultural production.* New York: International General.
35. WATERS, H. F. 1990. Family Feuds. *Newsweek* (Apr. 23): 38.
36. LEO, J. 1992. Sneer not at 'Ozzie and Harriet.' *U.S. News and World Report* (Sept. 14): 24.
37. MEDVED, M. 1992. *Hollywood vs. America: Popular culture and the war on traditional values.* New York: HarperCollins.
38. ZOGLIN, R. 1992. Sitcom politics. *Time* (Sept. 21): 44–47.
39. LASCH, C., cited in *Time* (Dec. 24, 1990): 59.
40. ROCKWELL, J. 1991. A bedazzled critic finds Oz, in Paris. *New York Times* (Apr. 7): 25–H.
41. HARRIS, L. 1992. Support for the arts is on the rise. *Philadelphia Inquirer* (Apr. 28): A–17.

12 **Other Forms of Play: Morally Marginal Leisure**

. . . these glittering new casinos [Mississippi riverboats with legalized gambling] have nothing to do with the Las Vegas and Atlantic City worlds of loan sharks, hookers and high-rolling drunks. Rather, these are advertised as wholesome family-fun places that repackage casinos as floating nineteenth-century theme parks. The boats' lure is of antebellum romance with river rogues clad in sharply tailored frock coats sporting gold watches and diamond studs. Under Iowa law just 30 percent of a ship's floor space can be devoted to gambling. There's even a $200-per-cruise loss limit to ensure no one gets carried away.[1]

The preceding chapters in this book describe three major forms of popular leisure pursuits today: outdoor recreation, travel, and tourism; sports; and arts and entertainment. Obviously, there are numerous other forms of recreation that Americans enjoy. The most common uses of leisure involve casual, inexpensive, and close-to-home activities, such as family interaction, watching television, reading, parties or companionship with friends, going for a drive or a walk, and picnicking. Beyond these pastimes, however, there are several forms of play that either involve criminal behavior or may—even when legal—be seriously destructive to individual or societal well-being. These include gambling, drug and alcohol abuse, and commercialized sex. This chapter examines each of these "morally marginal" forms of play in terms of their appeal and their outcomes, and society's ambiguous efforts both to sponsor and profit from them, and to contain their harmful outcomes.

■ INFORMAL LEISURE PURSUITS

In addition to the major types of organized recreation activities described earlier in this book, Americans spend their leisure time in varied unstructured ways. In the early 1980s, a survey on leisure conducted by United Media Enterprises defined the most popular casual free-time activities of adults (see Table 12.1).

Such pursuits, while usually carried on in unstructured and unsponsored ways, may involve considerable expenditure. For example, gardening spending amounts to an estimated $20 billion each year. Pet care—including food and related equipment and services for dogs, cats, birds, fish, and more exotic kinds of pets—is an $8 to $10 billion industry. The sale of toys and electronic games totaled $13 billion annually in the early 1990s. Card and table games, including such favorites as chess, checkers, Monopoly, Scrabble, and Trivial Pursuit, engage millions of participants, as do such hobbies as collecting, model building, dressmaking, and home crafts. Many Americans join clubs based on special interests ranging from astronomy to square dancing. It has been estimated that 80 percent of adults belong to such groups, with titles that range from "Aardvark Aficionados" to "The Diving Dentists' Society" to "Sarcastics Anonymous."[2]

TABLE 12.1
Percentage of adults who engage in activity daily or almost every day

Watch television	72%	Spend an evening just	
Read newspaper	70	talking to someone	30%
Listen to music at home	46	Read a book	24
Talk on phone to		Pursue a hobby	23
friends or relatives	45	Work in the garden	22
Exercise or jog	35	Engage in sexual activities	11

SOURCE: United Media Enterprises national poll, reported in *Time,* December 7, 1982, p. 70.

In addition to such widely found pursuits, many people seek to express their individuality by engaging in daring or unique forms of leisure activity as chronicled by *Time* magazine:

> Some adventuresome souls achieve fame by scaling the world's highest peaks or plumbing the oceans' deepest bottoms. Their feats faithfully find their way into the *Guinness Book of World Records,* as do the odysseys of marathon smoke-ring blowers, balloonists, goldfish swallowers, grape eaters, yo-yo spinners, Scrabble players, prune devourers, face slappers, Pogo-stick jumpers, leapfroggers, barrel jumpers, needle threaders and record-breakers in 10,000 other *Record*-worthy categories.[3]

■ MOTIVATIONS FOR LEISURE INVOLVEMENT

What accounts for this immense range of involvement in leisure activities? David Gray and Hilmi Ibrahim stress that recreation experience is much more than a casual, inconsequential time filler. Instead, it comprises a cluster of human experiences of great diversity and impact. They write:

> we have found that when people are asked to recount their most memorable recreation experiences they often recall intimate memories of extraordinary personal meaning. These experiences are so significant they are often a part of the personal identity of the individual and so memorable they last a lifetime. [They] shape not only what one can do but also who one is. Self-discovery is the most intimate, the most difficult, and the most significant of all learning. It comes in subtle ways and often in unexpected places. In [such narratives] largely unreported and often unanticipated, we find the recreation experience as a major source of self-discovery.[4]

Most persons would be likely to identify the essential purpose of recreation as "to have fun," or "pleasure." Although in the past, such a motivation was often regarded as trivial or childlike, we are beginning to realize the healthful values of humor and enjoyment as such. Columnist John Leo points out that researchers are finding that "regular injections of mirth are associated with fewer headaches, reduced stress, and even a longer life."[5] Similarly, Natalie Angier reports that scientists who followed a group of subjects through their lives found that those who were easygoing and enjoyed life lived significantly longer than those who did not. They conclude, she writes: "that euphoria unrelated to any ingested substance is good for the body, that laughter is protective against the corrosive impact of stress, and that joyful people outlive their bilious, whining counterparts."[6]

Summing up the literature on fun, Walter Podilchak concludes that although fun is dismissed as an aspect of leisure by classicists like Sebastian de Grazia, it is inescapably part of the social-interactional and emotional world. While not synonymous with leisure, fun is inherently a social process, an ongoing lived experience—a hedonistic, self-gratifying activity that is shared with others.[7] Obviously, however, it is not the total purpose or outcome of leisure involvement.

In 1980, Rick Crandall presented a list of leisure motivations that had been developed by a group of investigators at the University of Illinois. It consisted of seventeen motivation factors that had been identified in a systematic study of a cross-section of American adults. They included such factors as: enjoying nature and escaping civilization; change from routine and responsibility; physical exercise and health values; social contact and companionship; creativity and aesthetic expression; gaining a sense of power and influence; altruism and being of service to others; stimulus of excitement-seeking; self-actualization and enrichment of one's personality; and avoiding boredom.[8]

Other efforts to identify leisure motivations focused more narrowly on the goals and outcomes of leisure involvement for specific population groups or inherent in particular recreational activities. For example, Tinsley, Teaff, and Colbs identified the special values of recreation for elderly persons (see page 190). Gump and Friesen found that high school students reported that their reasons for taking part in extracurricular activities included competence development, novelty, and social contact.[9] Based on studies of adults in three communities, Kelly found that reasons for leisure involvement included such elements as: rest and relaxation, excitement, self-expression, enjoying companionship, or pressures from one's spouse.[10]

Studies of reasons for engaging in a specific leisure activity, such as recreational running, have yielded such motivations as maintaining fitness and weight control, the elevated mood obtained after running, companionship and social values, enjoyment of competition, and addiction to the activity. Some runners become so hooked on the pursuit that they are compelled to run even when it is medically, vocationally, or socially contraindicated.[11]

Benefits of Personal Leisure Involvement

Beyond the exploration of participants' motivation for taking part in given leisure activities, there is the question of what they actually *gain* from involvement.

For example, Haggard and Williams have studied the role of leisure as "symbols of the self," meaning that it is used to affirm one's own identity to oneself and to others.[12] Roggenbuck, Loomis, and Dagostino discuss the learning benefits of leisure, with emphasis on the outcomes of outdoor recreation involvement. These include: (1) learning specific recreational activities and skills in outdoor environments; (2) learning about the natural environment and developing more positive attitudes and behaviors toward resource management; (3) developing pride in the community and the nation and becoming a more involved citizen; and (4) learning more about the self.[13] Studies by the U.S. Department of Education have shown that participation in extracurricular activities and good grades are closely linked in high school students.[14]

Another area in which the values of leisure involvement have been convincingly documented is in the realm of physical fitness and health. Over the past three decades, Americans have pursued fitness almost as an obsession. In 1988, *Time* reported:

> Some 7 million Americans, most between the ages of 25 and 44, last year spent $5 billion on membership fees [in health clubs] to swim, grunt on exercise equipment and play racquetball. . . . Americans last year bought $738 million worth of exercise benches, light weights, exercise bikes and treadmills for their homes. A decade earlier sales were only $5 million.[15]

In addition to membership in health clubs and the use of personal exercise equipment, millions of American youth and adults run, jog, swim, bicycle, and engage in vigorous sports with health concerns as a primary motivation. There is increasing evidence that even moderate exercise has important health benefits. Physical inactivity has been shown as a major risk factor for heart disease, and varied sports and other active leisure pursuits help to reduce the incidence of coronary disease, high blood pressure, certain forms of cancer, and other health risks.[16] Research has also demonstrated that participants tend to drop out of exercise programs carried on for purely health-oriented reasons, but to continue in programs that include social and recreational satisfactions.[17]

■ THE SHADY SIDE OF LEISURE

What is not generally acknowledged in scholarly studies of leisure and its effects is that many of the most widely engaged in forms of play in American society have potentially negative outcomes.

ⅢⅢ➡ TO THE POINT

As earlier chapters have shown, leisure has historically been viewed from two sharply contrasting perspectives. On the one hand, it has been seen as socially desirable, contributing to cultural enrichment and the quality of life, and even linked to spiritual goals and personal self-actualization. On the other hand, throughout history, the work ethic has been sharply opposed to idleness and play; in successive eras societies have sought to control gambling, sexual activity, drinking, drug use, and other forms of morally marginal play. The term *marginal* is used here because most of these forms of leisure activity are on the fringe of social acceptability. In some cases, they are widely engaged in, legally permitted, and even sponsored by government and by religious authorities. In other cases, they are viewed as immoral, illegal, and to be resisted at all costs.

Such activities often become part of large, commercially driven businesses, sometimes legal but often illegal. Typically, criminal organizations like the Mafia have through the years been involved in the lucrative businesses of gambling and loan-sharking, drug distribution, illicit liquor trade (when Prohibition was in force), prostitution, and pornography. Indeed, federal crime studies show that the "mob" makes hundreds of billions of dollars in profit from such leisure-related enterprises.[18]

Many morally marginal leisure pursuits are carried on for reasons similar to the motivations prompting other forms of recreational participation. They may involve socialization with others, relaxing or escaping from tensions and pressures, the lures of excitement and challenge, risk, and reward. At the same time, each of these pursuits may lead to feelings of guilt and failure, to physical and economic self-destruction, to alienation from one's family, and even to criminal prosecution.

■ MARGINAL PLAY AS ADDICTIVE BEHAVIOR

What makes such forms of play so appealing? Anthropologist Lionel Tiger suggests that the search for primitive "sensory pleasures" has deep roots in humankind's past and that there is a significant relationship among power, pleasure, reproduction, and human nature. Indeed, he writes, a nation's success in providing an array of legitimately enjoyed pleasures may have much to do with its ability to survive in the modern world.[19] A unique aspect of morally marginal forms of play is that they often take the form of addictions. Gloria Hochman writes: "Most addictions begin as pleasurable activities. Hobbies and innocent pastimes start to become addictions when more and more time, energy and resources are needed to achieve the same effect."[20]

Similarly, Frederick Goodwin, a psychiatrist and administrator of the Alcohol, Drug Abuse and Mental Health Administration, points out that many behaviors begin as voluntary acts, but then become reflexive and automatic.[21] The most obvious examples are alcoholism and drug addiction, which most medical experts today view as chronic diseases with biological and perhaps even genetic underpinnings.

What causes some persons to become addicted and others not, despite similar family backgrounds or environmental circumstances? Research suggests that addicts resemble each other in certain ways. They tend to have difficulty in recognizing and expressing their feelings, in relating to other people, and in forming long-range goals because they focus too much on short-term, immediate gratification. They do not anticipate or respect possible harmful outcomes of risky behavior and are consequently unable to create a safe, healthy life-style. Many of them have been raised in dysfunctional families where parents or other siblings may be substance or physical abusers, where too little love has been expressed, and where there has been too much early discipline or too little.

William Bennett, editor of the Harvard Medical School *Health Letter,* points out that people are often addicted to habits that are not always "great fun." Compulsive human behavior may involve as much pain as pleasure, with a period of mounting anxiety followed by a period of release when the event is over. He suggests that a given stimulus, whether pleasant or aversive, may become addicting not only because of the way it feels but also because it leads to a powerful cycle of anticipation, sensation, and withdrawal that becomes the key element in creating dependency.[22]

■ GAMBLING AS LEISURE ACTIVITY

We turn now to an examination of several forms of addictive leisure behavior about which society is ambivalent. The first of these is gambling, defined as any sort of game or contest in which individuals wager money in the hope of financial gain.

In the early New England colonies, some forms of gambling, such as lotteries, were regarded as socially acceptable and in fact were used to finance worthwhile community projects. Others, like racetrack betting, cards, and dice, were regarded as a vice; the Puritans condemned them as akin to taking the Lord's name in vain, because they "prostituted the divine providence to unworthy ends."

In the early 1800s, gambling flourished in frontier saloons and big-city "sporting" settings. In a review of its history in America, John Findlay points out that there were no consistent efforts to control it, and that it was influenced by what he calls "climates of transiency."

> Historically [gambling] flourished where traditional restraints were loosened, in settings where "family and home-town inhibitions disappear." Thus, in the days when the country was expanding rapidly, when men were freed from small-town life to seek their fortunes to "make a killing," gambling became increasingly popular.[23]

Throughout the nineteenth and much of the twentieth century, efforts both to legalize and to control gambling followed a piecemeal pattern. The only state to permit legalized casino gambling was Nevada; however, numerous other states encouraged pari-mutuel betting on horse and dog races, allowed nonprofit organizations to operate Bingo games, and permitted other forms of gambling to exist.

In the decades after World War II, gambling became more popular as a recognized form of recreation, as a number of the legal restraints on it were withdrawn. Two major forms of play were at the heart of this trend—legalized casino betting and state-sponsored lotteries. In 1978, *U.S. News and World Report* described a "gambling spree across the nation," pointing out that the gambling industry, long hidden in the shadows of American society, was now making a bid for respectability:

> Pressures against tax increases and the growing quest for "easy money" have led to the legalization of some form of wagering in forty-four states over the past fifteen years. . . . Gambling-industry leaders consider the introduction of legalized casinos in New Jersey a breakthrough. That development brings the excitement and relatively favorable odds of casino gambling within five hours' drive of one quarter of the U.S.[24]

In states like New York, Florida, Pennsylvania, and California, advocates were pushing for more casinos, slot machines, race betting, and other games. By the early 1980s, doubts and fears about games of chance were falling by the wayside, as gambling became increasingly perceived both as a direct economic benefit to the states and communities that initiated it through taxes and employment and as a boost to tourism. In 1985, Americans legally wagered more than $177 billion at casinos, pari-mutuels, and state-owned lotteries, with another huge amount of illegal gambling that could only be guessed at. In city after city and state after state, citizen referendums were held to approve various forms of gambling—usually justified to gain revenue and provide a boost to employment.

Giant new casinos were built in both Atlantic City and Las Vegas, capped by Donald Trump's billion-dollar Taj Mahal and his rival Steve Wynn's $600 million Mirage. In the early 1990s, a number of states, beginning with Iowa, approved riverboat gambling along the Mississippi River, in the hope that floating casinos would not only bring new revenues but would also raise the image and stimulate the economy of depressed riverfront towns.

Increasingly, gambling casino chiefs like Nevada's spectacularly successful Steve Wynn are seeking to portray gambling as just another form of wholesome family recreation. Here, smiling adults enjoy blackjack, slot machines, and roulette on the luxurious *Dubuque Casino Belle,* longest passenger vessel and gambling boat on the Mississippi. Despite its popularity, gambling is recognized as a serious problem in Iowa, where the State Department of Human Services places warning posters in school corridors.

GAMBLING CAN LEAD TO
DANGER

Don't Sweat It Out
On Your Own!

Get Help.

Call 1-800-BETS-OFF

By 1991, every state except Utah and Hawaii had legalized lotteries or some other form of gambling or betting, and *Gaming and Wagering Business Magazine* reported that Americans had legally wagered $286 billion in the most recent year—more than $1,000 per capita and 6.2 percent of U.S. total personal income. A number of states had instituted off-track betting parlors for horse racing. In the same year, gross revenues from legalized gambling were more than five times the box office of the domestic movie industry.

In Duluth, Minnesota, a former Sears store was certified as an Indian reservation belonging to the Fond du Lac Chippewa tribe, solely to allow the operation of a casino downtown. In no state is gambling as diversified as in Iowa; in addition to craps, blackjack, roulette, and slot machines on its floating casinos, it offers a lottery, horse and dog racing, Bingo, and Las Vegas nights for charities.

■ THE DOWNSIDE OF LEGALIZED GAMBLING

While there was widespread support for new forms of legalized gambling, many civic groups opposed its spread and pointed out some of the negative outcomes of the new trend. In many cases, Bingo or Las Vegas nights that were sponsored by religious or charitable organizations were shown to be run by professional gambling groups linked to organized crime. In Philadelphia, for example, the professional operators of one of the city's largest Bingo operations (sponsored by a Roman Catholic church) were charged with racketeering, gambling violations, criminal conspiracy, and diverting almost $1 million that the church should have received.

When New Jersey's legislature first considered legalizing casino gambling in Atlantic City, it was argued that the move would curb illegal gambling activity. However, in the late 1980s, the state's highest-ranking police officer concluded that instead it had helped organized crime augment and expand its illegal gambling operations. New Jersey State Police Superintendent Clinton Pagano pointed out that gambling was still

> the primary, consistent source of revenue for traditional organized criminal enterprises . . . the wheel of organized crime. Casinos have exposed a broader base of people to the mechanics of gambling. This has created a larger number of prospective patrons for the illegal market.[25]

⇛ TO THE POINT

Beyond the stimulus it gives to mob-run illegal gambling, legalized casino gambling has also been linked to the growth of other types of crime in the areas where it has been established. In little Deadwood, South Dakota, where gambling was legalized in 1989 to raise funds to preserve the decaying historical district within the city, gambling revenues were much higher than anticipated. However, the unexpectedly large number of tourists and gamblers invading Deadwood caused an increase in crime, traffic, and noise, a change in the community's social fabric, and the loss of a number of businesses. The local state prosecutor reported that the 1989 legalization of poker, blackjack, and slot machines had helped raise the crime rate in Lawrence County, where Deadwood is located, by nearly 70 percent. Bad checks, felonies, and physical assaults increased; forgery crimes rose 480 percent, burglaries 300 percent, and grand theft 1,000 percent.[26]

The Problem of Compulsive Gamblers

It is estimated that two million Americans are compulsive gamblers, a problem defined in the *Diagnostic and Statistical Manual of Mental Disorders* of the American Psychiatric Association as a serious form of mental illness. Often, relatives or friends of compulsive gamblers recognize the problem belatedly because it is so often an invisible addiction. One director of a gamblers' treatment center comments:

> They're bright, carefree, aggressive, outwardly successful people, hard workers to the point of being workaholics. Often they're dynamite salespeople. But, underneath, there's a lack of confidence that they don't want anyone else to see, so they avoid any real intimacy and seek refuge in gambling.[27]

Indeed, one of the reasons gambling attracts as many apparently successful people as it does is that it encourages the kind of competitive, risk-taking behavior that is highly valued in the corporate world. According to the National Council on Compulsive Gambling, at least half of the nation's pathological gamblers eventually turn to illegal means of obtaining funds, from bad checks or phony insurance claims to embezzlement. Studies at two New Jersey prisons showed that over 30 percent of the prisoners were pathological gamblers.[28]

▐▌▶ TO THE POINT

There is growing awareness of the risk imposed by gambling on America's young people. A 1990 study of 2,700 high school students in New Jersey, Virginia, California, and Connecticut showed that half the students gambled occasionally, 13 percent financed their gambling with crimes, and 5 percent were classified as pathological gamblers, using American Psychiatric Association criteria. The easy accessibility of gambling and society's apparent acceptance of it for adults have led increasing numbers of teenagers to involvement with betting on sports, cardplaying, lotteries, and slot machines—with many lying about their age to gain admission to casinos from which they are barred by law.[29]

The casino industry has been slow to recognize its responsibility for helping to create this social problem, although over the last few years it has begun to contribute to treatment programs for addicts. In addition, a number of lottery-sponsoring states have set up special programs to aid compulsive gamblers.

Economic Realities of Gambling

The alluring assumption that gambling represents an easy and acceptable means of solving the financial problems of communities and states requires critical analysis. First, it is apparent that all forms of gambling—and particularly lotteries—prey heavily on the poor, who seek miraculous solutions to their economic problems. One authority, who has studied gambling for over twenty years, points out that the lottery system is "a fraud that preys on the lower classes." The reality is that players have a six times greater chance of being hit by lightning than of winning the lottery. Essentially, the lottery, which pays only a 50 percent return to betters, compared to bookies who skim less than 5 percent from their customers, is a tax on the poor. Seven of the nine biggest state lotteries are in states with a large number of urban poor, such as Pennsylvania, Ohio, and Massachusetts, with California having the highest volume of ticket sales.

Beyond such criticisms, there is evidence that legalized gambling is now taking so many forms and becoming so available that it has reached a saturation point and has drawn customers away from other forms of entertainment, including nightclubs and taverns, shows, racetracks, and other competitors for the sophisticated leisure dollar. In 1985, the owner of a casino and hotel complex in Atlantic City commented: "Basically, the market growth hasn't kept up with the growth in casino capacity. A lot of the operators are hurting, and it could get worse."[30]

In the early 1990s, Atlantic City's boardwalk casinos reported combined losses of over $260 million and two of Donald Trump's financially troubled casinos filed for bankruptcy in an effort to restructure their debts. Even casino owners in Las Vegas began to fear that they were chasing a dwindling number of high rollers during the recession, although the industry began to make a recovery in the following years.

Religious, civic, and other organizations note the bittersweet experience of Atlantic City where gamblers stay in the casinos while the surrounding city remains a devastated ghetto. Although the casinos brought in millions in taxes and created thousands of new jobs, economic spinoffs never developed for the resort city. There are fewer restaurants today in Atlantic City, for example, than there were before casinos were legalized. The risk factor for host communities as well as gambling patrons was vividly illustrated when a number of the riverboat casinos that had begun operations in Iowa were moved down the Mississippi to the Gulf Coast after only a year or two, in search of fewer restrictions and higher profits.

In numerous other cities and states, the expansion of legalized gambling has become a major policy issue. In Gary, Indiana, an economically depressed community, two hundred church leaders opposed a proposal to legalize casino gambling in 1991. For nearly its entire history, Indiana had a constitutional ruling against lotteries, but a proposition passed in 1990 to permit lotteries encouraged the legislature to consider other proposals for horse and dog track racing and casinos. Opponents of the proposal cited both moral and practical arguments against it, while Gary's mayor argued that gambling would bring tourism from Chicago and throughout the Midwest, and that the real moral issue was jobs. Others pointed out that there were clear racial overtones in the gambling industry's targeting Gary, which is predominantly black, with a high rate of unemployment and welfare dependency, for its proposal. A gambling analyst for a brokerage firm in Philadelphia confirmed the trend: "We think Gary presents the best opportunity that we've seen in ten years. . . . The conditions are right there . . . because it's so depressed."

Meanwhile, the casino industry seeks to broaden its market among all socioeconomic markets, with particular emphasis on cultivating the family and youth market. For example, in Las Vegas a number of major casinos are offering such attractions as continuous trapeze acts, nightly jousting tournaments, dolphins on display, a man-made volcano, and white tigers to draw sightseers of all ages, including a "no-nudes" policy. Some observers suggest that gambling companies anticipate good times ahead as baby boomers, raised on a credo of "sex, drugs, and rock 'n' roll" grow older and turn to gambling to meet their need for sensational forms of recreation. In the proposal for a Chicago gambling and theme park complex (see page 193), the rationale is to develop future customers:

> While children would not be allowed to gamble in the casino complex, having theme parks and other attractions around casinos familiarizes young people with gambling early in their lives, increasing the odds that they will grow up to be recreational gamblers.[31]

■ SUBSTANCE ABUSE AND LEISURE

We turn now to a second major form of morally marginal leisure activity: alcohol and drug abuse. Both are similar in that they involve ingesting substances to reach a "high," or a state of excitement or euphoria. Both are usually carried on in social situations, and both may be pursued over a lengthy period of time in a moderate, controlled way. However, addiction-prone individuals often become obsessively dependent on alcohol or drugs, using mind-altering substances more and more frequently to the point that they suffer extreme psychological, physical, and economic injury and can no longer function in healthy, autonomous ways.

Both kinds of substance use are often referred to as leisure pursuits. The term *social drinking* is commonly heard, and the press frequently describes such substances as marijuana as "recreational drugs." Indeed, during the Vietnam War, *Time* characterized heroin as a "plaything" of returning American service personnel.

Despite their similarities, the use of alcohol and of narcotic drugs differ in two respects: (1) alcoholic beverages are legally sold, while narcotic drugs are illegal and have become the driving force behind an immense network of criminal activity, both domestic and international; and (2) while drinking is a recognized part of many community and family-centered occasions, narcotic drug use is, with relatively few exceptions, perceived negatively by Western society and is carried on furtively. Although alcohol is generally regarded as less harmful and dangerous than drug use, there are many more alcoholics in American society than there are drug addicts, and the cost of drinking in physical, psychological, and economic terms is vastly greater than that of narcotic drug use.

Drinking and Leisure

When drinking becomes a habit, a necessity for the individual in his or her daily life, it represents an addiction. The American Medical Association declared alcoholism a disease in 1957, reversing the long-held view that alcoholics were not sick, but sinful. Later, the AMA defined it more precisely: "Alcoholism is an illness characterized by preoccupation with alcohol and loss of control over its consumption such as to lead usually to intoxication if drinking is begun, by chronicity, by progression, and by tendency to relapse."[32]

The old stereotype of the alcoholic as a red-nosed individual who drowns his or her sorrows in drink in a bar or on Skid Row is fallacious. Instead, Lucinda Franks writes:

> the myth that alcoholics are drunk all the time is giving way to the recognition that many of them remain undiscovered, working and living outwardly normal lives, until an alcohol-related disease suddenly cuts them down. The myth that alcoholism is always psychologically caused is giving way to the realization that it is, in large measure, biologically determined.[33]

Some authorities have recently contended that alcoholism is essentially a behavioral rather than a medical problem, and that the disease concept blurs the issue of moral responsibility. Most medical authorities, however, do not accept this position; there are growing evidences of biological as well as psychosocial causes of this form of addiction. One researcher, a professor of psychiatry at New York's Downstate Medical Center, has found abnormalities in brain-wave patterns of alcoholics that suggest physical rather than environmental influences in alcoholism.[34] Other scientists have discovered a gene that governs a part of the brain called the dopamine receptor, which plays a crucial role in Parkinson's disease, schizophrenia, and pleasure-seeking behavior such as drinking alcohol, suggesting a possible inherited tendency to alcoholism.[35]

Whatever the causes, there is no doubt that problem drinking represents a major source of concern in the United States. Fully 55 percent of the public report knowing someone who "drinks too much," and Louis Harris reports that 32 percent of the nation's households have someone at home with a drinking problem. Depending on the criteria used, national surveys indicate that there are between ten and eighteen million problem drinkers in the United States. By income, excessive drinking is found most frequently among those earning $35,000 to $50,000 a year—very much a middle-income affliction.[36] There is evidence that the national consumption of alcoholic beverages has declined over the past two decades. However, the number of persons seeking treatment for problem drinking has continued to rise and the physical and social fallout from drinking is tremendous. Drunkenness is involved in 30 to 50 percent of traffic deaths, 45 percent of all fatal falls, and 50 to 70 percent of homicides.

In particular, alcohol represents a growing problem for America's youth. Although their use of other "recreational" drugs has diminished since the end of the 1970s, alcohol's staying power as the intoxicant of choice among the young has made it the nation's most persistent problem drug. According to the *New York Times* in the early 1990s:

> Even as alcohol use has diminished over the last decade, a federal survey of students in eight states shows that 10.6 million of 29.7 million seventh through twelfth graders drink, though all states now prohibit drinking before the age of 21. Eight million of them drink at least once a week, and 450,000 drink at least five or more drinks at a sitting.[37]

The age of first alcohol use has steadily drifted downward. The age of first drinking in the 1930s was seventeen for males and nineteen for females; today it is much more common for children of twelve or thirteen to drink. A report issued in 1991 by the U.S. Surgeon General's office indicated that three thousand teens between fifteen and nineteen died annually in alcohol-related automobile accidents.

> Most students buy alcohol with fake IDs or from stores with young clerks. . . . The study found that teens' attitudes about alcohol are influenced by their parents, friends and ads. Two-thirds of those who drink said their parents tolerated drinking. Many students cited ads that make drinking look glamorous and fun. Several specifically noted [that] the ads had sexy people in them.[38]

The Surgeon General of the United States points out that alcohol advertising frequently shows people racing cars or surfing, ignoring the fact that drinking would make these activities perilous. She comments:

> It is no coincidence that sports such as boating, swimming, skiing, surfing, car racing and mountain climbing—which have strong links to alcohol-related injuries—are the very activities glamorized in alcohol beverage ads and promotions. I have asked them to stop using ads that lead our youth to think they can ski, swim, scuba dive or race cars better if they drink.[39]

Timothy Dwyer points out that from locker rooms to grandstands, from the postgame interview to the player-of-the-game award, alcohol and sports are as intertwined as the seams on a baseball. Anheuser-Busch, the largest brewer and advertiser, is a major sponsor for twenty-three of twenty-four domestic major-league baseball games, twenty-five National Basketball Association teams, thirteen of fourteen domestic National Hockey League teams, and other sports—paying hundreds of millions of dollars annually for broadcast ads and stadium billboards. Dwyer writes:

> Partly as a consequence, in most clubhouses, a beer in a ballplayer's hand is accepted as an extension of the uniform. While athletes with drug problems still generate spectacular attention and large headlines, alcohol is by far the drug of choice of men who play ball for a living. . . . One grisly count of how deeply alcohol abuse runs through sports is the expanding list of athletes who have been hurt or killed, or who have killed someone else, as a result of drinking and driving.[40]

Although there is obviously a strong connection between the use of alcohol and leisure as such, there has been relatively little research on the subject. Jussi Simpura, a Finnish social researcher, points out that in studies on the use of time, drinking is seldom mentioned

Entertainment and recreation
at Fun Without Alcohol Fair,
a national program created by
Dr. Connie O'Connor of California State University at Chico,
designed to educate young
people about alcohol and to
show that it is possible to have
fun without drinking. Seen
here: a karate demonstration,
an enactment of medieval
jousting and swordplay, and
a simulated car-crash unit
showing outcomes of a drunk-
driving accident.

even though drinking constitutes a significant part of activities in various contexts in many cultures . . . [particularly] leisure contexts. One reason for this neglect is that studies on the use of time often focus on activities that are commonly regarded as necessary or beneficial. So, for instance, drinking is not mentioned among the dozens of activity categories reported by Szalai in an international study on the use of time.[41]

One early study that did examine the relationship between alcoholism and leisure values and behavior was conducted by H. Douglas Sessoms and Sidney Oakley, who examined a select group of adult male alcoholics at a state rehabilitation center in North Carolina.

> The alcoholics' [time-use] patterns seem to be filled with additional work [including a high rate of moonlighting], spectator activities, and drinking. . . . The sample displayed a minimum of concern in current affairs, the performing arts, social dancing, and civic club activities.[42]

In general, the individuals studied showed little interest in activities that did not lend themselves to drinking, whereas they did participate in activities like bowling or billiards that did. As a rule they tended not to be joiners, but if they did join a club or organization, it was usually one in which alcoholic beverages were readily available before, during, or after the club meeting.

Despite the negative aspects of drinking, alcohol taken in moderation is an accepted form of sociability in many community settings. Indeed, in some residential settings, such as nursing homes, recreation therapists schedule modest cocktail parties or beer sessions, when residents may have a drink or two under controlled circumstances. Research reports in the British medical journal, *The Lancet,* have indicated that two drinks a day reduced the risk of heart attack by more than a quarter, according to a study of forty-four thousand men.

John Crompton, a Texas professor of recreation and park administration, has pointed out that a large majority of public recreation centers in Great Britain are licensed to sell a full range of alcoholic beverages, including beer, wine, and mixed drinks. He argues that the serving of alcohol is an important leisure experience for many participants, and continues:

> It is also the major income-generating service in the facilities. Without it, it is unlikely that operational viability can be achieved. In short, provision of opportunities for clients to have an alcoholic drink is widely accepted to be an integral part of providing recreation in the public sector.[43]

Similarly, a British sociologist writes approvingly of the role of drinking in popular culture and leisure pursuits. In a report published by Salford University, Bacon points out that the British pub is not simply a sales outlet for alcohol:

> rather it is a social and recreational locale which plays a key role in the continued vitality of the nation's popular culture. It is a commercial leisure centre where people go to talk, eat, drink, play darts, organize sporting trips and sometimes welfare activities. . . . [It is also a] flourishing leisure industry [which employs over 250,000 people].[44]

Crompton contends that American leisure facility managers should consider offering alcoholic beverages, to diversify recreation center offerings, to attract the public more effectively, and as a source of needed revenue. Despite this argument, the consensus of American park and recreation managers appears to be that public leisure agencies should not offer liquor to the public in community recreation centers. Some leisure professionals pointed out that, while consumption of alcoholic beverages was often permitted in private parties renting public facilities or in restaurants adjoining public golf courses, it would be contrary to the accepted values of public recreation agencies to sell liquor in community recreation centers.

At the same time, it is clear that other public policies regarding the use of alcohol in the United States are inconsistent and ambiguous. Five states and the District of Columbia, while outlawing the sale of alcohol to minors, do not specifically make its purchase by minors a crime. And in forty-four states, minors are allowed to sell and serve alcoholic beverages without adult supervision.

One of the key problems is that government itself has assumed the role of liquor entrepreneur in eighteen states, through state agencies that distribute and sell alcoholic beverages. The claim that state-run liquor stores help to reduce alcohol abuse and drinking-related auto accidents does not appear to be valid; Pennsylvania, which has a state-controlled system, has a higher rate of alcohol-related fatalities than nineteen states that do not have state liquor monopolies.

At the same time, drinking to excess is more widely condemned today than in the past. Corporate office parties are more likely to get along without alcohol, and there is a greater consciousness of the dangers of liquor in the workplace. The days of the "three-martini lunch" appear to be over. With the exception of a number of abstinent Protestant sects, American society seems to have accepted the view that drinking is acceptable in moderation, but that drinking to excess represents a social danger and must be overcome. As for the speculation that it is possible for carefully conditioned alcoholics to resume occasional social drinking—the findings of a since discredited research study—it is now agreed that "once an alcoholic, always an alcoholic," with total abstinence from liquor the only solution.[45]

Drug Abuse as Play

We turn now to the second major area of substance abuse that represents a morally marginal form of leisure activity—the use of narcotic drugs that initially create a sense of euphoria and escape, but then become powerful controlling agents in the lives of their users. For years, the use of drugs was regarded as a semi-respectable act; many doctors made personal use of heroin or cocaine, and women's patent medicines often contained narcotics.

Particularly during the era of the youth rebellion in the late 1960s and early 1970s, young people dismissed the possible health hazards of narcotics and argued that smoking pot was no worse than their parents' daily quota of cocktails. Realistically, the sensations gained from drug use provided—at least at the outset—pleasure that was more satisfying than other leisure activities could offer. One leading researcher commented:

> The simple fact is, marijuana is fun to smoke. . . . In my own study of marijuana users,
> pleasure emerged as the dominant motive for continued use. Almost 70 percent said

that sex was more enjoyable high. Almost 90 percent said that the simple act of eating became more fun. . . . Marijuana has become, and will continue to be, increasingly a *recreational* drug, and for larger and larger numbers of young (and not so young) people. This will not disappear, and it will not abate; drug "education" campaigns are doomed to failure. . . . Outlawing fun has always been a tough job.[46]

TO THE POINT

Despite such views and the widely expressed conviction that recreational drugs did little harm to their users, through the 1980s a series of studies documented their negative effects. In 1987, a study financed by the National Institute of Drug Abuse found that about 18.2 million Americans used marijuana regularly. In a report presented to the American Psychological Association, the researchers found that heavy users of marijuana had suffered decreases in concentration and short-term memory and had gravitated to less mentally demanding jobs.[47] In a 1988 study published by a UCLA psychologist, it was reported that heavy drug use as a teenager severely disrupted a person's emotional and social growth during the transition to adulthood, although occasional drug use of hashish and marijuana did not appear to have significant effects.[48] The unpredictable effects of drugs like cocaine, heroin, LSD, and other synthetic substances clearly involved major health risks, as evidenced by the deaths of numerous popular music stars over the past two decades and of athletes like Leonard Bias, an All-American basketball player who died of an overdose of cocaine on the brink of a lucrative professional career.

In 1988, a report by the U.S. Justice Department indicated that almost 60 percent of the juveniles incarcerated in long-term facilities had used drugs regularly. Nearly half were under the influence of drugs or alcohol when they committed the crime for which they were imprisoned.[49] In 1989, a study of 254 hard-core juvenile crack cocaine users in Florida's Dade County found that they had committed over 220,000 crimes a year, counting offenses such as robbery, assault, and shoplifting, in addition to drug possession itself.[50]

Until the post–World War II era, drug abuse tended to be thought of as a relatively minor social problem. In the 1970s, in addition to the great numbers of affluent white college and high school youth who began to experiment with drugs, it became apparent that millions of middle-class Americans were using narcotics in one form or another, including employees in large corporations, successful professionals, and members of highly respected families. Indeed, a 1986 study directed by the Harvard University School of Public Health revealed that a high proportion of doctors and medical students had used illegal drugs.

More than half the physicians and three-quarters of the medical students who participated in a Harvard University survey said they had used drugs at least once for self-treatment, to get high, or to help them stay awake. Nearly 40 percent of doctors under age 40 reported in the survey that they had used marijuana or cocaine to get high with friends, and a quarter of doctors of all ages said they had recently treated themselves with mind-affecting drugs.[51]

In the same year, it was reported that Americans consumed 60 percent of the world's production of illegal drugs. An estimated twenty million persons were regular users of marijuana, four to eight million more were cocaine abusers, and five hundred thousand were heroin addicts. Despite constant media images of black youths being arrested for drug-related crimes, some studies showed that white students were more likely to use drugs and alcohol than their African-American peers. Based on research conducted by federal agencies, Health and Human Services Secretary Louis Sullivan reported:

> white male high school seniors were almost twice as likely to use cocaine as were blacks (12 percent vs. 6.1 percent according to data from the government's National High School Senior Surveys from 1985 to 1989). Forty percent of white male seniors had used marijuana, compared with 30 percent of black male seniors. . . . The studies also found that 88 percent of white male students said they had consumed alcohol in the last year, compared with 73 percent of black males.[52]

Other studies questioned these findings and reported higher use of drugs and alcohol by black students on all grade levels.[53] Without question, drugs represent a severe problem in depressed minority neighborhoods in cities where African-American and Hispanic youth have a high rate of unemployment and harshly limited prospects for the future. The invasion of crack cocaine, beginning in the late 1980s, meant that whole areas of urban ghettoes and barrios were captured by drug dealers and gangs that terrorized law-abiding families. For many minority-group youth, a job in the underground drug economy, a businesslike, well-organized, and competitive operation, is a respected means of survival. A black minister, Cecil Williams, says that many teenagers are drawn to work in the cocaine trade simply because they want jobs. The drug business is seen as a "safety net," a place where it is always possible to make a few dollars.

> "Money and drugs are the obvious immediate rewards," Williams adds. "But there is another strong motivating force, and that is the desire to show family and friends that they can succeed at something . . . and they see no chance to find a well-paying job with career possibilities."[54]

By the end of the Reagan administration, there were confident assertions by federal officials that progress was being made in curbing drug use, and that the rate of drug use by the young had declined. However, it was apparent that despite the billions of dollars being spent each year, with over a million arrests annually, the "war on drugs" had barely dented addiction or violent crimes linked to narcotics.[55] In 1991, the National Household Survey on Drug Abuse reported that there *was* a decline in drug use among those who held jobs, were better educated, or lived in the suburbs. However, the overall drop was minor and prevention efforts had not reached hard-core addicts. And, in May 1992, the latest government figures showed a startling increase in the number of people admitted to emergency rooms for serious drug-use episodes during the past year.[56] In April 1993, a federally funded University of Michigan survey found that there was a significant increase in the use of marijuana, cocaine, LSD, and other illicit substances among eighth graders, most of whom are thirteen or fourteen years old.[57]

Efforts to Control Drug Use

Given the critical nature of this problem, what efforts are being made to solve it? The major emphasis in government-funded programs is on interdiction, with approximately 70 percent of federal dollars being spent on efforts to prevent drug trafficking, to intercept shipments, and to punish offenders. With tougher enforcement laws, since 1980 the average sentence length for federal drug offenses has climbed 20 percent to about 5.5 years, and prisons and local jails are overcrowded with offenders. It is obvious that a major aspect of the drug problem involves the African-American and Hispanic poor in American cities. However, authorities warn that the widespread myth of drugs as primarily a ghetto problem is misleading. It enables one to ascribe all the profound social problems of the inner city to drugs—blaming racial minorities for their involvement, while ignoring the deeper problems of unemployment and lack of education. Moreover, it permits middle-class white Americans to avoid responsibility for the widespread use of drugs among their own families and friends.

▐▶ TO THE POINT

> Government figures demonstrate that nearly three-quarters of inmates serving time in local jails on drug charges in 1992 were black or Hispanic—up from 54 percent in 1983. Yet roughly nine million white Americans regularly use illegal drugs, while the estimated number of regular black and Hispanic drug users is just one-third of that, about 3.1 million. Although the argument may be made that minority group members tend to be dealers and thus subject to arrest more often, two-thirds of the arrests are for possession—not sales—according to the Federal Bureau of Investigation. Beyond this, non-whites are disproportionately targeted for being stopped and frisked; black and Hispanic offenders tend to be sent to detention centers, while whites are more frequently given community-service alternatives or placed in treatment programs.

Summing up, nonprofit organizations like the Drug Policy Foundation and the National Center on Institutions and Alternatives conclude that the drug war is racially biased on all fronts.[58] A number of government officials and authorities on drug abuse have argued that the only way to attack the problem is to legalize narcotics as a number of other nations have done—thus removing the powerful profit motive that has made it a major industry in America. However, there has been little support for this position, and it seems unlikely that Congress or the American people would approve it.[59]

Linkage of Drug Abuse with Leisure

Relatively few research studies have explored the relationship of leisure and recreation with drug abuse. Seppo Iso-Ahola and Edward Crowley conducted one study that examined the role of leisure in the lives of adolescent substance abusers. Surprisingly (since one might assume that drug abusers would have fewer recreational interests), they found that

> substance abusers had a tendency to participate more frequently in leisure in general and physical recreation activities in particular. . . . Because of their personality predisposition toward sensation-seeking and low tolerance toward [repetitious] experiences, substance abusers presumably prefer active leisure lifestyles. But if leisure activities fail to satisfy their need for optimal arousal, leisure boredom results and drug use may be the only alternative.[60]

A second study, by Ann Rancourt, explored the relationships among recreation, leisure, and substance abuse in a treatment program for women. It focused on two issues: the past attitudes and behaviors of the subjects with respect to leisure and the potential role of recreation in residential treatment programs. The subjects revealed that, while their use of drugs was recreational in that they thought of it as "partying," it was rarely enjoyable. Instead, some said: ". . . it was like a job; I had to get high . . . to feel normal." . . . abuse ultimately became "like medication, not like recreation."[61]

Rancourt found that many women felt that they had missed out on their childhoods and that taking part now in such experiences as roller or ice skating, visiting parks or beaches, bowling or picnics, gave them the intense feeling of being young again. While "normal" kinds of play had meant little to them while abusing drugs, now they began to realize that it could make a positive contribution to their lives:

> they related that they could enjoy being "high" without using drugs; could do things they had never done before or thought they could do; felt accepted among peers; could have or experience fun while sober; were willing to try more things [and] when asked how important the recreation and leisure component was in their treatment indicated it was extremely important . . . "it's really exciting doing it sober/straight. . . ."[62]

The findings of these two studies suggest that the fuller use of positive and challenging recreation in school and community programs serving at-risk youth might provide a helpful weapon in the early prevention of substance abuse.

■ COMMERCIALIZED SEX

We turn now to a third major category of morally marginal play, involvement in commercialized sexual activity. Edwin Schur points out that over the past several decades many Americans developed a *Playboy*-influenced mentality, in which sex came to represent a symbol of competitive striving and acquisition and an omnipresent element in the mass media, advertising, and varied forms of entertainment. He writes that the hallmark of the *Playboy*-influenced life-style is consumption.

Women, much like the other fun-offering products, are to be consumed. The female is depicted as a concertedly sought and ultimately purchasable acquisition. [In *Playboy*] the issue was money. Men made it; women wanted it. . . . The message was simple: You can buy sex on a fee-for-service basis, so don't get caught up in a long-term contract.[63]

Playboy and other magazines like it encouraged men's tendency to view women primarily in sexual terms and to be preoccupied with detailed and heavily eroticized female body parts. Through their pictures, stories, and articles, these publications promoted a general life-style in which men "could have it all":

> . . . as part of "having it all" . . . men are being encouraged to engage in what might be called comparison shopping. These magazines seem to imply, as a basic operating principle for males: the more sex, and the more sexual partners, the better. Their highly depersonalized, almost combat-like, depiction of sexual relations, fuels the male's conquest mentality. . . . [64]

In America, Schur writes, entrepreneurs are constantly on the lookout for new business opportunities. The American obsession with sex presented many such opportunities. That sex—formerly viewed as an intimate and even sacrosanct activity—now can be seen as just another business field illustrates the degree to which all forms of leisure have been commodified in contemporary American life. Schur concludes:

> even without adding the enormous exploitation of sex by advertising and the beauty business . . . the sex industry is a "significant part" of the nation's economy. . . . [It] provides the basis for a major segment of the American labor market. For many people, sex is the substance of their daily work. And millions of Americans are customers of this industry.[65]

Sex for Sale

Probably the leading example of sex being used as a commodity for commercial gain is prostitution. In America's early history, prostitution flourished in frontier areas where there were many men and few women, but also in cities and towns where established "madams" and houses of prostitution were tolerated as necessary evils. In the 1820s, urban reformers in the United States declared prostitution a threat to municipal virtue and social order and conducted campaigns against brothels.

For a time, prostitutes were viewed primarily as victims of male predators. However, during World War I, with growing concern about venereal disease, the image of the prostitute was transformed from sex-victim to sex-villain. New laws against prostitution penalized women exclusively and frequently violated their civil rights. In describing this period, historian Barbara Hobson points out that men held all the power but took none of the responsibility for illicit sexuality or for the larger socioeconomic pressures that drove women into prostitution.[66]

During the post–World War I period, women charged with "crimes against chastity" were remanded to special penal institutions; inmates of such settings included not only alleged prostitutes but also "stubborn" or "wayward" girls. In the modern era, prostitution is often permitted tacitly to exist in the form of call-girl rings or escort services, along with massage parlors that advertise openly in many cities and are often a front for prostitution. Nevada is the only state that permits legal houses of prostitution in a number of its counties. The feminist movement is divided regarding this social problem. For many feminists, it represents sexual slavery and a vivid representation of women's economic and social subservence. But for others, the growing ethic of sexual independence for women, plus the fact that some women who engage in prostitution have vigorously defended their right to choose their occupation, challenges the underlying assumption of female sexual passivity that underlies much condemnation of prostitution.

In many cities today, prostitution is tolerated, provided that it is limited to certain streets or downtown neighborhoods or to avenues leading to the city's outskirts. When the problem becomes too blatant, police may crack down by harassing prostitutes. In some cases, as in Portland, Oregon, police seize and impound the cars of men caught patronizing street prostitutes. During the mid-1980s, organized-crime groups with Far East ties began to import thousands of women from South Korea and Taiwan, moving them through a network of American brothels, according to federal and state law enforcement officials.[67]

Pornography

A second leading example of commercialized sex in the United States today is pornography—the manufacture and sale of books, magazines, and videotapes depicting sexual activity in all its varieties. In the past, fascination with this kind of material was regarded as a sick and shameful kind of obsession. Today, interest in sexual materials is so widespread that it is no longer regarded by most individuals as evidence of sinfulness or mental disturbance.

Writing in *The Christian Century,* Mary Ellen Ross points out that pornography is readily available to all, including children, and in the privacy of our own homes. She writes:

> Pornographic images have been proliferating at a remarkable rate. What was a $5-million-a-year enterprise merely 25 years ago has boomed to a $7-billion to $10-billion-a-year industry today. . . . This surge is due in part to the discovery of new markets. While adult bookstores, peepshows and movie theaters still thrive, the fastest growing sectors of the industry are pornographic videocassettes, cable television, and phone sex.[68]

Exactly what *is* pornography? Joseph Slade points out that the word itself derives from the Greek word *pornographos,* meaning "writing about prostitutes," or a "tale told by prostitutes," and has been used more or less consistently to designate material specifically intended to arouse a person sexually. It has often been difficult to draw a line between books or pictures that have a legitimate artistic purpose in dealing with erotic themes and those that are intended simply to present sexual images to capitalize on prurient interests. Slade concludes:

> Only one thing seems clear: culture changes over time, and so do standards of sexuality. What appeared outrageous to earlier generations strikes modern audiences as quaint. Taboos erode, to be replaced by others: that is the dynamic of pornography, which continuously assaults limits, and that function is precisely its value to a culture in transition. At a minimum, pornography historically redefines taste.[69]

In recent years, radical feminists have tried to define pornography in law as an exclusively male phenomenon, in which women were invariably the victim of exploitation and brutality. However, this is clearly not the case, and there is evidence that a considerable number of women today enjoy pornography; 30 percent of those renting X-rated videos in a 1986 survey of retailers of "adult" films, for example, were women.

⫸ TO THE POINT

In 1986, Attorney General Edwin Meese's Commission on Pornography issued a report that concluded that there was a causal link between pornography and aggressive or violent behavior toward women—contradicting the findings of an earlier commission that it was *not* a cause of sexual crime. In the late 1980s, a growth in moral militancy in American society was evidenced in a series of restrictive Supreme Court decisions that enabled officials in a number of cities to close adult bookstores because of solicitation for prostitution or other offenses. Some cities enacted stricter ordinances controlling the display and sale of pornographic materials, or established "anti-porn" squads, putting pressure on real estate owners to shift their "sex-oriented" buildings to less offensive businesses. Citizen groups and religious coalitions joined the battle, as denominations like the Catholic Church, the Episcopal Church, the Evangelical Lutheran Church, and the Southern Baptist Convention all condemned pornography as undermining human dignity and subverting the common social good. However, writes Ross:

> the mainline Protestant churches have shied away from efforts to restrict expression, tending to recommend that church members register their objections with distributors of pornographic material (boycotting them, if necessary) and stressing the importance of education . . . and consciousness-raising.[70]

As a continuation of this effort, a bill was introduced in Congress in the spring of 1992. Known as the Pornography Victims' Compensation Act or, less formally, the Bundy bill (after serial killer Ted Bundy, who claimed that pornography had fueled his violent fantasies and rape/murders), it was designed to allow victims of sex crimes the right to sue producers and distributors of works judged to have been a "substantial cause" of their injury. Opponents of this measure argued that the bill was a dangerous incursion on First Amendment rights, shifted blame from the actual perpetrators of sexual violence, and did little to address the real causes of such crimes.[71]

In general, the X-rated industry has been in a slump since the late 1980s, with at least half of the nation's adult movie theaters closing down and the sales of magazines like *Playboy* declining sharply. Many forms of sex-oriented play, as described in Chapter 6, had been affected by growing fears of sexually transmitted disease, particularly the AIDS epidemic. Patronage of legal, health-inspected Nevada brothels was off by as much as 40 percent.

At the same time, other forms of exploiting sexual interest have continued to evolve. For example, in motion pictures there has been a distinct trend toward increasing nudity and the more open depiction or simulation of the sex act. Advertising is increasingly using scenes in which the human body is almost totally exposed. Stuart Elliott writes:

> Sex has long been at the heart of marketing. Pretty women decorated Coca-Cola calendars back in the 1890's. But sexual themes—particularly involving the undraped body— are being used by Madison Avenue as never before to cut through commercial clutter and grab the consumer's attention.[72]

While nudity was always available in furtive shows in country fairs, amusement parks, and burlesque shows, during the 1960s and 1970s such successful shows as *Hair* and *Oh! Calcutta* for the first time presented full frontal nudity on stage, without immediate police reprisal. Since then, nudity has been more or less taken for granted as entertainment in motion pictures, stage shows, and late-night television, and is part of the appeal of topless bars and nightclubs. In 1991, the Supreme Court ruled that the First Amendment protection of free expression is compatible with Indiana's law prohibiting total nudity in public places. This decision freed state legislatures and municipalities to enact and enforce rules against total nudity. However, patterns of enforcement vary greatly around the country, as do forms of sexually oriented entertainment.

Some forms of erotic play are less direct, relying on electronic means of communication. The use of 1-900 telephone lines for caller-paid conversations increased dramatically in the late 1980s, with revenues reaching several hundred million dollars each year. Barbara Rudolph writes:

> So far, sex has been the best seller, generating more than a third of the industry's revenues. The dial-a-porn lines offer everything from recorded fantasies to lusty personal ads. Bawdy party lines have also proliferated, though their popularity is fading. Many of the numbers are far from erotic, providing legitimate dating services or outlets for gentle conversation.[73]

Another development of the early 1990s was the introduction of erotic computer games that involve sexual themes. Such software is usually not handled by respectable retailers but is sold by mail order. Another trend of this period was the appearance of "do-it-yourself" porno movies, in which growing numbers of adult couples, following the example of successful television shows like "America's Funniest Home Videos," have used videocameras to record their own sexual activities. Anastasia Toufexis points out that technological advances have promoted this trend:

> Polaroids, for example, enable people to take seductive snapshots of their partners and themselves without having the pictures developed by strangers. . . . And when affordable, lightweight camcorders became commonplace during the past few years, X-rated home movies were the inevitable next step. No one keeps statistics on the trend, but psychologists say an increasing number of couples are making the tapes.[74]

◼ VIOLENCE, CRUELTY, AND CRIMINALITY AS ASPECTS OF LEISURE

A final form of leisure activity that must be regarded as morally marginal consists of those forms of play that center around violence and cruelty, or that actually are criminal pursuits.

While some might argue that it is impossible to regard any activity based on human or animal suffering as leisure or play, the reality is that throughout history, human beings have been fascinated by the suffering of others. They formed huge audiences to watch gladiators fighting each other or battling fierce animals in Roman arenas, and they attended with enthusiasm hangings, burnings at the stake, mass executions of pirates, and the flogging of criminals. Blood sports like bullfighting and cockfighting have been popular and continue today—legally in some countries, illegally in others. Fighting among youth gangs, beating or even wantonly killing drunken hobos, and rioting at times of sports-victory celebrations, all demonstrate the appeal of violence and cruelty as themes of play.

What accounts for the popularity of such pursuits? Ethologists and anthropologists have suggested an inherited ingredient in human nature, stemming from the time when it was necessary to defend one's tribe against savage animals or the incursion of human enemies. Even today, in preliterate cultures like the Yanomano Indians in Brazil or Highland tribes in Papua, New Guinea, violence is an everyday pursuit and aggressive and warlike men are highly honored by others. Fighting with serious weaponry is regarded almost as a scheduled form of sport in New Guinea, a land of fierce "mud men," sorcerers, and evil spirits. One Westerner comments: ". . . it is not at all unusual for men to call in sick when duty calls—'Can't make it to work today,' they would say, 'I've got a tribal war.'"[75]

American popular culture may include events centered around the idea of destruction—as in so-called demolition derbies, where cars and drivers collide with each other in successive heats to determine the winner, the last car running. Violence and physical confrontation can also be part of everyday life, as in the case of combat among motorists in the heavy traffic on California's freeways. Characterizing it as "war," psychiatrist Ange Lobue describes the machismo among motorists who tailgate each other, cut each other off, and demonstrate territoriality by passive-aggressive slowing, abrupt braking, or sudden lane changes. Lobue continues: "This is followed by an exchange of insults and an aggressive passing display. Insults escalate and lead to more dangerous maneuvers: speeding, weaving, attempts to pass and then bumping, throwing objects at each other and, if guns are on board, the alarming shoot-out."[76]

Sometimes the search for "kicks" through violence and illegal activity takes the form of arson. During the 1980s, there were numerous accounts of fires set in rural regions by members of volunteer fire companies. In a single year, for example, investigators reported that in western Virginia, over four hundred fires were deliberately set by volunteer fire fighters. In northern Pennsylvania, the state police fire marshal commented that hundreds of fires set by junior volunteer fire fighters were classified as "thrill-and-excitement," and "set for the fun of it." He continued: "You get an individual who joins a fire department to fight fires and isn't content unless he does. They'd get to drinking and decide they haven't had a fire for a while, so they'd set one. Then they'd go to fight it."[77]

While economic motives underlie such crimes as robberies, break-ins, and muggings, sociologist Jack Katz points out that crime also has a sensual, creative, almost magical appeal that is not found in most conventional, law-abiding acts. He describes crime as a "ludic" (gamelike) enterprise, with clear-cut winners and losers, accessible only to members of a daring elite. As an example, he suggests robbery—a crime that involves confrontation of a victim and the use or threat of force. Its appeal, Katz argues, lies not only in the money gained, but also in the thrill and danger of the episode and the ceremony of dominating and humiliating the victim.[78]

Other crimes involving personal assaults and sexual attacks seem to have similar motivations. Toufexis describes a wave of highly publicized crimes by groups of teenagers across the United States involving random attacks on others, arson sprees, and sexual assaults. She writes:

> More and more teenagers, acting individually or in gangs, are running amuck. In the Central Park incident [involving the rape and beating almost to death of a jogging female stockbroker] young toughs said they were "wilding," which apparently means marauding with no purpose in mind but to create havoc and hurt people. In Philadelphia packs of youths chant "Beat, beat, beat" as they roam the streets looking for victims.[79]

Columnist George Will described the attack on the Central Park jogger in detail. She was beaten and hacked with a pipe, a knife, and a brick, raped by seven or more boys, and lay undiscovered for nearly four hours, losing three-quarters of her blood before being found. Various experts offered opinions as to why this attack occurred—alienation, anomie, boredom, rage, peer pressure, inequality, status anxieties, television, advertising. Ignoring this psychobabble, Will points out that one of the boys finally revealed the reason for the attack. It was not rage; there was no sign of rage. Instead, he said: "It was something to do. It was fun." Will comments:

> Newspaper reports have repeatedly referred to the "wilding" attacks as "motiveless." But fun is a motive. Police officers, with their knack of the language of unvarnished fact, refer to "wildings"—packs of boys looting stores and inflicting random beatings— as a "pastime." Pastimes are adopted for fun.[80]

Unpleasant as the thought may be, crimes *are* often fun. The assaults against homosexuals that have been increasing throughout the United States in recent years by neo-Nazi skinheads are often carried out in a spirit of hate encouraged by societal indifference. The director of the antiviolence project of the National Gay and Lesbian Task Force in Washington comments: "These attacks are trivialized. They're viewed as sport, a form of entertainment—it's just boys being boys. For police, it's just not a priority."[81]

Numerous recreational pursuits illustrate the popular fascination with violence. College students play games such as Assassin, cloak-and-dagger pursuits in which each player is assigned a victim and at the same time is marked as a target. Murder

Mystery weekends are popular fare at many resorts and on ocean cruises, with players taking part in make-believe crimes. A game called Survival is popular among Hollywood motion picture directors and producers, who travel to the desert, wear camouflage makeup, and "eliminate" each other with paint-shooting guns.

In another example of violence and cruelty as themes of play, there has been a long history of indifference to animal suffering in the Western world, as illustrated in various forms of blood sports, like bullfighting and cockfighting. J. C. Furnas cites examples of fiestas in Spanish settlements in the early Southwest where caballeros and their demure sisters or sweethearts might join Indian serfs in "enjoying fights to the death between a bull and a grizzly bear; the bull's foreleg was chained to the bear's hind leg to make it an even, hence horribly prolonged match."[82]

More recently, there have been protests against mass shoots, such as an annual World Championship Prairie Dog Shoot in Nucla, Colorado, where thousands of the little rodents are killed by high-powered rifles in an event dreamed up to bolster the town's economy. Perhaps most repulsive of all are "canned hunts," the point-blank slaughter of captured animals like spotted or black leopards, Bengal tigers, mountain lions, or grizzly bears by would-be "big-game" hunters who pay thousands of dollars to shoot frightened creatures who are prodded out of cages into their gunsights. Kathy Schocket writes:

> In Texas . . . canned hunts are quick and dirty, most of them the work of "fly-by-night" promoters who find a cat at an exotic-animal auction and then put a deal together. . . . Increasingly, breeders are raising exotic animals specifically for hunting. Investigations of canned hunts and wildlife trafficking operations are under way . . . but weak and conflicting laws make officials' jobs harder.[83]

Such perversions of sport give final evidence to the point that while leisure may encourage the most positive and enriching kinds of human behavior and creative involvement, it may also be used for destructive and demeaning purposes. Here then we come to the question of the philosophy and goals underlying the provision of organized leisure-service programs. Of the eight major types of recreation sponsors in the United States today, public and nonprofit organizations tend to be the ones with the clearest and most positive statements of social purpose. Their goals and functions and the growth of the overall recreation and leisure-service field in the United States are described in detail in Chapter 13.

■ SUMMARY

While we usually think of leisure in positive terms, it may also provide the opportunity for harmful forms of play. Particularly when activities such as gambling or substance abuse are being carried to the point of addiction, they are literally life-threatening and are carried on at tremendous cost to the individual and society. The popularity of these and other morally questionable forms of leisure activity underlines the need for education to deal constructively with the issue of values, goals, and outcomes of leisure experience. The great number of children and youth who experiment with and ultimately become hooked on drugs, alcohol, and gambling or who experience shattering outcomes from careless or promiscuous sexual activity should make more purposeful and effective programs of leisure education a national necessity. Beyond this, they make it all the more essential that the organized leisure-service system of the nation accept as a commitment the task of providing positive and attractive alternatives to self-destructive play, particularly for youth and for the disadvantaged in society.

■ QUESTIONS FOR DISCUSSION

1. Based on the definition of leisure presented in this book, should casual and intermittent use of alcohol and drugs be regarded as forms of leisure? At what point, if any, do they cease being leisure?

2. In recent years, there has been a dramatic trend toward various forms of legalized gambling to provide income for social purposes and to promote tourism. Some argue that it is a tax on the poor, and that legalized gambling results in increased crime and greater numbers of gambling addicts. From a moral point of view, how do you view this issue? From a purely pragmatic view? What does the evidence say?

3. There has been an ongoing dialogue about legalizing narcotics. The argument is that varied forms of prevention and education do not work, and that only by removing the money-making incentive can crime and the wholesale distribution of drugs by criminal groups be reduced. How do you feel about this?

4. In many ways, society stimulates interest in sex and promotes it as a commodity—through advertising, entertainment, and other leisure-oriented settings. Is this healthy? Should controls on varied forms of commercial sex be further reduced? Should people be completely free to engage in any form of commercialized sex they choose—or should there be certain legal limits? Should this be a matter for local control only, or should there be national or state standards and legal principles involved?

5. This chapter cites a number of leisure pursuits that appeal to the cruel, sadistic, or sensation-seeking aspects of human personality, including a number of quasi-legal or actually illegal activities. What are some examples of such forms of cruel or destructive play? Would it be possible to divert such drives and channel them into other, comparable but less destructive kinds of leisure activity?

■ NOTES

1. PEIRCE, N. 1991. Bringing gambling to the river cities. *Philadelphia Inquirer* (Sept. 16): 11–A.

2. ROMANO, C. 1992. Getting together, dubbing it a club. *Philadelphia Inquirer* (Aug.3): E–1.

3. Oddball olympics. *Time* (May 13, 1974): 72.

4. GRAY, D., and H. IBRAHIM. 1985. The recreation experience: A source of self-discovery. *Journal of Physical Education, Recreation and Dance* (Oct.): 20.

5. LEO, J. 1989. One laugh = 3 tbsp. oat bran. *U.S. News and World Report* (Jan. 23): 55.

6. ANGIER, N. 1992. The anatomy of joy. *New York Times Good Health Magazine* (Apr. 26): 50.

7. PODILCHAK, W. 1991. Establishing the fun in leisure. *Leisure Sciences* 13: 123–124.

8. CRANDALL, R. 1980. Motivations for leisure. *Journal of Leisure Research* 12, 1: 45–54.

9. GUMP, P. V., and W. V. FRIESON. 1962. Satisfactions derived by juniors from non-class settings of large and small high schools. In Barker, R. G. *Big School-Small School*. Midwest Psychological Field Station. Lawrence, KA: University of Kansas.

10. KELLY, J. R. 1978. Leisure styles and choices in three environments. *Pacific Sociological Review* 21: 178–208.

11. CLOUGH, P., J. SHEPHERD, and R. MAUGHAN. 1989. Motives for participation in recreational running. *Journal of Leisure Research* 21, 4: 292–309.

12. HAGGARD, L. H., and D. W. WILLIAMS. 1992. Identity affirmation through leisure activities: Leisure symbols of the self. *Journal of Leisure Research* 24, 1: 1–8.

13. ROGGENBUCK, J. W., R. J. LOOMIS, and J. DAGOSTINO. 1990. The learning benefits of leisure. *Journal of Leisure Research* 22, 2: 112–124.

14. Link found between high school activities and good grades. *Associated Press* (Dec. 20, 1986).

15. BRAND, D. 1988. A nation of healthy worry-warts. *Time* (July 25): 66.

16. FITZGERALD, S. 1992. Physical inactivity now listed as a major heart disease risk. *Philadelphia Inquirer* (July 2): 1–A.

17. WANKEL, L. 1985. Personal and situational factors affecting exercise involvement: The importance of enjoyment. *Research Quarterly for Exercise and Sport* 56, 3: 281.

18. Dirty money in the spotlight. *Time* (Nov. 12, 1984): 85.

19. TIGER, L. 1992. The origins of pleasure. Conversation with Alvin Sanoff. *Time* (Feb. 13): 85.

20. HOCHMAN, G. 1988. The dangers of desire. *Philadelphia Inquirer Magazine* (Feb.21): 22.

21. GOODWIN, F. 1990. In Levine, A. America's addiction to addictions. *U.S. News and World Report* (Feb. 5): 62.

22. BENNETT, W. 1988. Patterns of addiction. *New York Times Magazine* (Apr. 10): 60.

23. ABT, V. 1986. Review of Findlay, J. 1986. *People of chance: Gambling in American society from Jamestown to Las Vegas*. New York: Oxford University Press. In *Philadelphia Inquirer* (May 18): P–8.

24. Gambling spree across the nation. *U.S. News and World Report* (May 29, 1978): 35.

25. ANASTASIA, G. 1987. Weighing the wages of gambling. *Philadelphia Inquirer* (Oct. 17): B–1.

26. STUBBLES, R. 1992. A question of gambling. *Parks and Recreation* (April): 64.

27. BLAIR, G. 1988. Betting against the odds. *New York Times Magazine* (Sept. 25): 57.

28. *Ibid.*, p. 76.

29. Playing the adolescent odds. *U.S. News and World Report* (June 18, 1990): 51. See also Belluck, P. 1992. Starting too young, getting in too deep. *Philadelphia Inquirer* (Aug. 16): A–1.

30. KLEINFIELD, N. R. 1990. The tables have turned on gambling. *New York Times* (Dec. 9): 3–1.

31. JOHNSTON, D. 1992. Big cities cast their lot with gambling. *Philadelphia Inquirer* (Mar. 29): D–1.

32. See *U.S. News and World Report* (November 30, 1987): 59.

33. FRANKS, L. 1985. A new attack on alcoholism. *New York Times Magazine* (Oct. 30): 47.

34. Court facing debate on alcoholism. *New York Times* (Oct. 25, 1987): 14.

35. Genes with a don't-drink label. *U.S. News and World Report* (Apr. 30, 1990): 15.

36. HARRIS, L. 1987. *Inside America*. New York: Vintage Books, pp. 60–62.

37. BANDY, L. 1991. 'Alarming trend' in U.S. teens. *Philadelphia Inquirer* (June 7): 18–A.

38. *Ibid.*

39. Surgeon General says ads for alcohol ignore danger. *Associated Press* (Mar. 24, 1992).

40. DWYER, T. 1991. Beer hall, the message from sports: Alcohol is drug of choice. *Philadelphia Inquirer* (May 9): 1–A.

41. SIMPURA, J. 1985. Drinking: An ignored leisure activity. *Journal of Leisure Research* 17, 3: 200.

42. SESSOMS, H. D., and S. OAKLEY. 1969. Recreation, leisure and the alcoholic.

Therapeutic Recreation Journal (Winter): 21–31.

43. CROMPTON, J. 1982. Why can't I get a beer when I go to the recreation center? *Parks and Recreation* (Aug.): 26.

44. BACON, A. W. 1980. *Leisure in the '80s.* Report of Centre for Leisure Studies, Salford University (England), p. 54.

45. TIMNICK, L. 1982. A sober finding: No social drinks for the alcoholic. *Los Angeles Times Service* (July 10).

46. GOODE, E. 1971. Turning on for fun. *New York Times* (Jan. 9): 27.

47. Study: Heavy users of marijuana dulled. *Associated Press* (Aug. 29, 1987).

48. Study: Heavy drug use hurts young. *Los Angeles Times Service* (July 21, 1988).

49. Study at youth correctional center spotlights home life and drug use. *Associated Press* (Sept. 19, 1988).

50. COLE, R. 1989. Study links young crack users, crimes. *Associated Press* (Aug. 4).

51. Poll measures use of drugs among doctors. *Philadelphia Inquirer* (Sept. 25, 1986): C–1.

52. MOORE, A. 1992. Sullivan: Drug use less for black teens. *Philadelphia Inquirer* (May 14): A–2.

53. Survey: Drug use is up among young. *Philadelphia Inquirer* (Oct. 19, 1992): A–2.

54. KLEINE, T. 1991. A portrait of the drug dealer as a young man. *Utne Reader* (May–June): 63.

55. SHANNON, E. 1990. Losing battle. *Time* (Dec. 3): 47.

56. ZUCCHINO, D. 1992. Sobering statistics in drug battle. *Philadelphia Inquirer* (May 17): C–1.

57. ISIKOFF, M. 1993. Study finds 8th grade drug use is up. *Philadelphia Inquirer* (April 14): A–2.

58. ZUCCHINO, D. 1992. Racial imbalance seen in war on drugs. *Philadelphia Inquirer* (Nov. 1): A–1.

59. WINK, W. 1990. Biting the bullet: The case for legalizing drugs. *The Christian Century* (Aug. 8–15): 736–737. See also Wilson, J. 1990. Against the legalization of drugs. *Commentary* (Feb.): 21–24.

60. ISO-AHOLA, S., and E. CROWLEY. 1991. Adolescent substance abuse and leisure boredom. *Journal of Leisure Research* 23, 3: 260.

61. RANCOURT, A. 1991. An exploration of the relationships among substance abuse, recreation, and leisure for women who abuse substances. *Therapeutic Recreation Journal* (Third Quarter): 15.

62. *Ibid.,* p. 17.

63. SCHUR, E. 1989. *The Americanization of sex.* Philadelphia: Temple University Press, pp. 86–87.

64. *Ibid.,* p. 87.

65. *Ibid.,* p. 94.

66. HOBSON, B. 1988. *The politics of prostitution and the American reform tradition.* New York: Basic Books.

67. CORWIN, M. 1986. Asian gangs tied to prostitution. *Los Angeles Times Service* (Sept. 16).

68. ROSS, M. E. 1990. Censorship or education? Feminist views of pornography. *The Christian Century* (Mar. 7): 244.

69. SLADE, J. 1989. Pornography. In Inge, M. T. *Handbook of American popular culture* (Vol. 2). Westport, CN: Greenwood Press, p. 958.

70. ROSS, *op. cit.*

71. BEALE, L. 1992. Porn bill in Senate fueling debate. *Philadelphia Inquirer* (Apr. 12): N–15.

72. ELLIOTT, S. 1991. Has Madison Ave. gone too far? *New York Times* (Dec. 15): 3–1.

73. RUDOLPH, B. 1988. Business: Who ever said talk was cheap? *Time* (Sept. 19): 44.

74. TOUFEXIS, A. 1990. Sex lives and videotape. *Time* (Oct. 29): 104–105.

75. LOEB, V. 1992. A violent prelude to tribal haggling. *Philadelphia Inquirer* (Aug. 2): A–2.

76. LOBUE, A. 1987. Mayhem on the highways. *U.S. News and World Report* (Sept. 28): 9.

77. DVORCHAK, B. 1983. Charges of firefighters as arsonists. *Philadelphia Inquirer* (Mar. 10): 8–B.

78. KATZ, J. 1988. *Seductions of crime: Moral and sensual attractions of doing evil.* New York: Basic Books.

79. TOUFEXIS, A. 1989. Our violent kids: A rise in brutal crimes by the young shakes the soul of society. *Time* (June 12): 52.

80. WILL, G. 1989. No psycho-socio babble lessens the fact that evil was the crux of Central Park rape. *Philadelphia Inquirer* (May 1): 10–A.

81. MAYKUTH, A. 1991. Rising tide of anti-gay violence. *Philadelphia Inquirer* (Nov. 10): 1–A.

82. FURNAS, J. C. 1969. *The Americans: A social history of the United States.* New York: G. P. Putnam's Sons, p. 371.
83. MITCHELL, E. 1991. Shooting leopards in a barrel. *Time* (June 10): 61.

PART FOUR

The Leisure-Service System: Goals, Professionalism, and Future Challenges

13 The Leisure-Service System: Agencies, Philosophy, and Professionalism

In the last decades of the twentieth century, leisure service agencies [are] challenged to develop a more flexible and client-oriented comprehensive delivery system to better respond to the dynamic context of community life. There is ample evidence that our communities are changing; indeed, they are more diverse in ethnicity, culture and lifestyle than ever before. Community life, represented by the diverse and changing composition of individuals and families, results in an ongoing barrage of shifting values, interests, beliefs, and lifestyle preferences. Agencies must monitor carefully and respond to these changes if they are to provide relevant services and programs to their constituents.[1]

Earlier chapters in this book deal with leisure as a phenomenon of growing importance in national and community life. It is clear that, while it may be viewed from a purely personal perspective, leisure also has significant economic, health-related, and social implications in contemporary culture, and has become the responsibility of thousands of different agencies throughout the nation. Taken all together, the emergence of this network of leisure-service organizations and the realization of leisure's importance in national life have given rise to a new but rapidly growing profession. This chapter examines the leisure-service system, its varied specialized objectives, and its practitioners.

■ EIGHT TYPES OF LEISURE-SERVICE SPONSORS

In the mid- and late-1980s, a number of analyses were done of the overall leisure-service system. One such analysis provides a statistical picture of several different kinds of recreation sponsors, within both profit and nonprofit sectors (see Table 13.1). These agencies involve eight different kinds of groups under public, private, and commercial sponsorship, which are in some cases part of national chains or federations and in other cases autonomous units.

■ PUBLIC LEISURE-SERVICE AGENCIES

This category includes numerous governmental departments, bureaus, and other agencies that are primarily supported by public taxes, although they may also gain revenue from fees or charges, grants, contracts, and contributions. They operate on federal, state, and local levels of government.

On the federal level, leisure-service agencies include the National Park Service in the Department of the Interior, the Forest Service in the Department of Agriculture, the Bureau of Land Management, the Fish and Wildlife Service, the U.S. Army Corps of Engineers, and the Tennessee Valley Authority. Numerous other offices or bureaus have functions related to environment, commerce, tourism, and the needs of special populations, such as youth, the aging, or disabled persons.

All fifty states have departments or administrative units responsible for parks and outdoor recreation, as well as other offices concerned with tourism, cultural programs, and the needs of special populations. Typically, states maintain hospitals, special schools, and correctional institutions that include recreation as a basic service. In addition, state agencies serve as a liaison between the federal and local governments within several areas of leisure-service programming, such as services for the elderly or disabled. State universities also have a major responsibility for preparing professional workers in the leisure-service field.

The most important type of public leisure-service agency in terms of meeting the everyday needs of most Americans consists of recreation and park departments sponsored by local government, either on the township or municipal level, or by counties or special park districts. Specialized leisure programs are offered by the public schools, departments of human services, libraries, and other educational, cultural, or social-service departments linked to local government.

TABLE 13.1
Characteristics of leisure-service agencies: Sponsorship, size, revenues

Type of Establishment	Private For-Profit Sector	Private Nonprofit Sector	Other	Mean Size of Establishment	Mean Monthly Customers	Mean Gross Revenues
Campground/trailer park	78.4%	8.5%	13.1%	176 sites	9,040	$447,800
Multi-unit housing development	65.8	26.7	7.5	1,905 units	5,026	3,892,780
Public golf course (non-municipal)	75.9	5.7	18.4	280 daily capacity	6,751	491,524
Racquet/health club*	62.4	30.6	7.0	879 membership	5,304	778,856
Resort hotel/motel	80.6	5.1	14.3	209 rooms/units	6,291	2,703,046
Theme/amusement park	65.0	15.4	19.4	14,889 daily capacity	77,479	2,693,398
Corporate recreation/fitness center	29.1	48.9	22.0	2,038 users weekly	4,148	401,844
Private golf/country club	28.3	66.4	5.3	572 memberships	2,707	1,415,147
Retirement/life care center	22.2	67.5	10.3	309 units	567	2,994,950
Sport/recreation camp	29.1	61.7	9.3	488 daily capacity	2,131	407,773
YMCA/YWCA	1.3	77.6	21.1	3,917 memberships	8,252	1,529,783

SOURCE: "The recreation, fitness and leisure industry in 1988." *Recreation, Sports and Leisure*, 1988 (July-August), pp. 5–12.
*This category is dealt with inconsistently, with some headings referring to "racquet/tennis clubs," and others to "health/fitness clubs."

Public local recreation and parks agencies have three major areas of responsibility: (1) *operating facilities for public use,* such as parks, playgrounds, indoor recreation centers, outdoor sports facilities, swimming pools, nature centers, art centers, senior centers, and such other specialized units as skating rinks, ski centers, marinas, and riding stables; (2) *providing recreation programs under leadership,* involving instruction, supervision, and organizational direction of such programs as after-school and summer playground and day-camp activities, adult classes, sports leagues, performing arts workshops, and a host of other activities; and (3) *promoting and stimulating recreation in the community at large,* by assisting other agencies, training leadership, coordinating volunteer efforts, providing facilities for use by other groups, and working closely with other environmental, educational, and social-service organizations.

Philosophy of Park and Recreation Agencies

While each public park and recreation department is likely to have its own mission statement or set of goals, most would subscribe to the fundamental belief that the opportunity for healthful and constructive recreation is a basic right of all citizens, whether young or old, and that it is the responsibility of local government to ensure that a reasonable level of opportunity is available to all persons, regardless of economic status or other special conditions. In addition, beyond the obvious purpose of providing fun and creative challenge for community residents, the specific goals of local park and recreation departments are to:

1. *Improve the overall quality of life for residents* by helping them use leisure in creative and fulfilling ways;
2. *Promote mental and physical fitness* through a broad range of sports, outdoor recreation, and other free-time pursuits;
3. *Encourage positive social and moral values* that are keyed to the dominant values held by the community at large, and to present desirable adult role models for children and youth;
4. *Help prevent and control juvenile delinquency* and other forms of youthful deviant behavior by working closely with "at-risk" youth and offering them alternative, constructive forms of play;
5. *Strengthen family and neighborhood cohesiveness* by encouraging or sponsoring events and volunteer-based programs that build pride and a sense of community belonging;
6. *Serve mentally and physically disabled persons* either directly in recreation programs for special populations, or by working with organizations, residences, or treatment centers that meet their leisure needs;
7. *Sponsor and assist programs and institutions in the arts* to promote community awareness and support and to enrich cultural life for all ages and social classes;
8. *Protect and improve the natural environment* by maintaining parks, nature centers, zoos, and ecologically fragile sites, and by offering educational programs and services to promote environmental awareness;

9. *Strengthen the community's economic base* by making it a more pleasant and more attractive place to live, and by attracting tourists and others to sports events, historic celebrations, and other programs and institutions that contribute to the local economy and to employment;

10. *Build better understanding and cooperative relationships* among those of different races, ethnic and national backgrounds, religions, socioeconomic classes, and generations; and

11. *Blend all of these values or benefits together holistically*, so that leisure becomes a positive force in daily life for individuals, families, neighborhoods, or the community at large.[2]

Programs of Public Agencies

To achieve these goals, local public departments' programs may include a host of sports leagues, day camps, cultural and civic events and celebrations, special activities for the elderly or for disabled persons, and cooperative relationships with many community organizations. In some cases, municipal or county recreation and park departments may offer a range of classes that introduce members of the public to varied leisure activities and give them the opportunity to practice them on increasingly more advanced levels of skill and satisfaction. For example, the Montgomery County, Maryland, Department of Recreation offers hundreds of classes in local recreation centers or on a countywide basis, in such areas as children's fitness, arts and crafts, dance, youth and adult fitness, music, and other such varied interests as:

> Amateur radio, bike repair, bridge, cake decorating, clowning, dog obedience, flower arranging, garden design, herbs, magic, mah jongg, modeling, photography, puppetry, storytelling, tracing one's family, Aikido, bay fishing, fencing, karate, motorcycling, tumbling and dozens of other special interests.[3]

In the area of crafts, the Montgomery County program gives instruction in twenty-one different skills, ranging from basketry and porcelain dollmaking to hand-crafted pottery and stained glassmaking. In dance, it offers forty different skills, including such specialties as "Kinder Pre-Ballet," Viennese Waltzes and Ragtime Twosteps, side by side with Appalachian Clogging and Mambo and "Dirty Dancing." Many courses are offered in several different locations throughout the county. In addition to classes, Montgomery County sponsors dozens of holiday events, sports tournaments, swap meets, parades, parties, youth and adult leagues, clubs and events for seniors, and an extensive range of activities for disabled persons. Programs are offered in public schools throughout the county, as well as in parks and recreation centers, libraries, and private racquet, swim, tennis, and golf clubs.

There is strong evidence that the public at large supports such local park and recreation programs. A 1992 study sponsored by the National Recreation and Park Association (NRPA) found a high level of use and support for public recreation and park facilities, as shown in Figure 13.1.

- 75% of U.S. population uses public park and recreation facilities
- 69% of population supports park and recreation funding derived from both taxes and user fees
- over 75% of population agreed that local park and recreation services were worth more than the national average expenditure on parks ($45 per person per year)
- 71% of the population has a park or playground within walking distance
- 60% of the population said their community as a whole benefited substantially from local park areas, a position supported even by park non-users

FIGURE 13.1
Nationwide study of public perceptions of local recreation and park services (October 1992).
SOURCE: From "Study indicates that the U.S. public uses and supports public park, recreation services," *Dateline: NRPA* (October, 1992), p. 1. (Telephone survey of 1,300 older youth and adults, conducted by Dr. Geoffrey Godbey and Dr. Alan Graefe of Pennsylvania State University.)

At the same time, it should be made clear that many communities, particularly older cities with depressed economic conditions, *lack* adequate recreation and park facilities and programs. In Camden, New Jersey, for example, municipal and county budget cuts have reduced support for public leisure services sharply. Although an outstanding, $32 million New Jersey State Aquarium was recently constructed on the edge of Camden, along the Delaware River waterfront, the city's children and youth—thirty-six thousand of them under the age of twenty—play amid vacant and crumbling houses on potholed streets and lots strewn with broken glass and ringed by abandoned cars. Dwight Ott writes:

> these people . . . have no movie theater, no bowling alley, no mall and few organized activities to keep them off the streets. Sometimes they fall prey to the lure of the excitement of selling drugs and trying to outrun police. In some neighborhoods, small groups of children who are not yet teen-agers. . . . shout a warning to drug dealers [or become involved in dealing drugs themselves].[4]

■ VOLUNTARY, NONPROFIT SOCIAL AGENCIES

A second major type of leisure-service organization involves voluntary nonprofit community agencies, such as YMCAs, YWCAs, Boys and Girls Clubs, scouting groups, sports leagues, programs sponsored by major religious denominations or individual churches or synagogues, arts organizations, settlement houses, and a host of other special-interest groups.

Such groups are not tax-supported directly, although in some cases they may conduct programs funded by government through special contracts. Instead, they rely for fiscal support on membership fees and charges for participation, annual grants by United Way or similar bodies, fund-raising drives, or assistance from business or foundation sources. The term *voluntary* means that they represent the voluntary, independent effort of community residents. They are usually managed by paid professional staff members, although many youth organizations like the Boy Scouts and Girl Scouts rely heavily on adult volunteers for face-to-face leadership.

The goals of voluntary agencies vary greatly. Those serving youth tend to center about the promotion of constructive and morally sound personal values, and many such organizations are known as "character-building" groups. Associations like the Police Athletic League often stress citizenship values and seek to prevent juvenile delinquency in urban slums. Religiously oriented agencies may seek to promote family togetherness (see page 192) or to reinforce moral values in leisure. Some may strive to enrich the folk heritage and religious identification of their members; for example, many Jewish community centers sponsor classes or clubs dealing with Jewish history, customs, and literature. In addition to recreation as such, many churches today sponsor varied counseling and support groups or related social services. For example, Kristin Holmes describes activities at the 3,500-member Bryn Mawr, Pennsylvania, Presbyterian church:

> Monday: singles volleyball. Tuesday: violin music class. Wednesday: older adults walking club. Thursday: career transition support group. Friday: Alcoholics Anonymous. Saturday: managing chronic illness seminar. Sunday: church services . . . Most recently [the church created] a new singles council to organize programs for the congregation's rising number of unmarried members.[5]

Not far away, the First African Methodist Episcopal Church in Darby Township houses a medical center, a day-care center, food-and-clothing-giveaway programs, and a newly organized youth group—all illustrating a trend among many congregations to provide programming that meets the needs of local residents. The "one-stop" approach to programming by religious organizations stems, one sociologist suggests, from several factors:

> A decline in "natural communities" that has caused people to look elsewhere for a sense of belonging. . . . The emphasis on personal growth and fulfillment that started with the Encounter movement. . . . The increasingly serious problem of addiction, which is the basis for many such groups. . . . The realization that empty churches and synagogue buildings could be put to good—and perhaps profitable—use on weekdays.[6]

■ ARMED FORCES RECREATION

A third major type of organized recreation sponsor involves the nation's military forces, and consists of programs and facilities operated by the Morale, Welfare and Recreation (MWR) Program within the Department of Defense. In the 1980s this program served approximately nine million people, including active-duty, reserve, and retired military personnel, civilian personnel, and dependents. Operating on virtually all 923 Department of Defense installations in the United States and 363 bases in twenty-nine foreign countries, the Morale, Welfare and Recreation program at this time had a total budget of approximately $3 billion, much of it derived from self-generated revenues, and employed 215,000 people, including 8,700 military personnel, 8,900 civilian employees on government-funded salaries, and almost 200,000 employees on nonappropriated salaries.[7]

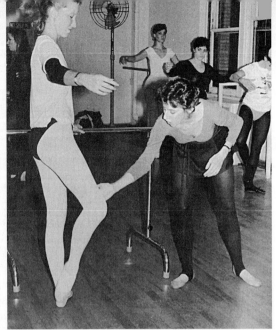

Voluntary nonprofit organizations serve youth and adults with a wide range of recreational, educational, and other human-service program elements. Until the 1950s, most such groups were racially segregated; today they are usually integrated. Here, members of the New York YWCA take computer classes geared for career needs, study ballet, and use fitness equipment.

Recognizing that the MWR program contributes significantly to the quality of life in the military community, the Department of Defense is mandated to conduct a varied program of activities that:

- Maintain a high level of esprit de corps; enhance job proficiency; contribute to military effectiveness; aid in recruitment and retention by making military service an attractive career; and aid service personnel in the transition from civilian to military life.
- Promote and maintain the physical, mental and social well-being of military members, their families, and other eligible members of the military community.
- Encourage constructive use of off-duty leisure time with opportunities for acquiring new talents and skills that contribute to the military and civilian community.
- Provide community support programs and activities for military families, particularly when the service member is on an unaccompanied tour or involved in armed conflict.[8]

Within each of the major branches of service, the MWR program typically covers a broad range of physical, social, cultural, and entertainment pursuits. For example, the Special Services program of the U.S. Air Force provides such activities and facilities as: (1) sports, including self-directed, competitive, instructional, and spectator events; (2) motion pictures; (3) service clubs and entertainment, including parties and special events, dramatic and musical activities; (4) crafts and hobbies; (5) family activities, particularly for children and youth; (6) special-interest groups, such as aero, automotive, motorcycle, and power-boating clubs, and hiking, skydiving, and rod and gun clubs; (7) rest centers and recreation areas; (8) open messes; and (9) libraries.

Special efforts are made throughout the armed services to compensate for the stress and boredom of military life and to overcome problems of drug and alcohol abuse that have affected many servicemen and women. Consistently, studies have shown that armed forces recreation programs have contributed to the morale of military personnel and their dependents and are an important factor in the retention and reenlistment of men and women within the Department of Defense.

■ EMPLOYEE SERVICES AND RECREATION

A fourth important segment of the leisure-service system consists of recreation and fitness programs sponsored by corporations for their employees and often their families. In the latter half of the nineteenth century, such programs began as the severe work ethic and "sweatshop" conditions of many factories were replaced by a new concern for worker well-being and the quality of life in American communities. Many industrial concerns, insurance companies, banks, and other employers sponsored recreation programs to promote the loyalty of their employees, create a sense of fellowship and high morale, and promote physical and mental well-being. By the mid-twentieth century, estimated expenditures for employee recreation were estimated by the *Wall Street Journal* at $800 million, and by 1963, the National Industrial Recreation Association had a total membership of over eight hundred large corporations.

Each specialized type of recreation agency tends to have its own unique goals and program emphases. In armed forces recreation, the mission is to promote physical fitness and team morale, serve the needs of families of military personnel, and counteract possible negative forms of play. Left, sailors play volleyball on an aircraft carrier flight deck during the Persian Gulf war. Below, program activities at the Orlando, Florida, Naval Training Center include holiday parties and other social events, as well as a youth soccer league.

Throughout this period, employee recreation—which was generally regarded as an integral part of personnel management—varied in its administrative sponsorship. Some companies took complete responsibility for organized recreation programs providing facilities and leadership, sometimes with an advisory council of employees. Others provided facilities and a degree of financial support, with employees taking responsibility for planning and conducting programs. Some corporations built large gymnasiums, meeting rooms, and recreation centers; activity programs included varied sports, classes and clubs in hobby interests and areas of personal development, family activities, parties, picnics, and a wide range of other pastimes.

In the 1980s and early 1990s, the range of employee services broadened to include clinics and support groups dealing with health needs, stress management, drug and alcohol abuse; some companies provided a greater diversity of services, such as discount buying clubs and chartered travel programs. By the mid-1980s, the National Employee Services and Recreation Association (NESRA) had almost three thousand member companies that offered such human resources programs as employee assistance, health and fitness activities, sports, travel, education, and pre-retirement planning. Michael Murphy summed up NESRA's basic philosophy:

> that employee services, recreation, and fitness programs make good business sense. That a work environment which satisfies its users' physical and psychological needs is conducive to greater productivity. That happy and healthy employees result in reduced absenteeism and turnover, and higher workforce morale. That the time for a humanized workplace is now.[9]

■ LEISURE SERVICES IN SCHOOLS AND COLLEGES

A fifth major group of sponsors of organized recreation programs involves educational institutions. As Chapter 3 points out, many public schools began to build playgrounds and develop summer and after-school recreation programs during the early decades of the twentieth century. Although few school systems deliberately set out to achieve the goals of leisure education enunciated in the Cardinal Principles of Secondary Education in 1918 (see page 47) in their formal curricula, many promoted these goals in their extracurricular activities.

During the post–World War II years, many school districts gave up the primary responsibility for sponsoring community recreation programs that they had held until that time. However, they continued to offer extensive after-school and enriched adult education programs—often in cooperation with local park and recreation departments.

In addition, numerous colleges and universities throughout the nation sponsor varied leisure opportunities for their students, staff, and community residents, through what is usually called "campus recreation." This may be carried on through various auspices—either through a department of athletics (especially for sports and outdoor recreation activities) or under the supervision of a dean of students or division of student life. Campus recreation covers a wide range of activities and purposes, ranging from networks of fraternities and special-interest or social clubs, to intramural and intercollegiate sports, cultural programs that include concerts, theater, dance, and other performing groups or spectator events, outings, publications, and volunteer service projects.

⫸ TO THE POINT

Often leisure activities are housed in college unions or campus recreation centers. For example, at San Diego State University in California, the

> Associated Students Organization sponsors a remarkable range of films, concerts, recreation and athletic programs, legal services and other activities. This multi-million dollar corporation, funded by annual student fees . . . operates the Aztec Center, the college's student union building. In addition, it runs a highly successful travel service, intramurals and sports clubs, special events, leisure skills classes, lectures, movies, concerts, an open-air theater, a large aquatics center, a campus radio station, a child-care center, a black students council, a general store, a campus information booth, and many other services and activities. Within this spectrum, the bulk of the leisure activities on the San Diego campus are operated directly by the Recreation Activities Board, a unit within the overall Associated Students Organization.[10]

The goals of colleges and universities in providing or assisting such services are in part to fulfill the responsibility of *in loco parentis*—that is, to oversee the lives of young men and women entrusted to their care by attempting to control negative or destructive forms of play, and by providing positive alternative leisure opportunities. In addition, the image and reputation of institutions may be enhanced by student activities that help to build public awareness and assist in the recruitment and retention of students. Various student programs contribute to the learnings stressed by the formal curriculum, including programs in the arts, humanities, sciences, and social sciences, as well as in career-related subject fields.

■ THERAPEUTIC RECREATION SERVICE

A sixth important component of the organized leisure-service field involves therapeutic recreation service. Historically, this field was known either as "hospital recreation" or as "recreation for the ill and handicapped," and tended to provide recreation as a morale-related service for individuals with physical or mental disabilities or illnesses, in residential treatment settings. In time, it broadened its scope to include those with a broader range of disabilities, and to embrace the purpose of equipping individuals with disabilities to live independently in community settings.

Today, recreation provided as part of treatment service is often closely linked to other treatment functions. Within the "clinical" or "prescriptive" approach to therapeutic recreation, patients are carefully evaluated and treatment plans are developed to achieve specific objectives linked to the physical, emotional, social, or cognitive skills that are needed for recovery or rehabilitation.

Viewing therapeutic recreation as a form of psychosocial rehabilitation provides the common ground underlying all recreational therapy—whether in mental health or in physical medicine and rehabilitation settings, which are the predominant arenas in which recreation as therapy is practiced. Regardless of the cause of the health condition requiring treatment, everyone contending with an illness or disability must learn to cope and adapt [including dealing with such factors as] the individual's self-perceptions and the elements in the environment that may contribute to poor self-esteem. They also involve traits associated with illness and disability, such as "learned helplessness," playing a "sick role" and excessive dependency, perceptions of being "different" from others and inability to recover from losses and grief.[11]

The role of therapeutic recreation in helping persons who are disabled gain or regain skills of independent living related to self-care and maintenance, travel, shopping, attending public events, and developing satisfying leisure pursuits and social lives is related to the field's second important function: assisting disabled persons who live in the community setting. Here, so-called special recreation programs are provided by community organizations like Special Olympics, the Easter Seal Society, and other groups that serve specific populations like those with physical, mental, or visual disability, or that provide activities for different categories of disabled persons. In general, their goal is to promote mainstreaming of such persons, having them participate in nonsegregated community recreation programs wherever possible. A leading example of such organizations for the past four decades has been the Recreation Center for the Handicapped in San Francisco, a unique agency founded by Janet Pomeroy, which has gained immense community support and enriched the lives of many thousands of participants through the years (see Figure 13.2).

Now known as RCH Inc., in addition to recreation, this organization provides vocational, counseling, and other important services. Through the years, sixteen thousand center participants have been successfully integrated into community life. Programs of this kind are critical for persons with disabilities; since so many such individuals do not work, they tend to have an inordinate amount of free time, which is often spent in isolated, boring, and nonproductive ways. Given encouragement and opportunity, individuals with disability have achieved remarkable success in sports, outdoor pursuits, the creative arts, and other leisure interests, and in gaining the fullest degree of satisfaction and personal growth that they are capable of, in both treatment-centered and community-based settings.

■ PRIVATE MEMBERSHIP ORGANIZATIONS

This seventh category of leisure-service agencies consists of groups or clubs that provide recreation for their members, rather than for the community at large. As was pointed out in Chapter 7, country clubs have served middle- and upper-class Americans for many years, specializing in such pursuits as golf, tennis, yachting, and social events for member families. In addition, many private-membership clubs are based on other outdoor recreation interests, such as hunting and fishing, skiing, family camping, riding, and similar pastimes. Usually, such clubs own their own land and are not as restricted in terms of membership policies as country clubs are.

Enrollment
1952   6 young adult participants, most with cerebral palsy
1992   1,800 community residents of all ages — kindergarten through elderly, with 77 types of disabling conditions

Volunteers
1952   a total of 2
1992   100–150 each month, with approximately 350 people who contribute over 20,000 hours of volunteer service annually

Staff
1952   2 part-time staff
1992   120 full-time, 56 part-time, for a total of 176

Transportation
1952   one station wagon, taxicabs, Red Cross, and other volunteer drivers to cover 720 miles each month
1992   a fleet of 32 vehicles owned and operated by the center, with 28 full-time and part-time staff covering 40,000 miles each month

Food Service
1952   lunches served 12 times a month
1992   breakfast, lunch and dinner served daily — 4,100 meals a month

Financing
1952   approximately $12,500 provided through a foundation grant
1992 $4 million annually, through a public-private partnership involving city, state, and federal contracts, government grants, and contributions from foundations, businesses, service clubs, and individuals

Facilities
1952   one room
1992   main recreation building, with swimming pool complex, gymnasium, training and development center, children's annex, and respite care facility, plus on-site accessible children's playground — a total of 80,000 square feet on 5 ½ acres; plus off-campus locations.

FIGURE 13.2
Forty-year summary: Recreation Center for the Handicapped
SOURCE: *Annual Report* (1992). San Francisco, Ca.: Recreation Center for the Handicapped, Inc.

Some private membership organizations are structured nationally or regionally, to promote participation and influence public attitudes within a given area of leisure activity. For example, in the field of outdoor recreation and conservation, membership organizations like the Sierra Club, Appalachian Mountain Club, and the Audubon Society may maintain networks of facilities, sponsor tours and training programs, and at the same time promote environmental causes and lobby for needed legislation.

A unique type of private-membership organization involves the provision of recreation programs for people based on residence. Many wealthy families live in resort communities or have vacation homes in developments that provide skiing, sailing, or other forms of outdoor play, making use of facilities that are restricted to property owners. However, such private-membership leisure opportunities are not necessarily limited to the affluent. In one giant development, Starrett City, in Brooklyn, New York, middle-income tenants drawn from various ethnic populations—approximately half of Hispanic, African-American, and Asian backgrounds—enjoy a variety of sports, aquatic, fitness, and club activities that are limited to families in residence.

■ COMMERCIAL RECREATION

Finally, the largest and most extensive form of leisure-service today, in terms of variety of programs offered and the sheer scope of participation and revenues earned, is provided by commercial recreation. Many thousands of leisure-service businesses large and small offer fitness and health-related activities, travel and tourism, and opportunities for participation in such pursuits as bowling, racquetball, horseback riding, and a host of other pastimes. In the broadest sense, all forms of commercially sponsored entertainment and hospitality, including admission to for-profit theater and concerts and the operation of nightclubs and bars, are part of this field.

⇒ TO THE POINT

The services offered by recreation businesses are varied; they may include instruction, the rental of equipment or use of special facilities, the provision of entertainment, hospitality, and social contacts, and other kinds of leisure-related opportunity. In some cases, recreation is the sole element that is offered to the public; in others, it is part of a complex of offerings. In some huge shopping malls that have been built in recent years, recreation is a major attraction that helps to draw great numbers of people to the overall facility. For example, the West Edmonton Mall, in Alberta, Canada, is the world's largest shopping complex. This sprawling indoor facility is crammed with 836 stores, 110 restaurants, 20 movie theaters, and a large hotel. An appealing destination for tourists in its own right, the mall attracts as many as a hundred thousand visitors a day, about 40 percent from the United States. Its recreation facilities include a mammoth amusement park (entry free of charge) with forty-seven rides; a miniature golf course; a $5 million skating rink; a huge water park with a surf pool, an artificial lake, submarines that take tourists on underseas adventures, and a replica of Columbus's ship, the *Santa Maria*.[12]

Similarly, the Mall of America, the nation's largest shopping mall, recently built in Bloomington, Minnesota, has numerous recreation attractions, including a huge amusement park, Camp Snoopy. Such enterprises demonstrate the degree to which leisure has become part of the commercial structure of the nation, both as a highly profitable business in its own right, and as a "threshold" attraction that draws customers to other businesses.

■ LEISURE AS A SYSTEM

These eight major types of recreation sponsors illustrate the diversity of the leisure-service field. Each such category clearly has its own characteristic philosophy or sense of mission. Some are chiefly concerned with serving their own members or with clearing a financial profit; others are more broadly motivated by altruistic goals that contribute to community health and social well-being.

Although they are described as a system, most leisure-service agencies do not work together in a coordinated way. Indeed, they may be highly competitive or even hostile toward each other, as in a number of cases where private health, sports, or racquet clubs have sued YMCAs, claiming that the latter are essentially operating as "for-profit" fitness centers, and should be denied tax-exempt status.

However, the trend is toward a fuller degree of cooperation among different types of recreation organizations. For example, in some metropolitan areas, councils of social agencies have identified priorities and gaps in recreation and other social services, and have helped area agencies coordinate their efforts. Increasingly, public and private functions in the leisure-service field are being merged through the process of privatization. This term refers to the subcontracting of formerly public functions—such as the design and construction of facilities, maintenance, food service, and program operation—to private firms. It may include joint efforts in the building of stadiums or other major facilities, the operation of golf courses, or the rehabilitation or new development of harbor areas and marinas.

Examples of Cooperation

Numerous examples of cooperation within the leisure-service field may be cited. Crompton and Richardson point out that many state and local government departments of commerce or tourism work closely with private entrepreneurs in the joint promotion of tourism.[13] Publicly owned parks, seashores, historic monuments, gardens, marinas, zoos, and historic mansions attract tourists, who also patronize commercial cruises, tours, theme parks, and other attractions. Public and private agencies may also cooperate in carrying out festivals or other events that encourage tourist visits.

Many private companies assist by funding sports programs for children, youth, or special populations, locally or as part of nationwide programs. A useful example is Hershey's National Track and Field Youth Program, which is designed to introduce children between the ages of nine and fourteen to physical fitness through track and field events, and which is run in cooperation with the National Recreation and Park Association, the President's Council on Physical Fitness and Sport, and many local public recreation and park agencies. Timber and utility companies cooperate with park authorities in making their lands and water-based recreation sites available for camping, boating, and other forms of outdoor recreation. Still other companies or voluntary agencies sponsor or assist special camping for physically and mentally disabled persons. In numerous communities, public, voluntary, educational, and armed forces bases exchange facilities to maximize the leisure opportunities of different age groups.

Over the last several years, the U.S. Forest Service has developed a National Recreation Strategy to involve major corporations in special projects that facilitate recreational uses of major forest areas. For example, McDonald's, the fast-food chain, has cooperated with managers of the Lassen National Forest in northern California and the Golden Arches Association to provide camping programs in the heart of the national forest for seriously ill children.

Diversity and Complexity in Leisure-Service Programming

Such efforts are all part of a widespread effort on the part of public recreation and park agencies to join other elements in the leisure-service system to provide new recreational opportunities through imaginative entrepreneurship approaches. This effort has been accompanied by a surge in new kinds of recreation businesses offered by private-sector sponsors, including:

- high-adventure and high-risk activities (whitewater rafting, hang gliding, wind surfing, flying ultra-light aircraft, mountain bicycling [and other outdoor pursuits]).
- personal growth centers and self-development programs, bookstores, specialty schools. Leisure information and related services (video instructional programs, articles for specialty magazines, retirement career planning workshops).
- Social clubs and programs (dating services, recreation programs for singles and seniors); entertainment and eating establishments (fast-food services, theme-type eating establishments); travel and tourism services.
- Home entertainment (electronic hardware and software retail stores, videocassettes rental, video games); fitness, wellness, and leisure (nutrition, diet, fitness programs, health clubs, home exercise equipment).[14]

Commercial recreation entrepreneurs have become increasingly innovative in their marketing efforts. For example, Crossley and Ellis describe new marketing approaches in sports stores, where a weak link in the retail process has traditionally been the customer's inability to test a product before deciding to buy it. A Denver-based chain of sports equipment stores has created so-called Sports Castles that have basketball courts, tennis courts, golf putting greens, fly casting areas, archery ranges, and treadmill ski machines for testing equipment and learning skills. Crossley and Ellis continue:

> They also have a large multipurpose classroom where they teach fly tying, hunter safety and other classes related to the equipment sold. In addition [they offer] a full service travel agency, sell tickets to concerts and ski areas, and sponsor a variety of community sports events. In sum, [the company] sells a total recreation experience, not just sports equipment.[15]

However, such innovative approaches to programming are not restricted to commercial leisure-service businesses. Public recreation and park managers must be alert to recognize new community needs and to develop programs and services keyed to changing social conditions and demographic factors. As a single example, the Long Beach, California, Department of Parks, Recreation and Marine sponsors successful environmental cleanup projects, Senior Olympics, fitness and "adaptive" recreation programs, and an unusual Park Ranger Gang project (see page 362)—all in addition to a full range of typical activities. Recognizing population shifts, the Long Beach Department offers numerous language classes, including conversational Russian and Japanese and no fewer than five different courses in Spanish to meet speed, conversational, law enforcement, medical, and business needs.[16]

These examples make clear that the traditional provision of leisure services by all kinds of sponsors has become increasingly complex and sophisticated to satisfy a wide range of audiences and to market programs successfully in a competitive atmosphere. As a consequence, there has been a continuing effort to develop a higher level of professionalism in the overall leisure-service field and within its specialized delivery systems.

■ PROFESSIONALISM IN RECREATION, PARKS, AND LEISURE SERVICE

Although people have been employed for thousands of years in the provision of recreational experiences—as entertainers, fencing and dancing masters, zookeepers, gardeners, and sports coaches and in hundreds of other leisure-related roles—the emergence of professionalism in this field has essentially been a twentieth-century phenomenon.

During the early decades of the twentieth century, as growing numbers of public recreation and park agencies were established, most recreation leaders were drawn from the fields of education and physical education. Park personnel were trained in fields like forestry, agriculture, and, in some cases, civil engineering. Schools of education offered courses in playground leadership, and the National Recreation Association sponsored one-year graduate training for recreation and park administrators. With the expansion of federally funded recreation programs during the Great Depression of the 1930s, there was increased awareness of the special role of leisure in society.

The American Association for the Study of Group Work published an important report in 1939 stating that the "leisure of the American people constitutes a central and crucial issue of social policy." Its author, Eduard Lindeman, a key federal official during the Depression, pointed out that American workers were gaining a huge "national reservoir" of leisure amounting to hundreds of billions of hours a year. If this free time were not to become "idleness, waste, or opportunity for sheer mischief," Lindeman urged that a national plan for leisure be developed, including the widespread preparation of professionally trained recreation leaders:

> I have no doubt that a distinct profession of recreation leadership is now coming into being. Indeed, it is my expectation that this newer occupation will enlist recruits at an accelerated rate of speed and that in the next quarter century there will be a demand for at least one hundred thousand trained recreation professionals. Some of these will be concerned with problems of administration and planning; others will work in research; others will be engaged in developing newer forms of facilities; some will be supervisors, recreation teachers and trained specialists.[17]

Beginning in the late 1930s and in the years after World War II, a number of major universities around the nation initiated specialized curricula in recreation and park leadership and management. By the mid-1960s, there were several dozen such programs—many housed in departments of schools of physical education, but others administratively attached to agriculture, conservation, or resource management departments. James Charlesworth, president of the American Academy of Political and Social Science, urged that the public administration of recreation and park services be reorganized with state departments of leisure comparable to state education, health, and highway units. With respect to staffing of leisure-service agencies, Charlesworth wrote:

> A department of leisure should have a staff as varied as that of a large city-planning commission . . . [including] psychologists, sociologists, educators, statisticians, administrators, sportsmen, recreationists, naturalists, and hobbyists, to name only the more obvious. . . .
>
> Even in the more specific field of recreation, we need broadened perspectives. Just as city planning will not achieve its full potential as long as it is dominated by architects, so recreation will not realize its full possibilities as long as most of its practitioners are physical educationists. A comprehensive, pervasive recreation program should contain elements drawn from all the behavioral and related sciences.[18]

With growing awareness of the burgeoning number of job opportunities in professional recreation, park, and leisure services, curricula in this overall field expanded rapidly in the late 1960s and 1970s. By the end of the 1970s, it was estimated that there were approximately five hundred such programs in the United States and Canada, including many two-year community college curricula, four-year bachelor's programs, and graduate degree programs. While the majority of these continued to be linked to health and physical education, most were now relatively independent, in terms of having their own faculty members, separate courses, and counseling and placement services.

With the merging of the recreation and park fields, which was symbolized by the formation of the National Recreation and Park Association in the mid-1960s, many formerly separate government agencies joined forces. Gradually, management-oriented degrees replaced degree requirements that had been concerned with programming and leadership. A growing number of specialized degree options replaced the earlier "generalist" curricula. For example, therapeutic recreation, which had formerly been a relatively minor area of concern, now expanded rapidly in response to national interest in disabled populations. Other specialized curricula appeared, including courses dealing with armed forces, employee, commercial, and campus recreation. Along with this development, there was increased concern about professionalism within the leisure-service field.

Progress toward Professionalism

What did it mean to be professional, and why did those working or teaching in the recreation, park, and leisure-service field seek this designation—apart from the higher degree of status that it implied? A position paper of the Society of Park and Recreation educators defined *profession* as follows:

A profession is a vocation whose practice is founded upon an understanding of the theoretical structure of some department of learning or science and upon the abilities accompanying such understanding. This understanding and these abilities are applied to the vital practical affairs of man. . . . The profession . . . considers its first ethical imperative to be altruistic service to the client.[19]

⏩ TO THE POINT

More recently, H. Douglas Sessoms identified the following elements, which are generally accepted as criteria of professionalism in contemporary society:

1. Professions align themselves with a social concern, the ameliorating of some social ill, and they frequently result from a major social movement.
2. Professions establish their body of knowledge, a set of concepts and procedures generally known to those within the profession.
3. Specified programs of education and training, generally involving internships, are needed in order for one to learn the necessary concepts and practices of the profession.
4. To assure that programs of professional preparation are reliable, that individuals have the prerequisite skills and understandings to practice, programs of accreditation and certification are created.
5. Those within the profession create organizations to serve it. These organizations often establish codes of ethics, norms of practice which are enforced by the profession.[20]

Through the period extending from the mid-1960s to the early 1990s, park, recreation, and leisure-service professionals made significant progress in meeting these criteria. First, a growing body of published research identified the unique functions and competencies attached to leadership in the field. Journals related to leisure concepts, administrative methods, and a host of other theoretical and practical concerns add to this body of knowledge each year.

Trends in Professional Preparation

Professional authority based on formal academic training has been achieved through the expansion of a higher education system of college and university curricula ranging from two-year community college programs to institutions that offer the doctorate in this field. Through the 1980s, professional preparation in recreation, parks, and leisure studies was consolidated, as a number of weak or marginal programs discontinued their offerings and others shifted their institutional affiliations. At the same time, as M. Deborah Bialeschki points out in a 1992 report on higher education in the field, college and university programs have continued to respond to important community needs. Based on an Educational Resources Survey conducted by the Society of Park and Recreation Educators, statistics on student enrollment in specialized areas of concern are provided in Table 13.2.

TABLE 13.2
Percentage of student majors in areas of emphasis

Emphasis	Associate's	Bachelor's	Master's	Ph.D.
General/administration	21%	32%	36%	32%
Therapeutic recreation	29	28	27	37
Commercial/tourism	11	13	11	11
Outdoor recreation	18	16	14	21
Programming/leadership	21	10	10	—

SOURCE: Bialeschki, M. D. 1992. "The state of parks, recreation and leisure studies curricula," *Parks and Recreation* (July): 73.
NOTE: Although this survey did not measure other conceptual areas of study, graduate programs in many institutions also focus on study and research in such fields as sociology of leisure, psychology of play, and similar concerns.

A key factor in the field's meeting the criterion of formal academic training has been its recognition and approval as an appropriate area of professional study by the Council of Postsecondary Accreditation (COPA) in the mid-1980s. This means that parks, recreation, and leisure studies are now validated as a legitimate field of academic specialization; today, approximately one hundred colleges and universities have met the requirements of the Council on Accreditation (a joint function of the National Recreation and Park Association and the American Association for Leisure and Recreation).

Credentialing in Recreation, Parks and Leisure Services

On the national level, the National Recreation and Park Association's National Certification Board began in 1990 to conduct a Certified Leisure Professional Examination, to serve as the basis for identifying individuals as qualified practitioners in the field. In addition, forty-three states and the National Therapeutic Recreation Society conduct NRPA-recognized certification programs. A number of other specialized professional societies, such as the National Employee Services and Recreation Association (NESRA) maintain certification requirements, usually based on a combination of professional education and experience.

While curriculum accreditation and personnel certification procedures have upgraded professionalism in the leisure-service field, the reality is that they do not control the admission or continuing employment of many recreation and park workers. Table 13.3 presents current employment statistics within this overall field and in related fields. In several cases, recreation personnel are lumped together indiscriminately with other specialists, making it difficult to determine how many are recreational practitioners and how many are in related fields. In addition to these job categories, there are substantial numbers of therapeutic recreation specialists, workers in museums, zoos, membership organizations, and similar agencies, who are part of the total leisure-service field.

It is safe to say that there are at least several hundred thousand individuals who have recreation programming as a primary job function in the United States today.

TABLE 13.3

Number of employees in recreation and related fields

Park and recreation civilian workers in federal, state, and local agencies	336,000
Amusement and recreation services	1,089,000
Social, recreation, and religious workers	1,124,000
Writers, artists, entertainers, and athletes	1,957,000

Source: *Statistical Abstract of the United States*, 1992. Washington, DC: U.S. Department of Commerce, Bureau of the Census, pp. 305, 392, 396–397.

A relatively small segment of this overall group consists of practitioners who should be classified as professionals, in terms of their specialized job functions, academic training, certification status, and other criteria. Chiefly, these are managerial personnel in recreation and park departments, recreation therapists or supervisors, members of armed forces MWR units, school and college program managers, and specialists in employee recreation programs. A substantial number of government recreation workers must meet Civil Service requirements, usually based on a combination of education and professional experience, or, if they work in health-care settings, must satisfy state personnel requirements. Finally, a substantial number of recreation professionals employed in voluntary agencies like the YMCA, YWCA, or YM-YWHA, Boy and Girl Scouts, Boys and Girls Clubs, and similar national federations must meet hiring requirements and take part in training and continuing education programs established by these groups.

Work of Professional Societies

As in other fields of professional service that have improved their higher education curricula and standards for admission to practice over time, recreation, parks, and leisure services continue to make steady progress. In large measure, this is due to the work of such organizations as the National Recreation and Park Association and its specialized components, such as the American Park and Recreation Society, the National Therapeutic Recreation Society, and the Society of Park and Recreation Educators. Other professional societies include the American Therapeutic Recreation Association, the Armed Forces Recreation Society, the American Association for Leisure and Recreation, the National Employee Services and Recreation Association, the National Intramural and Recreational Sports Association, and dozens of other organizations and trade associations concerned with promoting specialized branches of commercial recreation.

NRPA in particular has been effective in promoting public awareness of the leisure-service field, pressing for sound legislation related to urban needs, open space and other environmental concerns, and juvenile delinquency, and drawing attention to the needs of the aging and other special populations and similar recreation-related issues. It has constantly stimulated research and publication and has been instrumental in establishing numerous special schools and workshops across the United States that provide in-service education for practitioners.

Employment Trends: Numbers, |

Labor statisticians agree that leisure wil|
employment in the United States in the y·
and World Report presented estimates of |
next ten years in several key industries (see '|

Within this overall growth, patterns of ε
graphic factors linked to ethnicity and gend
indicated that members of racial and ethnic
in the recreation and parks field, but that re
of public or voluntary agency administratic
this pattern changed as numerous large c'
African-American and Hispanic-American |
as directors of public park and recreation d
dent in federal agencies like the National Pa·· ᴊervice and the Forest Service, aπ·
many state recreation, park, and conservation departments. Fuller representation on
all levels of employment for members of racial and ethnic minorities and the
improvement of recreation programs serving minorities are the continuing concern
of the Ethnic Minority Society.

A somewhat similar situation is evident with respect to the role of women as
leisure-service professionals in the United States. Henderson, Bialeschki, and
Sessoms point out that in the early years of the playground and recreation movement, most program leadership was provided primarily by women, and men were
not the majority staff members until the 1930s.[22] Particularly with the merger of the
park and recreation movements, however, men took over the bulk of management
positions—especially those entailing facilities development and maintenance responsibilities. Women were relegated to direct program leadership positions for the most
part, often working with preschool groups, the elderly, or girls' and women's pro-

TABLE 13.4

Ten-year outlook in selected key industries

Industry	Expected Jobs in 1995	Change from 1984
Health care	8.3 million	+29%
Banking, financial	5.7 million	+19%
Printing, publishing	1.7 million	+20%
Textiles, apparel	1.5 million	−18%
Computers, electronics	1.5 million	+35%
Leisure, recreation services	1.5 million	+27%
Food, beverages	1.4 million	−10%
Auto making	828,000	−4%

Sᴏᴜʀᴄᴇ: Bureau of Labor Statistics, U.S. Department of Labor; "Where the jobs will be." *U.S. News and World Report* (Dec. 23, 1985): 45.

grams. This situation began to change in the 1970s, as women moved increasingly into a range of supervisory and management roles. A professional profile survey of women employed in the recreation and park profession revealed in the late 1980s that a substantial percentage of women were employed on administrative levels, and that they were generally positive about their career development.[23]

However, Henderson, Bialeschki, and Sessoms report that pay inequity still exists through much of the leisure-service field, and that men continue to dominate executive levels of employment—particularly within the private or commercial sector.[24] And, in 1992, Henderson stresses that women continue to face the glass ceiling that hinders their advancement in recreation and parks careers, just as in other areas of employment. In many job settings, women are subject to sexual harassment, and the problem may also be exacerbated by other demographic factors. She writes:

> Gender discrimination in the workplace must also be addressed as it relates to discrimination related to race, disability, or any other factor that makes people be perceived as different. . . . Discrimination against women of color . . . may result in different and greater discrimination than against white women. . . . While little is known about the extent of overt discrimination against women of color or women with disabilities in leisure services, professionals must be aware of the implications of multiple discrimination for women.[25]

DEFINITION OF PROFESSIONAL IDENTITY AND ROLE

Despite the evidences of professional growth that have been described throughout this chapter, it is probable that many Americans are not yet familiar with the field of leisure service *as* a profession. While they recognize the specific occupations in which people work—recreation therapist, travel agent, tourist guide, playground director, or parks manager—the likelihood is that they are not aware of leisure as a generic field of employment.

Similarly, H. Douglas Sessoms points out that the precise role of the professional in recreation, parks, and leisure service has yet to be defined. It is certainly not simply the act of leading activities or managing operations. Like members of other professions, he writes, practitioners in this field must have the ability to identify the goals of their agencies consistent with accepted professional values or mission statements. They must also have the ability to solve problems and create action plans to achieve their goals. Sessoms continues:

> Such action implies an understanding of the required resources, the method appropriate for utilization of those resources for goal achievement and the ability to monitor the process. It also implies the utilization of other professions, trades and even volunteers in the accomplishment of those objectives. The role set suggests management responsibilities, but management is not a unique role function. Others also manage. What it does require is an understanding by both the profession and the public of the role the profession is to assume and the major social concerns to be addressed.[26]

In addition to paid professional leaders and managers, millions of Americans young and old work as volunteers or trainees in leisure-service agencies ranging from Boy Scouts and Girl Scouts to programs serving disabled participants, like Special Olympics. Here, senior citizen volunteers teach swimming to youngsters in a Westchester County, New York, public pool, and junior high school girls in Minnesota learn to plan and officiate in youth sports leagues. Below, leader aides in Portsmouth, Virginia, gain horticulture and nursery management skills.

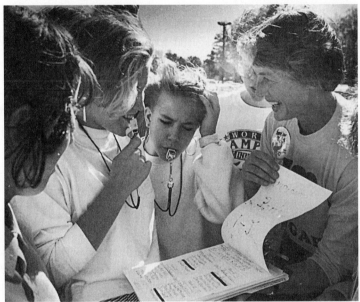

Clearly, the single unifying element that brings together varied kinds of practitioners within the eight major sectors of the leisure-service field has to do with the unique nature of leisure and with its potential for improving the quality of life in contemporary society. Whatever the special goals of different types of sponsoring agencies, a key task of the professional worker in each of them is to clarify the important contribution made by leisure involvement to individual participants, to neighborhoods, and to communities at large. As this text has shown, these benefits help to promote physical and mental health, improve intergroup relationships, stimulate economic well-being, and protect the environment. However, it is becoming increasingly necessary for leisure-service professionals to make hard choices between conflicting needs and priorities. Should recreation and leisure be viewed primarily from an entrepreneurial or a human-service perspective?

This issue, with its implications for managerial strategy, is discussed in fuller detail in the final chapter of this text, along with an examination of the political, social, and economic trends that our nation is likely to face in the decades that lie ahead.

■ SUMMARY

This chapter has presented an overview of eight major types of leisure-service organizations, together with details of their sponsorship arrangements, goals, and programs. The overall field is not a highly coordinated or structured body, but consists of numerous specialized groups, which both compete and cooperate with each other. Similarly, the overall occupation of leisure service, which has grown dramatically over the past four decades, includes several million individuals, many of whom do not identify with the field in terms of higher education or affiliation with its professional societies. However, the core of individuals who *are* professionally affiliated provide strong leadership to recreation and park agencies, as they seek to carry out their shared social mission.

■ QUESTIONS FOR DISCUSSION

1. Describe leisure service as a system, including its components and their chief characteristics. To what degree do these represent a formal system with defined relationships and to what degree are they independent elements in a loosely organized field?

2. Select any two or three of the major types of leisure-service sponsors, such as local government park and recreation departments, commercial businesses, or therapeutic recreation agencies. Compare them systematically, in terms of goals, populations served, sources of funding, and program elements.

3. What are the reasons for the emergence of leisure and recreation as a distinct professional field in American society? Identify several criteria of professionalism suggested by Sessoms and others, and assess the degree to which leisure-service professionals meet these expectations.

4. How have the roles of women and minorities changed in recent years within the leisure-service professions? In terms of the kinds of changes that the overall society has undergone and will continue to experience, what do you see as their special contributions?

5. Some leisure educators have challenged the continuing effort to promote professionalism in leisure service, seeing it as a negative force within the field. What are their reasons, and how valid do you believe they are?

■ NOTES

1. MURPHY, J. F., and R. F. DAHL. 1991. The right to leisure expression. *Parks and Recreation* (Sept.): 106.

2. For a fuller discussion, see Chapter 14, Social functions of community recreation, in Kraus, R. 1990. *Recreation and leisure in modern society.* Glenview, IL: Scott, Foresman, pp. 378–396.

3. *Guide to recreation and leisure service.* Fall 1992. Rockville, MD: Montgomery County, Md., Department of Recreation.

4. OTT, D. 1991. It keeps them out of trouble. *Philadelphia Inquirer* (Dec. 23): B–1.

5. HOLMES, K. 1991. Programs help churches foster sense of belonging. *Philadelphia Inquirer* (Nov. 10): 1–B, 5–B.

6. *Ibid.*

7. KORB, L. J. 1982. *Morale, welfare and recreation program overview.* (March) Washington, DC: U.S. Department of Defense, p. 3.

8. *Ibid.* See also Lankford, S., and D. DeGraaf. 1992. Strengths, weaknesses, opportunities and threats in morale, welfare and recreation organizations: Challenges of the 1980s. *Journal of Park and Recreation Administration* (Spring): 31–45.

9. MURPHY, M. 1984. The history of employee services and recreation. *Parks and Recreation* (Aug.): 38.

10. See *Breakaway: Recreational guide to San Diego State University.* (n.d.) San Diego, CA.

11. KRAUS, R., and J. SHANK. 1992. *Therapeutic recreation service: Principles and practices.* Dubuque, IA: Wm. C. Brown, p. 95.

12. HENRY, G. 1986. Welcome to the pleasure dome. *Time* (Oct. 20): 75.

13. CROMPTON, J., and S. RICHARDSON. 1986. The tourism connection: Where public and private leisure services merge. *Parks and Recreation* (Oct.): 38.

14. BULLARO, J. 1987. Recreation and leisure service: Entrepreneurial opportunities and strategies. *Journal of Physical Education, Recreation and Dance* (Feb.): 64.

15. CROSSLEY, J., and T. ELLIS. 1988. An entrepreneurial application: Systematic innovation. *Journal of Physical Education, Recreation and Dance* (Oct.): 35.

16. *Fall schedule.* 1992. Long Beach, CA: Department of Parks, Recreation and Marine.

17. LINDEMAN, E. C. 1939. *Leisure: A national issue.* New York: American Association for the Study of Group Work, p. 32.

18. CHARLESWORTH, J. C. 1964. *Leisure in America: Blessing or curse?* Lancaster, PA: American Academy of Political and Social Science, p. 45.

19. *Education for leisure.* 1975. Position statement of Society of Park and Recreation Educators. Cited in *Proceedings of the 1975 Dallas-SPRE Institute,* ed. D. Weiskopf. Arlington, VA: National Recreation and Park Association, p. 18.

20. SESSOMS, H. D. 1990. The professionalization of parks and recreation: A necessity? In *Recreation and leisure: Issues in an era of change,* ed. T. L. Goodale and P. A. Witt. State College, PA: Venture, p. 248.

21. GODBEY, G., and D. HENKEL. 1976. The manpower study: A report. *Parks and Recreation* (Nov.): 25.

22. HENDERSON, K., M. D. BIALESCHKI, and H. D. SESSOMS. 1990. Occupational segregation? Women and the leisure services. *Journal of Physical Education, Recreation and Dance* (Oct.): 49–52. See also Henderson, K., and M. D. Bialeschki. 1993. Professional women and equity issues in the 1990s. *Parks and Recreation* (March): 55–59.

23. CRAWFORD, C. C. 1988. *Professional profile survey of women employed in the recreation and park profession.* Rocky Hill, CN: NRPA N.E. Service Center.

24. HENDERSON, BIALESCHKI, AND SESSOMS, *op. cit.,* p. 50.

25. HENDERSON, K. A. 1992. Being female in the park and recreation profession in the 1990s: Issues and challenges. *Journal of Park and Recreation Administration* 10, 2: 18.

26. SESSOMS, H. D. Professionalization of parks and recreation, *op. cit.,* p. 259.

14 Conflict in Leisure Values: Charting the Future

The century to come, and the centuries to follow, will be complex, fast-paced and turbulent. Human beings everywhere have learned to live with, even thrive on, explosive increases in the volume of knowledge, the capacities of technology, the potential for travel, the electronic immediacy of once distant cultures. Change has become almost addictive, a jolt to energy and creativity. . . .

The tribal must give way to the global. Yet will it? To make the dreamed-for future work, people everywhere are going to have to know much more about, and demand much more from, themselves. The change that sparks the future is rooted in discovering what sparked the past and present. To embrace the future fully, one must give to it the very best of oneself. For the future to be bright, it must be lit by the lamp of learning, the true Olympic torch.[1]

As we move toward the twenty-first century and the immense challenges that the year 2000 will bring, society faces the certainty that the era ahead will dramatically transform all our lives. An integral part of the changes that occur will have to do with leisure and recreation. This chapter outlines a number of the key changes that are occurring now and some of the most significant ones that are predicted for the years ahead. First, however, it defines the most pressing problem that faces the leisure and recreation field today—whether it is to continue to adopt a marketing-oriented, entrepreneurial approach or to renew recreation's historic mission of meeting significant social needs.

■ LEISURE AS SOCIAL CONCERN

In a detailed history of the origins of the urban parks and recreation movement, Wayne Stormann shows how the playground and play pioneers during the late 1800s were part of a generation of social reformers who linked the need for public parks and recreation with other important causes, such as working conditions, crime, family life, and community health.[2] Similarly, Mary Duncan points out that the key pioneers of the play movement in the early 1900s were radical reformers like Joseph Lee, Jane Addams, and Luther Gulick, who sought to overcome slum problems and social injustices with political action and innovative community programs.[3]

Throughout the twentieth century, during the Great Depression of the 1930s and the Civil Rights era and the War on Poverty of the 1960s, recreation programs were consistently mounted to overcome social problems, particularly in urban ghettoes. The National Urban Recreation Study, conducted in 1978 by the U.S. Department of the Interior, made clear that the provision of adequate park and recreation facilities and programs was closely linked to other vital urban concerns, such as housing, transportation, education, crime prevention, and others.[4] Based on field studies of the nation's most highly populated metropolitan areas, it emphasized that well-distributed systems of parkland and other recreational spaces were essential to community well-being. However, it found that the greatest deficiencies for recreation land and facilities were in the inner cores of the cities studied:

> In the growing cities, the greatest need is for development of new parkland and facilities; in the older cities, lack of funds for programs and maintenance has restricted recreation opportunities and has resulted in the loss of large investments in park facilities as these facilities deteriorate and become unusable.[5]

Despite the efforts of professionals and citizen groups, inner-city recreation and park programs continued to decline dramatically through the 1980s. In 1990, Foley and Pink described what they called "recreation apartheid," the ugly contrast between suburban and small-town settings, where leisure-service programs for all age groups are provided with effective leadership in attractive, safe settings, and the ghetto conditions of decayed parks and playgrounds. They cite a *Los Angeles Times* article, "The Dead Parks":

In scores of city parks across Los Angeles—mostly cramped sites in poor neighbor-hoods—the fear is high. So pervasive are gangs, drug dealers and drunks, so limited are the programs and facilities, that the sites are known to parents and even some recreation directors as "dead parks."[6]

The causes of this trend were obvious: property tax initiatives that had sharply reduced funding support for community social programs and services, along with growing statistics of crime and delinquency, gang violence, drug abuse, and family breakup. In 1992, R. Dean Tice, executive director of the National Recreation and Park Association, described the growing gap between haves and have-nots in American society and the alienation between many government institutions and their constituents. He wrote:

> Antisocial behavior and unrest in many forums spill over to public recreation programs and places, reducing the broader social value and degrading the environment. Public recreation budgets are too often stripped of the capacity to respond rather than enhanc-ing our ability to respond to danger. . . . We must aggressively link the values of recre-ation and resources to other basic needs like economic security, shelter and education [and adopt] an advocacy agenda embracing "children, youth and family" issues.[7]

Strikingly, it is not only public recreation and park agencies that have deteriorated dramatically in inner-city neighborhoods. Other types of sponsors, such as Little League, Pony League, AAU swimming and track clubs, that use public facilities often do not exist in communities like Camden, New Jersey (see page 336), or South Los Angeles. Jack Foley and Veda Ward write:

> Boys and girls clubs, YMCAs and YWCAs, scouts, and so forth, which [are widely found] in suburban America, do not exist in South Los Angeles. . . . there is no com-mercial recreation, i.e., movie theaters, malls, video arcades, skating rinks or bowling alleys [and] few of the amenities such as cultural centers, art museums and theatres which often spur private development.[8]

But at the heart of the problem is the inability of financially strapped, skeletonized public recreation and park agencies in many older cities to provide a comprehensive network of effective leisure facilities and programs.

A Broad Social Agenda for Leisure Services

The primary responsibility of public, local recreation and park agencies should be to serve the community at large—meaning residents of all ages, socioeconomic classes, racial and ethnic backgrounds, and neighborhoods. Obviously, in most communi-ties, this will include substantial numbers of economically comfortable, stable fami-lies who, at the same time that they use public facilities, may also belong to private clubs and use commercial recreation resources. Beyond this group, however, there is a pressing need to provide constructive and satisfying recreation opportunities to individuals with special personal, health-related, and economic needs. These include such groups as impoverished inner-city residents, those with physical or mental dis-abilities, at-risk youth, survivors of childhood sexual abuse or parental alcoholism, the homeless, and other special populations. With the passage of the Americans with Disabilities Act and related legislation, the priority to serve special populations has become increasingly clear. More and more, recreation is being recognized as a health-related field. Godbey writes: "New understandings of what constitutes health and healthy lives have drawn the concepts of 'health' and 'recreation' or 'leisure' so close together they are practically synonymous."9

Instead of thinking of health in purely medical terms, Godbey points out that a much broader concept of wellness prevails today. While the view of disease as an outside agent that invades the body has generally dominated scientific thinking and government policy, there is growing acceptance of the idea that illness stems both from such causes and from an imbalance between physical, psychological, and social aspects of the individual within his or her environment. Clearly, recreational experiences play a major role in promoting positive personal and public health-related attitudes and life-styles.

Leisure and At-Risk Youth

Historically, one of the most compelling arguments for the provision of playgrounds, day camps, and other recreational programs for children and youth was that they helped to reduce antisocial or delinquent behavior. Many youth-service organizations continue to have this as a major goal. Pamela Robinson-Young describes recreation programs carried out in Dallas, Texas, as a form of gang intervention. In that city, Campfire, Inc., and the Exall Recreation Center involve teenagers from the inner city, not in a program that preaches about good citizenship and lawful behavior, but one that meets their needs for excitement and challenge by involving them in activities such as rock climbing, camping, and rappelling. Such experiences help young people learn about safety, leadership, and responsibility. However, Robinson-Young cautions that recreation alone will not be successful in overcoming deviant social values and behavior among youth:

> Recreation service delivery should emphasize adventurous leisure education, exciting recreational opportunities, parenting skills, communication skills, drug awareness workshops, employment assistance, education, crises intervention, self-esteem building workshops, and other life skills training.10

The Long Beach, California, Department of Parks, Recreation and Marine has established a Park Ranger Program designed specifically to work with various youth gangs in the city, including Hispanic-American and Asian-American gangs, warring groups like the "Crips" and the "Bloods," and other factions like "Stoners" and "Skinheads." The rangers play a complex role with gangs, involving both armed and unarmed approaches, linkage with local enforcement authorities, and intensive work with citizen groups and other service agencies. Recognizing that much of the intergang rivalry stems from racial antagonisms—with hundreds of deaths a year from gang violence in Los Angeles County—the Long Beach Rangers strive to reduce such frictions, to monitor gang activity and control it in park settings, and to fight the escalation of drug activity. When it is feasible, gangs and their leaders are encouraged to join in organized sports and other community recreation programs.

Given the tremendous overcrowding in many penal and correctional institutions and their apparent ineffectiveness in overcoming the increase of crime and delinquency, criminal justice authorities are exploring new sentencing alternatives and methods of rehabilitating convicted offenders. One promising new approach is the boot camp method, in which young male offenders are sentenced to an intense ninety-day experience as a condition of probation. In the state of Georgia, for example, five inmate and six probation boot camps were established in the early 1990s, with a total of more than three thousand beds, for several levels of offender control. Each camp operates under military-like supervision, with emphasis on rehabilitative efforts to reduce recidivism, including behavior modification and values orientation.

Recognizing that youthful offenders typically engage in deviant acts during their leisure, the Georgia Department of Corrections developed a leisure education curriculum for each boot camp, consisting of lesson plans in the following areas: Introduction to leisure education; leisure awareness; decision-making; leisure skills (indoor and outdoor); leisure resources; social interactions; aerobics and fitness; and nutrition, health and wellness.[11]

At another level of prevention, Wayne Munson describes the growing role of therapeutic recreation specialists as ecological change agents in working with family groups to prevent dysfunctional behavior and juvenile delinquency.[12] Such practices reflect increasing public concern about various types of social problems that were rarely discussed or dealt with meaningfully in the past. Cynthia Carruthers and Colleen Hood, for example, describe in detail the role of leisure in the recovery of alcoholics and in working with the children of alcoholics.[13] Typically, they write, exposure to significant family dysfunction at an early age may interfere with the development of trust, autonomy, favorable self-concepts, and the ability to function as an individual separate from the family unit. Because many children with alcoholic family backgrounds experience play deprivation, leisure is an important area for intervention, offering assistance in experiencing cooperative play and impulse control and helping children develop balanced life-styles and satisfying social relationships.

Other investigators have examined the role of leisure in the lives of adult survivors of childhood sexual abuse. Such individuals tend in adulthood to be isolated from others and to lack a stable network of personal friendships because of their inability to trust. Leisure education experiences that include values clarification, social interaction, and relationship building are an important part of treatment programs for childhood-abuse survivors.[14]

Another special group that has been identified in recent years as having special needs with respect to leisure involves homosexual youth. Arnold Grossman points out that lesbian and gay youth are two to three times more likely to attempt suicide than heterosexual youth:

> This is one dramatic fact among the many that result from society's exclusion and stigmatization of lesbian, gay, and bisexual youth from its mainstream institutions. Other results of exclusion often include physical and verbal abuse, emotional stress, educational failure, rejection, and isolation from family and peers.[15]

As a result, many lesbian, gay, and bisexual youth undergo severe loneliness and pain, conceal their identities, and often become involved in self-destructive behavior. Grossman suggests that sensitive recreational and educational professionals can provide appropriate transitional experiences to such youth, to help them move toward a young adulthood of self-worth and acceptance, rather than self-denial and shame. Through drop-in centers, teen council activities in schools, leisure counseling, and "rap" groups, lesbian, gay, and bisexual youth can socialize in a healthy environment, receive accurate information about homosexuality and bisexuality, and develop positive peer and adult role models. Such experiences may include HIV/AIDS prevention education programs, which are desirable today for all youth groups, but especially important for gay, lesbian, and bisexual young people.

Intercultural Aspects of Leisure Service

Another critical area of socially oriented leisure service today concerns racial and ethnic minorities. James Murphy and Rene Dahl point out that many leisure-service professionals continue to operate as if they were programming for a traditional, homogeneous, white, middle-class public. The reality is that in the early 1990s, there were in the United States 30 million African Americans, 7.3 million Asian Americans, 22.4 million Hispanic Americans, and 2 million Native Americans—and that these totals are continuing to rise steadily.

Murphy and Dahl point out that leisure-service providers have customarily had four chief kinds of functions: (1) direct programming and leadership; (2) information and referral assistance; (3) enabling and facilitating, including leisure education and cooperative programming; and (4) advocacy. Today, these roles should be extended to ensure that members of ethnic and racial minorities have the opportunity to serve on recreation boards and commissions and to assist in developing programs that meet their unique needs and interests.[16]

The needs of newly entered immigrants from other regions of the world represent a pressing concern for recreation and park professionals. Louise Whelan, coordinator of the Open Door Society in Saskatoon, Saskatchewan, Canada, points out that substantial numbers of new Canadians are refugees from such areas as Africa, Central and South America, and Southeast Asia. While their initial needs center about housing, medical care, language difficulties, and employment assistance, their successful cultural readjustment soon requires that they begin to enter into the social and recreational fabric of their host communities. One effective way of dealing with such new Canadians, Whelan writes, has been to use crosscultural contacts made through a one-to-one matching system, with volunteers who provide English tutoring, friendship, and support and serve as a key to make Saskatoon's work and leisure opportunities more accessible.[17]

Beyond such efforts, many leisure-service agencies and government departments have made concerted efforts to improve the public's understanding and respect for those of different racial and minority backgrounds. In the United States, for example, such parks and historic sites as the Booker T. Washington National Monument, the San Antonio Missions National Historical Park, the Canyon de Chelly National

Monument, the Thaddeus Kosciuszko National Memorial, the Clara Barton National Historic Site, and Ellis Island are all elements of the National Park System that focus on ethnic and racial minorities or women who have played leading roles in American history. Local park and recreation departments may offer courses or events dealing with ethnic or racial history, arts, music, dance, cultural traditions, cooking, and similar subjects, along with folk festivals designed to promote intercultural understanding and fellowship (see Figure 14.1).

Needs of Other Groups

At another level, growing numbers of recreation and park professionals and leisure-service educators have begun to press for fuller attention to the needs of the homeless and the unemployed. Paula Dail points out that it is extremely difficult for homeless or runaway youth to function successfully either in school or interpersonally. She writes:

Slavic Heritage Celebration

Sunday, July 31, 1983   1 PM — 7 PM
Tibbetts Brook Park, Yonkers

Featuring:
- Pilsner Brass Band
- Limbora Slovak Dancers
- Ukrainian Band—Evatra (Bonfire)
- Harvest Moon Ball — Polish Polka Champions
- Troika Russian Balalaika
- Cultural Exhibits and Slavic Food

Rain site: Lemko Hall, 556 Yonkers Ave, Yonkers

Free admission
Parking charge $1.00 before 5 P.M.

Co-sponsored by:

Joseph M. Caverly
Commissioner
Department of Parks,
Recreation & Conservation
Westchester County

United Slavonian American League
President: Nicholas Benyo
Chairman: Paul Kubawsky
Co-Chairmen: Stephen Trusa
Dorothy Turchinsky
Hon. Chairman: Andrew P. O'Rourke

Hispanic Heritage Celebration 1983

Sunday, July 10th, 4 to 8 PM
Tibbetts Brook Park, Yonkers, N.Y.

Featuring:
- Johnny Colon Orchestra and East Harlem Workshop Band
- Hispanic Delicacies
- Spanish American Folk Lore Dance Group
- The Menudo Babes

Admission is free
Parking charge $1.00 before 5 PM

Please bring blankets or chairs

Rain site: Westchester County Center White Plains, N.Y.

Co-Sponsored by:

Andrew P. O'Rourke
County Executive
Joseph Caverly
Commissioner
Department of Parks
Recreation and Conservation
Westchester County

Westchester Hispanic Coalition Inc.
948-8466

FIGURE 14.1
Examples of ethnic heritage celebrations
SOURCE: Westchester County, New York, Department of Parks, Recreation and Conservation

males frequently join gangs, enter into a life of crime and encounter the juvenile justice system at a very early age. Adolescent females, who are more vulnerable to street life, often engage in prostitution to earn money, and become involved with individuals who will "protect" or "defend" them. . . . Without intense, ongoing social support, and interpersonal caring, the probability that they will continue this lifestyle into adulthood is high.[18]

Recreation programs may be invaluable in helping such individuals learn important social skills, use their time constructively, and establish links to self-help community agencies. Robin Kunstler points out that a number of such projects have been successfully established in cities like New York, making use of city shelters, youth and mental-health centers, and hospitals as initial contact sites. Since homeless persons are often fiercely protective of their independence and resist agencies that treat them as helpless "clients," Kunstler writes:

> Recreation and leisure service professionals who can connect with [homeless] individuals by establishing contact, listening, developing a trust relationship and providing opportunities for recreation participation . . . may well be at the forefront of successful intervention. . . .[19]

⏩ TO THE POINT

Summing up the social mission that challenges the park and recreation field today, H. Douglas Sessoms and Dennis Orthner point out that many leisure-service professionals are seeking to rediscover their traditional goals as they deal with such problems as an influx of immigrants, the presence of street people, migrant workers, and the trauma of drug abuse, youth gangs, and urban crime. They continue:

> Discussions about management strategies, pricing policies and risk management simply do not do the job of instilling a sense of place and purpose for what parks and recreation is about. They may be critical professional issues, but they leave us short as we communicate to our constituents the importance of what we are doing and why parks and recreation is an essential public service. . . . Has parks and recreation lost its soul? Has it become so institutionalized and administratively focused that it has lost a sense of purpose and direction? Has it become so middle class that it has forgotten those who are unable to pay its entry fees or program charges; that it is no longer a service to all? Many say "yes," and that is why some say our leisure service delivery system is in crisis.[20]

■ INFLUENCE OF THE MARKETING ORIENTATION

In sharp contrast to the human-service emphasis just described, a so-called marketing orientation has become increasingly influential in the leisure-service field over the past two decades.

Initially, recreation was regarded as an essentially free public service like highways, police protection, and elementary and secondary education—paid for through taxes, but without charges at the point of service delivery. Gradually, as more varied and elaborate facilities began to be built—such as swimming pools, tennis courts, golf courses, indoor skating rinks, and marinas—it became customary to charge modest fees for their use. Throughout the decades after World War II, the use of fees and charges—for registration, admission, instruction, use of equipment, and other services—was the subject of an ongoing debate. Those opposed to them argued that they represented a form of double taxation and that they tended to exclude children, the elderly, the disabled, and the poor from participation. Those in favor of fees and charges argued that they were essential to maintain and expand programs in an era of fiscal austerity.

In time, the argument became moot, as most public recreation and parks systems on local, state, and federal levels imposed fees and charges on a wide range of program activities. Community residents tended to accept such policies without objection. For example, in a study conducted by Economic Research Associates in the mid-1970s, most citizens interviewed felt that more recreation services should be on a pay-as-you-go basis.[21] Recreation and park administrators reported that although initial resistance to new or increased fees was reflected in a short-term decline in usage, this effect tended to disappear in two or three years. In some cases, higher fees were followed by *increased* attendance at facilities.

In a 1988 report, Howard and Cable found that although members of the public generally selected the lowest price alternative when asked what they would be willing to pay for a given recreation service, they indicated readiness to pay higher fees when given fuller information about the need for such charges.[22] Techniques such as public relations campaigns, gradual increments in charges, fee-by-fee analysis to determine appropriate pricing levels, and annual passes with higher charges for nonresidents were all used to gain public support.

▮▶ TO THE POINT

An outstanding example of contemporary marketing approaches of public recreation and park departments may be found in Prince William County, Virginia, where the Chinn Aquatic and Fitness Center offers a huge, spectacular indoor pool with whirlpools, saunas, and an outdoor sunbathing deck, along with a large gymnasium and fitness room equipped with the latest weight-training technology. Services provided at the Chinn Center include aerobic classes, dance programs, computerized fitness assessments, child care, birthday parties and facility rentals, youth activities, and other family program features. Built at a cost of $10.4 million, the complex makes use of varied fee structures, including youth, senior, and couple discounts; daily admissions charges; and six-month and one-year pass plans. Annual membership charges in the publicly owned facility ranges fom $160 for senior residents of Prince William County to $655 for nonresident couples.

Such efforts were not unique to public recreation and park agencies. Many organizations, like voluntary youth associations, religious federations, and others, began to use high-powered promotional techniques to gain public support and increase their revenue sources. For example, in the past, armed forces recreation programs had been financed by a combination of appropriated funds (tax moneys allocated by Congress) and nonappropriated funds (derived from on-base revenues from messes, vending machines, and post-exchange stores). Gradually, during the 1980s, the level of appropriated funds for recreation in the military was cut back. In 1991, Bill Mullins wrote:

> Few of us could have predicted a decade ago that military recreation programs would obtain additional operating funds by literally turning trash into cash, soliciting corporate sponsorships, or promoting, administering and operating leisure travel services. These enterprises, among other initiatives, are helping military recreation professionals manage their fiscal transition into the twenty-first century.[23]

Recreation and park educator John Crompton rejects the notion that the term *marketing* is a euphemism for *hucksterism,* and that it is concerned only with "selling" programs or gathering revenues. In his view, the key benefits of marketing-oriented revenue-generating approaches to recreation and park management are that they:

- Provide increased resources which can be directed to favored projects for which there would otherwise be no funds.
- Are lauded by elected officials because tax support is reduced (or services are increased/enhanced without a tax increase).
- Offer a wider range of services to citizens without increasing taxes, which increases the department's citizen/political constituency support.
- Enhance political strength which may be associated with generating revenues from non-tax sources.
- Enhance reputation for being an innovator/leader in the city.
- Increase incentive for staff to offer high quality and relevant services. Pricing services builds in accountability. The services have to meet a real need and their quality has to be high or people will not pay for them.
- Offer staff a new challenge and thus induce an atmosphere of vitality, energy, and excitement in the agency.[24]

■ CHALLENGES TO THE MARKETING ORIENTATION

At the same time, a number of critics have expressed serious concerns about the implications of the leisure-service field's having moved so sharply into an entrepreneurial mode. For example, Dustin, McAvoy, and Schultz argue strongly that the chief purpose of the recreation and park profession must be to promote human growth and development. When the need for profitability takes over, they write: "we are concerned about the possibility that the values and purposes underlying the traditional public delivery of park and recreation services will be undermined by the values and purposes underlying business practices."[25]

⫸ TO THE POINT

In a study of the fiscal policies of park and recreation agencies in several hundred cities in the United States, Mark Havitz and Clarence Spigner asked whether these agencies offered discounts or free admissions to members of five categories of individuals: senior citizens, children, low-income people, students, and the unemployed. It was found that while a majority of agencies offered discounts to children and the elderly, relatively few offered them to unemployed persons. No data were reported with respect to free-admission policies, and it was apparent that the leisure needs of economically disadvantaged persons did not represent a significant concern for the agency managers surveyed—in comparison to park and recreation directors in other nations, such as Great Britain, where sports leagues were often targeted for communities with high unemployment rates.[26]

Clearly, there is a sharp contrast between the two administrative approaches—one that assigns heavy priority to public leisure-service agencies seeking to meet important social needs within their communities, and the other that stresses marketing and revenue-source management goals. How are these two conflicting orientations to be reconciled?

Combining Marketing and Human-Service Approaches

Ronald Riggins suggests that public recreation has several distinctive functions that should supersede purely economic concerns. First, he writes, public recreation and parks must consider the leisure needs of *all* citizens and must advocate and protect the broadest possible fabric of recreation opportunity within the community setting:

> It is charged with the responsibility to consider more than the economic attraction of an activity, the size and "purchasing power" of the group seeking participation, or the social, political and economic status of the persons in that group. This obligation lies at the root of the public parks and recreation movement.[27]

Riggins makes clear that commercial recreation businesses have no such responsibility, and that bringing the profit-oriented drive of entrepreneurism into the public sector with the result of neglecting the legitimate leisure interests of any group of citizens is a questionable trend. The need to serve the public interest, Riggins writes, is the basis of the social contract that has long existed between recreation and park managers and their constituents. For professionals to take on a commercial mentality that responds almost exclusively to those who can afford to pay for leisure services is wrong. The task is to balance the need for economic viability and agency efficiency with a renewed commitment to the profession's traditional service mission. Riggins concludes:

We must revitalize the message that recreation services in the public sector exist, not solely because of their economic value, but in response to the basic right of all Americans to pursue happiness, a pursuit inextricably bound to the quest for a meaningful life. A socially responsible government has the fundamental obligation to respond to demands fostered by this right.[28]

Clearly, all leisure-service agencies that hope to survive—and flourish—within a difficult economic climate *must* take into account the principles and methods of entrepreneurial marketing in planning programs and facilities. However, these must be blended with the traditional social mission of recreation and parks, applied to the problems that face contemporary society. Efforts must be made to encourage or cosponsor neighborhood revitalization projects, experimental programs like Chicago's midnight basketball league for at-risk youth, innovative employment opportunities in human services and community beautification, and similar ventures. Beyond this, some authorities argue that the harsh disparities between inner cities and their surrounding suburbs can only be overcome if regional approaches are adopted in the planning and provision of education, health, transportation, recreation, and other services. And this process must inevitably deal with the rapidly changing social, economic, and demographic conditions of the nation that will take shape as we move into the twenty-first century.

■ CHARTING THE FUTURE: CHALLENGES OF THE YEARS AFTER 2000

The rate of change over the past century has been immense, in terms of population growth, the improvement of medical care and the extension of life expectancy, technological advancement, and the growth of cities. What changes can we look forward to in the future, and how will these affect our life-styles, our social values, and our patterns of leisure and recreational participation? Predicting the future is always uncertain, and yet it is possible to define a number of oncoming trends with reasonable assurance by extending current population shifts and economic and technological developments.

In 1990, the United Way of America's Strategic Institute, working with its volunteer Environmental Scan Committee, identified more than one hundred specific trends in contemporary society and grouped them into nine major "change-drivers" for the 1990s. These forces included the steady maturation of American society in terms of aging and social and political changes; increasing diversity moving the nation from a "mass" to a "mosaic" society; redefinition of individual and societal roles, with a blurring of the differences between public and private-sector functions; continued growth of an information-based economy; the increased globalization of business and economic activity; personal and environmental health becoming key areas of public concern; a major restructuring of global economic patterns and American businesses; redefinition of traditional concepts of family and home; and, finally, a rebirth of social activism.[29]

In 1992, writing in the *Journal of Park and Recreation Administration,* Daniel McLean and Ruth Russell discussed a number of other projected trends that social scientists believe lie ahead. These include such elements as a stronger "greening movement" based on continuing environmental decline; increased economic dislocation and social malaise for many families; the emergence of new leadership, based on "powershifts" involving the knowledgeable, the news media, and the innovator. McLean and Russell write:

> Anticipatory democracy will be more prevalent at all levels. There will be a decentralization of power in all organizations with a disappearance of large sectors of middle management. Visionary leaders will be the leaders of the future—those who can share and empower others in their vision. [There will be a] social revolution different from any experienced before. . . . promoted by humans who have evolved into opportunity creators—people who imagine, create, and implement opportunities for better futures.[30]

Clearly, not all of these dramatic predictions are likely to prove correct. However, both social scientists and the public at large do expect major shifts to take place in every area of social, personal, and economic life. This was illustrated in an issue of *Time* published in October 1992, which dealt with predictions for the new millennium. The American public was polled with the question: "If you had to predict, which of the following are likely to occur in the twenty-first century?" Percentages of affirmative answers were:

- Scientists will find a cure for AIDS (75%)
- Scientists will find a cure for cancer (80%)
- The average American will live to be 100 (57%)
- A woman will be President of the U.S. (76%)
- A black will be President of the U.S. (76%)
- Automobiles will no longer run on gasoline (75%)
- Computers will be as smart as humans and have personalities like humans (44%)
- Humans will make regular trips to other planets (43%)
- Beings who live on other planets will come in contact with us (32%)

Some public expectations were negative; those polled felt that there would be more environmental disasters, poverty, and disease in the twenty-first century. However, they also felt that there was hope for the future, and that religion would play a greater role in the lives of Americans after the year 2000.[31]

■ PREDICTIONS AFFECTING AMERICAN LIFE-STYLES AND LEISURE BEHAVIOR

Apart from such global concerns, numerous social scientists, futurists, and planning groups have projected contemporary trends to identify probable changes with respect to population shifts, family life, patterns of employment, changing social values, and other factors affecting leisure in American life.

Expected Population Changes

In a summary of demographic shifts expected to occur over the next three decades, *Fortune Magazine* predicted: (1) that life expectancy for both men and women would increase steadily in this period, with a dramatic rise in Medicare costs; (2) that by 2010, areas like New England and Florida would have the highest proportion of elderly citizens, with baby-boomers reaching sixty-five and the number of retirees rising to thirty-three million citizens, compared to twenty-five million in 1991; and (3) the cost of Social Security payments would reach $558 billion in 1991 dollars in 2020, almost double the level in 1995.[32]

A 1990 report published by the Hudson Institute and the Retirement Policy Institute warned that America could face a retirement crisis, as the burden of financing retirees' benefits falls on a steadily declining working force. However, earlier predictions that the birthrate would continue to decline were reversed in 1992, when Census Bureau reports documented a new "baby boomlet," which, if the trend continued, would result in ten million more children being born by the year 2000 than the bureau had originally predicted.[33]

Other predicted demographic changes will affect the male/female balance in American society in the years ahead. In the late 1980s, it was reported that the scarcity of American males of marriageable age and the abundance of females that had characterized the 1970s and 1980s was shifting, and that through the twenty-first century there would be a surplus of adult males and an undersupply of females. This change is likely to affect the social behavior of men and women. According to University of Houston social scientists Marcia Guttentag and Paul Secord, when eligible males are comparatively rare, there is a tendency for them to exploit the situation.

> In such a society, men have multiple relationships with women and become less willing to commit themselves to one woman in marriage. But when young males are more numerous than females, the situation turns around and men are more eager to pursue marriage.[34]

During the late 1980s, the average age at first marriage for women began to drop, and the number of family households increased. With the expected rise in the birthrate and a leveling off of divorces, the growing number of families with young children will have important implications for recreation and leisure. Jib Fowles writes:

> the new marrieds will be allocating dollars for the improvement of their homebound leisure activities. Systems that get movies into living rooms by one means or another will do well, and so will subscription magazines and recreational equipment for families with children. Vacations will involve travel to sites of family recreation. The national parks are going to be even more heavily used, and Disneyland will find others trying to move in on its expanding market. The travel will be done in mid-sized vehicles; the family van is the wave of the future.[35]

At the same time, other social scientists predict that family life will continue to become increasingly complex and diverse. The typical nuclear family of the 1950s and 1960s will become a phenomenon of the past. Instead, growing numbers of families in the twenty-first century will be divided by divorce, multiplied by remarriage, expanded by new birth technologies—or perhaps all of the above. Single parents and working mothers will be more common, as will out-of-wedlock babies, although the concept of the "illegitimate" child will diminish as the patriarchal nuclear family disappears. While couples who remain together through a lifetime will still be a major sector of the family spectrum, serial monogamy will become increasingly accepted, as the extended family becomes more prevalent.

The number of never-married individuals increased steadily from 1970 to 1991, according to a 1992 Bureau of the Census report. About one-fourth of American adults eighteen and older—41.5 million—have never married, and the total number of single persons, including divorced, widowed, and never married, rose from thirty-eight million to seventy-one million, proportionately from 28 percent to 39 percent.[36]

Life may become more difficult for middle-aged couples who will be part of extended family networks of crisscrossing loyalties and obligations. As life spans lengthen and marriages multiply, they could find themselves caring all at once for aging parents, frail grandparents, children still in school, and perhaps even a step-grandchild or two. It is predicted that the number of Americans sixty-five and older will reach sixty-five million by the year 2030, compared with thirty million in the early 1990s. As the number of those who are eighty-five and older increases fivefold to fifteen million within the next three decades, there will be a boom in the number of retirement communities for the affluent and nursing homes for many others.

Particularly as the baby-boom generation joins the ranks of the elderly in the next century, an "elder culture"—a return to the values and life-styles that these individuals experienced during the 1960s—is likely to appear. Writing in *The Christian Century,* Wade Roof suggests that the "boomers," who grew up with tightly defined peer groups and experimented with communes and life-style enclaves in their teenage and early adult years and who later dealt with a myriad of crises and addictions, are likely to seek out a variety of new communities. Roof predicts that in a land of extended old age, we can:

> Expect elderhostel programs to flourish, offering opportunities to meet and socialize with like-minded people. The search for community will take many forms in many places: expect a mushrooming of gatherings in shopping malls, libraries, churches and other public centers, wherever groups can assemble around common concerns. . . .
>
> "Networking" will become an even more encompassing concept. Boomers will not lack for therapists if that's what they want, and many will. They will pursue recreation and celebrate nature: expect more camping, sailing, gardening, bird-watching, recycling. The generation that popularized the backpack, gave us the ecology movement and inspired Earth Day is not likely to back away from such concerns in their old age.[37]

Where People Will Live: Urban Trends and "Edge" Cities

Linked to predictions of population shifts are new expectations of where many people will live. The post–World War II years saw major shifts in residential patterns, with millions of middle-class Americans moving from central cities to suburbs, and many others moving from the older, colder Rust Belt states of the Northeast and Midwest to Sun Belt states in the South, West, and Southwest. The 1990 census showed, for example, how California's population grew to almost thirty million people, while Texas and Florida grew respectively by 20 and 30 percent during the preceding decade.

The 1980s ended with 75 percent of the nation's population living in big cities or their suburbs. In part, the urban growth was caused by an influx into the cities of immigrants and small-town dwellers fleeing depressed economic conditions and limited job opportunity. But it was also a result of so-called urban sprawl—the gradual envelopment of suburban and rural areas by larger cities. Inescapably, there is the problem of fiscal crises affecting all levels of government as a result of economic recessions and increased costs of education, social services, and city management. In 1991, *Business Week* reported:

> Across the country, state and local governments are grappling with budget deficits adding up to more than $40 billion—and still rising. Localities large and small are hiking taxes and slashing budgets. . . . Some 30 states face deficits, as do dozens of cities, towns, and counties. . . . In the 1980s, almost every state found its budget being pulled upward, willy-nilly, by the relentless rise in education, medicaid, and prison expenses.[38]

While attention has chiefly been focused on the social problems of large cities, the reality is that many smaller communities are suffering as well. Long-term poverty is more severe in rural areas, with a substantial underclass of both blacks and whites in southern states, from Appalachia to the Mississippi Delta. Throughout the Midwest and the plains states, many small towns have lost substantial numbers of their populations, and rural organizations like the Grange, which typically offered rich leisure opportunities to farm families, are declining in number.

At the same time, a new kind of American living environment has been steadily emerging—the so-called edge city. In *Edge City: Life on the New Frontier,* Joel Garreau describes the new kind of community that has resulted from the mushrooming office–corporate–shopping mall–residential development encircling many of America's largest cities.[39] In these new urban centers, we see "the culmination of a generation of individual American value decisions about the best ways to live, work and play." Edge cities usually do not fall within a single governmental unit's control, but operate under quasi-nongovernmental associations that act as "shadow governments." Heavily dependent on automobile access, and with enforcement policies that keep out the homeless, the poor, the beggars, and others who are unattractive or "inconvenient," these new American "Main Streets," contrast sharply with older cities. At the same time, they lack the grand parks, boulevards, concert halls, museums, and other amenities of central cities—and are described by many residents as "plastic," a "hodgepodge," or "sterile."

Racial and Ethnic Diversity

Another critical aspect of the oncoming twenty-first century will be the way America responds to the continuing growth of its racial and ethnic minorities. Between 1980 and 1990, the Census Bureau reported that Asian Americans in six ethnic groupings grew from 2.5 million to 7.2 million. The expectation is that Hispanic Americans will increase from fifteen million in 1980 to approximately fifty-five million in 2020, passing African Americans, who will total about forty-two million in the same year. Census demographers predict a more crowded, ethnically diverse America:

Imagine a United States crowded with 128 million more people than there are today, where one in five citizens is Hispanic, where Asians are gaining in numbers on blacks, and non-Hispanic whites represent only a bit more than half of the population.[40]

➨ TO THE POINT

The overall challenge will be to upgrade the level of educational achievement of all minority groups and to improve their occupational status in order to ameliorate the conditions that have made substantial segments of these populations a deprived "underclass" in American society. During the early 1990s, there was evidence that African Americans in particular were making progress in terms of years of schooling completed, political involvement and offices held, reduction of racist values within the society at large, and acceptance of outstanding African Americans as cultural heroes through sports and the mass media of entertainment. Harvard sociologist and prize-winning author Orlando Patterson makes a strong case that racism and discrimination are declining in the United States:

> America, while still flawed in its race relations and its stubborn refusal to institute a rational, universal welfare system, is now the least racist white-majority society in the world; has a better record of legal protection of minorities than any other society, white or black; offers more opportunities to a greater number of black persons than any other society, including all of Africa; and has gone through a dramatic change in its attitude toward miscegenation. . . . [41]

At the same time, with greater numbers of nonwhites, it is probable that frictions among these different groups will mount. In Florida, for example, there have been sharp clashes between African Americans and Hispanics—particularly Cuban Americans—over jobs and political influence. In other regions, hostility has mounted between Korean shopkeepers and black residents in urban ghettoes. Friction exists among different segments of the overall Asian-American community. And, strikingly, feminism and the general concept of multiculturalism may be increasingly at odds, as many of the traditional values of Eastern and African-influenced cultures with respect to women clash with American values and life-styles.

For example, women occupy a markedly inferior position in fundamentalist Islamic communities. In Hispanic and some Asian cultures, male machoism or dominance within the family structure accepts the view that a wife's infidelity should be punished by death at the betrayed husband's hands. Cathy Young writes of the immolation of widows and female infanticide in Hindu society, and cliterodectomy, polygamy, and the acceptance of wife-beating in much of Africa, pointing out that advocates of multiculturalism rarely refer to such practices, while at the same time criticizing America for discrimination against minorities and women. She concludes:

> The double standard is blatant. The only civilization that has made an effort to overcome its sexist traditions, the West is berated for failing to do away with them com-

pletely. The Third World cultures are treated as static; it is noble to try to protect the primitive tribes' ancestral customs from the onslaught of Western ways.[42]

As the proportion of non-Western and nonwhite families grows in the United States, issues of acculturation become acute. Young points out that current "politically correct" thinking urges that immigrants and their children be encouraged to preserve their cultural values; assimilation is viewed as a form of psychic warfare. But what if these values include polygamy, arranged marriages of nine-year-old girls, or wife-slaying to redeem the husband's "honor"? Such issues are likely to confront leisure-service managers as they seek to work constructively to reduce interracial tensions and help in the building of integrated social relations in American communities.

Shifting Patterns of Employment

Meanwhile, what of work itself—the key element that determines how much free time people have, and how much discretionary income they have to indulge their recreational interests?

During the 1970s and 1980s, the U.S. Bureau of Labor Statistics predicted a continuing but gradual rise in the size of the labor force, with women becoming an increasingly larger segment of job-holders. The nature of work itself was expected to be influenced by a proliferation of "knowledge workers," who prepare newsletters, tapes, information transmission materials, and similar products for education, training, and other business uses. In general, a long-term trend from blue-collar to white-collar jobs was expected, along with a decline in farm work and manufacturing employment and an increase in service industries.

Other trends that were predicted at this time included the growth of part-time jobs and job-sharing, particularly for men and women who sought to combine paid work with family responsibilities. Moonlighting—the holding of more than one position—was expected to remain fairly constant, with multiple jobholders about 4.5 percent of the work force. Because of technological changes, it was anticipated that there would be a high rate of job obsolescence, compelling many individuals to seek new jobs or enter second, third, or even fourth career fields during their working lives.

In a study of job trends reported in *The Futurist* in 1991, it was predicted that the highest percentage of increase in new jobs would be in technical fields related to health and human services. Leisure-related job fields designated as among the fifty fastest-growing of all job titles recognized by the Labor Department were: travel agents, human-services workers, recreational therapists, childcare workers, social workers, and landscape architects.[43]

Impact of Automation

Clearly, any vision of what the future holds, in terms of job availability and employment patterns, will depend on the degree to which automation supplants human effort. Each year, there are increasingly impressive accounts of new industrial automatons—or, to use the more popular term, *robots*. Unlike the versions portrayed in science fiction, industrial robots are not strange, exotic beings. Instead, they are machines that can be programmed to carry out simple, repetitive tasks that are usually performed by human workers. Hess, Markson, and Stein write:

> Like people, robots can be moved from one job to another and can learn new tasks. Unlike people, they can work two or three shifts a day, six or seven days a week, and do not take coffee breaks, vacations, sick leave, expect to be paid, or argue with management. Nor are they affected by industrial hazards such as radioactivity, toxic wastes, or pollution.[44]

Japan in particular has pioneered in the use of giant computerized machines; in 1981, Steve Lohr described the night-shift scene in a Japanese machinery works:

> . . . the machines work unassisted. The place is rather dimly lit. One solitary human sentinel—the night watchman—patrols the factory floor, armed with a flashlight, as the machines labor on. Each machine works independently, making an individual part different from its neighboring machining center. The computer tells a machine tool to drop one task, pick up another, speed up, slow down, or whatever—all in sync with the overall, computerized production plan. The scene here is one of eerie, antiseptic efficiency. Everything is clean, oiled and steely. No coffee cups, cigarette butts or the other flotsam of human activity is to be found.[45]

Ten years later, Japanese engineers have moved almost to the point of creating robots that will be able to assemble other robots. If all goes according to plan, Vernon Loeb writes:

> a new generation of [Japanese] robots with artificial intelligence could actually start reproducing within five years, assembling other robots like brooms in *The Sorcerer's Apprentice*. These neurocomputer-equipped automatons would be so sophisticated that they could actually deduce what task needed to be accomplished next, paving the way for far more complex responsibilities. "Absolutely no people are necessary," Yoshinori Kozai, a senior vice president, says with quiet satisfaction.[46]

TO THE POINT

The implications are tremendous. In an article on "The Workless Society" in *The Futurist,* it is predicted that in the twenty-first century, intelligent machines will replace almost all workers, and people will get paid for doing nothing, in a life of ease and abundance.[47] Of course, the use of automation will apply to some fields, such as manufacturing, agriculture, mining, and transportation, more fully than it will to service fields that involve working directly with people.

Despite *The Futurist*'s predictions, the wholesale replacement of human workers by machines is still not an immediate threat in the United States. Apart from their widespread use in automobile manufacturing, robots have not been widely introduced to the American workplace. The National Service Robot Association had about 250 individual and corporate members in 1992, most trying to develop machines that would clean hazardous-waste sites, deliver food in hospitals, or assist the disabled. However, as new functions for the application of artificial intelligence are discovered and machines to carry them out are created, it seems probable that economic reasons for applying them will outweigh social concerns about displaced workers.

If this occurs, and if large numbers of working men and women are displaced from the nation's economy, it is clear that American society will face a critical choice. Historian Christopher Lasch points out that the prospect of universal abundance made progress a morally compelling ideology in the past. But, writes Lasch, affluence for all now appears unlikely, even in the distant future; the emergence of a global economy, far from eliminating poverty, has widened the gap between rich and poor nations, and poverty is spilling over into the developed nations from the Third World. The increase in the numbers of homeless, unemployed, illiterate, drug-ridden, and other effectively disfranchised people is a clear indication of this trend in America. He continues:

> The well-being of democracy, a political system that implies equality as well as liberty, hangs in the balance. A continually rising standard of living for the rich, it is clear, means a falling standard of living for everyone else. Forcible redistribution of income on a massive scale is an equally unattractive alternative. The best hope of reducing the gap between rich and poor lies in the gradual emergence of a new consensus, a common understanding about the material prerequisites of a good life. Hard questions will have to be asked. Just how much do we need to live comfortably? How much is enough?[48]

Lasch asks whether we can afford to continue the trend of the 1980s, which saw the rich get richer and the poor get poorer. Similarly, Hess, Markson, and Stein suggest that if work tasks are not distributed more evenly, a society could arise made up of a busy elite of professionals and a "useless" majority unable to master the critical skills of the job world:

> . . . an elite of "gods" doing the work and a majority of "clods" getting in the way. An extreme example of such a society was described by the novelist Kurt Vonnegut in *Player Piano,* where the gods are PhDs in engineering in control of an almost automated world, the clods are either in the army where they march endlessly or engaged in digging purposeless ditches and filling them once again.[49]

■ FUTURE LEISURE TRENDS

Assuming that advancing automation provides expanded amounts of free time—whether wanted or not—for substantial segments of the population, how will this discretionary time be spent?

Influence of Technology

It seems clear that technology will continue to shape our recreational experiences in novel new ways. In the recent past, new kinds of equipment and modes of transport have enabled us to expand our outdoor pursuits by traveling through the air with ballooning, parasailing, hang gliding, and skydiving, or over and under the water with jet skis and scuba gear. Now, just as Americans became familiar with computers

Reflecting contemporary leisure interest in technologically based forms of play and future-oriented career pursuits, the unique U.S. Space Camp program, affiliated with NASA, familiarizes young people with astronaut and mission training and space technology. Above and left, students at its Huntsville, Alabama, Aviation Challenge camp learn aerobatics, instrument navigation, air-to-air intercepts and simulated water survival techniques. Below, adult enthusiasts learn auto racing skills at popular Skip Barber Racing School in Connecticut.

and VCRs in recent years, they will learn to use CD-ROMs (compact disc-read only memory) in the decades ahead. First introduced to the book industry in the early 1990s, this technological device is a form of electronic book that is capable of providing access to all twenty-six volumes of a major encyclopedia on a single five-inch disc, and combining text, high-resolution color pictures, stereo sound, and video in unified presentations.

In another application of electronic technology, computer consultants have now developed the concept of the "electronic coffeehouse," in which "cyberpunks" (computer enthusiasts) are able to meet and chat with their counterparts in dozens of other cafes hooked up to a common network. This concept builds on the existing use of computer dating services and electronic bulletin boards to provide a new means of sociability in contemporary society.[50]

Other forms of leisure activity, Philip Elmer-Dewitt writes, are likely to fit into familiar forms over the years immediately ahead. However, after a few decades, they will begin to blend together and lose their distinct identities. TVs, VCRs, CD players, computers, telephones, video games, newspapers, and mail-order catalogues will merge to create new products and services that can only be dreamed about today. New versions of transportation, communication, game-playing, and even love-making, Elmer-Dewitt writes, will all be transformed by emerging technologies. For example, it will be possible to play Ping-Pong or any other sport with phantasms that look and talk like the celebrity of your choice. Or, more romantically, one might enjoy sex over the telephone by slipping into undergarments lined with sensors and miniature actuators, dial one's partner, and, while whispering endearments, fondle each other over long-distance lines.[51]

Popular entertainment is likely to diversify in a bewildering way in the years ahead. Fiber-optic cable will bring hundreds, even thousands, of TV channels into the home, and interactive computer technology will give viewers almost total control over what they wish to see. Richard Zoglin suggests that the oncoming wave of pop-culture images borrowed from "quick-cut" and "in-your-face" style sitcoms and music videos is likely to affect Americans and make them less literate. While the visual image will be more familiar and communicative to people, at the same time, there will be a general decline of language. He continues:

> Our connection with the real world may grow ever more tenuous as images increasingly supplant words and symbolic gestures overwhelm rational argument. The portent is ominous. How can an electorate conditioned by MTV ever have the patience to solve the budget deficit?[52]

Trends in Managed Recreation Programs

It is likely that globally distributed forms of entertainment will become even more prevalent, and giant conglomerates will increasingly control tourism, home entertainment, and other commercial amusements. The use of outdoor recreation resources will become more and more congested with population growth, and distinctly different travel patterns will emerge in terms of distance covered, activities enjoyed, and cost factors—all influenced by participants' age and economic and family status.

Government agencies like the Forest Service or the Bureau of Land Management have sought to anticipate these changes and to expand their efforts to meet the outdoor recreation needs of varied population groups while maintaining the ecological health of the nation's natural resources. For example, the Bureau of Land Management has developed a set of priorities for the year 2000, which includes such strategies as upgrading visitor information and interpretation, monitoring resource protection, improving access to scattered or fragmented public land, developing partnerships with volunteers and volunteer groups, and working effectively with tourism organizations and the travel industry.

Other public recreation sponsors will continue to diversify their offerings, including redesign of major aquatic and sports facilities. Swimming pool designers, for example, will abandon the rectangular lap-pool concept in favor of the leisure-pool idea, with an ocean-cruise or tropical-beach ambience and with a variety of water-based fun experiences. Al Turner describes some of the elements that will be found in such public pools in the years ahead:

> In addition to a serpentine flume [the] community aquatic center might contain a teen/adult pool with a thriller speed slide, lily pad or log walk, water cannons and fountains, and still have room for the occasional lap swimmer. . . . spray-and-splash jungle gyms, miniature waterslides. . . . can provide kids—and their parents—with hours of fascination. The resurgence of the American family spirit means that families want to enjoy interaction.[53]

Clearly, sports and fitness activities will continue to represent a major form of leisure interest in the decades ahead. Whether home viewing becomes the major form of sports spectatorship through pay-for-view and cable television cannot be predicted. While it might make more sense from a commercial vantage point to eliminate or sharply cut back live audiences and frame major sports events within a studio-like format, the appeal of fans cheering and the spectacle of marching bands, cheerleaders, costumed mascots, and similar paraphernalia undoubtedly would be missed in such spartan presentations.

Adult Education

For all groups, education will continue to be an important aspect of leisure in the twenty-first century. However, as Fred Best and Ray Eberhart write, education needs to transform itself from a youth-oriented institution to one that serves growing numbers of adults. In part, the future of adult education will be shaped by the needs of the economy, in terms of meeting skills gaps in a rapidly changing work world. In addition, it will also contribute to parents' ability to raise children, deal with medical and health problems, and make intelligent decisions about increasingly complex social and public issues. Beyond such "useful" purposes, continuing education throughout the life span will bring fuller awareness of the arts, of human culture, of history, languages and a host of other aspects of contemporary life that will enrich and bring pleasure to persons of every age. Best and Eberhart point out that in the future, education will be provided by many different types of organizations:

Employer-provided education and training; proprietary schools and private colleges; community organizations; voluntary and foundation-supported education; public and private higher-education extension programs; and publicly funded adult education (adult schools, community colleges, prison and correctional education, job-training programs, public and state libraries).[54]

It is likely that municipal and county recreation and park departments will continue to provide impressive arrays of adult classes in the arts, sports and fitness activities, family-living skills, investment and finance, current events, and various other areas of personal enrichment. Television will play an important role in this process. For example, in the early 1990s, the Children's Television Workshop developed a new program titled "Ghostwriter"—a suspenseful, literacy-training adventure series designed to be used in cooperation with 4-H Clubs, the YMCA, the Girl Scouts, Boys and Girls Clubs, and other community agencies.

Leisure and Economic Growth

Finally, it is clear that in the future, leisure will continue to provide a key force in the national economy and in international trade. As earlier chapters have shown, over the past several decades, numerous cities whose manufacturing and industrial bases had declined found that their economic health depended increasingly on varied forms of leisure activity. Urban waterfront development, the preservation of historic neighborhoods, conventions, sports, festivals, and performing arts programs all serve not only to bring visitors to cities, but also to enhance the cities' image in the public eye. On the international scene, regional businesses will continue to be sustained by the flow of tourism—including American citizens and growing numbers of visitors from other nations.

Beyond this, American forms of entertainment and popular culture are presently dominating the leisure hours of numerous other countries and bringing sizable revenues that help to overcome the nation's balance-of-trade deficit. All indications are that this favorable situation will accelerate in the years ahead.

■ CHALLENGES FACING LEISURE AND RECREATION IN THE TWENTY-FIRST CENTURY

Given the dramatic population, social, and economic changes that futurists predict for the United States in the twenty-first century, what kinds of policies and decisions are likely to assist the nation in adapting to the world of tomorrow? Six major challenges face planners and administrators within the broad field of leisure services as well as other policymakers in the nation at large.

Leisure Haves and Have-Nots: The Distribution of Free Time

If we continue on the road to increased automation, it seems inevitable that more and more people will either be permanently unemployed or will work only periodically at low-level jobs in the economy. The implications of this trend for the living standards and morale of those at the lower end of the socioeconomic scale are frightening. One might envision a replay of the decline of the Roman empire in modern dress—with new versions of "bread and circuses" devised to keep the poor reasonably content in their nonproductive roles and their too-abundant leisure. By the same token, the problem of the harried upper classes—lavish incomes offset by a growing time famine—is unenviable.

Will it be possible to develop a system of social and economic planning that will ensure that there will be an adequate supply of work for all classes and that no single group is burdened either by excess toil or by interminable leisure? While this may appear to be an unrealistic expectation, it is clear that the human consequences of having a major portion of the nation's adult population unemployed and living on the dole will be socially and psychologically demoralizing.

Cultural Diversity and the American Mosaic

The second challenge will be to recognize that the old image of the American melting pot has really disappeared and that the stereotypical image of the nuclear family with mom, dad, and the kids living in a comfortable home on a tree-lined street in a warm and friendly small town does not conform to reality. As America's racial and ethnic minorities have steadily grown in numbers and influence, we have become the world's most diverse nation. The task of leisure and recreation in the years ahead will be to creatively reflect the differing cultural values, customs, and contributions of all the social groups that make up the American mosaic—and to use them to promote intercultural understanding and acceptance.

Beyond this, the roles of leisure and recreation in serving different kinds of families, individuals with alternative life-styles, those with varying sexual orientations, and the physically, mentally, and socially disabled, will also be critical. Here, the task will be to merge the two kinds of priorities discussed earlier—the need to fulfill recreation's historic social mission and to do so in an economically viable way.

Environment as a Continuing Concern

A third important challenge will be to renew our concern with the nation's environment through continuing efforts to protect and restore wilderness areas, streams, lakes, and rivers, historic sites, and open space surrounding our cities. Here, the need will be to control the outdoor recreation pursuits that imperil the environment—such as the overcrowding of national and state parks and forests, the use of off-road vehicles that threaten wildlife and vegetation, and the pollution of streams and lakes by harmful boating practices.

At the same time, it will be necessary to broaden our understanding of the environment. For too many people, environment consists of crowded and ugly tenements, streets and alleys, abandoned factories, and decayed and unused waterfronts. Some cities have achieved brilliant success in restoring such areas and making them appealing both for residents and for tourists, and rehabilitating local parks and playgrounds to make the daily environment of people attractive and safe. Communities throughout the nation must follow their example and enlist organizations of every kind in volunteer, cooperative efforts to restore both urban and rural environments.

Public Leisure Values and "Morally Marginal" Play

While it is tempting to think of leisure only in terms of the healthy pleasures and creative social values it offers, another major side of it consists of the public's wholesale involvement in pursuits such as gambling, substance abuse, and commercialized sex.

⏵ TO THE POINT

In the past, our efforts to control such negative forms of play through government control and interdiction have proven largely unsuccessful, as in the cases of Prohibition or the current effort to stop narcotic drug trafficking. While such efforts must continue, it seems clear that they should be accompanied by a major, comprehensive thrust toward educating people, both about the dangerous and negative aspects of such pursuits and about the positive and enriching benefits of other forms of recreation. The mandate to educate our nation's youth for leisure that was first expressed in the *Cardinal Principles of Secondary Education* (see page 47) has never been fully accepted or carried out. As discretionary time grows in the years ahead, it is essential that agencies of all kinds—schools, colleges, community recreation departments, employee services programs, and others—join together to promote fuller leisure awareness and healthy participation for all age groups in society. The task will be to inculcate positive leisure values and to equip people, whether young or old, with the knowledge and skills to enjoy leisure to the fullest, and to see it as the source not only of pleasure but of personal enrichment and social benefits as well. In schools and colleges, this can be done by appropriate curriculum planning in such fields as the arts, physical education, and social studies, and by providing a rich variety of extracurricular offerings. In community agencies serving young adults, the middle-aged, and the elderly, both public and nonprofit voluntary agencies will have the responsibility for offering courses, clinics, and ongoing recreation programs that will meet leisure education goals at each age level.

Coordination of Leisure Services

A fifth challenge in the twenty-first century will be for all the diversified elements in the leisure-service delivery system to coordinate their efforts and to work cooperatively to provide the richest and most effectively managed base of recreational opportunity for the American public. While government regulation would be neither appropriate nor legally possible, public leisure-service agencies may well take the lead in conducting studies of leisure needs and interests. Joint sponsorship of activities, coordination of program schedules and special events, leadership training, and sharing of facilities and other resources are all possible outcomes of such efforts. In cities where the financial resources of government are too limited to carry out traditional recreation and park functions, it may be necessary for volunteer community groups of neighborhood residents to take fuller responsibility for managing leisure facilities and operating programs. In such situations, the role of some recreation and park professionals may shift from direct management to becoming catalysts and enablers.

Advancing Professionalism

A final challenge that confronts those who work in the broad field of leisure services is to continue to advance the level of professional practice. In some specializations, such as therapeutic recreation, this is being done with improved programs of professional preparation, the application of sound job credentialing systems, and the work of professional societies.

However, if the field of leisure service is to gain fuller public recognition as a significant area of social responsibility, it must do certain things. First, the training of its practitioners should incorporate fuller exposure to relevant disciplines such as psychology and social psychology, social work, urban planning, political science, and management theory. Recognizing the need for leisure services to adapt to a truly multicultural society, there must be fuller emphasis on issues of human growth and development, population diversity, gender issues, and the greatest possible range of social outcomes in leisure planning and programming.

At the same time, leisure professionals must continue to respect the simple human appeal of recreational involvement for most persons—the desire for fun and pleasure, the need for a sense of personal achievement, the delight in outdoor play and in sports competition, the rewards of group involvement and sociability, and the ultimate triumph of having realized one's own creative potential through leisure experience. Along with the social and economic values of recreation that have been stressed in this chapter, the unique appeal of leisure for the individual and its potential for spiritual re-creation and recovery from stress are elements that will persist in the years to come.

■ SHIFT IN PUBLIC VALUES: THE "SIMPLE LIFE"

In the early 1990s, there was growing evidence that Americans had turned away from the gaudy dreams, materialism, and consumerism of the preceding years and were beginning to turn toward simpler pleasures and homier values. Psychologists, social critics, and theologians were reporting a movement toward quieter and more relaxed life-styles, less-pressured careers, and more meaningful family involvement. In a *Time*/CNN poll of representative adults, 61 percent agreed that earning a living today "requires so much effort that it is difficult to find time to enjoy life." Only a few thought it important to keep up with fashions, trends, and status-symbol products, while a strong majority agreed that it was important to give personal interests and hobbies a high priority. Janice Castro concluded that many Americans were

> thinking hard about what really matters in their lives, and they've decided to make some changes. What matters is having time for family and friends, rest and relaxation, good deeds and spirituality. For some people that means a radical step: changing one's career,

living on less, or packing up and moving to a quieter place. For others it can mean something as subtle as choosing a cheaper brand of running shoes or leaving work a little earlier to watch the kids in a soccer game.[55]

Certainly, leisure-service professionals can do much to promote such positive values and changing life-styles, as part of their overall mission in American life. If they are able to meet the six challenges that have been presented in this chapter successfully, the words of President W. A. Griswold of Yale University, cited earlier in this text, will have renewed meaning:

> Now we stand on the threshold of an age that will bring leisure to all of us, more leisure than all the aristocracies of history, all the patrons of art, all the captains of industry and kings of enterprise ever had at their disposal. . . . What shall we do with this great opportunity? In the answers that we give to this question the fate of our American civilization will enfold.[56]

■ SUMMARY

Two conflicting priorities exist in recreation and leisure service: (1) the human-service orientation, which sees the provision of leisure programs for the disadvantaged, at-risk youth, and other special populations as a primary mission; and (2) the entrepreneurial, marketing approach that has gained influence in the field over the last two decades, and has relatively little concern about leisure's social agenda. These two sets of priorities must be reconciled in leisure-service managers' principles and strategies, if the field is to maintain its fundamental identity and at the same time retain fiscal viability. This chapter concludes with a number of economic and social forecasts for the century that lies ahead, with accompanying predictions with respect to leisure's role and trends in the future. The key issue has to do with society's willingness to distribute work responsibilities more equitably, so that all have a reasonable share of both work and leisure—as opposed to the possibility that a relatively small number of people will have long work hours and secure economic futures, while many others do not work and are dependent on public subsidy for support. Linked to this, the chapter suggests six major challenges that face both leisure-service planners and managers and the society at large, in the decades ahead.

■ QUESTIONS FOR DISCUSSION

1. Make a strong case for emphasizing socially oriented programs in community recreation agencies to meet critical neighborhood needs related to crime and delinquency, health trends, social relationships, and other concerns. Then present a positive rationale for the marketing emphasis found throughout the leisure-service field today. Can the two approaches exist side by side, or are they mutually incompatible?

2. What are some of the key changes in society that are predicted for the years ahead, in terms of population shifts and technological development, that will affect leisure programming? How should leisure-service planners and managers prepare to meet such changes?

3. Inadequate public support for organized public leisure services and the popularity of varied types of self-destructive and essentially negative pastimes suggest a need for a renewed effort to promote education for leisure in American society. Support this argument, if you can, and suggest how such educational efforts might be implemented.
4. This chapter describes a tradeoff between the benefits of economic progress that might be made possible through fuller automation, and the negative effects of reducing work, particularly for a substantial segment of the population. What would it mean to society to have a huge mass of more or less permanently unemployed adults? How could work and free time be fairly redistributed in ways acceptable to the public at large?
5. Express in your own words the key priorities facing recreation, park, and leisure-service professionals in the years ahead, and suggest ways in which these varied challenges might best be met.

■ NOTES

1. HENRY, W. 1992. Ready or not, here it comes! *Time* (Fall, special issue): 32.
2. STORMANN, W. 1991. The ideology of the American urban parks and recreation movement: Past and future. *Leisure Sciences* 13: 137–151.
3. DUNCAN, M. 1990. Back to our radical roots. In *Recreation and leisure: Issues in an era of change,* ed. T. L. Goodale and P. A. Witt. State College, PA: Venture, pp. 407–415.
4. *National urban recreation study: Summary.* February 1978. U.S. Department of Interior Report. Washington, DC: U.S. Government Printing Office.
5. *Ibid.,* p. 14.
6. FOLEY, J., and H. PINK. 1992. Taking back the parks: Addressing 'recreation apartheid.' *Leisure Watch* 5, 3 (Fall): 1–5.
7. TICE, R. D. 1992. NRPA perspective: The urban challenge. *Parks and Recreation* (April): 6.
8. FOLEY, J., and V. WARD. 1993. Recreation, the riots and the healthy LA. *Parks and Recreation* (March): 68.
9. GODBEY, G. 1991. Redefining public parks and recreation. *Parks and Recreation* (Oct.): 57.
10. ROBINSON-YOUNG, P. 1992. Recreation's role in gang intervention. *Parks and Recreation* (March): 55.

11. GRIMES, P., and M. FAIN. 1992. Leisure education: Does it work in boot camp? *Parks and Recreation* (March): 46.
12. MUNSON, W. 1991. Juvenile delinquency as a societal problem and social disability: The therapeutic recreator's role as ecological change agent. *Therapeutic Recreation Journal* (Second quarter): 19–30.
13. CARRUTHERS, C., and C. HOOD. 1992. Alcoholics and children of alcoholics: The role of leisure in recovery. *Journal of Physical Education, Recreation and Dance* (April): 48–51.
14. MEISTER, T., and A. PEDLAR. 1992. Leisure patterns and needs of adult survivors of childhood sexual abuse. *Journal of Physical Education, Recreation and Dance* (April): 52–55.
15. GROSSMAN, A. 1992. Inclusion not exclusion: Recreation service delivery to lesbian, gay and bisexual youth. *Journal of Physical Education, Recreation and Dance* (April): 45.
16. MURPHY, J., and R. DAHL. 1991. The right to leisure expression. *Parks and Recreation* (Sept.): 106–109.
17. WHELAN, L. 1987. Working with refugee newcomers in Saskatchewan. *Recreation Canada* (Oct.): 30–33.
18. DAIL, P. 1992. Recreation as socialization for the homeless: An argument for inclusion.

Journal of Physical Education, Recreation and Dance (April): 37.

19. KUNSTLER, R. 1992. Forging the human connection: Leisure services for the homeless. *Parks and Recreation* (March): 45.

20. SESSOMS, H. D., and D. ORTHNER. 1992. Parks and recreation and our growing invisible populations. *Parks and Recreation* (Aug.): 62.

21. *Fees and charges handbook.* 1979. Washington, DC: U.S. Department of the Interior, Heritage Conservation and Recreation Service, p. 15.

22. HOWARD, D., and S. CABLE. 1988. Determining consumers' willingness to pay for park and recreation services. *Trends* (NRPA and National Park Service) (Second quarter): 32.

23. MULLINS, B. 1991. Managing fiscal transition. *Parks and Recreation* (Oct.): 38.

24. CROMPTON, J. 1988. Are you ready to implement a comprehensive revenue-generating program? *Parks and Recreation* (March): 56.

25. DUSTIN, D., L. McAVOY, and J. SCHULTZ. 1990. Recreation rightly understood. In Goodale and Witt, *op. cit.,* pp. 97–105.

26. HAVITZ, M., and C. SPIGNER. 1992. Access to public leisure services: A comparison of the unemployed with traditional target groups. *Journal of Physical Education, Recreation and Dance* (April): 41.

27. RIGGINS, R. 1988. Social responsibility and the public sector entrepreneur. *Journal of Physical Education, Recreation and Dance* (Oct.): 60.

28. *Ibid.,* p. 61.

29. United Way Strategic Institute. 1990. Nine forces reshaping America. *The Futurist* (July-Aug.): 9–16.

30. McLEAN, D. D., and R. V. RUSSELL. 1992. Future visions for public park and recreation agencies. *Journal of Park and Recreation Administration* 10, 1: 48–49.

31. The future poll. *Time* (Special issue, Fall 1992): 12–13.

32. How America will change over the next 30 years. *Fortune* (June 17, 1991): 12.

33. SPIERS, J. 1992. The baby boomlet is for real. *Fortune* (Feb 10): 101–104.

34. GUTTENBERG, M., and P. SECORD. 1988. In J. Fowles, Coming soon: More men than women. *New York Times* (June 5): F–3.

35. *Ibid.*

36. DUBIN, M. 1992. Unaltered states: More and more have not married. *Philadelphia Inquirer* (July 17): A–2.

37. ROOF, W. 1990. The spirit of the elderculture. *The Christian Century* (May 16): 529.

38. The sad state of the states. *Business Week* (April 22, 1991): 24–25.

39. GARREAU, J. 1991. *Edge city: Life on the new frontier.* New York: Doubleday.

40. BLONSTON, G. 1992. Study sees a more crowded, ethnically diverse America. *Philadelphia Inquirer* (Dec. 4): A–25.

41. PATTERSON, O. 1992. Cited in L. Harrison, The black success story isn't being told. *Philadelphia Inquirer* (June 27): A–9.

42. YOUNG, C. 1992. Feminism and multiculturalism: An uncomfortable coexistence. *Philadelphia Inquirer* (April 2): A–21.

43. Work: Fastest growing jobs in America. *The Futurist* (July-Aug. 1991): 49.

44. HESS, B., E. MARKSON, and P. STEIN. 1988. *Sociology.* New York: Macmillan, p. 619.

45. LOHR, S. 1981. New in Japan: The manless factory. *New York Times* (Dec. 13): 3–1.

46. LOEB, V. 1991. Building the worker of the future. *Philadelphia Inquirer* (April 14): D–1.

47. TOTH, K. 1990. The workless society. *The Futurist* (May-June): 33.

48. LASCH, C. 1992. Is progress obsolete? *Time* (Fall, special issue): 71.

49. HESS, MARKSON, and STEIN, *op. cit.*

50. BISHOP, K. 1992. The electronic coffeehouse. *New York Times* (Aug.2): v-3.

51. ELMER-DEWITT, P. 1992. The century ahead: Dream machines. *Time* (Fall, special issue): 39–40.

52. ZOGLIN, R. 1992. Beyond your wildest dream. *Time* (Fall, special issue): 70.

53. TURNER, A. 1991. Public pool 2000. *Parks and Recreation* (Nov.): 48.

54. BEST, F., and R. EBERHARD. 1990. Education for the era of the adult. *The Futurist* (May-June): 23.

55. CASTRO, J. 1991. The simple life. *Time* (April 8): 58.

56. GRISWOLD, W. A. 1959. Special issue on leisure. *Life Magazine* (Dec.): 59.

Bibliography

ANDRE, JUDITH, and DAVID JAMES. 1991. *Rethinking College Athletics*. Philadelphia: Temple University Press.

ARIAN, EDWARD. 1989. *The Unfulfilled Promise: Public Subsidy of the Arts in America*. Philadelphia: Temple University Press.

BAKER, WILLIAM J. 1988. *Sports in the Western World*. Urbana, IL: University of Illinois Press.

BALTZELL, E. DIGBY. 1964. *The Protestant Establishment: Democracy and Caste in America*. New York: Random House.

BAMMEL, GENE, and LEI LANE BAMMEL. 1991. *Leisure and Human Behavior*. Dubuque, IA: Wm. C. Brown.

BELL, DANIEL. 1959, 1988. *The End of Ideology*. Cambridge, MA: Harvard University Press.

BODE, CARL. 1959. *The Anatomy of American Popular Culture, 1840–1861*. Berkeley, CA: University of California Press.

BRIGHTBILL, CHARLES. 1961. *Man and Leisure: Philosophy of Recreation*. Englewood Cliffs, NJ: Prentice Hall.

BULLARO, JOHN, and CHRISTOPHER EDGINTON. 1986. *Commercial Recreation Service*. New York: Macmillan.

BUTLER, GEORGE. 1959. *Introduction to Community Recreation*. New York: McGraw-Hill.

BUTSCH, RICHARD, ed. 1990. *For Fun and Profit: The Transformation of Leisure into Consumption*. Philadelphia: Temple University Press.

BYRNE, EDMUND. 1990. *Work, Inc.: A Philosophical Inquiry*. Philadelphia: Temple University Press.

CAILLOIS, ROGER. 1961. *Man, Play and Games*. London: Thames and Hudson.

CALDERONE, MARY. 1970. *Sexuality and Man*. New York: Charles Scribner's Sons.

CAVALLO, DOMINICK. 1981. *Muscles and Morals: Organized Playgrounds and Urban Reform*. Philadelphia: University of Pennsylvania Press.

CHARLESWORTH, J. C., ed. 1964. *Leisure in America: Blessing or Curse?* Lancaster, PA: American Academy of Political and Social Science.

CHU, D. 1989. *The Character of American Higher Education and Intercollegiate sport.* Buffalo, NY: University of New York Press.

CHUBB, MICHAEL, and HOLLY CHUBB. 1981. *One Third of Our Time: An Introduction to Recreation Behavior and Resources.* New York: John Wiley.

CROSS, GARY, ed. 1988. *Worktime and Industrialization: An International History.* Philadelphia: Temple University Press.

DE BEAUVOIR, SIMONE. 1965. *The Second Sex.* New York: Bantam.

D'EMILIO, J., and E. FREEDMAN. 1988. *Intimate Matters: A History of Sexuality in America.* New York: Harper and Row.

DE GRAZIA, SEBASTIAN. 1952. *Of Time, Work and Leisure.* New York: Twentieth Century Fund.

DULLES, FOSTER. 1965. *A History of Recreation: America Learns to Play.* New York: Appleton Century Crofts.

DUMAZEDIER, JOFFRE. 1974. *Sociology of Leisure.* Amsterdam: Elsevier.

DURSO, JOSEPH. 1975. *The Sports Factory.* New York: Quadrangle.

EDWARDS, JERRY. 1973. *Sociology of Sport.* Homewood, IL: Dorsey Press.

ELLIS, M. J. 1973. *Why People Play.* Englewood Cliffs, NJ: Prentice Hall.

ELLIS, TAYLOR, and RICHARD NORTON. 1988. *Commercial Recreation.* St. Louis: Times-Mirror Mosby.

EPPERSON, ARLIN, ed. 1986. *Private and Commercial Recreation.* State College, PA: Venture.

FALUDI, SUSAN. 1992. *Backlash: The Undeclared War Against American Women.* New York: Crown.

FINDLAY, J. 1986. *People of Chance: Gambling in American Society from Jamestown to Las Vegas.* New York: Oxford University Press.

FINE, R. 1987. *The Forgotten Man: Understanding the Male Psyche.* New York: Haworth.

FRAZIER, E. FRANKLIN. 1957, 1962. *Black Bourgeoisie.* New York: Collier.

FURNAS, J. D. 1969. *The Americans: A Social History of the United States.* New York: G. P. Putnam's Sons.

GALBRAITH, J. K. 1958. *The Affluent Society.* Boston: Houghton Mifflin.

GANS, HERBERT. 1962. *The Urban Villagers: Group and Class in the Life of Italian-Americans.* New York: Free Press.

GARREAU, JOEL. 1991. *Edge City: Life on the New Frontier.* New York: Doubleday.

GLAZER, NATHAN, and DANIEL MOYNIHAN. 1963. *Beyond the Melting Pot: The Negroes, Puerto Ricans, Jews, Italians and Irish of New York City.* Cambridge, MA: M.I.T. Press.

GODBEY, GEOFFREY. 1989. *The Future of Leisure Services: Thriving on Change.* State College, PA: Venture.

GODBEY, GEOFFREY. 1990. *Leisure in Your Life: An Exploration.* State College, PA: Venture.

GODBEY, GEOFFREY, and STAN PARKER. 1976. *Leisure Studies and Services.* Philadelphia: W. B. Saunders.

GOODALE, THOMAS, and GEOFFREY GODBEY. 1988. *The Evolution of Leisure: Historical and Philosophical Perspectives*. State College, PA: Venture.

GOODALE, THOMAS, and PETER WITT. 1990. *Recreation and Leisure: Issues in an Era of Change*. State College, PA: Venture.

GRAEFE, ALAN, and STAN PARKER, eds. 1987. *Recreation and Leisure: An Introductory Handbook*. State College, PA: Venture.

GREENBERG, D. 1988. *The Construction of Homosexuality*. Chicago, IL: University of Chicago Press.

GUTTMANN, ALLEN. 1988. *A Whole New Ball Game: An Interpretation of American Sports*. Chapel Hill, NC: University of North Carolina Press.

GUTTMANN, ALLEN. 1991. *Women's Sport: A History*. New York: Columbia University Press.

HACKER, A. 1992. *Two Nations: Black and White, Separate, Hostile, Unequal*. New York: Charles Scribner's Sons.

HAMPER, BEN. 1991. *Rivethead: Tales from the Assembly Line*. New York: Warner.

HARRIS, LOUIS. 1987. *Inside America*. New York: Random House, Vintage.

HARRIS, MARVIN. 1981. *America Now: The Anthropology of a Changing Culture*. New York: Simon and Schuster, Touchstone.

HENDERSON, KARLA, M. DEBORAH BIALESCHKI, SUSAN SHAW, and VALERIE FREYSINGER. 1989. *A Leisure of One's Own: A Feminist Perspective on Women's Leisure*. State College, PA: Venture.

HOBERMAN, JOHN. 1984. *Sports and Political Ideology*. Austin, TX: University of Texas Press.

HOLLINGSHEAD, A. B. 1949. *Elmtown's Youth: The Impact of Social Class on Adolescents*. New York: John Wiley.

HUIZINGA, JOHAN. 1950. *Homo Ludens: A Study of the Play Element in Culture*. Boston: Beacon.

HUNNICUTT, BENJAMIN. 1988. *Work Without End: Abandoning Shorter Hours for the Right to Work*. Philadelphia: Temple University Press.

INGE, M. THOMAS. 1989. *Handbook of American Popular Culture*. Westport, CT: Greenwood.

ISO-AHOLA, SEPPO. 1980. *The Social Psychology of Leisure and Recreation*. Dubuque, IA: Wm. C. Brown.

JACKSON, EDGAR, and THOMAS BURTON, eds. 1989. *Understanding Leisure and Recreation: Mapping the Past, Charting the Future*. State College, PA: Venture.

JAFFE, CAROLE. 1986. *The Regulation of Sexuality*. Philadelphia: Temple University Press.

JURY, MARK. 1977. *Playtime: Americans at Leisure*. New York: Harcourt Brace Jovanovich.

KANDO, THOMAS. 1980. *Leisure and Popular Culture in Transition*. St. Louis: C. V. Mosby.

KASSON, J. 1978. *Amusing the Millions: Coney Island at the Turn of the Century*. New York: Hill and Wang.

KELLY, JOHN. 1985. *Recreation Business*. New York: John Wiley.

KELLY, JOHN. 1987. *Freedom to Be: A New Sociology of Leisure*. New York: Macmillan.

KELLY, JOHN. 1990. *Leisure*. Englewood Cliffs, NJ: Prentice Hall.

KNAPP, RICHARD, and CHARLES HARTSOE. 1979. *Play for America: The N.R.A., 1906–1965*. Arlington, VA: National Recreation and Park Association.

KNUDSON, DOUGLAS. 1980. *Outdoor Recreation*. New York: Macmillan.

KRAUS, RICHARD. 1990. *Recreation and Leisure in Modern Society*. Glenview, IL: Scott, Foresman.

KRAUS, RICHARD, and JOSEPH CURTIS. 1990. *Creative Management in Recreation, Parks and Leisure Services*. St. Louis: Times-Mirror Mosby.

LARRABEE, ERIC, and ROLF MEYERSOHN, eds. 1958. *Mass Leisure*. Glencoe, IL: Free Press.

LASCH, CHRISTOPHER. 1979. *The Culture of Narcissism: American Life in an Age of Diminishing Expectations*. New York: Warner.

LEE, ROBERT. 1964. *Religion and Leisure in America*. Nashville, TN: Abingdon.

LINDER, STAFFAN. 1970. *The Harried Leisure Class*. New York: Columbia University Press.

LYNES, RUSSELL. 1949, 1980. *The Tastemakers: The Shaping of American Popular Taste*. New York: Simon and Schuster.

MANNING, ROBERT. 1986. *Studies in Outdoor Recreation: Search and Research for Satisfaction*. Corvallis, OR: University of Oregon Press.

MEDVED, MICHAEL. 1992. *Hollywood vs America: Popular Culture and the War on Traditional Values*. New York: Harper Collins.

MESSNER, MICHAEL, and DONALD SABO. 1990. *Sport, Men and the Gender Order: Critical Feminist Perspectives*. Champaign, IL: Human Kinetics Books.

MILLAR, SUSANNAH. 1968. *The Psychology of Play*. New York: Penguin.

MOORE, JOAN. 1978. *Home Boys: Gangs, Drugs and Prison in the Barrios of Los Angeles*. Philadelphia: Temple University Press.

MURPHY, JAMES, E. WILLIAM NIEPOTH, LYNN JAMIESON, and JOHN WILLIAMS. 1991. *Leisure Systems: Critical Concepts and Applications*. Champaign, IL: Sagamore.

NASH, JAY B. 1960. *Philosophy of Recreation and Leisure*. Dubuque, IA: Wm. C. Brown.

NEALE, ROBERT. 1969. *In Praise of Play: Toward a Psychology of Religion*. New York: Harper and Row.

NELSON, MARIAH. 1991. *Are We Winning Yet? How Women Are Changing Sports and Sports Are Changing Women*. New York: Random House.

NEUMEYER, MARTIN, and ESTHER NEUMEYER. 1936, 1949. *Leisure and Recreation: A Study of Leisure and Recreation in Their Sociological Aspects*. New York: A. S. Barnes.

OGLESBY, CAROLE, ed. 1978. *Women and Sports*. Philadelphia: Lea and Febiger.

OUTDOOR RECREATION RESOURCES REVIEW COMMISSION. 1962. *Report to the President and Congress*. Washington, DC: U.S. Government Printing Office (27 volumes).

OXENDINE, JOSEPH. 1988. *American Indian Sports Heritage*. Champaign, IL: Human Kinetics Books.

PARKER, STANLEY. 1976. *The Sociology of Leisure*. London: George Allen and Unwin.

PEISS, KATHY. 1986. *Cheap Amusements: Working Women and Leisure in Turn-of-the-Century New York*. Philadelphia: Temple University Press.

PIEPER, JOSEF. 1952. *Leisure: The Basis of Culture*. New York: Mentor-Omega: New American Library.

RADER, BENJAMIN. 1983. *American Sports from the Age of Folk Games to the Age of Spectators*. Englewood Cliffs, NJ: Prentice Hall.

RADER, BENJAMIN. 1984. *In Its Own Image: How Television Has Transformed Sports.* New York: Free Press.

RAINES, J., and D. DAY-LOWER. 1986. *Modern Work and Human Meanings.* Philadelphia: Westminster.

RAPOPORT, ROBERT, and RHONA RAPOPORT. 1975. *Leisure and the Family Life Cycle.* London: Kegan Paul.

REISSMAN, LEONARD. 1959. *Class in American Society.* Glencoe, IL: Free Press.

ROCKEFELLER PANEL REPORT. 1965. *The Performing Arts: Problems and Prospects.* New York: McGraw-Hill.

ROJEK, CHRIS. 1985. *Capitalism and Leisure Theory.* London: Tavistock.

ROSENBERG, BERNARD, and DAVID WHITE. 1957. *Mass Culture: The Popular Arts in America.* Glencoe, IL: Free Press.

RUSKIN, HILLEL, ed. 1984. *Leisure: Toward a Theory and Policy.* Rutherford, NJ: Fairleigh Dickinson University.

RYBCZYNSKI, WITOLD. 1991. *Waiting for the Weekend.* New York: Viking.

SCHOR, JULIET. 1991. *The Overworked American: The Unexpected Decline of Leisure.* New York: Basic Books.

SCHUR, EDWIN. 1988. *The Americanization of Sex.* Philadelphia: Temple University Press.

SESSOMS, H. DOUGLAS. 1984. *Leisure Services.* Englewood Cliffs, NJ: Prentice Hall.

SHIVERS, JAY. 1981. *Leisure and Recreation Concepts: A Critical Analysis.* Boston: Allyn and Bacon.

SINGER, JUNE. 1976. *Androgyny: Toward a New Theory of Sexuality.* New York: Anchor.

SMIGEL, ERWIN, ed. 1962. *Work and Leisure.* New Haven, CT: College and University Press.

TIGER, LIONEL. 1969. *Men in Groups.* New York: Random House, Vintage.

TOFFLER, ALVIN. 1964. *The Culture Consumers.* New York: St. Martin's Press.

VANNEMAN, REEVE, and LYNN CANNON. 1987. *The American Perception of Class.* Philadelphia: Temple University Press.

VEAL, A. J. 1987. *Leisure and the Future.* London: Allen and Unwin.

VEBLEN, THORSTEIN. 1899, 1912. *The Theory of the Leisure Class.* New York: Macmillan.

WARNER, W. LLOYD, and P. S. LUNT. 1941. *The Social Life of a Modern Community.* New Haven, CT: Yale University Press.

WILLIAMS, ROBIN M., JR. 1970. *American Society: A Sociological Interpretation.* New York: Knopf.

WYSZOMIRISKI, MARGARET. 1987. *Congress and the Arts: A Precarious Alliance.* New York: American Council for the Arts.

Photo Credits

(t) = top; (c) = center; (b) = bottom; (l) = left; (r) = right

page 6: (t) International Association of Amusement Parks and Attractions; (c) White Water, Inc., Columbus, Ohio, courtesy Renee Heuss; (b) Marketing Group, for Sylvan Pools, Doylestown, Pennsylvania, courtesy Amy Smith.

page 62: (t) Zoological Society of San Diego, California, Ron Garrison, photographer; (c) Larson Company, Tucson, Arizona, courtesy Suzy Tipton and Dennis Farris; (b) Department of Parks, Recreation and Conservation, Westchester County, New York, courtesy Karen Sposato.

page 72: (t) Leisure Services Department, Portsmouth, Virginia, courtesy Dr. L. Pettis Patton; (c, b) Department of Parks, Recreation and Conservation, Westchester County, New York, courtesy Karen Sposato.

page 91: (tl) Robert Kaiser, Eugene, Oregon; (tr) courtesy Edd Davis, U.S. Space and Rocket Center, Huntsville, Alabama; (c) Prof. Al Jackson, Chico, California; (b) courtesy Ralph Cryder, Director, Department of Parks, Recreation and Marine, Long Beach, California.

page 130: (tl, tr) courtesy Prof. Sue Durrant, Washington State University, Pullman; (b) Smith College Archives, Northhampton, Massachusetts, Carolyn Dash, photographer.

page 140: Kathy Borchers, photographer, *The Providence Journal*.

page 148: Ferrari Publications, Phoenix, Arizona, courtesy Marianne Ferrari.

pages 168, 169: (all) Ron Tarver, staff photographer, *Philadelphia Inquirer*.

page 178: (t, c) courtesy Ralph Cryder, Director, Department of Parks, Recreation and Marine, Long Beach, California; (bl) Sugarbush Resort, Warren, Vermont, Dennis Curran, photographer; (br) Robert Leake, Church of Jesus Christ of Latter-Day Saints, Salt Lake City, Utah.

page 195: (t, c) San Francisco R.C.H., Inc., courtesy Ola Kupka, Bill Cogan, photographer; (bl, br) Department of Parks, Recreation and Marine, Long Beach, California.

page 207: (tl) Rivers Resort Complex, Lansing, West Virginia; (tr) Woodswomen, Inc., Minneapolis, Minnesots, courtesy Denise Mitten; (bl, br) National Outdoor Leadership Schol, Lander, Wyoming, courtesy Sukey Hohl, Maurice Witsch, photographer.

page 210: (tl) Rio Parismina Lodge, Costa Rica; (tr) Allagash Guide Service, Allagash, Maine, courtesy Bob Condon; (b) Winterhawk Outfitters, Silt, Colorado, courtesy Larry Amos.

page 223: (tl) Randall West, photographer; (tr) Richard Twarog, photographer, courtesy Steve Sandoval; (bl, br) Royal Caribbean Cruises, Ltd., Cocoanut Beach, Florida.

page 229: (t, l) Silver Springs, Florida, courtesy Lisa Westerfield; (r) Busch Entertainment Corporation, courtesy Robyn de Ridder (©1992 Florida Cypress Gardens, Inc., all rights reserved).

page 242: Aquatic Center, University of Minnesota, courtesy Duane Proell, Wendell Vanderlee, photographer.

page 258: (t) Nick Bollettieri Tennis Academy, Inc., Bradenton, Florida, courtesy Bill Rompf, photograph by James Bollettieri; (bl) Arthur Ashe Tennis Center, Philadelphia, courtesy Wendy Tank-Nielsen; (br) National Foundation of Wheelchair Tennis, San Clemente, California, courtesy Wendy Parks.

page 260: (t) Hershey Foods Corporation, Hershey, Pennsylvania, courtesy Lisa Schlegel; (bl, br) Plainfield, Indiana, Community Middle School, courtesy Jerry Goldsberry, principal.

page 273: (t) Children's Theatre, courtesy Tracy Evans; (c, b) Vero Beach Center for the Arts, courtesy Joe Ellis.

page 275: (t) Krannert Center for the Performing Arts, University of Illinois, courtesy Jan McCracken; (c) courtesy Mike Anderson and Ottawa Department of Recreation and Culture; (b) Randolph-Macon Women's College, Lynchburg, Virginia, courtesy Elizabth Shipp.

page 304: Roberts River Rides, Dubuque, Iowa, courtesy Kathy Bearce.

page 311: (all) courtesy Prof. Connie O'Connor, California State University at Chico.

page 338: (all) YWCA of City of New York, courtesy Paulette Crowther; (tl) Jonathan Snow, photographer; (tr) Bettye Lane, photographer.

page 340: (t) Morale, Welfare and Recreation Division, U.S. Navy, courtesy Ed Pratt; (bl, br) Orlando, Florida, Naval Training Center, courtesy Steve Gergick.

page 355: (t) Department of Parks, Recreation and Conservation, Westchester County, New York, courtesy Karen Sposato; (c) John Cross, photographer, *The Free Press*, Mankato, Minnesota; (b) Leisure Services Department, Portsmouth, Virginia, courtesy Dr. L. Pettis Patton.

page 379: (tl, tr, c) U.S. Space Camp, Aviation Challenge Program, courtesy Edd Davis; (b) Skip Barber Racing School, Canaan, Connecticut, courtesy Rick Roso.

Author Index

Lynd, Robert and Helen, 49, 158
Lynes, Russell, 160
Lyng, Stephen, 219

McAvoy, Leo, 197, 206, 216–217, 368
Maccoby, Michael, 32
McDonald, Dwight, 268
McDonough, Maureen, 111
McGuire, Frank, 186, 209
McLean, Daniel, 370–371
Mancini, J., 191–192
Mann, F., 139
Manning, Robert, 216
Marshall, Thurgood, 88
Massengale, J., 246–247
Mathiesen, James, 239
Mazzarella, S., 182–183
Mechling, Jay, 141
Meyer, Harold, 92
Mills, C. Wright, 60
Mobily, Kenneth, 184
Mullins, Bill, 368
Munson, Wayne, 363
Murphy, James, 364
Murphy, Michael, 341
Murphy, Teresa, 38–39
Myrdal, Gunnar, 51

Nash, Jay B., 48
Nash, Roderick, 219–220
Neugarten, Bernice and Dail, 176
Neumeyer, Martin and Esther, 48
Northrup, Solomon, 41–42

Oakley, Sidney, 312
O'Connor, John, 104
O'Connor, Kathleen, 134
O'Leary, J., 186, 209
Orlean, Susan, 24
Orthner, Dennis, 191–192, 366
Osgood, Nancy, 176–177, 185, 187

Packard, Vance, 159
Pancner, Carol, 111
Pantopinto, J., 127
Parks, Frances, 104
Peiss, Kathy, 50, 124
Peterson, Don, 220
Pieper, Josef, 8–9

Pink, H., 360
Pitts, Brenda, 145–146
Podilchak, Walter, 299
Prebish, Charles, 240

Rader, B. G., 98, 239, 247–248, 255
Rancourt, Ann, 317
Rannells, J., 124
Ranney, S. R., 206
Ravitch, D., 85, 90
Reich, Robert, 164
Reissman, L., 159
Richardson, S., 346
Riesman, David, 161
Riggins, Ronald, 369–370
Robinson-Young, Pamela, 362
Roggenbuck, J. W., 300
Rojek, Chris, 15–16, 170
Roof, Wade, 176, 373
Rosaldo, Renato, 89
Rubarth, Lisa, 135
Ruskin, John, 30
Rybczynski, Witold, 23, 26, 76–77
Rynder, J., 197

Sabo, D., 127
Sage, George, 238
Samuelson, Robert, 75
Schleien, Stuart, 197
Schor, Juliet, 74–75
Schroedel, J., 121
Schultz, John, 368
Schur, Edwin, 148, 317–318
Scott, D., 186
Seefeldt, Vern, 261
Sessoms, H. Douglas, 312, 350, 353–354, 366
Seton, Ernest, 108
Shank, John, 125–126
Shaw, Susan, 125
Short, J. F., 95–96
Sifford, Darrell, 211
Smith, Ralph, 194
Snyder, E. E., 70
Sobel, Robert, 75
Spigner, Mark, 369
Spock, Benjamin, 181–182
Spreitzer, E. A., 70
Stalnaker, Deborah, 141
Stamps, S. M., 141

Stormann, Wayne, 360
Strausfeld, D., 108
Strodtbeck, F. L., 95–96
Stubbles, R., 307, 326
Sylvester, Charles, 46
Szwak, Laura, 177, 192

Taylor, Glenda, 141
Teaff, Joseph, 190, 300
Tedrick, Ted, 96
Thorstenson, Clark, 192–193
Tice, R. Dean, 361
Tinsley, H. E., 190, 300
Tocqueville, Alexis de, 39
Turner, Al, 381

Veal, A. J., 161
Veblen, Thorstein, 9, 18

Wankel, L., 246, 301, 326
Ward, Veda, 361
Warner, W. Lloyd, 157–158
Warnick, Rodney, 96, 187
Wartella, E., 182–183
Washington, Sharon, 115–116
Webb, James, 134
Weissinger, Ellen, 196
West, P. C., 97
White, R. Clyde, 158–159
Whitson, D., 138
Wiggins, David, 99–100
Will, George, 21–22, 323
Williams, D. W., 300
Williams, J. R., 116–117
Williamson, Nancy, 127
Willits, F., 186
Winn, Marie, 179–180
Wolf, Esther, 108
Wolfenstein, Martha, 60
Wong, R., 215
Woodard, Michael, 96
Woodward, C. Vann, 51
Wrisberg, C., 134

Yuhill, Ji-Yeon, 89–90

Zeigler, E., 194
Zoglin, Richard, 254
Zuckerman, Marvin, 218

Subject Index

ISBN 0-02-366302-2